W9-CJX-776

Reform, War, and Reaction: 1912–1932

the text of this book is printed
on 100% recycled paper

DOCUMENTARY HISTORY OF THE UNITED STATES

Edited by Richard B. Morris

Chronological Volumes:

David B. Quinn THE DISCOVERY OF AMERICA HR/1505
Alden T. Vaughan: THE PURITAN TRADITION IN AMERICA
Charles Gibson: THE SPANISH TRADITION IN AMERICA HR/1351
Y. F. Zoltvany: THE FRENCH TRADITION IN AMERICA HR/1425
Milton M. Klein: THE DUTCH AND QUAKER TRADITIONS IN AMERICA
Aubrey Land: BASES OF PLANTATION SOCIETY HR/1429
Jack P. Greene: GREAT BRITAIN AND THE AMERICAN COLONIES, 1606-1763 HR/1477
Richard B. Morris: THE AMERICAN REVOLUTION, 1763-1783 HR/1504
Forrest McDonald: CONFEDERATION AND CONSTITUTION HR/1396
Noble E. Cunningham, Jr.: THE EARLY REPUBLIC, 1789-1828 HR/1394
Jack M. Sosin: THE OPENING OF THE WEST HR/1424
Gilbert C. Fite: THE WEST, 1830-1890
Robert V. Remini: THE AGE OF JACKSON
Stanley Elkins & Gerald Mullin: DOCUMENTS IN THE HISTORY OF SLAVERY
Walter Hugins: THE REFORM IMPULSE (1828-1847)
James P. Shenton: THE CIVIL WAR
La Wanda and John Cox: RECONSTRUCTION, THE NEW SOUTH, AND THE NEGRO
John A. Garraty: THE TRANSFORMATION OF AMERICAN SOCIETY, 1870-1890 HR/1395
Richard M. Abrams: THE ISSUES OF THE POPULIST AND PROGRESSIVE ERAS, 1892-1912 HR/1428
Earl Pomeroy: THE FAR WEST IN THE TWENTIETH CENTURY
Stanley Coben: WORLD WAR, REFORM, AND REACTION
William E. Leuchtenburg: THE NEW DEAL: *A Documentary History* HR/1354
Louis Morton: UNITED STATES AND WORLD WAR II
Robert E. Burke: DOMESTIC ISSUES SINCE 1945

Topical Volumes:

Alan F. Westin: THE SHAPING OF THE CONSTITUTION (2 volumes)
Herbert G. Gutman: THE LABOR MOVEMENT (2 volumes)
Robert D. Cross: THE IMMIGRANT IN AMERICAN HISTORY
Douglass C. North & Robert Paul Thomas:
THE GROWTH OF THE AMERICAN ECONOMY TO 1860 HR/1352
William Greenleaf: AMERICAN ECONOMIC DEVELOPMENT SINCE 1860 HR/1353
Hollis R. Lynch: THE AMERICAN NEGRO IN THE TWENTIETH CENTURY
I. B. Cohen: HISTORY OF SCIENCE IN AMERICA
Richard C. Wade: THE CITY IN AMERICAN HISTORY
Robert H. Ferrell: FOUNDATIONS OF AMERICAN DIPLOMACY, 1775-1872, Volume I HR/1393
Robert H. Ferrell: AMERICA AS A WORLD POWER, Volume II HR/1512
Robert H. Ferrell: AMERICA IN A DIVIDED WORLD, Volume III
Stanley J. Reisor: HISTORY OF MEDICINE
Robert T. Handy: RELIGION IN AMERICA

Reform, War, and Reaction: 1912–1932

Edited by
Stanley Coben

HARPER & ROW, PUBLISHERS
New York, Evanston, San Francisco, London

REFORM, WAR, AND REACTION: 1912–1932.

For information address Harper & Row, Publishers, Inc., 49 East 33rd Street, New York, N.Y. 10016. Published simultaneously in Canada by Fitzhenry & Whiteside Limited, Toronto.

A hardcover edition of this book is published by University of South Carolina Press.

First HARPER PAPERBACK edition published 1972.

LIBRARY OF CONGRESS CATALOG CARD NUMBER: 72–75847

STANDARD BOOK NUMBER: 06–1384178

Contents

IV United States Civilization during the 1920s

V Politics in the 1920s

VI The Economy during the 1920s

Introduction

THIS BOOK covers a time span not especially long; but during these twenty years Americans lived through what for most was a bewildering series of shocks: the great mass of progressive legislation accompanied by demands for further social and cultural change, World War I, the postwar reaction and the threat of revolution, the variety of ethnic and intellectual conflicts during the 1920s, the stock market crash of 1929 and the economic depression that followed. At the end of the period American civilization, to those who had voted in 1912, seemed to have passed from a time of glorious promise in their youth to one of utter ruin. All the ostensible achievements of the era—the triumph of progressivism, victory in a war to make the world safe for democracy, a fairly successful movement for 100 percent Americanism, the neutralization of potentially radical movements by socialists, communists, Negroes, and feminists, the rationalization of business by large corporations with governmental assistance, and other federal efforts to smooth out the business cycle—seemed to have had trivial, if not negative, results. Western Europe, with the galling exception of the Soviet Union, had been dragged into depression by the economic collapse of the United States. The trend in Europe, and perhaps throughout the world, was toward totalitarian dictatorships, not democracy. War more devastating than ever before threatened the great nations. A dull attitude of hopelessness pervaded the United States, where most of the old truths appeared to have been proven wrong. The greatest industrial and financial system ever created suffered from near paralysis, and after years of cheerful predictions that renewed prosperity lay just around the corner, no one could be certain that conditions would not become even worse.

A collection of forty-two documents can do no more than illuminate some of the ways that Americans experienced these momentous events and permit insight into the intentions of the leaders of the society. Moreover, it may serve to liberate the reader from the narrative and analysis written by historians. Even the finest historical writing suffers as much as it benefits from the author's awareness of what happened next, necessarily giving him a different perspective from those present at the time, who did not know. Furthermore, those who wrote these documents were products of a culture that differed significantly from that in which we live. For this reason also, the original documents can give discerning students greater empathy with the Americans who took part in events that occurred forty to sixty years ago.

I. The Flowering of Progressivism

Although four major candidates took part in the 1912 presidential campaign—Socialist Eugene V. Debs, the new Progressive party's Theodore Roosevelt, Republican William H. Taft, Democrat Woodrow Wilson—only two stood a serious chance of winning. To voters in 1912 Roosevelt and Wilson presented two different paths for the future course of the progressive movement. In a speech charged with high emotion Roosevelt submits his plan for a New Nationalism in Selection 1. This program would have taken the country far in the direction of government control and paternalistic aid achieved later by the New Deal. Wilson's plans, on the contrary—developed largely during the campaign—stressed governmental efforts to bring back the high degree of individual economic opportunity which supposedly existed before the wholesale intervention in the economy of huge, frequently monopolistic, corporations. Wilson's program is set forth in Selection 2. The Socialist alternative to these capitalistic programs is presented in Debs's speech, Selection 3.

Wilson's plans underwent considerable change during his first term, as a report in the *Catholic Charities Review* reveals in Selection 4. Because of these shifts—most of them in the direction of Roosevelt's New Nationalism—former Progressives flocked to the Democratic party in 1916, making possible Wilson's reelection. Selection 5 explains the movement of one of the most influential Progressives, Walter Lippmann, into the ranks of Wilson's supporters.

The progressive attitudes also encompassed areas virtually unaffected by politics: religion, literature, scholarship, the philosophy, and techniques of education, and even most of the fine arts. James Harvey Robinson offers a progressive suggestion for the teaching and writing of history in Selection 6, and the editors of *The Seven Arts* presented a manifesto, reprinted as Selection 7, calling for cultural progressivism in the first issue of that remarkable magazine.

II. World War I

Historical questions connected with United States participation in World War I can be divided into two categories: the reasons for United States entrance into the conflict and the perplexing problem of the Peace Treaty, which was designed to bring America into the League of Nations. In Selection 8 William Dean Howells, the American author most highly respected by the nation's educated business and political leaders, attempts to explain why men of his class and ethnic origins—the men who still ruled America—almost intuitively sided with England and France. Yet Howells, like the majority of the old-stock American social leaders he represented, hoped in 1915 that the United States would refrain from entering the war until "Zeppelins infest our atmosphere and begin dropping bombs on Boston." More bloodthirsty partisans of the Allies, like Theodore Roosevelt, might demand immediate American participation, but so long as men like Howells—and Woodrow Wilson—refused to consider war unless Germany actually invaded the United States, no American troops would fight in Europe.

Although Howells in 1915 refused to contemplate belligerency until the country had borne everything from Germany "short of invading our shores after sinking all our ships," he did insist that protests be registered and accounts kept for a postwar reckoning, as after the Civil War, when Great Britain paid an indemnity for constructing Confederate cruisers that took a terrible toll of Union ships. Wilson adopted a similar policy, protesting with increasing bitterness against infringements of American rights by both sides.

To some Americans protests against German policies and actions seemed much harsher than those directed at British incursions upon American rights. Moreover, the drastic warnings to Germany seemed to be leading inevitably toward war. Among those who objected to the tone and the tendencies they discerned in Wilson's notes to Germany was Secretary of State William Jennings Bryan. Wilson's angry protests to Germany after a submarine sank the British liner *Lusitania,* which had been carrying munitions as well as passengers from New York, was issued despite objections to its strong language from Bryan. The Secretary of State's consequent letter of resignation, his public explanation, and his appeal for a foreign policy that would guarantee peace for America comprise Selection 9.

Less pacifistic Americans, led by Theodore Roosevelt, took exception to Bryan's position. Contemptuous of those who applied the optimistic ideals of domestic progressivism to world affairs, they demanded preparedness for war. The derisive attack on American pacifists reprinted in Selection 10 was representative of many similar statements made by those who supported Roosevelt on this issue.

As Bryan had predicted, Wilson's decisions led to war. While the government—and the nation—poised on the brink of the European conflagration, one of the country's foremost intellectuals, philosopher John Dewey, perceived great significance in America's long hesitation. Beyond the reasons usually given for this reluctance to fight, Dewey sensed something deeper. In Selection 11 he describes a widespread but barely conscious feeling that the United States finally had become an entity distinct from Europe, willing, although not anxious, to enter the war only when vital American interests were seriously endangered. In the long run, Dewey concluded, the grounds for the hesitation might prove to be more important than the decision to act.

For two and a half years Woodrow Wilson had resisted a variety of provocations from the belligerents, and in 1916 the claim that he had "kept us out of war" made possible his reelection. As late as January 1917, the President informed his closest adviser, Colonel Edward House, that "it would be a crime against civilization for us to go in." Wilson made up his mind firmly in favor of intervention about March 30, 1917, and he then was obliged to devise an explanation for this crucial decision, an explanation that would persuade previously unconvinced Americans that they should enter the war wholeheartedly. Wilson offered this explanation in a speech asking a joint session of Congress for a declaration of war on April 2. Among the factors influencing Wilson that he failed to mention in this address (Selection 12), was his conviction that he, more than any other world leader and perhaps he alone among them, possessed the determination and the popular support needed to create a peace settlement that would "make the world safe for democracy." Only by taking part in the now certain Allied victory could the American President be assured of a prominent place at the peace conference.

Most congressmen hitherto opposed to war now either rallied to Wilson's support or fell silent. A comparatively small proportion of those who had urged continued neutrality still opposed American intervention after the President spoke. Even the Socialist party divided on the issue. Only a handful of congressmen spoke against the war resolution. (The votes for belligerency were 82 to 6 in the Senate and 373 to 50 in the House of Representatives.) Perhaps the most effective of these antiwar speeches, and therefore the most disturbing to advocates of intervention, came from the highly respected Senator from Nebraska, George W. Norris (Selection 13). A hint of the repression ahead appeared at the conclusion of Norris' address, when a string of United States Senators took the floor to charge him with treason even before war was declared.

With a large segment of the United States population only nominally in support of war and a highly vocal minority of pacifists, radicals, and sympathizers with the German cause openly opposed to it, the American government organized a vast campaign to persuade previously neutral citizens that high moral purposes as well as military necessity made an all-out American military effort necessary. A progressive journalist and editor, George Creel, was placed in charge of the government propaganda effort. Creel's account of the activities of his committee (Selection 14) suggests why dissent in the United States was put down even more fiercely than in most of the European nations on whose soil the war was fought. This mobilization of moral fervor affected postwar attitudes also, and its success made a deep impression on specialists in public relations and advertising and even on intellectuals like Walter Lippmann, who sought to understand the formation of public opinion.

At the conclusion of the war Wilson entered the peace conference with high purposes and demonstrations of public support for his policies. He emerged with a treaty about as close to his suggested fourteen points as a reasonable man could have expected. Especially, he returned to the United States with a commitment from the European powers to join a potentially powerful League of Nations. Yet it was in America, where support for an organization like the League had appeared overwhelming, that the treaty was rejected. Most influential in organizing this unexpected rebuff was

Republican Senator Henry Cabot Lodge of Massachusetts. Lodge explained the ostensible reasons for his opposition in a Senate speech, reprinted in Selection 15. Wilson replied in a series of cogent addresses in various parts of the country. He seemed to be making headway in cutting through the objections raised against the treaty and the League when he collapsed and suffered a disabling stroke following a particularly moving talk in Pueblo, Colorado (Selection 16). From that point on Wilson's illness and the physiological and psychological symptoms that accompanied it played a critical role in preventing a compromise which would have brought the United States into the League of Nations.

III. Postwar Reaction

Fear of imminent mongrelization of the "Nordic" race that had made America great reached hysterical proportions after World War I, obliging Congress to place severe limitations on immigration from Eastern and Southern Europe and to prevent Japanese immigration altogether. No one did more to arouse this fear than Madison Grant, author of *The Passing of the Great Race* (Selection 17), the most influential racist volume in twentieth-century United States history. Published in 1916, before the scale of the internal Negro migration became apparent, Grant concentrated on what he considered the deterioration of the ruling race in America because of the casual mixing of European races. Critical of democracy, Christian ideals, and even national pride for their contribution to this destruction of racial purity, Grant insisted that race was the foundation of all that was worthwhile in America's national and cultural heritage. Grant's influence can be seen in the widespread postwar insistence on stringent immigration restriction.

Although the movement for 100 percent Americanism continued to gather strength well into the 1920s, the peak of emotional intensity came in 1919–1920, when millions of otherwise sane Americans, including almost every member of Wilson's Cabinet, expected a revolution that would attempt to topple the United States government. These fears were fed by warnings from the government official in the best position to evaluate the strength of revolutionary forces, Attorney General A. Mitchell Palmer. Condemned by the Senate in the fall of 1919 for his inactivity against radicals and informed by the antiradical division of his

Bureau of Investigation, under the direction of J. Edgar Hoover, that a powerful revolutionary movement might attack the government at any time, Palmer initiated a series of mass roundups of suspected alien communists. Many nonalien, non-communists citizens were caught in the gigantic dragnet, which flagrantly violated several sections of the Bill of Rights. Palmer explains the necessity for this drastic action in Selection 18.

While Palmer planned his raids, a series of nationwide strikes—in the coal, steel, and railroad industries—threatened Americans already disturbed by postwar shortages, unemployment, and runaway prices. The first of these strikes, part of an A.F. of L. attempt to organize the steel industry, where wages had fallen far behind rising living costs and working conditions generally were terrible, broke out in September 1919. With the aid of charges that the strike was a part of a communist conspiracy to paralyze American industry, the steel companies beat back the attempt at organization and in most respects won the conflict. Investigators from the Industrial Department of the Interchurch World Movement, an association of Protestant church organizations, traveled through the steel manufacturing areas carrying out a lengthy study of the causes of the strikes, its effects, and the charges made by both sides. The long report, published in 1922, in general condemned the labor practices of the steel companies, including the unfounded charges of radical influences used to break the strike. The report also supported most of the strikers' demands. Its conclusions are reprinted as Selection 19. Although this report appeared much too late to affect the strike, it did mobilize public opinion against the policies of the steel industries, obliging major steel companies to adopt the eight-hour day and to end their most flagrant abuses of labor.

Other organizations, periodicals, authors, and politicians also refused to bow before the demands of 100 percent Americans. A large group of associations, their journals, and their spokesmen objected to proposals for immigration restriction and fought what amounted to guerrilla warfare against the Americanization campaigns conducted by patriotic organizations. The efforts to homogenize Americans were opposed politely but firmly by groups representing large immigrant or Negro constituencies like the National Catholic Welfare Council, the American Jewish Committee, and the NAACP. Associations like the Sons of Italy, the

Jewish Labor Bund, Marcus Garvey's huge black nationalist organization, the United Negro Improvement Association, and, in some areas, the Knights of Columbus were less patient with the activities of the 100 percenters. The most systematic assault of the theory that minority ethnic groups ought to subordinate their peculiarities to conventional American values, traditions, dress, and speech, was written by Horace Kallen (Selection 20). America's distinction, Kallen insisted, lay in the rich variety of ethnic strains that existed side by side, contributing the best of each tradition to the American heritage.

A more caustic counterattack against the 100 percenters was launched by H. L. Mencken, essayist, critic, and editor of *The American Mercury*, the most popular journal of dissent in the United States during the 1920s. In his essay "Star Spangled Men" (Selection 21), Mencken poured contempt upon patriots of every variety, including superpatriotic General George Pershing, the Ku Klux Klan, and A. Mitchell Palmer. As a result of a strident literary counterattack, by the mid-1920s no would-be intellectual dared defend America's most cherished ideals and heroes, unless he was willing to risk being set down as an incurable member of what Mencken referred to as "homo boobiens," or the "boobeoisie."

IV. United States Civilization during the 1920s

To a very high proportion—perhaps a majority—of white, native-born, Protestant Americans, most of whom had been born in rural areas or in small towns, American civilization seemed in danger of serious deterioration. Their complaints ranged far beyond the usual clichés about a hell-bound younger generation. Fundamental moral precepts were being transgressed by people of all ages. Shameless intellectuals condemned the whole society in witty articles that appeared in prestigious magazines, as well as in books available to susceptible young people. The most sacred aspects of the true religion were ridiculed freely. The crime-ridden big cities appeared to resemble Sodom and Gomorrah. A casual stroll through any of these cities revealed that almost every one was being occupied by invaders from Eastern and Southern Europe. It took little investigation, either in person or through trusted newspapers and magazines, to reveal that these swarthy foreigners, and the Negroes who continued to crowd in among them, were responsible for the mounting crime and drunkenness. They supplied the illegal liquor, the prostitutes, gambling dens, and the licentious motion pictures. They sent their children to parochial schools that taught loyalty to a foreign Pope or to international Jewry. Unrestrained Negroes were dangerous enough, but when these intellectually childlike but physically powerful people were mixed with debauched Papists and radical Jews, the combination might well be explosive.

To combat these dangers to American civilization a number of organizations arose. By far the most formidable was the Ku Klux Klan. Out of the white Protestant stronghold of Atlanta, Georgia, came the Kleagles of the Klan, over two hundred experienced organizers, most of whom already had served the Elks, the Moose, the Oddfellows, the Woodmasons of America, or some such fraternal organization. They entered towns and cities from Maine to California, uncovering from conversations with Methodist and Baptist ministers and sympathetic newspaper editors the chief grievances of the white Protestant population. The Kleagles then proceeded to spread the word by public meetings, sermons, newspaper stories, and advertisement that the Klan had arrived in the community and was prepared to help solve the most pressing local problems. Any white Protestant native-born male could join the crusade. The only requirements were his signature on a membership application and ten dollars (of which the Kleagle retained four dollars for a initiation fee).

To a marvelous degree the fears of Klan members throughout the country coincided with those expressed by Klan leaders, especially after these leaders had assimilated the results of their Kleagles' market research. An early emphasis on the need to squelch "uppity" Negroes practically disappeared from Klan pronouncements. In Selection 22 Hiram Evans, the Klan's Imperial Wizard, summarizes the reasons (as of 1926) for the Klan's existence and its objectives.

An impression of what the Klan was up against, even among white Protestants of the more sensitive and educated variety, can be gleaned from the satirical account of a small-town American's intellectual evolution printed in the *New Republic* shortly after the modern Klan's formation (Selection 23). The common species of intellectual rebellion described in this journal became much more widespread and the participants more self-confident and persistent in their revolt during the 1920s.

The diary of a cultural dissenter written during the '20s almost certainly would have mentioned the drinking of bootlegged liquor. Violation of the prohibition laws was a convention observed by rebels, not only of thirst, boredom, or alcoholism, but because it was expected—much like an acquaintance with Freud's ideas and Joyce's literary techniques. Klan leaders' suspicion of intellectuals was not without foundation, although in violating the prohibition laws they were joined by much of America's urban population. The Klan's complaints about the role of "foreign" elements in criminal activity like bootlegging were justified also, as the list of Chicago gang leader Frank Torrio's associates reveals. Dion O'Banion, Louie Alterie, Hymie Weiss, and Al Capone all were ineligible for Klan membership, but at times during the 1920s they practically ruled Chicago, especially after Capone succeeded Torrio. The story of Torrio's rise to power and his subsequent abdication when the financial stakes rose and the need for organizational powers and ruthlessness increased, is described in Selection 24.

Although Torrio, O'Banion, Capone, and their counterparts in other cities contributed to drastic changes in the economic as well as the power relationships among ethnic groups, they hardly qualified as cultural rebels. In fact, except for his distinct New York-Italian accent, Capone sounded like an auto or chemical industry executive when he spoke of systematizing, consolidating, and diversifying his interests. He thought highly of mergers and joint enterprises, as well, although his methods of inducing them might have been considered crude (but admirably effective) even by Standard Oil.

In addition to the political radicals and immigrant groups discussed in Section III, rebellious elements among Negroes, women, and literary and academic intellectuals conducted steady warfare against the dominant culture during the 1920s.

The most startling aspect of the Negro rebellion was the sudden appearance of a huge black nationalist organization, the United Negro Improvement Association, under the leadership of Marcus Garvey. A fascistic type organization (Garvey boasted that Mussolini had copied his methods) with an ideology resembling Zionism, the UNIA demonstrated an enormous appeal for American Negroes, who had been told and shown from birth that were inferior to whites. Now they heard Garvey boast to enormous crowds that "I am the equal of any white man," and they watched thousands of militant UNIA members march through the streets of Harlem. Although Garvey's written words hardly capture the charismatic qualities—and perhaps not the ideas—that all but mesmerized his audiences, the selections from editorials in his newspaper *The Negro World* reprinted as Selection 25 reflect important aspects of his ideology and program.

While Garvey's legions multiplied, a much smaller group of Negro intellectuals self-consciously sought to develop themselves as artists, while seeking an answer to the question of what negritude meant in America. This Harlem Renaissance included musicians Louis Armstrong and Duke Ellington, singers Josephine Baker and Paul Robeson, sculptors and painters, as well as a remarkable group of writers. The renaissance almost literally was called into being by W. E. B. Du Bois, editor of the most influential Negro journal, *The Crisis*, of the NAACP. Du Bois now attempted to bring the Negro movements to fruition by shifting the policies and emphasis of *The Crisis*, as he explains in Selection 26. The renaissance itself is analyzed by Alaine Locke in an introduction (Selection 27) to the first anthology of articles, poems, stories, and excerpts from novels and plays by the young black authors. Locke's collection, published in 1925, was called *The New Negro*.

In Selection 28 feminist Sophia Breckinridge dispassionately describes a quiet revolution that obviously had not gone as far as the author would have liked: the movement of women into legitimate employment outside the home. The reasons for the failure of the feminist movement to take advantage of woman suffrage to press successfully for further gains along the lines described by Miss Breckinridge, perhaps through the equal rights amendment to the Constitution advocated by the Woman's party, are analyzed by Ethel Puffer Howes in Selection 29.

The most devastating critics of American society during the 1920s were not angry feminists or blacks; but, rather, the most lively, perhaps the most talented, and certainly the largest group of gifted writers the country ever had produced. A highly dramatic summary of the widespread denunciation of American civilization by two generations of authors was delivered by Sinclair Lewis in accepting the Nobel Prize for literature in 1930 at Stockholm

(Selection 30). To a large extent unfairly, Lewis used William Dean Howells as a symbol of the crushing inhibitions to honest creativity that America imposed upon all her artists save those who worked in architecture or films. Through representatives like Howells, he proclaimed American civilization tried to force its writers to adhere to "the code of a pious old maid." Lewis acknowledged hope, nevertheless, for the future of American literature. Not only were established writers, such as Theodore Dreiser and Eugene O'Neill, proving immune to the heavy hand of societal repression and the discouraging influence of popular indifference, but a rising generation was producing passionate and authentic work of a high order. He mentioned specifically Ernest Hemingway, Thomas Wolfe, Thornton Wilder, John Dos Passos, Stephen Benét, Michael Gold, and William Faulkner.

Other American writers were less hopeful about the future of their civilization. The best-known collection of pessimistic viewpoints appeared in *Civilization in the United States*, thirty essays on diverse topics edited by Harold Stearns in 1922. Few of the essays in Stearn's volume still seem worth reprinting. A more searching analysis, written from a comparably gloomy viewpoint, can be found in the essays by John Dewey and Joseph Wood Krutch, reprinted as Selections 31 and 32. Dewey explains the limitations that American moralism necessarily places upon free intellectual inquiry—what he defines as "the illiberalism which is deep-rooted in our liberalism." Krutch, even more cynical, and, perhaps, more resigned about the limitations of American civilization, seems to have struck a highly responsive chord within the American intelligentsia with his *The American Temper*, the conclusion of which is reprinted as Selection 32. Discouraged by the apparent failure of intellectuals in Europe as well as the United States to promulgate values which would revitalize their decaying civilization, Krutch took a negative view about the possibility of such an invigoration.

A reminder that intellectuals were part of American culture, sharing most of the important values and goals, was provided by the reaction of almost every sector of the population to the transatlantic air flight of Charles A. Lindbergh. In only a few respects was Lindbergh's flight remarkable. Others had completed longer and more dangerous air trips; a number already had crossed the

Atlantic. Lindbergh, however, flew alone from New York to Paris, and his modest demeanor contrasted with the brashness shown by most of his competitors for international fame as aviators. These factors obviously are insufficient in themselves to explain the outpouring of people and emotion that greeted Lindbergh everywhere upon his return to the United States, and the phenomenon has drawn the attention of several historians of American culture. They must reckon not only with the popular frenzy, but also with attitudes like that expressed by Malcolm Cowley, semi-official literary chronicler of the "lost generation" of writers. Cowley, who upon reading *Ulysses* declared that he would rather see Joyce than any man alive, finally came upon his hero in Paris three times in one day. He felt, Cowley recalled "the same emotions as when Lindbergh arrived." Selection 33 describes the unprecedented response when Lindbergh returned to New York City, after being greeted first by an incredibly large and enthusiastic crowd in Washington.

V. *Politics of the 1920s*

Outside the South and a few enclaves in the urban North, the Republican party controlled the United States at every political level during the 1920s, although not without some interesting challenges. However, behind this superficial hegemony, shifts in population and in voter affiliation were taking place and discontent was gathering that would all but destroy the Republicans in the decade to follow.

Herbert Hoover, the most active and popular and, with the possible exception of Andrew Mellon, the most influential member of the Harding and Coolidge administrations, voiced the predominant philosophy of his party in a speech on American government delivered during his campaign for the presidency in 1928. In this address, reprinted as Selection 34, Hoover claimed that he described "those fundamental principles and ideals upon which I believe the United States should be governed." Except for Hoover's comparatively urbane style and an absence of nativistic rhetoric, the speech could have been made by any of the three Republican Presidents of the decade and by most of their party's leaders. Domestic tax reduction, tariff increases, highway construction, and encouragement to American industry's foreign trade all were described as "progressive" policies. Stimulation of individual initiative in business and government, while maintaining some regulation of various types of monopolistic public utilities, Hoover proclaimed as the foundation of wise federal administration. This combination of freedom mixed with a minimum of necessary control Hoover termed "our American system." As a consequence of its application the candidate boasted, "We are nearer today to the ideal of the abolition of poverty and fear from the lives of men and women than ever before in any land." Almost exactly a year later the stock market collapsed.

Even more typical of the style of thought and expression that marked the Republican party at the high tide of its modern authority is Calvin Coolidge's description of his assumption the presidency (Selection 35). The contemporary picture of a phlegmatic, curt President has been overdrawn, but the character who emerges from Coolidge's own words is unmistakably that which drove men like Mencken and Sinclair Lewis to fits of satire.

Two major political rebellions took place during the 1920s against the triumph of the dominant culture in general and the political power of the established business classes in particular. The first of these—the Progressive party campaign of 1924—was potentially the more dangerous, as the party's platform (Selection 36) reveals. That platform might have been even more radical, except for charges of communist domination which constituted the main theme of Republican attacks on Senator Robert La Follette's candidacy. Meanwhile the Communists, on orders from Moscow to reject this new temptation to accommodation with a bourgeois party, hammered at La Follette's movement as a tool of the capitalist order.

The second important challenge came from the ethnic minorities that increasingly found a home within the Democratic party. Al Smith, Irish, Catholic, wet ("The question isn't whether Al Smith drinks, but whether Al Smith drinks too much," a critic remarked), visibly proud of his Tammany affiliations, flouting his "foreign" New York accent and mannerisms, assumed leadership of these groups and thereby won the Democratic presidential nomination in 1928. The response of a Protestant leader to Smith's candidacy, reprinted in Selection 37, indicates the depths as well as the breadth of the cultural fears that candidacy aroused.

VI. The Economy During the 1920s

Although the details of economic change and development in the 1920s are discussed in another volume of this series, several tendencies are so entwined with general cultural shifts that they warrant presentation here. The dominant philosophy of the period idealized the businessman. Bruce Barton's enormously popular reinterpretation of Jesus Christ in terms of business values (Selection 38) was symptomatic of this general approbation. Barton presented Jesus as the supreme business executive without offending the highly sensitive proponents of a fundamentalist interpretation of the New Testament.

Among the fascinating economic changes of the postwar era was the channeling of discretionary income into leisure activities. With the aid of this income, time made available by shrinking workweeks and longer vacations and the increase in mobility made possible by the automobile and highways, Americans made a huge industry out of new forms of entertainment. Large crowds assembled in more accessible movie theatres. And much larger audiences gathered to watch athletic events, turning into national heroes an Italian orphan who could hit a baseball phenomenal distances and an Irish draft dodger with a devastating left jab and right hook. The greatest number of large crowds paid to watch college football games. Colleges, impressed with the funds that flowed into their treasuries as a result of this previously marginal student activity and conscious of the correlation between the football team's success and alumni donations, competed for promising athletes in a fashion that made a mockery of the ostensible purposes of their institutions. This competition and some of its consequences are described by an involved observer in Selection 39.

The best minds among American economists managed to retain some degree of dispassionate judgment as the stock market soared, and wages as well as business profits rose steadily during the decade. In Selection 40 Wesley Mitchell, appointed by President Hoover to head an investigation of the American economy, presents his committee's conclusions. These are especially interesting because they were published at the height of public confidence—which in too many cases approached ecstasy—in 1929. Mitchell's group discovered great disparities between the fortunes of people in different occupations, industries, and geographic sections. In sum, he found that an undeniably prosperous period for the country as a whole had not significantly improved the economic condition of a sizeable minority of the population.

President Hoover publicly downgraded the importance of the stock market catastrophe in October 1929, although privately he warned business, labor, and government officials of possible disaster ahead. Those involved as brokers, customers, or bankers hardly needed to be warned about the dimensions of the tragedy or its possible consequences. Fear seeps through every firsthand account of the crash, including the *New York Times* description of market activity, on Thursday, October 30, 1929 (Selection 41), which turned out to be far from the bottom of the market's decline.

Although the precise nature of the relationship between the stock crash and the subsequent depression remains cloudy, the connection is undeniable. A summary of unemployment and of suggestions for alleviating both its rapid increase and the accumulating distress was presented to the National Conference of Social Work in June 1931 and is reprinted in Selection 42. Needless to say, despite such suggestions and a flow of cheerful predictions from Washington, the conditions described in this selection steadily worsened throughout the following year. The world of the 1920s ended with both a bang and a whimper.

Reform, War, and Reaction: 1912–1932

I

The Flowering of Progressivism

1. The New Nationalism: Theodore Roosevelt

THEODORE ROOSEVELT's *speech, delivered before a convention audience that reacted almost like participants in a revival meeting, is his official acceptance of the Progressive party nomination for President. The nomination and acceptance took place June 22, 1912, almost immediately after the renomination of President Taft by the Republicans, which Roosevelt's supporters considered fraudulent. The speech expressed a concept of governmental control over the economy that Roosevelt had been developing since his first term in office. Many of these ideas had been presented to Congress in the form of recommendations, especially in 1908, but conservative legislative leaders virtually ignored most of them. Then, perhaps stimulated by* New Republic *editor Herbert Croly's* The Promise of American Life, *Roosevelt moved still further in the direction of executive intervention during his four years out of public office.*

To you, men and women who have come here to this great city of this great State formally to launch a new party, a party of the people of the whole Union, the National Progressive party, I extend my hearty greeting. You are taking a bold and a greatly needed step for the service of our beloved country. The old parties are husks, with no real soul within either, divided on artificial lines, boss-ridden and privilege-controlled, each a jumble of incongruous elements, and neither daring to speak out wisely and fearlessly what should be said on the vital issues of the day. This new movement is a movement of truth, sincerity, and wisdom, a movement which proposes to put at the service of all our people the collective power of the people, through their governmental agencies, alike in the nation and in the several States. We propose boldly to face the real and great questions of the day, and not skilfully to evade them as do the old parties. We propose to raise aloft a standard to which all honest men can repair, and under which all can fight, no matter what their past political differences, if they are content to face the future and no longer to dwell among the dead issues of the past. We propose to put forth a platform which shall not be a platform

SOURCE: *The Works of Theodore Roosevelt*, National Edition XVII (New York, 1926): 254–259, 262–266, 268–270, 272–273, 278–279, 281, 283–284, 292–293, 298–299.

of the ordinary and insincere kind, but shall be a contract with the people; and, if the people accept this contract by putting us in power, we shall hold ourselves under honorable obligation to fulfill every promise it contains as loyally as if it were actually enforceable under the penalties of the law.

The prime need today is to face the fact that we are now in the midst of a great economic evolution. There is urgent necessity of applying both common sense and the highest ethical standard to this movement for better economic conditions among the mass of our people if we are to make it one of healthy evolution and not one of revolution. It is, from the standpoint of our country, wicked as well as foolish longer to refuse to face the real issues of the day. . . .

I especially challenge the attention of the people to the need of dealing in far-reaching fashion with our human resources, and therefore our labor power. . . . In the last twenty years an increasing percentage of our people have come to depend on industry for their livelihood, so that today the wage-workers in industry rank in importance side by side with the tillers of the soil. As a people we cannot afford to let any group of citizens or any individual citizen live or labor under conditions which are injurious to the common welfare. Industry, therefore, must submit to such public regulation as will make it a means of life and health, not of death or inefficiency. We must protect the crushable elements at the base of our present industrial structure.

The first change on the industrial statesmanship of the day is to prevent human waste. The dead weight of orphanage and depleted craftsmanship, of crippled workers and workers suffering from trade diseases, of casual labor, of insecure old age, and of household depletion due to industrial conditions are, like our depleted soils, our gashed mountainsides and flooded riverbottoms, so many strains upon the national structure, draining the reserve strength of all industries and showing beyond all peradventure the public element and public concern in industrial health. . . .

We hold that under no industrial order, in no commonwealth, in no trade, and in no establishment should industry be carried on under conditions inimical to the social welfare. The abnormal, ruthless, spendthrift industry or establishment tends to drag down all to the level of the least considerate.

Here the sovereign responsibility of the people as a whole should be placed beyond all quibble and dispute. . . .

We stand for a living wage. Wages are subnormal if they fail to provide a living for those who devote their time and energy to industrial occupations. The monetary equivalent of a living wage varies according to local conditions, but must include enough to secure the elements of a normal standard of living—a standard high enough to make morality possible, to provide for education and recreation, to care for immature members of the family, to maintain the family during periods of sickness, and to permit of reasonable saving for old age.

Hours are excessive if they fail to afford the worker sufficient time to recuperate and return to his work thoroughly refreshed. We hold that the night labor of women and children is abnormal and should be prohibited. . . . We hold that the seven-day working week is abnormal, and we hold that one day of rest in seven should be provided by law. We hold that the continuous industries, operating twenty-four hours out of twenty-four, are abnormal, and where, because of public necessity or of technical reasons (such as molten metal), the twenty-four hours must be divided into two shifts of twelve hours or three shifts of eight, they should by law be divided into three of eight. . . .

It is abnormal for any industry to throw back upon the community the human wreckage due to its wear and tear, and the hazards of sickness, accident, invalidism, involuntary unemployment, and old age should be provided for through insurance. This should be made a charge in whole or in part upon the industries, the employer, the employee, and perhaps the people at large to contribute severally in some degree. . . . What Germany has done in the way of old-age pensions or insurance should be studied by us, and the system adapted to our uses. . . .

Working women have the same need to combine for protection that working men have; the ballot is as necessary for one class as for the other; we do not believe that with the two sexes there is identity of function; but we do believe that there should be equality of right; and therefore we favor woman suffrage. Surely, if women could vote, they would strengthen the hands of those who are endeavoring to deal in efficient fashion with evils such as the white-slave traffic. . . .

The present conditions of business cannot be accepted as satisfactory. There are too many who do not prosper enough, and of the few who prosper greatly there are certainly some whose prosperity does not mean well for the country. . . . Our aim is to promote prosperity, and then see to its proper division. We do not believe that any good comes to any one by a policy which means destruction of prosperity; for in such cases it is not possible to divide it because of the very obvious fact that there is nothing to divide. We wish to control big business so as to secure among other things good wages for the wage-workers and reasonable prices for the consumers. Wherever in any business the prosperity of the business man is obtained by lowering the wages of his workmen and charging an excessive price to the consumers, we wish to interfere and stop such practices. . . .

It is utterly hopeless to attempt to control the trusts merely by the antitrust law, or by any law the same in principle, no matter what the modifications may be in detail. . . . What is needed is the application to all industrial concerns and all cooperating interests engaged in interstate commerce in which there is either monopoly or control of the market of the principles on which we have gone in regulating transportation concerns engaged in such commerce. The antitrust law should be kept on the statute-books and strengthened so as to make it genuinely and thoroughly effective against every big concern tending to monopoly or guilty of antisocial practices. At the same time, a national industrial commission should be created which should have complete power to regulate and control all the great industrial concerns engaged in interstate business—which practically means all of them in this country. This commission should exercise over these industrial concerns like powers to those exercised over the railways by the Interstate Commerce Commission, and over the national banks by the comptroller of the currency, and additional powers if found necessary. . . .

There can be no greater issue than that of conservation in this country. Just as we must conserve our men, women, and children, so we must conserve the resources of the land on which they live. We must conserve the soil so that our children shall have a land that is more and not less fertile than that our fathers dwelt in. . . .

Surely there never was a fight better worth making than the one in which we are engaged. It little matters what befalls any one of us who for the time being stands in the forefront of the battle. I hope we shall win, and I believe that if we can wake the people to what the fight really means we shall win. But, win or lose, we shall not falter. Whatever fate may at the moment overtake any of us, the movement itself will not stop. Our cause is based on the eternal principle of righteousness; and even though we who now lead may for the time fail, in the end the cause itself shall triumph. . . . Now to you men, who, in your turn, have come together to spend and be spent in the endless crusade against wrong, to you who face the future resolute and confident, to you who strive in a spirit of brotherhood for the betterment of our nation, to you who gird yourselves for this great new fight in the never-ending warfare for the good of mankind, I say in closing . . . : We stand at Armageddon, and we battle for the Lord.

2. Program to Restore Economic Opportunity: Woodrow Wilson

DURING THE *1912 campaign the primary difference between Wilson and Roosevelt appears in the Democratic nominee's emphasis on the importance of individual opportunity for the "little man." Roosevelt mocked this New Freedom as "the very old freedom to cut your neighbor's throat." In his inaugural address reprinted below, Wilson continued to advocate programs designed to further economic competition: tariff schedules written to expose inefficient large corporations to incursions by more effective smaller firms, meanwhile lowering prices to consumers; a federal reserve system meant to curb the power of huge big-city banks and make credit more accessible to businessmen, including farmers, outside the great centers of commerce; and legislation simplifying federal efforts to restore competition in industries monopolized by one or even by a few firms, through antitrust action. In the most vague terms Wilson also mentioned the necessity for federal action to aid men, women, and children too unorganized or otherwise too weak to protect themselves adequately against exploitation, impure food, and unsanitary living conditions.*

SOURCE: Ray Stannard Baker and William E. Dodd, eds., *The New Democracy*, I (New York, 1926): 1–5. Reprinted by permission of Harper & Row, Publishers, Inc.

First Inaugural Address as President of the United States

DELIVERED MARCH 4, 1913
FROM OFFICIAL PUBLICATION IN MR. WILSON'S FILES

MY FELLOW CITIZENS:

There has been a change of government. It began two years ago, when the House of Representatives became Democratic by a decisive majority. It has now been completed. The Senate about to assemble will also be Democratic. The offices of President and Vice-President have been put into the hands of Democrats. What does the change mean? That is the question that is uppermost in our minds today. That is the question I am going to try to answer, in order, if I may, to interpret the occasion.

It means much more than the mere success of a party. The success of a party means little except when the Nation is using that party for a large and definite purpose. No one can mistake the purpose for which the Nation now seeks to use the Democratic Party. It seeks to use it to interpret a change in its own plans and point of view. Some old things with which we had grown familiar, and which had begun to creep into the very habit of our thought and of our lives, have altered their aspect as we have latterly looked critically upon them, with fresh, awakened eyes; have dropped their disguises and shown themselves alien and sinister. Some new things, as we look frankly upon them, willing to comprehend their real character, have come to assume the aspect of things long believed in and familiar, stuff of our own convictions. We have been refreshed by a new insight into our own life.

We see that in many things that life is very great. It is incomparably great in its material aspects, in its body of wealth, in the diversity and sweep of its energy, in the industries which have been conceived and built up by the genius of individual men and the limitless enterprise of groups of men. It is great, also, very great, in its moral force.

Nowhere else in the world have noble men and women exhibited in more striking forms the beauty and the energy of sympathy and helpfulness and counsel in their efforts to rectify wrong, alleviate suffering, and set the weak in the way of strength and hope. We have built up, moreover, a great system of government, which has stood through a long age as in many respects a model for those who seek to set liberty upon foundations that will endure against fortuitous change, against storm and accident. Our life contains every great thing, and contains it in rich abundance.

But the evil has come with the good, and much fine gold has been corroded. With riches has come inexcusable waste. We have squandered a great part of what we might have used, and have not stopped to conserve the exceeding bounty of nature, without which our genius for enterprise would have been worthless and impotent, scorning to be careful, shamefully prodigal as well as admirably efficient. We have been proud of our industrial achievements, but we have not hitherto stopped thoughtfully enough to count the human cost, the cost of lives snuffed out, of energies overtaxed and broken, the fearful physical and spiritual cost to the men and women and children upon whom the dead weight and burden of it all has fallen pitilessly the years through. The groans and agony of it all had not yet reached our ears, the solemn, moving undertone of our life, coming up out of the mines and factories and out of every home where the struggle had its intimate and familiar seat. With the great Government went many deep secret things which we too long delayed to look into and scrutinize with candid, fearless eyes. The great Government we loved has too often been made use of for private and selfish purposes, and those who used it had forgotten the people.

At last a vision has been vouchsafed us of our life as a whole. We see the bad with the good, the debased and decadent with the sound and vital. With this vision we approach new affairs. Our duty is to cleanse, to reconsider, to restore, to correct the evil without impairing the good, to purify and humanize every process of our common life without weakening or sentimentalizing it. There has been something crude and heartless and unfeeling in our haste to succeed and be great. Our thought has been "Let every man look out for himself, let every generation look out for itself," while we reared giant machinery which made it impossible that any but those who stood at the levers of control should have a chance to look out for themselves. We had not forgotten our morals. We remembered well enough that we had set up a policy which was meant to serve the humblest as well as the most powerful, with an eye single to the standards of justice and fair play, and remembered it with pride. But we were very heedless and in a hurry to be great.

We have come now to the sober second thought. The scales of heedlessness have fallen from our eyes. We have made up our minds to square every process of our national life again with the standards we so proudly set up at the beginning and have always carried at our hearts. Our work is a work of restoration.

We have itemized with some degree of particularity the things that ought to be altered and here are some of the chief items: A tariff which cuts us off from our proper part in the commerce of the world, violates the just principles of taxation, and makes the Government a facile instrument in the hands of private interests; a banking and currency system based upon the necessity of the Government to sell its bonds fifty years ago and perfectly adapted to concentrating cash and restricting credits; an industrial system which, take it on all its sides, financial as well as administrative, holds capital in leading strings, restricts the liberties and limits the opportunities of labor, and exploits without renewing or conserving the natural resources of the country; a body of agricultural activities never yet given the efficiency of great business undertakings or served as it should be through the instrumentality of science taken directly to the farm, or afforded the facilities of credit best suited to its practical needs; watercourses undeveloped, waste places unreclaimed, forests untended, fast disappearing without plan or prospect of renewal, unregarded waste heaps at every mine. We have studied as perhaps no other nation has the most effective means of production, but we have not studied cost or economy as we should either as organizers of industry, as states men, or as individuals.

Nor have we studied and perfected the means by which government may be put at the service of humanity, in safeguarding the health of the Nation, the health of its men and its women and its children, as well as their rights in the struggle for existence. This is no sentimental duty. The firm basis of government is justice, not pity. These are matters of justice. There can be no equality or opportunity, the first essential of justice in the body politic, if men and women and children be not shielded in their lives, their very vitality, from the consequences of great industrial and social processes which they can not alter, control, or singly cope with. Society must see to it that it does not itself crush or weaken or damage its own constituent parts. The first duty of law is to keep sound the society it serves. Sanitary laws, pure food laws, and laws determining conditions of labor which individuals are powerless to determine for themselves are intimate parts of the very business of justice and legal efficiency.

These are some of the things we ought to do, and not leave the others undone, the old-fashioned, never-to-be-neglected, fundamental safeguarding of property and of individual right. This is the high enterprise of the new day: To lift everything that concerns our life as a Nation to the light that shines from the hearthfire of every man's conscience and vision of the right. It is inconceivable that we should do this as partisans; it is inconceivable we should do it in ignorance of the facts as they are or in blind haste. We shall restore, not destroy. We shall deal with our economic system as it is and as it may be modified, not as it might be if we had a clean sheet of paper to write upon; and step by step we shall make it what it should be, in the spirit of those who question their own wisdom and seek counsel and knowledge, not shallow self-satisfaction or the excitement of excursions whither they can not tell. Justice, and only justice, shall always be our motto.

And yet it will be no cool process of mere science. The Nation has been deeply stirred, stirred by a solemn passion, stirred by the knowledge of wrong, of ideals lost, of government too often debauched and made an instrument of evil. The feelings with which we face this new age of right and opportunity sweep across our heartstrings like some air out of God's own presence, where justice and mercy are reconciled and the judge and the brother are one. We know our task to be no mere task of politics but a task which shall search us through and through, whether we be able to understand our time and the need of our people, whether we be indeed their spokesmen and interpreters, whether we have the pure heart to comprehend and the rectified will to choose our high course of action.

This is not a day of triumph; it is a day of dedication. Here muster, not the forces of party, but the forces of humanity. Men's hearts wait upon us; men's lives hang in the balance; men's hopes call upon us to say what we will do. Who shall live up to the great trust? Who dares fail to try? I summon all honest men, all patriotic, all forward-looking men, to my side. God helping me, I will not fail them, if they will but counsel and sustain me!

3. The Socialist Alternative: Eugene V. Debs

EUGENE VICTOR DEBS, *former railroad worker and organizer of the American Railway Union, received an opportunity for sustained study and thought about socialism when he was jailed for contempt of court as a result of his participation in the Pullman strike of 1894. Thereafter Debs acted as the leading Socialist spokesman in the United States, and he was five times the party's candidate for President (1900, 1904, 1908, 1912, 1920). Despite the presence on the ballot in 1912 of two dynamic arch-Progressive candidates, Wilson and Roosevelt, Debs won almost 900,000 votes out of about 15,000,000 cast, by far the largest proportion of the total that the Socialist party ever has obtained in the United States. Splits engendered by World War I and the Communist Revolution in Russia played the most important role in disrupting this promising alternative to the essentially capitalistic major parties.*

The appeal of the Socialist party is to all the useful people of the nation, all who work with brain and muscle to produce the nation's wealth and who promote its progress and conserve its civilization.

Only they who bear its burdens may rightfully enjoy the blessings of civilized society.

There are no boundary lines to separate race from race, sex from sex, or creed from creed in the Socialist party. The common rights of all are equally recognized.

Every human being is entitled to sunlight and air, to what his labor produces, and to an equal chance with every other human being to unfold and ripen and give to the world the riches of his mind and soul.

Economic slavery is the world's greatest curse today. Poverty and misery, prostitution, insanity and crime are its inevitable results.

The Socialist party is the one party which stands squarely and uncompromisingly for the abolition of industrial slavery; the one party pledged in every fiber of its being to the economic freedom of all the people.

SOURCE: Debs' speech accepting the Socialist presidential nomination in 1912, in *Socialist Campaign Book* (Chicago, 1912), pp. 14–15. Reprinted by permission of the U.S. Socialist Party.

So long as the nation's resources and productive and distributive machinery are the private property of a privileged class the masses will be at their mercy, poverty will be their lot, and life will be shorn of all that raises it above the brute level.

The infallible test of a political party is the private ownership of the sources of wealth and the means of life. Apply that test to the Republican, Democratic and Progressive parties and upon that basic, fundamental issue you will find them essentially one and the same. They differ according to the conflicting interests of the privileged classes, but at bottom they are alive and stand for capitalist class rule and working class slavery.

The new Progressive party is a party of progressive capitalism. It is lavishly financed and shrewdly advertised. But it stands for the rule of capitalism all the same.

When the owners of the trusts finance a party to put themselves out of business, when they turn over their wealth to the people from whom they stole it and go to work and make an honest living, it will be time enough to consider the merits of the Roosevelt Progressive party.

One question is sufficient to determine the true status of all these parties. Do they want the workers to own the tools they work with, control their own jobs, and secure to themselves the wealth they produce? Certainly not. That is utterly ridiculous and impossible from their point of view.

The Republican, Democratic and Progressive parties all stand for the private ownership by the capitalists of the productive machinery used by the workers, so that the capitalists can continue to filch the wealth produced by the workers.

The Socialist party is the only party which declares that the tools of labor belong to labor and that the wealth produced by the working class belongs to the working class.

Intelligent workingmen are no longer deceived. They know that the struggle in which the world is engaged today is a class struggle and that in this struggle the workers can never win by giving their votes to capitalist parties. They have tried this for many years and it has always produced the same results to them.

The class of privilege and pelf has had the world by the throat and the working class beneath its iron-shot hoofs long enough. The magic word of freedom is ringing through the nation and the spirit of intelligent revolt is finding expression in every land beneath the sun.

The solidarity of the working class is the silent force in the social transformation of which we behold the signs upon every hand. Nearer and nearer they are being drawn together in the bonds of unionism; clearer and clearer becomes their collective vision; greater and greater grows the power that throbs within them.

They are the twentieth century hosts of freedom who are to destroy all despotisms, topple over all thrones, seize all sceptres of authority and hold them in their own strong hands, tear up all privilege by the roots, and consecrate the earth and all its fulness to the joy and service of all humanity.

It is vain to hope for material relief under the prevailing system of capitalism. All the reforms that are proposed by the three capitalist parties, even if carried out in good faith, would still leave the working class in industrial slavery.

The working class will never be emancipated by the grace of the capitalist class, but only by overthrowing that class.

The power to emancipate itself is inherent in the working class and this power must be developed through sound education and applied through sound organization.

It is as foolish and self-destructive for workingmen to turn to Republican, Democratic and Progressive parties on election day as it would be for them to turn to the Manufacturers' Association and the Citizens' Alliance when they are striking against starvation wages.

The capitalist class is organized economically and politically to keep the working class in subjection and perpetuate its power as a ruling class. They do not support a working class union nor a working class party. They are not so foolish. They wisely look out for themselves.

The capitalist class despise a working class party. Why should the working class give their support to a capitalist class party?

Capitalist misrule under which workingmen suffer slavery and the most galling injustice exists only because it has workingmen's support. Withdraw that support and capitalism is dead.

The capitalists can enslave and rob the workers only by the consent of the workers when they cast their ballots on election day.

Every vote cast for a capitalist party, whatever its name, is a vote for wage slavery, for poverty and degradation.

Every vote cast for the Socialist party, the workers' own party, is a vote for emancipation.

4. Social Reform: Woodrow Wilson

A LARGE *body of social legislation already had been passed by the states when Wilson took office in 1913. This legislation included laws regulating the wages and hours of working women and children, working conditions, workmen's compensation legislation, minimum wages, health insurance, and public assistance to mothers with dependent children. During the first years of his administration, Wilson avoided advocating federal social welfare legislation on the grounds that, constitutionally, most suggestions of this kind either were illegal or were matters to be decided by the individual states. Wilson's ideas changed somewhat around 1915, perhaps prodded by Roosevelt's return to the Republican party and the obvious necessity of winning votes from former Progressives if he expected reelection in 1916. This report, from the* Catholic Charities Review, *describes some of the more important legislative consequences of Wilson's shift in policy.*

The Federal Law for Workmen's Compensation

After more than three years of agitation on the part of its friends, the Kern-McGillicuddy bill became a law just before the adjournment of Congress last September. It provides for the compensation of injured workmen in the service of the Government of the United States. These number about one half a million. Among its main provisions are the following: a reasonable amount of medical, surgical, and hospital services and supplies are to be furnished to all injured civil servants, beginning with the fourth day of their disability; a workman who is totally disabled receives two-thirds of his regular wages during the whole time of his incapacity, even though it should last until his death; in case of partial disability the worker is to be paid two-thirds of the loss of wages due to

SOURCE: "Social Questions," *The Catholic Charities Review*, 1 (January 1917): 11–14. Reprinted by permission of the publisher.

the injury; for example, a person who can now earn only twenty-five dollars a month instead of the one hundred dollars that he regularly commanded before his injury, gets as compensation under the law two-thirds of the lost seventy-five dollars, thus receiving as combined wages and compensation a monthly income of seventy-five dollars; if the workman's injury results in his death, his widow receives thirty-five percent of his former wage rate, and an additional ten percent for each child, but her total payments must not exceed two-thirds of her deceased husband's wages; these payments continue until the widow dies or marries, and until the children die, marry, or reach the age of eighteen years. Not the least important feature of the law is that its benefits are extended to the victims of certain occupational *diseases*. In the great majority of the State laws, compensation is restricted to injuries caused by accidents; workers who become partially or totally disabled from diseases contracted at their work are given no relief whatever.

This law is the most liberal of its kind ever enacted in any country. It should prove effective as an example to those States that have not yet provided compensation legislation for workers in private employments, as well as to those States whose present laws on the subject are inadequate.

The Federal Child Labor Law

The provisions of the law against child labor enacted by Congress last summer are designed to prevent young persons from being employed in industrial occupations before they are fourteen years of age, or at night, or longer than eight hours a day. In hazardous occupations the minimum age at which they may go to work is sixteen years. While the standards set up by this law are fairly high, they are found in the statutes of more than half the States. The striking thing about the measure is not the nature of its restrictions upon child labor, but the manner of attempting to secure them.

In the distribution of powers between our State and Federal governments, the latter can enact only those kinds of laws that are allotted to it by the Federal Constitution. All matters not specifically mentioned in that document are reserved to the several States. Now there is nothing in the Federal Constitution authorizing our national Congress to make laws explicitly concerning the conditions of labor or industry. All such regulations belong properly to the States. For this reason the advocates of child labor regulation at first appealed to the States, and within the last fifteen or twenty years have succeeded in getting most of them to enact reasonably good laws of this nature. But certain of the Southern States refused to bring their legislation on this subject up to the standard of reasonable requirements. Therefore, the friends of proper child labor restriction turned for assistance to Congress. They believed that what the latter body was unable to do directly and explicitly, it might accomplish by indirection. In the eighth section of the first article of the Constitution of the United States, Congress is empowered to "regulate commerce among the several States." The power to regulate commerce includes the power to prohibit commerce; therefore, let Congress forbid the transportation from one State to another of articles made by child labor. Hence the new Federal law simply prohibits any establishment that employs children in conditions contrary to the standards set up in the law, from shipping its products in interstate commerce. No establishment is prevented from selling its products, whether made by child labor or not, within the State in which it is located; for Congress has no power to make such a regulation. Its authority extends only to goods that pass from one State to another. Practically all important employers of child labor in mills, factories, canneries, workshops, mines and quarries, however, do an interstate business. Rather than give this up, they will comply with the law in the matter of child labor restrictions, or will cease entirely to employ children. In a word, the law seeks to abolish child labor by making it unprofitable.

The law will be attacked in the courts on the ground that it is not authorized by the interstate commerce clause of the Constitution. The argument will be that this clause merely empowers Congress to regulate the *instrumentalities* of commerce, such as railroads, cars, and ships, and that it does not authorize interfering with the content or subject matter, the goods shipped; or at any rate, that it does not give Congress the right to prohibit commerce entirely under the guise of regulation. It is a nice constitutional question. In the minds of the men who wrote the Constitution there was probably no intention of enabling Congress to exercise any such power as is contemplated by the law that we are considering. Nevertheless, this would not be the first instance in which the language of the Constitution has been interpreted to mean more than the Fathers intended it to include. The Constitution has been more than once amended by the process of judicial construction. With a Constitution that is so difficult of formal amendment as ours, it is not only desirable but necessary that the Supreme Court should utilize this method of virtual amendment. Otherwise, our social and industrial life would be strangled by a Constitution that was made to fit the conditions of the eighteenth century. It is the belief of the friends of the Federal child labor law that the Supreme Court has already virtually amended the interstate commerce clause of the Constitution sufficiently to provide a basis for declaring the present measure constitutional. When it is decided that the law forbidding the transportation of lottery tickets from one State to another was within the power of Congress, it seems to have sanctioned the principle that the constitutional authority to regulate commerce among the States includes the power to prohibit such interstate commerce as is harmful to the public welfare.

The Movement for a Federal Eight Hour Law

It is proposed to apply the principle underlying the Federal child labor law to the working day of women. A few States have already passed laws limiting the hours of labor for female workers to eight per day, and these have been sustained by the United States Supreme Court as a legitimate exercise of the police power by the States. But it will be a long time before all, or even a majority, of the States will follow the good example set by California, Washington, and Oregon. Hence the advocates of the shorter work day for women are agitating for a Federal law to make at one stroke the eight hour day universal. Like the child labor statute, such a law would prohibit the shipment in interstate commerce of goods made or handled in establishments employing women for a longer work day than eight hours. The National Consumers' League, the Women's Trade Union League, and other organizations have within the last few months held largely attended meetings in the interest of such legislation. If the Supreme Court should uphold the Federal child labor law, it would probably sustain an eight hour day law enacted by Congress, and applying only to women. If it declares constitutional the Oregon minimum wage law, it would probably sanction a Federal statute forbidding the interstate transportation of goods by establishments employing women at less than a minimum living wage. Thus the way would be open for national and uniform regulation of all the conditions of labor for women and children. A little later, if the Supreme Court should declare minimum wage laws and eight hour day laws constitutional when enacted by the States for men, we should be able to apply such legislation to the whole country by means of Federal statues embodying the principle of the Federal child labor law. In this way we should have at last and by indirection a condition that ought to have been attainable at first, and by direct Federal action. Inasmuch as both the employers and the employees of one State are affected by the labor regulations of almost every other State, our industrial legislation should be uniform throughout the whole country. Inasmuch as it will not be feasible for a long time yet to amend the Federal Constitution so as to enable Congress to pass such laws directly, the interstate commerce clause of the Constitution should be utilized as far as the Supreme Court will permit. Perhaps, after all, this is the safer and more acceptable way; for it will be less obnoxious to those who dislike to see radical changes in the phraseology of the Constitution.

The Social Insurance Conference

The Conference on social insurance called by the International Association of Industrial Accident Boards and Commissions was held at Washington, D.C., December 5th to December 9th. During the first two days the attention of the Conference was devoted to the various problems arising out of the Administration of Workmen's Compensation Legislation in this country. Under this head the relative merits and demerits of the Industrial Accident Board System, the Industrial Commission System and the District System of administering compensation laws were discussed. Other problems coming up for discussion were the advantages and the disadvantages of the different insurance carriers, the principles of rate-making, the physical examination of employees, limitations of American compensation laws and occupational diseases. The discussion of the relative merits and demerits of the different methods of carrying Workmen's Compensation Insurance lead to a heated controversy between the representatives of the private stock companies and the State Insurance Associations. Considerable interest was manifested in the papers on the physical examination of employees and on occupational diseases. It was the consensus of the Conference that occupational diseases should be included within the scope of the compensation laws. One important subject, the prevention of industrial accidents, seems to have been entirely overlooked.

On the third day the Conference turned its attention to Sickness Insurance. The various agencies for sickness insurance in this country at the present time formed the subject of interesting papers. In regard to the feasibility of adopting compulsory sickness insurance for wage earners in this country the members of the Conference were by no means unanimous. The representatives of the American Association for Labor Legislation favored the immediate introduction of compulsory sickness insurance. The representatives of insurance companies were in favor of a voluntary system of sickness insurance. The representatives of the American Federation of Labor bitterly denounced all systems of compulsory sickness insurance. The fourth day of the Conference was devoted to the consideration of the existing agencies for old age and invalidity insurance, Maternity Benefits and Mothers' Pensions, the problems receiving the greatest amount of attention being the relation of private pension funds established by employers to the welfare of their workers and the administration of mothers' pension laws in the different States. At the final session of the Conference held Saturday morning, December 9th, interesting papers were read on the British National System of Unemployment Insurance and the Massachusetts System of Savings Bank Life Insurance.

5. The New Wilsonian Coalition: Walter Lippmann

AFTER ROOSEVELT'S *return to the Republican party and Wilson's adoption of much of the New Nationalism, the editors of the* New Republic, *formerly Roosevelt's most effective intellectual supporters, shifted in varying degrees to support of Woodrow Wilson's reelection. Walter Lippmann's article explaining this shift was the most concise and perhaps the most eloquent of a series of similar essays by* New Republic *staff members. These were symptomatic of a wholesale move into the Wilson camp of social workers, intellectuals, feminists, and others impressed with Wilson's social welfare policies.*

Not Mr. Wilson's eloquence but his extraordinary growth has made the case for him. I shall vote not for the Wilson who has uttered a few too many noble sentiments, but for the Wilson who is evolving under experience and is remaking his philosophy in the light of it, for the Wilson who is temporarily at least creating, out of the reactionary, parochial fragments of the Democracy, the only party which at this moment is national in scope, liberal in purpose, and effective in action.

He was the nominee of a party which was divided between the machine which almost selected Champ Clark, and the unilluminated provincialism of Bryan. Its stock in trade was a tradition of hostility to organized action, of laissez faire in government, of the crudest kind of eighteenth-century amateur democracy. In foreign affairs it was a party of isolation and irresponsibility. It seemed to lack all power of cohesion, it showed no signs of any ability to plan comprehensively, and in the test of action it seemed to have an irresistible tendency to fly apart into sulky groups. It rested on the tragic solidarity of the South, the corrupt machines of the cities, and a helpless radicalism in other parts of the country.

That was the condition which confronted Woodrow Wilson, the

SOURCE: Walter Lippmann, "The Case for Wilson," *The New Republic* (October 14, 1916), pp. 263–264. Reprinted by permission of the author.

condition of his own party and the traditions in his own mind. The worst faults of his administration are clearly due to it. The state of his party explains the Bryan appointment as well as the halting of administrative progress. The ugly fact is that Mr. Wilson had to purchase the unity of his party by yielding to its hunger. He stooped to conquer. But he conquered. He did not yield as Taft did out of mere lazy good humor and conventionalism. He yielded enough to turn the Democratic Congress into the most constructive legislative instrument which has been at the Capitol in generations. What is more, he did not continue to yield, for the later appointments are of an altogether different quality than the earlier ones. Once he had unified his party, subdued Bryanism and the machine, he began to substitute purpose where there had been mere partisanship. He became the master of his party, and he has used the mastery for ends which are on the whole so undeniably good that Mr. Hughes has hardly dared to attack them. This fashioning of an old party into something like a national liberal organization is, it seems to me, in a government by parties a large accomplishment. With all Mr. Roosevelt's skill he failed to do it with the Republicans in the nation as Mr. Hughes failed in New York. The weak, impractical doctrinaire has proved to be one of the great party leaders of American history. On that record I cannot believe that Mr. Wilson is entirely inept.

While this transformation was taking place, Mr. Wilson was also shifting his ground. What the hostile critics call his tendency to change his mind is not mere caprice. The changes on the whole are consistent with Mr. Wilson's growth from a laissez faire Democrat into a constructive nationalist. The Federal Reserve act, Rural Credits, the Federal Trade Commission, Preparedness, the Child Labor bill, the Tariff Board, the League to Enforce Peace, may represent a change of mind, but it is a change of mind in the same direction. They are the landmarks of a man's evolution from the impossibilism of a party tradition to a franker acceptance of the necessities of modern life. Why then in the name of sanity should a progressive object because experience is turning Mr. Wilson into a progressive? Why is it weakness for a President to learn? I can see no virtue in the picture of the strong, obstinate, consistent man who never learns and never forgets; and far from turning against Mr. Wilson because facts teach him wisdom, I find in that talent the chief reason for reelecting him.

The next years will bring us to the settlement of the war, and the infinite difficulties of the reconstruction. The man who made a fetish of consistency in such times would be a fool. To navigate the seas we shall want above all else a mind capable of learning quickly from experience. Most emphatically we shall not want a mind that lays down a policy evolved half consciously out of early education and class prejudices and then sticks to it no matter what the cost. Woodrow Wilson's sensitiveness to changing conditions, his quick imagination and real flexibility of mind are, it seems to me, a necessity in the immediate future. I should not claim that he always sees the facts truly, or that he has that resourcefulness and invention which produces the greatest statesmanship, but that he has them in higher degree than his opponent is fairly clear.

Not only is his mind better fitted for the kind of difficulty that the next years will produce, his underlying purposes seem to me to justify considerable confidence in him. He has seen, as I believe Mr. Hughes has not seen, that wealth and privilege have inordinate power, and I believe he has grown in sympathy with the desire to redress the balance of classes within the nation. In Mexico he has no doubt blundered many times, and has not succeeded even now in translating his purpose into an adequate policy. But at bottom he has been wise about Mexico, infinitely wiser than his critics. He has understood that the problem of order in Mexico was deeper than the question of armed protection of American property and lives, that permanent stability and progress could never be attained by intervention, and that Mexico would never be a good neighbor until the Mexicans had achieved a measure of self-government. Conquest would merely mean decades of insurrection against the American conqueror, and a perversion not only of Mexico's life but our own. There was no peace to be had by intervention or by the establishment of Huerta. It was to be had only by the success of a government something like Carranza's which can win and hold the confidence of the Mexican people. When Mr. Hughes talks about protecting American interests as if that were the whole problem he betrays the limitations of his mind.

Granting errors in the technique of foreign policy, Mr. Wilson's attitude towards the European war has been as sound as American tradition permitted. He has not been neutral in thought or action, though he talked about it. He has been consistently and courageously benevolent to the Allies. Indeed he may have sacrificed his political future because he would not fall into the easy temptation of twisting the lion's tail. So when Mr. Hughes goes to Milwaukee and allows the German-Americans to believe that he would have broken the British blockade, he may be honest, but he is not entitled to the votes of that powerful section of American opinion which believes that the cause of the western Allies is in a measure our cause. It seems to me fundamentally trivial that people who damn Mr. Wilson for failure to coerce Germany enough should be voting for a candidate who implies, though he is afraid to state it, that Mr. Wilson did not coerce the Allies enough. I do not understand it. I do not understand what Mr. Roosevelt and the others meant by all their talk these last two years that they should be bent on overturning the man who has stretched neutrality to the breaking point, in order to put in office a man who has never dared to face the issue which they told us was paramount.

Mr. Hughes on his campaign and the Republican party on its record do not deserve to win. Firmness—firmness, indeed! Is it firmness that characterized Mr. Hughes at Milwaukee? Vacillation—what of California? Good men in office—what of the men who surround Mr. Hughes today? Inept—is it possible to equal his treatment of Governor Johnson? Is there either courage or wisdom in Mr. Hughes's campaign? Has he faced any issue but the eight-hour law? Has he said one word about international affairs that shows a hint of statesmanship? Has he said anything about the tariff which McKinley wouldn't have said, or about labor to which Mr. Taft wouldn't assent?

Why then are we called to make the change, to defeat a man who has grown, who has mastered his party and recast his beliefs? There ought to be some very good reason for making a change now. Defeat Mr. Wilson in November; from November to March no nation on earth will know what our policy is. If Mr. Hughes takes office in March two or three months will be consumed in displacing incompetent Democrats and at least six in teaching Mr. Hughes the problems of his office. Those months are likely to be the most crucial months of our time, for in those months the settlement will be formulated. A change of government ought to take place only if there is a sharp necessity and a real alternative. The necessity may exist, but the alternative doesn't. No human being, probably not even Mr. Hughes himself, knows how he would alter the policy of the nation. It would be mere restlessness to make the change.

Mr. Hughes was nominated in the dark, but he ought not be to be elected in the dark, not today, not in these difficult times.

6. Progressive Scholarship: James Harvey Robinson

JAMES HARVEY ROBINSON, *along with Charles Beard, Carl Becker, Harry Elmer Barnes, and Frederick Jackson Turner led the demand for a "new history," a history which would deal with the larger issues of contemporary life, attempting to explain their origin, using tools developed by social scientists in appropriate cases. When put into practice, Robinson's ideas made history an important intellectual weapon in the progressive movement. Certain of Charles Beard's works, especially* An Economic Interpretation of the Constitution *(1913), played an effective role in the reform movement.*

The Spirit of Conservatism in the Light of History

I

It is a long, long time since human history began, when a species of apes, probably closely allied to the gorilla and chimpanzee of the African forests, found itself able to go on its hind legs without the assistance of its fore limbs, leaving these free to become ever more dexterous arms and hands. This new being, with his good, big brain case, found that his ability to do things with his hands begat a tendency to use his advantages in novel ways. Accidentally casting bits of flint into the fire, he perceived that they would crack into convenient pieces for cutting and scraping, and so he perhaps made his first tools. What manner of creature he was—whether still hairy, and sleeping, mayhap, in trees like his congeners, the apes of today—is a matter of conjecture. The veteran French archaeologist, de Mortillet, conjectures that the earliest of the chipped stone tools found in the drift along river banks may be assigned to a period extending back two hundred and forty thousand years. Sup-

SOURCE: James Harvey Robinson, *The New History* (New York, 1912), pp. 236–266. Reprinted by permission of the estate of James Harvey Robinson.

pose we allow some two hundred and fifty thousand years back of that for the ancestors of paleolithic man, the makers of the so-called dawn stones (eoliths), we arrive at the conclusion that man and his upright forerunners have lived on the earth for at least half a million of years.[1] I think that few versed in prehistoric archaeology or in biology would feel inclined to reduce this period, although we have no way of determining it with any satisfactory degree of accuracy. Now to judge from the cavern remains, it would appear that no very great progress was made except in the skill with which the flints were chipped, in the variety of their forms, and in the decoration of bone objects, until perhaps ten thousand years ago, when the so-called neolithic or ground stone period, with its pottery, its agriculture, and its rude dwellings, comes clearly into sight. The American aborigines were still in the neolithic age when the first Europeans arrived in the late fifteenth century.

These facts about man's past are still such comparatively recent discoveries that they have not as yet so fundamentally revolutionized our thought as they should and will. Lyell's famous book on *The Antiquity of Man*, which first brought the great age of the human species to the knowledge of intelligent English readers, was published in 1863. It is true that Augustine found it necessary, in order to secure precedence for the Hebrew prophets, to refute the "lying vanity" of certain authors who maintained that the Egyptians had been carrying on their astronomical observations for no less than a hundred thousand years. How was this possible, he scornfully asks, when not six thousand years have elapsed since the creation of the first man?[2] This estimate of the great church father was somewhat reduced by an English prelate, Archbishop Usher, in the time of Cromwell. With laudable precision he assigned to Friday, October 28, 4004 B.C. the creation of all the terrestrial animals and the appearance of Adam, who, wholly inexperienced as he was, was called upon to devise a complete zoological nomencla-

1. De Mortillet, G. et A., *La Préhistoire*, Paris s. d. (1910), pp. 663 sq. Even archaeologists who are unconvinced that the so-called eoliths indicate human adaptations do not usually question the fact that man had probably used flint and shells long before the "fist hatchet" was elaborated.

2. *De Civitate Dei*, ed. Dombart (Teubner edition), lib. XVIII, cap. 40: "De Aegyptiorum mendacissima vanitate, quae antiquitati scientiae suae centum milia ascribit annorum."

ture. Before the close of the day Eve was created to solace his loneliness, and the nuptials, duly performed, constituted the last act of the first working week.[3] Although some thoughtful philosophers and theologians of the early church had expressed doubts as to the literal truth of this account, Archbishop Usher's exactitude found favor in the eyes of Protestants in the seventeenth century, and it was left for Darwin, Lyell, Huxley, and the anthropologists fundamentally to readjust our historical perspective, not half a century since.

In order to understand the light which the discovery of the vast age of mankind casts on our present position, our relation to the past and our hopes for the future, let us borrow, with some modifications, an ingenious device for illustrating modern historical perspective.[4] Let us imagine the whole history of mankind crowded into twelve hours, and that we are living at noon of the long human day. Let us, in the interest of moderation and convenient reckoning, assume that man has been upright and engaged in seeking out inventions for only two hundred and forty thousand years. Each hour on our clock will then represent twenty thousand years, each minute three hundred and thirty-three and a third years. For over eleven and a half hours nothing was recorded. We know of no persons or events; we only infer that man was living on the earth, for we find his stone tools, bits of his pottery, and some of his pictures of mammoths and bison. Not until twenty minutes before twelve do the earliest vestiges of Egyptian and Babylonian civilization begin to appear. The Greek literature philosophy, and science of which we have been accustomed to speak as "ancient," are not seven minutes old. At one minute before twelve Lord Bacon wrote his *Advancement of Learning*, to which we shall recur presently, and not half a minute has elapsed since man first began to make the steam engine do his work for him. There is, I think, nothing delusive about this reduced scale of things. It is much easier for us to handle and speculate upon than the life-sized picture, which so transcends our experience that we cannot grasp it.

Two reflections are obvious: In the first place, those whom we

3. *Annales veteris Testamenti a prima mundi origine deducti*, London, 1651, p. 1.

4. One of Haeckel's students, Heinrich Schmidt, seems to have first hit upon this method of representing "cosmological perspective." See Lester F. Ward, *Pure Sociology*, 1907, p. 38n.

call the ancients—Thales, Pythagoras, Socrates, Plato, Aristotle, Hipparchus, Lucretius—are really our contemporaries. However remote they may have seemed on Archbishop Usher's plan of the past, they now belong to our own age. We have no reason whatever to suppose that their minds were bettter or worse than ours, except in point of knowledge, which has been accumulating since their day. In the second place, we are struck by the fact that man's progress was at first shockingly slow, well-nigh imperceptible for tens of thousands of years, but that it tends to increase in rapidity with an ever accelerating tempo. Our forefathers, the drift men, may have satisfied themselves for a hundred thousand years with a single stone implement, the so-called *coup de poing* or fist hatchet, used, as Sir John Lubbock surmises, for as many purposes as a boy's jackknife. In time they learned to make scrapers, borers, arrowheads, harpoon points, and rude needles of flint and bone. But it was scarcely more than half an hour before twelve by our clock that they can be shown to have invented pottery and become the possessors of herds. The use of bronze and iron is much more recent, and the men of the bronze age still retained a pious devotion to the venerable stone hatchet, which the priests appear to have continued to use to slay their victims, long after the metals began to be used.

The Greeks were the first of all peoples, so far as we know, to use their minds freely. They unquestionably demonstrated the capacity of our intellects in ethics, metaphysics, logic, and mathematics, but the incalculable importance of the common things round about them escaped them in the main. Aristotle seems to have conceived that all the practical arts had already been discovered. He was willing that the slaves should be left to carry them on, while the philosophers reasoned on the ideals of a contemplative life,—on the good, the true, and the beautiful. Doubtless some advance was suggested in what we should call applied science, especially at Alexandria, but conditions were unpropitious, and mankind had no better ways of meeting his practical needs in Roman times than he had before Aristotle summed up all the achievements of the preceding Greek thinkers. The great Christian fathers, Jerome, Augustine, Ambrose, if they did not think material things absolutely bad, at least had no interest in them.[5] Their gaze was fixed on the relation of the soul to God. This transcended knowledge. Their

5. Henry Osborn Taylor, *The Mediaeval Mind*, 1911, Ch. IV.

contemporaries, the Neoplatonists, maintained that the highest truth came through intuition. Reason could reveal at best only unimportant matters. Both Neoplatonists and Christians were far more interested in miracles and various magical and sacramental methods of promoting man's heavenly interests than in a study of God's world. It was with this heritage that the Middle Ages began. A great part of what had been known in the Father's time was forgotten. The textbooks handed down a little Greek knowledge, half understood and mixed with incredible errors. The natural world was looked upon as at best a sort of gigantic allegory. The minerals possessed moral and magical virtues, rather than chemical and physical. The alleged habits of the lion recalled the death and resurrection of Christ, and those of the wren illustrated our dependence on the past. With the rediscovery of Aristotle's works, which were prayerfully studied in the universities in the thirteenth century and elaborately explained and interpreted by the great Dominican friars, Albert the Great and Thomas Aquinas, a new barrier was erected to the fruitful study of nature and the application of knowledge to man's material welfare. All of Aristotle's mistakes as well as all of the mistakes of his new interpreters, became sanctified.

Roger Bacon, the first person, so far as we know, to express an unbounded confidence in the possibilities of experimental science, impatiently declared that it would be far better if all the works of Aristotle were destroyed than that the universities should be engaged in attempting to get at the sense of the bad Latin translations upon which they were dependent. Aristotle, he concedes, certainly knew a great deal; but at best he only planted the tree of knowledge, and it had still many branches to put forth. "If we mortals could continue to live for countless centuries, we could never hope to reach full and complete knowledge of all that is to be known." Bacon held that the intelligent man of science should acquaint himself with the simple, homely things that farmers and old women know about. While in many ways the victim of his age, Roger Bacon, a little over six hundred years ago, gave first expression to the promise of man's happiness that lay in a study of plain material things. Experimental science,[6] he prophesied, would en-

6. Perhaps the most striking presentation of Bacon's view is to be found in the following words: "Quia licet per tria sciamus, videlicet per auctoritatem, et rationem, et experientiam, tamen auctoritas non sapit nisi detur ejus ratio,

able men to move ships without rowers, carriages might be propelled at an incredible speed without animals to draw them, flying machines could be devised to navigate the air like birds, and bridges might be constructed without supports ingeniously to span rivers.[7]

These tentative and seemingly fantastic suggestions came—to revert to our clock—about two minutes before twelve. A whole minute more was required before the expostulations of Roger Bacon was really heeded. The leaders of Protestantism had no heart in what we call progress. Luther decried reason as a "pretty harlot" who would blind us to the great truths God had revealed in the Bible. Melanchthon reedited with enthusiastic approval an ancient astrology. Calvin declared man innately and unspeakably bad and corrupt, utterly incapable of essentially bettering himself. But Pomponazzi and Giordano Bruno, and then Francis Bacon and Descartes, about one minute before twelve, began to batter down the great edifice which the scholastic doctors had reared from the blocks they had appropriated from Aristotle. They pleaded for reason and denounced the senseless respect for tradition. Descartes, at the close of his immortal treatise on *The Method of Seeking Truth*, says that he is writing in his own native French instead of the Latin of his Jesuit instructors because he hopes to reach those who use their own good wits instead of relying on old books. A little earlier Lord Bacon published his wonderful *Advancement of Learning*, also in his own mother tongue, and at the end of his life his *Novum Organon*, in Latin. In both he deals with what he calls "the kingdom of man." Augustine knew only of a kingdom of God and a kingdom of the devil. Lord Bacon was the first to popularize, in his varied and resourceful English, the promises of experimental science. He says:—

> Antiquity deserveth that reverence, that men should take a stand thereupon and discover what is the best way; but when the discovery is well taken, then to make progression. And to speak truly, *Antiquitas saeculi juventus mundi*. These times are the ancient times,

---

nec dat intellectum sed credulitatem; credimus enim auctoritati, sed non propter eam intelligimus. Nec ratio potest scire an sophisma vel demonstratio, nisi conclusionem sciamus experiri per opera." *Compendium studii*, Opera Inedita, ed. Brewer, p. 397.

7. "Epistola Fratris Rogerii Baconis de secretis operibus artis et naturae," *loc. cit.*, pp. 532 sqq.

when the world is ancient, and not those which we account ancient *ordine retrogrado*, by a computation backward from ourselves. . . .

Another error that hath also some affinity with the former, is the conceit that of former opinions or sects, after variety and examination, the best hath still prevailed and suppressed the rest; so that if a man should begin the labor of a new search, he were but like to light upon something formerly rejected, and by rejection brought into oblivion: as if the multitude, or the wisest for the multitude's sake, were not ready to give passage rather to that which is superficial, than to that which is substantial and profound; for the truth is, that time seemeth to be of the nature of a river or stream, which carrieth down to us that which is light and blown up, and sinketh and drowneth that which is weighty and solid. . . .

Another error hath proceeded from too great a reverence and a kind of adoration of the mind and understanding of man; by means whereof, men have withdrawn themselves too much from the contemplation of nature, and the observations of experience, and have tumbled up and down in their own reason and conceits. Upon these intellectualists, which are notwithstanding commonly taken for the most sublime and divine philosophers, Heraclitus gave a just censure, saying, "Men sought truth in their own little worlds and not in the great and common world;" for they disdain to spell, and so by degrees to read in the volume of God's works. . . .

But the greatest error of all the rest is the mistaking or misplacing of the last or furthest end of knowledge. For men have entered into a desire of learning and knowledge, sometimes upon a natural curiosity and inquisitive appetite; sometimes to entertain their minds with variety and delight; sometimes for ornament and reputation; and sometimes to enable them to victory of wit and contradiction, and most times for lucre and profession; and seldom sincerely to give a true account of their gift of reason, to the benefit and use of men; as if there were sought in knowledge a couch whereupon to rest a searching and restless spirit . . . or a shop for profit and sale; and not a rich storehouse for the glory of the Creator and the relief of man's estate.[8]

Bacon thus undermines reverence for the past by pointing out that it rests on a gross misapprehension. Living before us, the ancients could not be expected to be our peers in knowledge or experience. He would have the universities give up worshiping Aristotle and his commentators, cease "tumbling up and down" in their own metaphysical exaltations, and turn to the study of real things in the world about them. The reason for such study should be, first and foremost, the bright prospect of relieving man's estate.

8. *Advancement of Learning*, Bk. I, Ch. V, sections 1–11, *passim*.

Like Sir Thomas More, Bacon wrote a Utopia, the *New Atlantis*. The central feature of his ideal community was a national academy of sciences, a sort of Carnegie Institution, in which all sorts of experiments were carried on with a view to making discoveries designed to better the people's lot. Bacon has often been reproached with making no real contributions to science.[9] The criticism is probably just, but his role was that of a herald, as he himself recognized. He was the trumpeter who announced the dawn of our own day.

It was in 1605 that the *Advancement of Learning* was first published. And we may safely say that it is scarcely three centuries since the idea of the possibility of indefinite progress through man's own conscious efforts first clearly emerged in the minds of a very few thoughtful persons. And it is to Francis Bacon that the glory is due, as we have said, of first popularizing this great idea—the greatest single idea in the whole history of mankind in the vista of possibilities which it opens before us.

The idea of conscious progress was not only essentially new; it could only develop in an obviously dynamic social environment and with the growth of historic perspective. The Greek thinkers did not have it at all in its modern form, so far as we can judge. It is true that Herodotus had a lively appreciation of the general debt of Greek civilization to the Egyptians, and Plato now and then refers to Egypt, but there is no clear comprehension of just what we call progress. Aristotle was keenly aware of the development of Greek philosophy since the Ionian philosophers, but there is nothing to indicate that he thought of mankind as going on indefinitely discovering new truth, and he had none of Lord Bacon's interest in seeing the results of natural science applied to the gradual amelioration of the general lot of mankind. Lucretius, the Epicurean philosopher of Cicero's time, doubtless reflecting earlier Greek speculations, guessed that there had been a stone age, a bronze age, and an iron age.[10] But his was no philosophy of progress. Men

9. For example by Draper, in his *History of the Intellectual Development of Europe*.

10. In the oft-quoted and remarkable lines:—

> Arma antiqua manus, ungues, dentesque fuerunt
> Et lapides, et item sylvarum fragmina rami,
> Posterius ferri vis est aerisque reperta;
> Sed prior aeris erat quam ferri cognitus usus.
>
> —*De rerum natura*, Bk. V, vv. 1281 sqq.

might, it is true, understand the universe so far as to perceive that it was the result of a fortuitous concourse of atoms, limited in kinds and obeying certain fixed laws. But the chief significance of this to Lucretius lay in abolishing all fear of the gods and of death. He did not discover in his mechanistic universe any promise of steady human progress. Indeed, he thought that a degeneration was setting in which foreboded the complete dissolution of the universe as we know it. In short, the Greek and Roman philosophers would have agreed with the medieval theologians in accepting the stationary character of the civilization with which they were familiar.

Augustine and his disciple, Orosius, gave history a new background, and illustrated God's dealings with man, from the Garden of Eden to the sack of Rome by Alaric; but they knew little or nothing of man's long history and unconscious progress in the past, nor did they anticipate any future improvement, for to the ardent Christian no earthly betterment could compare with the overwhelming issue which awaited man after death, when every one entered into eternal and unchanging bliss or misery. Accordingly, emulation consisted at best, until the opening of the seventeenth century, in striving to reach standards set by the past. The mere age of an institution or a belief came to be its surest sanction. The present might consider itself fortunate if it was at any point as good as the past. Only with Giordano Bruno and Lord Bacon did the strength of authority and tradition begin to be weakened, in spite of the hostility and consistent opposition of those who believed that they were defending God-given arrangements against the attacks of infidels, freethinkers, and rationalists.[11]

The process of weakening authority has been very rapid, considering its novelty and its fundamental character. It went on apace in the eighteenth century. Beccaria, the Italian jurist, who pleaded so eloquently for the revision of the horrible criminal law, foresaw that the conservatives would urge that the practices which he sought to abolish were ratified by a hoary past; he begged them to recollect that the past was after all only an immense sea of errors

11. This cursory treatment of a great theme, the origin of the idea of progress, may be supplemented by Delvaille, J., *Essai sur l'histoire de l'idée de Progrès jusqu'à la fin du XVIIIième Siècle*, 1910; Laurent, *Études sur l'histoire de l'humanité*, 1866, Ch. XII, pp. 63 sqq.; and Flint, *History of the Philosophy of History*, pp. 88 sqq.

from which there emerged here and there an obscure truth.[12] During the early years of the French Revolution, and under most discouraging circumstances, Condorcet wrote his famous treatise on the indefinite perfectibility of man. In it he seeks to trace the steps which humanity has taken in the past toward truth and happiness.

> "Ces observations," he trusts, "sur ce que l'homme a été, sur ce qu'il est aujourd'hui, conduiront ensuite aux moyens d'assurer et d'accélérer les nouveaux progrès que sa nature lui permet d'espérer encore. Tel est le but de l'ouvrage que j'ai enterpris, et dont le résultat sera de montrer, par le raisonnement et par les faits, qu'il n'a été marqué aucun terme au perfectionnement des facultés humaines, que la perfectibilité de l'homme est réellement indéfinie; que les progrès de cette perfectibilité, désormais indépendent de toute puissance qui voudrait l'arrêter, n'ont d'autre terme que la durée du globe où la nature nous a jetés."[13]

These genial speculations tending to turn men's eyes toward the future rather than the past were tremendously reenforced by the scientific discoveries of the nineteenth century. These proved, first, that man was learning a great deal more than any one had ever known before about the world and his place in it. Secondly, he was applying his knowledge in such a way as to make older methods of manufacture and transportation and communication appear very crude and antiquated. Lastly, Darwin, Lyell, Boucher de Perthes, Huxley, G. de Mortillet, Haeckel, and the rest established the fact that long before historic times man had proved himself capable of the most startling progress. He had not only made his way from savagery to civilization, but from the estate of an animal to that of a man. Not only had his ancestors gone on all fours and lived as the beasts of the field, but their remoter ancestors had mayhap lived in the sea and, as Darwin conjectures, resembled a so-called Ascidian larva, a tadpole-like creature not yet supplied with an unmistakable backbone. Roger Bacon, Francis Bacon, Descartes, Beccaria, Condorcet,—these and many like them stoutly maintained that man could learn indefinitely more than any of his predecessors had known, and could better his estate indefinitely by the use of this

12. Beccaria, *An Essay on Crimes and Punishments*, 1788, p. 113.
13. "Esquisse d'un tableau historique des progrès de l'esprit humain," 1797, p. 4.

knowledge and the desertion of ancient prejudices and habits. The nineteenth century proved conclusively that he *had* been learning and *had* been bettering himself for hundreds of thousands of years. But all this earlier progress had been *unconscious*. For the first time, close upon our own day, progress became an ideal consciously proclaimed and sought. So, whatever the progress of man has been during the twelve hours which we assign to him since he became man, it was only at about one minute to twelve *that he came to wish to progress, and still more recently that he came to see that he can voluntarily progress, and that he has progressed*. This appears to me to be the most impressive message that history has to give us, and the most vital in the light that it casts on the conduct of life.

II

If it be conceded that what we rather vaguely and provisionally call social betterment is coming to be regarded by large numbers of thoughtful persons as the chief interest in this game of life, does not the supreme value of history lie for us today in the suggestions that it may give us what may be called the technique of progress, and ought not those phases of the past especially to engross our attention which bear on this essential point? History has been regularly invoked, to substantiate the claims of the conservative, but has hitherto usually been neglected by the radical,[14] or impatiently repudiated as the chosen weapon of his enemy. The radical has not yet perceived the overwhelming value to him of a real understanding of the past. It is his weapon by right, and he should wrest it from the hand of the conservative. It has received a far keener edge during the last century, and it is the chief end of this essay to indicate how it can be used with the most decisive effect on the conservative.

So far as I know, no satisfactory analysis has ever been made of the conservative and radical temperaments. It is commonly assumed that every boy and girl is born into one or the other party, and doubtless as mere animals we differ greatly in our bravery, energy, and hopefulness. But nurture is now seen to be all that separates even the most uncompromising radical from a life far lower than that of any savage that exists on the earth at the present

14. The Marxian socialist, of course, uses his version of the past in support of his plan of social amelioration.

time. Even the recently extinct race of Tasmanians, still in a paleolithic stage of development, represented achievements which it took man long ages to accumulate. The literally uneducated European even today could neither frame a sentence nor sharpen a stick with a shell. A great part, then, of all that goes to make up the conservative or radical may be deemed the result of education in the broadest sense of that term, including everything that he has got from associating since infancy with civilized companions. I think that the modern anthropologist and psychologist would agree on this point; at least, every one who allows his mind to play freely over the question must concede that a great part of what has been mistaken for *nature* is really *nurture*, direct and indirect, conscious or, more commonly, wholly unconscious.

Now it has been the constant objection urged by the conservative against any reform of which he disapproved that it involved a change of human nature. He has flattered himself that he knew the chief characteristics of humanity and that, since it was hopeless to alter any of these, a change which seemed to imply such an alteration was obviously impracticable. This argument was long ago met by Montaigne, who declared that one who viewed Mother Nature in her full majesty and luster might perceive so general and so constant a variety that any individual and even the whole kingdom in which he happened to live must seem but a pin's point in comparison.[15] But there is a wholly new argument now available. Whether the zoologists are quite right or no in denying the possibility of the hereditary transmission of acquired traits, there is no reason to think that one particle of culture ever gets into the blood of our human species; it must either be transmitted by imitation or inculcation, or be lost, as Gabriel Tarde has made clear. We doubtless inherit the aptitudes of our parents, grandparents, and remoter ancestors; but any actual exercise that they may have made of the faculties which we share with them cannot influence us except by example or emulation. *Those things that the radical would alter and the conservative defend are therefore not traits of human nature but artificial achievements of human nurture.* Accordingly, the anthropologist and historian can rule out this fundamental conservative appeal to human nature by showing that the most extraordinary variety has existed and still exist in the habits, insti-

15. "On Education," *Essays*, Bk. I, Ch. XXV.

tutions, and feelings of various groups of mankind; and the student familiar with the chief results of embryology will see that the conservative has constantly mistaken the artificially acquired and hereditarily nontransmissible for constant and unalterable elements in our native outfit. And, indeed, it may be asked, if it has proved possible to alter an invertebrate tadpole-like creature living in the sea into an ape-like animal sleeping in a tree, and to transform the ape-like animal into an ingenious flint-chipping artist, able to paint pictures of bison and deer on the walls of a cave, and to derive from the flint chipper of the stone age a Plato able to tell a most edifying tale about a cave full of conservatives, what becomes of the argument for the fixity of human nature in any important sense?

While it is then highly unscientific and unhistorical to consider the way in which men behave and feel at any particular time as exhibiting the normal and immutable principles of human nature, history and anthropology nevertheless concur in proving that each new generation is indebted to the previous generation for very nearly all that it is and has. This is true of even the most rapidly progressing societies, and there is reason to suppose that a group of mankind could live indefinitely adhering to an unchanged scheme of civilization so long as they were undisturbed and their environment remained constant. We have seen how very recently the idea that progress is possible has dawned upon a small portion of mankind. The alterations which any people can effect within a half century in its prevailing ideas and institutions, and in the range and character of its generally diffused knowledge, are necessarily slight when compared with the vast heritage which has gradually been accumulating during hundreds of thousands of years. In order to make the nature and variety of our abject dependence on the past clear, we have only to consider our language, our laws, our political and social institutions, our knowledge and education, our view of this world and the next, our tastes and the means of gratifying them. On every hand the past dominates and controls us, for the most part unconsciously and without protest on our part. We are in the main its willing adherents. The imagination of the most radically-minded cannot transcend any great part of the ideas and customs transmitted to him. When once we grasp this truth, we shall, according to our mood, humbly congratulate ourselves that, poor pygmies that we are, we are permitted to stand on the giant's shoulders and enjoy an outlook that would be quite hidden from us if we had to trust to our own short legs; or we may resentfully chafe at our bonds and, like Prometheus, vainly strive to wrest ourselves from the rock of the past, in our eagerness to bring relief to the suffering children of men.

> Es erben sich Gesetz' und Rechte
> Wie eine ew'ge Krankheit fort.

In any case, whether we bless or curse the past, we are inevitably its offspring, and it makes us its own long before we realize it. It is, indeed, almost all that we can have. The most frantic of us must follow the beaten path; we are like a squirrel in his revolving cage.

There is no space here to discuss the general relation of history to the causes and technique of progress, but a word may be said of the effect which our modern outlook should have on our estimate of the conservative mood. Mr. John Morley has given an unpleasant but not inaccurate sketch of the conservative, "with his inexhaustible patience of abuses that only torment others; his apologetic word for beliefs that may not be so precisely true as one might wish, and institutions that are not altogether so useful as some might think possible; his cordiality towards progress and improvement in a general way, and his coldness or antipathy to each progressive proposal in particular; his pygmy hope that life will one day become somewhat better, punily shivering by the side of his gigantic conviction that it might well be infinitely worse." How numerous and how respectable is still this class! It is made up of clergymen, lawyers, teachers, editors, and successful men of affairs. Doubtless some of them are nervous and apologetic, and try to find reasons to disguise their general opposition to change by taking credit for improvements to which they contribute nothing, or by forwarding some minor changes which exhaust their powers of imagination and innovation. But how rarely does one of them fail, when he addresses the young, to utter some warning, some praise of the past, some discouragement to effort and the onward struggle! The conservative is a perfectly explicable and inevitable product of that long, long period before man woke up to the possibility of conscious betterment. He still justifies existing conditions and ideas by the standards of the past rather than by those of the present or future. He neither vividly realizes how mightily things have advanced in times gone by, nor has he the imagination to see how easily they could be indefinitely bettered, if the temperament which he represents could cease to be artificially fostered.

Should the conservative be roused to defend himself, having been driven from the protection which his discredited conception of "human nature" formerly offered, he may ask peevishly, "what does progress mean anyway?" But no one who realizes the relative barbarism of our whole civilization, which contains, on a fair appraisal, so little to cheer us except promises for the future, will have the patience to formulate any general definition of progress when the most bewildering opportunities for betterment summon us on every side. What can the conservative point to that is not susceptible of improvement?

There is one more solace, perhaps the last, for the hard-pressed conservative. He may heartily agree that much improvement has taken place and claim that he views with deep satisfaction all deliberate and decorous progress, but ascribe to himself the modest and perhaps ungrateful function of acting as a brake which prevents the chariot of progress from rushing headlong down a decline. But is there any reason to suppose that any brake is necessary? Have fiery radicals ever got possession of the reins and actually driven for a time at a breakneck speed? The conservative would find it extremely difficult to cite historic examples, but doubtless the Reign of Terror would occur to him as an instance. This certainly has more plausibility than any other alleged example in the whole recorded history of mankind. But Camille Desmoulins, one of its most amiable victims, threw the blame of the whole affair, with much sound reasoning, on the precious conservatives themselves. And I think that all scholars would agree that the incapable and traitorous Louis XVI and his runaway nobles, supported by the threats of the monarchs of Prussia and Austria, were at the bottom of the whole matter. In any case, as Desmoulins urges, the blood shed in the cause of liberty was as nothing to that which had been split by kings and prelates in maintaining their dominion and satisfying their ambitions.[16]

So even this favorite instance of o'er-rapid change will scarcely bear impartial scrutiny, and we may safely assert that so far the chariot of progress has always been toiling up a steep incline and that the restraining brake of the conservatives has been worse than

16. "Vieux Cordelier," No. 3, December, 1793.

useless. Maeterlinck exhorts us never to fear that we shall be drawn too far or too rapidly; and there is certainly nothing in the past or present to justify his fear. On the contrary, as he says, "There are men enough about us whose exclusive duty, whose precise mission, is to extinguish the fires that we kindle." "At every crossway on the road that leads to the future, each progressive spirit is opposed by a thousand men appointed to guard the past. Let us have no fear lest the fairest towers of former days be sufficiently defended. The least that the most timid among us can do is not to add to the immense deadweight which nature drags along."

History, the whole history of man and of the organic universe, seems now to put the conservative arguments to shame. Indeed it seems to do more; it seems to justify the mystic confidence in the future suggested in Maeterlinck's *Our Social Duty*. Perhaps, as he believes, an excess of radicalism is essential to the equilibrium of life. "Let us not say to ourselves," he urges, "that the best truth always lies in moderation, in the decent average. This would perhaps be so if the majority of men did not think on a much lower plane than is needful. That is why it behooves others to think and hope on a higher plane than seems reasonable. The average, the decent moderation of today, will be the least human of things tomorrow. At the time of the Spanish Inquisition, the opinion of good sense and of the just medium was certainly that people ought not to burn too large a number of heretics; extreme and unreasonable opinion obviously demanded that they should burn none at all."

Here again we may turn to the past for its authenticating testimony. A society without slaves would have been almost incomprehensible to Plato and Aristotle. To the latter slavery was an inevitable corollary of human society. To Innocent III a church without graft was a hopeless ideal. To Richelieu a foreign service without bribery was a myth. To Beccaria a criminal procedure without torture, and courts without corrupt judges, were a dream. It would have seemed preposterous enough to Franklin to forecast a time when a Philadelphian could converse in his home with friends far beyond the Mississippi, or to assert that one day letters would be carried to all parts of the earth for so small a sum that even the poorest would not find the expense an obstacle to communication. But all these hopeless, preposterous dreams have come to pass and that in a little more than a hundred years.

From forwarding these achievements the conservative has hitherto held himself aloof, whether from temperament, ignorance, or despair. But let us exonerate him, for he knew no better. He had not the wit to see that he was a vestige of a long, unenlightened epoch. But history would seem to show that this period of exemption from service is now at an end. It is plain that his theory that human nature cannot be altered is exploded, as well as his belief that a fractious world needs him to apply the brakes.

The conservative has, in short, been victimized by a misunderstood past. Hitherto the radical has appealed to the future, but now he can confidently rest his case on past achievement and current success. He can point to what has been done, he can cite what is being done, he can perceive as never before what remains to be done, and, lastly, he begins to see, as never before, how it will get done. It has been the chief business of this essay to suggest what has been done. If there were time, I might try to show that progress in knowledge and its application to the alleviation of man's estate is more rapid now than ever before. But this scarcely needs formal proof; it is so obvious. A few years ago an eminent French litterateur, Brunetière, declared science bankrupt. This was on the eve of the discoveries in radioactivity which have opened up great vistas of possible human readjustments if we could but learn to control and utilize the inexhaustible sources of power that lie within the atom. It was on the eve of the discovery of the functions of the white blood corpuscles, which clears the way for indefinite advance in medicine. Only a poor discouraged man of letters could think for a moment that science was bankrupt. No one entitled to an opinion on the subject believes that we have made more than a beginning in penetrating the secrets of the organic and inorganic world.

In the fourth canto of the *Inferno* Dante describes the confines of hell. Here he heard sighs which made the eternal air to tremble. These came of the woe felt by multitudes, which were many and great, of infants and of women and men who, although they had lived guiltless lives, were condemned for being born before the true religion had been revealed. They lived without hope. But in the midst of the gloom he beheld a fire that conquered a hemisphere of darkness. Here, in a place open, luminous, and high, people with eyes slow and grave, of great authority in their looks, sat on the greensward, speaking seldom and with soft voices. These were the ancient philosophers, statesmen, military heroes, and men of letters. Neither sad nor glad, they held high discourse, heedless of the wails of infants, unconscious of the horrors of hell which boiled beneath them. They knew nothing of the mountain of purgatorial progress on the other side of the earth, which others were climbing, and heaven was forever inaccessible to them. Yet why should they regret it—were they not already in the only heaven they were fit for?

As for accomplishing the great reforms that demand our united efforts—the abolition of poverty and disease and war, and the promotion of happy and rational lives—the task would seem hopeless enough were it not for the considerations which have been recalled above. Until very recently the leaders of men have looked backward for their standards and ideals. The intellectual ancestors of the conservative extend back in an unbroken line to the very beginning of human history. The reformer who appeals to the future is a recent upstart. He belongs to the last half minute of our historical reckoning. His family is a new one, and its members have often seemed very black sheep to the good old family of conservatives who have found no names too terrible to apply to the Anthony Collinses, the Voltaires and Tom Paines, who now seem so innocent and commonplace in most of their teachings. But it is clear enough today that the conscious reformer who appeals to the future is the final product of a progressive order of things. While the conservative sullenly opposed what were in Roger Bacon's time called "suspicious novelties," and condemned changes either as wicked or impracticable, he was himself being gradually drawn along in a process of insensible betterment in which he refused consciously to participate. Even those of us who have little taste for mysticism have to recognize a mysterious unconscious impulse which appears to be a concomitant of natural order. It would seem as if this impulse has always been unsettling the existing conditions and pushing forward, groping after something more elaborate and intricate than what already existed. This vital impulse, *élan vital*, as Bergson calls it, represents the inherent radicalism of nature herself. This power that makes for experimental readjustment,—for *adventure* in the broadest sense of the term,—is no longer a conception confined to poets and dreamers, but must be reckoned with by the most exacting historian and the hardest-headed man of science. We are only just coming to realize that we can cooperate with and direct this innate force of change which has so long been silently operating, in spite of the respectable lethargy, indifference, and even protests of man himself, the most educable of all its creatures.

At last, perhaps, the long-disputed sin against the Holy Ghost has been found; it may be the refusal to cooperate with the vital principle of betterment. History would seem, in short, to condemn the principle of conservatism as a hopeless and wicked anachronism.

If what has been said above is true, or any considerable part of it, is not almost our whole education at fault? We make no consistent effort to cultivate a progressive spirit in our boys and girls. They are not made to realize the responsibility that rests upon them—the exhilaration that comes from ever looking and pressing forward. They are still so largely nurtured upon the abstract and the classical that we scarcely yet dare to bring education into relation with life. The history they are taught brings few or none of the lessons the past has to offer. They are reared with too much respect for the past, too little confidence for the future. Does not education become in this way a mighty barrier cast across the way of progress, rather than a guidepost to betterment? Would not most of those in charge of the education of our youth tremble before the possibility of having them realize fully what has been hinted in this essay? What would happen if the teachers in our schools and colleges, our theological seminaries and law schools, should make it their business to emphasize the temporary and provisional character of the instruction that they offer, and urge the students to transcend it as fast as a progressive world permitted? The humorous nature of such a suggestion shows how far we are still from any general realization and acceptance of the great lesson of history.

"Let us," to quote Maeterlinck once more, "think of the great invisible ship that carries our human destinies upon eternity. Like the vessels of our confined oceans, she has her sails and her ballast. The fear that she may pitch or roll on leaving the roadstead is no reason for increasing the weight of the ballast by stowing the fair white sails in the depths of the hold. They were not woven to molder side by side with cobblestones in the dark. Ballast exists everywhere; all the pebbles of the harbor, all the sand of the beach, will serve for that. But sails are rare and precious things; their place is not in the murk of the well, but amid the light of the tall masts, where they will collect the winds of space."

7. Toward a New Culture: Editorial from *The Seven Arts*

THE SEVEN ARTS editors, along with contributors like Amy Lowell, John Dos Passos, H. L. Mencken, John Dewey, and Randolph Bourne, formed a cross section of those who optimistically sought a cultural renaissance in the United States; even as other intellectuals, like Lippmann, worked for political regeneration. Outspoken criticism of American participation in the World War, especially by Bourne—an editor in 1917—caused such a furor that the magazine lost its financial support and died, a glorious symbol of wartime repression.

During the summer months, we sent out the following statement to American authors:

It is our faith and the faith of many, that we are living in the first days of a renascent period, a time which means for America the coming of that national self-consciousness which is the beginning of greatness. In all such epochs the arts cease to be private matters; they become not only the expression of the national life but a means to its enhancement.

Our arts shown signs of this change. It is the aim of *The Seven Arts* to become a channel for the flow of these new tendencies: an expression of our American arts which shall be fundamentally an expression of our American life.

We have no tradition to continue; we have no school of style to build up. What we ask of the writer is simply self-expression without regard to current magazine standards. We should prefer that portion of his work which is done through a joyous necessity of the writer himself.

The Seven Arts will publish stories, short plays, poems, essays and brief editorials. Such arts as cannot be directly set forth in a magazine will receive expression through critical writing, which, it is hoped, will be no less creative than the fiction and poetry. In this field the aim will be to give vistas and meanings rather than a monthly survey or review; to interpret rather than to catalogue. We hope that creative workers themselves will also set forth their vision and their inspiration.

In short, *The Seven Arts* is not a magazine for artists, but an expression of artists for the community.

SOURCE: Editorial, *The Seven Arts* (November 1916) pp. 52–53.

Some of the response to this may be seen in this number. But we are only at a beginning. Such a magazine cannot be created by either work or wishing. It must create itself, by continuing to exist. Its presence then becomes a challenge to the artist to surpass himself. He reads his contemporaries, and a sportsmanlike rivalry springs up which evokes his best effort. So a community spirit arises: and out of this once again, as it has before, among the cathedral builders, among the Elizabethans, a genuine and great art may spring.

II

World War I

8. Support for the Allies: William Dean Howells

WILLIAM DEAN HOWELLS, *elder statesman of American men of letters during the first two decades of the twentieth century, no longer spoke for the younger generation of American writers by 1915. Howell's long record of encouragement and sponsorship for promising realistic and naturalistic authors like Hamlin Garland, Theodore Dreiser, Frank Norris, and Stephen Crane antedated the memories as well as the careers of his young critics. Most educated Americans, however, still regarded him with the respect due a writer whose own artistic successes—such as* The Rise of Silas Lapham *(1885),* A Hazard of New Fortunes *(1890),* A Traveler from Altruria *(1894), and* Through the Eye of the Needle *(1907)—had not prevented him from championing innovators whose less constricted realism outraged conventional readers and critics.*

After these nine months of the manifold murder in Europe begun by Germany, we who hold her guilty of all the harm that can flow from the largest evil ever let loose upon the world may fitly take stock of our reasons and convictions, not so much as against Germany as in favor of England and France, and especially England. Why do we still believe as powerfully in her cause as at the first? It is easy to say because it is the cause of liberty, of humanity, of Christianity; that it is something like a last hope of mankind; that if it fails civilization will no longer be free in Europe or America, but will become the dismal condition of soldier-slaves enthralling and enthralled. But to say this does not seem enough. One wishes to count and recount one's convictions, to repeat again that the party of the Allies is the party, above everything, of peace, the party of hope, of the equal right to life, liberty, and the pursuit of happiness, of everything endeared by the Declaration and guarded by the Constitution. That was what we felt at the first, but as the bright days of the early resistance to the German ravage of Belgium and plunge into France dulled into days of dogged endeavor to hold the water-soaked trenches of the fighting line, and the blind artillery duel continued by telescope and telephone between the adversaries; when victory and defeat were doled out by

SOURCE: William Dean Howells, "Why?" *North American Review*, 201 (May 1915): 676–682. Reprinted by permission of the publisher.

inches to one side or the other in the West, and in the East the sudden triumph of the Russian millions turned into rout which not even the change of name from St. Petersburg to Petrograd could stay, we Americans who were with the Allies heart and soul began involuntarily to ask ourselves why.

We did not ask why so much, if at all, with regard to France. That remained the perfectly clear case it was at the beginning. Her home had been invaded and her very life threatened by Germany as the sole escape from the pretended menace or danger of Russia. The same atrocious contempt of neutral rights which animated her in her invasion of Belgium was the savage impulse that carried her over the French border almost to the forts of Paris. There was everything in the French situation to move us in behalf of France, and we who are not a very generous nation could individually give our moral support to the most generous of the nations without qualification. Usually we forget that we owe our national existence to France, but in that moment of her insult and outrage we did remember that we were alive because of that foster mother of ours. We had remembered more constantly the unnatural severity of our own natural mother, and if we had not felt so strongly that she was fighting the same battle which her oppression had forced us to fight against her, we might have hesitated to give her our whole hearts.

I do not think we did hesitate in that hour of her appeal to the instincts of all free peoples. The English, though not nearly so much as the Germans, have since felt the need of instructing our preference; but they have not waited our asking to tell us that they were fighting our battle against militarism, and that if they fell under its iron hoofs it would be our turn next, and it would be an easy walkover for those hoofs. I do not believe that we took counsel of our fears in the matter, though we had great reason to do so in our defenselessness. We who were for the Allies gave England our sympathy as unstintedly as we gave it to France, and with no fear of the German success shaken in our faces. We did not expect that success, and we do not expect it now; we have steadfastly trusted in the righteousness of England's cause, and in the power which has enabled her to compass the lands and seas of the whole world, and hold them fast in the fear or affection of the mightiest empire in history. Let Germany rage her little hour with her millions of conscripts, her submarines shattering peaceful ships, and her aeroplanes dropping bombs on the roofs of undefended towns and murdering women and children at their doors and in their beds. The hour will be little indeed beside that spacious day which must come as surely as the dawn follows the dark, when the English spirit of freedom shall lastingly prevail against her convulsive force and hold her homicidal epilepsy in sanative control.

I do not forget, in this prophesying, all the guilt and all the greed of England in the past. I do not forgive her the destruction of the South African republics in the recent past which is almost the present. That indeed was the effect of the greed, the insatiate lust of dominion of the imperial appetite which had come with eating. Still less do I forget the injuries which we suffered from her in our nonage, the manifold oppressions and repressions which welded our colonial disunity into the unity of these sovereign States. Still harder to forget are the slights and snubs which she put upon us in our national infancy, the insolent disregard of our international equality, and finally and most unforgetable of all, her laugh of exultation when our fear came, and she could hope that slavery might be the death of that freedom which we had learned from her to love, and which was the life breath of the Republic devoted by her ill will to destruction. No American who has read American history can be ignorant of the treacheries and atrocities she practised against us in both her wars with us; the loosing of cruel savages upon our frontiers, the hiring of German mercenaries to meet our armies in battle; the imprisonment of our seamen by thousands, and the horrors of the prison-ships; the contempt of our appeal to arms till the prowess of our Yankee privateers on every sea and the aim of our Kentucky riflemen at New Orleans taught her to respect us a little; and then in the Civil War the eager rush of English sympathy with the slaveholders, and the destruction of our commerce by the Confederate cruisers fitted and manned in English ports. The tale is long and need not be told in full, but if we were to vent our sense of injury from England in a hate song, such as the Germans have used to keep their anger warm, our reasoned grievances would make that detestable outburst appear the explosion of senseless passion in Bedlam.

We need not run back for quantity in our memories of injury from the England of that class which has hitherto been her ruling class. In our keenest sense of that injury we have always, unless we were very stupid and ignorant, been aware of two Englands, of another and a better England than that ruling England, the England which has been our friend, and the friend of every righteous cause. In our struggle for Independence the wisest and truest and kindest of Englishmen were our friends; in our struggle for Union these again were of our side. There are indeed two Englands: one that never forgets a friend once accepted, and one that never makes a friend whom injustice and insult could alienate. Hitherto it is the spirit of that evil England which has ruled England; but in these latest years we who have loved English liberty and hoped that somehow "in the far-off divine event" it would become American equality, have learned to believe that the better England had come into her own. We have seen a more equal tax wrung, however grudgingly, from the great nobles who had left the commons to pay an unjust share; we have seen, with shame for ourselves, national pensions voted to outworn labor, and the growth of good will between the classes and the masses. We have seen such things as these, and through the storm of obloquy poured out on the sturdy Celt who has forced this justice from the hand of Norman and Saxon we have made bold to hope for a day when the eyes of England should be purged of the dazzle of kings and nobles which has kept her blind to the glory of common manhood. We knew that our vision must be vain for yet a time indefinitely long, but we kept saying to ourselves, "Why not, at the end of this volcanic uprush of hell over the lands so long peaceful, should not there be a federation of the world which should at least prophesy, if not establish, the universal republic and make 'the game of kings' forever impossible?"

That was the secret at the bottom of true American hearts in their prayer for England's success in the war, and it is still the hope that animates us, though we deny it or avow it with shrinking and something like shame. From militarized Germany, from that dead corpse of medieval oppression, galvanized into an ecstasy of murder and rapine, humanity can hope nothing; but from England it can hope something, not everything, perhaps not much, but something.

It is because we hope for this something, much or little, that we wish England godspeed on the hard, perhaps long, road before her. It is because we love humanity, and hope from English liberty American equality that we earnestly desire her success in yonder hideous carnage. It is not because we hate the Germans or love the English; many of us love the Germans, and feel them *gemüthlich*, though they dine at one o'clock and eat with their knives. Most of us love England and love her dearly; we know home and mother when we breathe her air and feel her stinted sunshine; but do many of us love the English, say, in the lump, or do we any of us? We love certain Englishmen when we get to know them, as much as they will let us, but for the English in general, or even in particular, not all of us have much use. We have no use at all for their patriotism; for England as the head of the British Empire we do not care, but we care everything for her as the hope of the human race; everything, everything. The Englishman, especially the English journalist or poet, or other vocal person, seems not to understand this, and addresses us lively reproaches because we do not share his insular or imperial patriotism, not realizing in his own case that the patriotism of another is something almost offensive, like the warmth of another's person. It astonishes him, therefore, that we should say we are with him heart and soul, and yet look it so little. He cannot understand why we should not be ashamed to bother him with protest and question when we see him so busy fighting for his life and our own lives. Well, I, for one, wish we could have forborne those protests and questions, though I do not see how we could; or how without a word we could let England sweep our commerce from the seas as thoroughly as her Confederate cruisers did in our Civil War that she should not be hampered by it in her struggle for mankind against the enemy of mankind. I, for one, am ashamed that we seem already to have forgotten the abominable violence to all law by the Germans in their raids by sea and sky against defenseless towns, Belgian, French, and English, or that we must address Berlin in the same diplomatic terms of question as London. Of course, I know that I speak for no larger portion of the Republic than resides in any one citizen of it, but I know other citizens who think like me, many others. At the same time I know this will not satisfy the English. They want a great deal more good will from us than this; more than, for instance, they showed for us when they framed a treaty with Japan to support her in a certain event if she was at war with us. Nothing, in fact, would really satisfy the English short of our going to war with Germany, and that I hope we shall not do till the German submarines attack our home-keeping navy and their Zeppelins infest our atmosphere and begin dropping bombs on Boston.

But in spite of the unreasonableness of such Englishmen, every

American who loves the liberty which his own country represents must heartily, prayerfully wish England well in this Titanic struggle with the Satanic powers of Germany. Apparently it is the affair of Belgium, who has fought on to her political extinction in it, though we know she shall rise again in a glorious resurrection. Still more apparently it is the affair of France, which is pushing the invader with dogged (one might say bull-dogged) self-devotion from her soil. Apparently it is the affair of Russia in the incessant vicissitudes of progress and regress through that Eastern war scene which shine as triumphs at Petrograd and darkle as routs at Berlin. It seems even the affair of Portugal, but just how we cannot say. But above all and through all it is England's job to beat down, if not to bind, those forces of evil which the Allies are fighting. That is distinctly her job, as one hundred years ago it was her job to beat down and bind the forces which a far less formidable enemy of mankind had loosed upon the world. Success will come to her now as surely as it came to her then, and with success will come the question of what to do with her success. There is no St. Helena which can jail the malignant spirit of militarism, but somehow it can and must be destroyed. England, by and with the advice and consent of France and Belgium, will know how to deal with the question, and, leaving Japan and Portugal out of the matter, she will doubtless know how to deal with her fellow victor Russia; for somehow that strange mass of apparent inability must finally be dealt with. We have just seen how France and England have tried to undo their united work of sixty years ago and open to Russia the sea which they then closed against her, and doubtless they will find some way of utilizing in the great dénouement their unwieldy partner in the tremendous drama now enacting. Russia may represent to dramatic criticism the humorous element which Shakespeare finds the relief and contrast of his tragedy, but almost anything is predictable of that vast despotism which ought logically to be as bad as Prussian militarism, or worse. A people converted to Christianity by sovereign mandate, and baptized at one plunge in the river whither they were herded for salvation, have now been devoted to prohibition by the same power and saved a second time, while other nations are still striving toward that ideal by a course of moderate drinking. Who knows, then, but in the day of reckoning for Germany the Czar may not issue a ukase declaring his subjects the citizens of a free and independent Republic, and endowing them with the Initiative and Referendum, the Recall and Woman Suffrage, with himself for their first President ineligible for re-election?

In the forecast which I am here indulging anything appears possible, and it is not morally impossible but England may submit the inevitable Russian question to the arbitration of these States. She may remember the cherished fable of friendship between that Empire and this Republic, tacitly attested by sealed instructions to the Russian fleet which visited our shores during the Civil War to defend us against an attack of the French and English, and she may conceive it graceful to leave the Russian case to us. England has more of the virtues that convince the reason than the charms that win the affection of other nations; but a graceful thing is not beyond her, as we have lately seen in her letting our contraband ship *Dacia* fall a prey to our ancient ally France instead of capturing and confiscating the vessel herself. That was a delicate forbearance worthy of our ideal of ourselves; and throughout our exchange of civilities with her concerning neutral rights it seems to me that England has behaved with signal patience and polite forbearance when we could not have helped ourselves if she had done otherwise. To have done otherwise we should have tended to cast our lot where our will could never be, with Germany. We cannot, indeed, cast our lot with the Allies, but our will must be with them always because, as I began by saying, they are in the right, if there is any such thing as right or wrong. If it is wrong to build up a ruthless power by a system of worldwide espionage, to fortify a bad cause by every art of treachery and deceit, and then to use that power with arrogant disregard of all the international traditions, and all the laws of religion, and all the impulses of humanity, Germany is wrong and England is right, and that is why we must wish England well, whatever becomes of our questions and protests.

My own neutrality is of such measure and make that I would have our nation bear everything from the belligerents short of invading our shores after sinking all our ships. But I would have our Government continue registering its protests as a sort of charges to be paid off at some day of reckoning in the future. Something like this was managed in the case of England and her *Alabama*, which she settled without breach of the peace, from a conscience quickened by our insistence. Meanwhile the great Because which answers my Why is that England is—

> the land that freemen till,
> That sober-suited Freedom chose,
> The land where, girt with friends or foes,
> A man may speak the things he will.—

and that in Germany he may not without danger of going to jail for it.

9. This Is Not Our War: William Jennings Bryan

The great orator and champion of populism and expanded democracy, William Jennings Bryan, obtained appointment as Secretary of State in Wilson's cabinet largely because of Bryan's enormous popularity within the still-divided Democratic party. Furthermore, in 1913 Bryan's moralistic attitude toward foreign relations coincided with Wilson's. It seems doubtful, however, that the appointment would have been made had Wilson suspected at the time that the most important decisions of his administration would be in the realm of foreign policy. Once executive decisions in international relations began to have critical worldwide ramifications, an open clash between these two high principled politicians separated by wide differences in background and training probably was inevitable.

Mr. Bryan's Letter of Resignation

My Dear Mr. President:

It is with sincere regret that I have reached the conclusion that I should return to you the commission of Secretary of State with which you honored me at the beginning of your administration.

Obedient to your sense of duty and actuated by the highest motives, you have prepared for transmission to the German government a note in which I can not join without violating what I deem to be an obligation to my country, and the issue involved is of such moment that to remain a member of the cabinet would be

Source: William Jennings Bryan, *Heart to Heart Appeals* (New York, 1917), pp. 90–97. Reprinted by permission of Fleming H. Revell Company.

as unfair to you as it would be to the cause which is nearest my heart, namely, the prevention of war.

I, therefore, respectfully tender my resignation to take effect when the note is sent, unless you prefer an earlier hour. Alike desirous of reaching a peaceful solution of the problems arising out of the use of submarines against merchantmen, we find ourselves differing irreconcilably as to the methods which should be employed.

It falls to your lot to speak officially for the nation; I consider it to be none the less my duty to endeavor as a private citizen to promote the end which you have in view by means which you do not feel at liberty to use.

In severing the intimate and pleasant relations which have existed between us during the past two years, permit me to acknowledge the profound satisfaction which it has given me to be associated with you in the important work which has come before the state department, and to thank you for the courtesies extended.

With heartiest good wishes for your personal welfare and for the success of your administration, I am, my dear Mr. President, very truly yours,

W. J. BRYAN

Washington, June 8, 1915

Two Points of Difference

My reason for resigning is clearly stated in my letter of resignation, namely, that I may employ as a private citizen the means which the president does not feel at liberty to employ. I honor him for doing what he believes to be right, and I am sure that he desires, as I do, to find a peaceful solution of the problem which has been created by the action of the submarines.

Two of the points on which we differ, each conscientious in conviction, are:

First, as to the suggestion of investigation by an international commission, and,

Second, as to warning Americans against traveling on belligerent vessels or with cargoes of ammunition.

I believe that this nation should frankly state to Germany that we are willing to apply in this case the principle which we are bound by treaty to apply to disputes between the United States and thirty countries with which we have made treaties providing for investigation of all disputes of every character and nature.

These treaties, negotiated under this administration, make war practically impossible between this country and these thirty governments, representing nearly three-fourths of all the people of the world.

Among the nations with which we have these treaties are Great Britain, France and Russia. No matter what disputes may arise between us and these treaty nations, we agree that there shall be no declaration of war and no commencement of hostilities until the matters in dispute have been investigated by an international commission and a year's time is allowed for investigation and report. This plan was offered to all the nations without any exception whatever, and Germany was one of the nations that accepted the principle, being the twelfth, I think, to accept. No treaty was actually entered into with Germany, but I can not see that that should stand in the way when both nations endorsed the principle. I do not know whether Germany would accept the offer, but our country should, in my judgment, make the offer.

Such an offer, if accepted, would at once relieve the tension and silence all the jingoes who are demanding war. Germany has always been a friendly nation, and a great many of our people are of German ancestry. Why should we not deal with Germany according to this plan to which the nation has pledged its support?

The second point of difference is as to the course which should be pursued in regard to Americans traveling on belligerent ships or with cargoes of ammunition.

Why should an American citizen be permitted to involve the country in war by traveling upon a belligerent ship when he knows that the ship will pass through a danger zone? The question is not whether an American citizen has a right under international law to travel on a belligerent ship; the question is whether he ought not, out of consideration for his country, if not for his own safety, avoid danger when avoidance is possible.

It is a very one-sided citizenship that compels a government to go to war over a citizen's rights, and yet relieves the citizen of all obligations to consider his nation's welfare. I do not know just how far the President can go legally in actually preventing Americans from traveling on belligerent ships, but I believe the government should go as far as it can, and that in case of doubt it should give the benefit of the doubt to the government.

But even if the government could not legally prevent citizens from traveling on belligerent ships, it could, and in my judgment should, earnestly advise American citizens not to risk themselves or the peace of their country, and I have no doubt that these warnings would be heeded.

President Taft advised Americans to leave Mexico when insurrection broke out there, and President Wilson has repeated the advice. This advice, in my judgment, was eminently wise, and I think the same course should be followed in regard to warning Americans to keep off vessels subject to attack.

I think too, that American passenger ships should be prohibited from carrying ammunition. The lives of passengers ought not to be endangered by cargoes of ammunition, whether that danger comes from possible explosions within or from possible attacks from without. Passengers and ammunition should not travel together. The attempt to prevent American citizens from incurring these risks is entirely consistent with the effort which our government is making to prevent attacks from submarines.

The use of one remedy does not exclude the use of the other. The most familiar illustration is to be found in the action taken by municipal authorities during a riot. It is the duty of the mayor to suppress the mob and to prevent violence, but he does not hesitate to warn citizens to keep off the streets during the riots. He does not question their right to use the streets, but, for their own protection and in the interest of order, he warns them not to incur the risks involved in going upon the streets when men are shooting at each other.

The President does not feel justified in taking the action above suggested. That is, he does not feel justified, first, in suggesting the submission of the controversy to investigation, or, second, in warning the people not to incur the extra hazards in traveling on belligerent ships or on ships carrying ammunition. And he may be right in the position he has taken, but as a private citizen I am free to urge both of these propositions and to call public attention to these remedies in the hope of securing such an expression of public sentiment as will support the President in employing these remedies if in the future he finds it consistent with his sense of duty to favor them.

From statement issued after resignation as Secretary of State.

Persuasion vs. Force

To the American People:

You now have before you the text of the note to Germany—the note which it would have been my official duty to sign had I remained Secretary of State. I ask you to sit in judgment upon my decision to resign rather than to share responsibility for it. I am sure you will credit me with honorable motives, but that is not enough. Good intentions could not atone for a mistake at such a time, on such a subject and under such circumstances. If your verdict is against me, I ask no mercy; I deserve none if I have acted unwisely. A man in public life must act according to his conscience, but however conscientiously he acts he must be prepared to accept without complaint any condemnation which his own errors may bring upon him; he must be willing to bear any deserved punishment from ostracism to execution. But hear me before you pass sentence.

The President and I agree in purpose, we desire a peaceful solution of the dispute which had arisen between the United States and Germany. We not only desire it, but with equal fervor we pray for it, but we differ irreconcilably as to the means of securing it. If it were merely a personal difference, it would be a matter of little moment, for all the presumptions are on his side—the presumptions that go with authority. He is your President; I am a private citizen without office or title—but one of 100,000,000 inhabitants.

But the real issue is not between persons; it is between systems, and I rely for vindication wholly upon the strength of the position taken.

Among the influences which governments employ in dealing with each other there are two which are preeminent and antagonistic—force and persuasion. Force speaks with firmness and acts through the ultimatum; persuasion employs argument, courts investigation and depends upon negotiation. Force represents the old system—the system that must pass away; persuasion represents the new system—the system that has been growing, all too slowly, it is true, but growing, for 1,900 years. In the old system war is the chief cornerstone—war which at its best is little better than war at its worst; the new system contemplates a universal brotherhood established through the uplifting power of example.

If I correctly interpret the note to Germany, it conforms to the standards of the old system rather than to the rules of the new, and I cheerfully admit that it is abundantly supported by precedents—precedents written in characters of blood upon almost every page of human history. Austria furnishes the most recent precedent; it was Austria's firmness that dictated the ultimatum against Serbia which set the world at war. Every ruler now participating in this unparalleled conflict has proclaimed his desire for peace and denied responsibility for the war, and it is only charitable that we should credit all of them with good faith. They desired peace, but they sought it according to the rules of the old system. They believed that firmness would give the best assurance of the maintenance of peace, and faithfully following precedent, they went so near the fire that they were, one after another, sucked into the contest.

Never before have the frightful follies of this fatal system been so clearly revealed as now. The most civilized and enlightened—aye, the most Christian—of the nations of Europe are grappling with each other as if in a death struggle. They are sacrificing the best and bravest of their sons on the battlefield; they are converting their gardens into cemeteries and their homes into house of mourning; they are taxing the wealth of today and laying a burden of debt on the toil of the future; they have filled the air with thunderbolts more deadly than those of Jove, and they have multiplied the perils of the deep. Adding fresh fuel to the flame of hate, they have daily devised new horrors, until one side is endeavoring to drown noncombatant men, women and children at sea, while the other side seeks to starve noncombatant men, women and children on land. And they are so absorbed in alternate retaliations and in competitive cruelties that they seem, for the time being, blind to the rights of neutrals and deaf to the appeals of humanity. A tree is known by its fruit. The war in Europe is the ripened fruit of the old system.

This is what firmness, supported by force, has done in the Old World. Shall we invite it to cross the Atlantic? Already the jingoes of our own country have caught the rabies from the dogs of war. Shall the opponents of organized slaughter be silent while the disease spreads?

As a humble follower of the Prince of Peace, as a devoted

believer in the prophecy that "they that take the sword shall perish with the sword," I beg to be counted among those who earnestly urge the adoption of a course in this matter which will leave no doubt of our government's willingness to continue negotiations with Germany until an amicable understanding is reached, or at least until, the stress of war over, we can appeal from Philip drunk with carnage to Philip sobered by the memories of an historic friendship and a recollection of the innumerable ties of kinship that bind the Fatherland to the United States.

Some nation must lift the world out of the black night of war into the light of that day when "swords shall be beaten into plowshares." Why not make that honor ours? Some day—why not now?—the nations will learn that enduring peace can not be built upon fear—that good will does not grow upon the stalk of violence.

Some day the nations will place their trust in love, the weapon for which there is no shield; in love, that suffereth long and is kind; in love, that is not easily provoked, that beareth all things, believeth all things, hopeth all things, endureth all things; in love which, though despised as weakness by the worshippers of Mars, abideth when all else fails.

From statement issued after resignation as Secretary of State.

10. The Argument for Preparedness: Hudson Maxim

BEHIND THE *progressive movement lay a belief in man's basic goodness and in the eventual triumph of Christian virtues. A curious dichotomy in the minds of many progressives, however, led to the attitude that this triumph might entail violent battle. When Theodore Roosevelt proclaimed to the Progressive Convention in 1912 that "We stand at Armageddon, and we battle for the Lord," he spoke figuratively, of course. But the worldwide victory of Anglo-Saxon democracy over the "bully" nations required the use of military force inappropriate for a domestic political crusade. Roosevelt and his admirers, including the author of the essay below, believed also that war and preparation for war toughened a people's moral fiber, leaving it better prepared for domestic as well as international travail.*

SOURCE: Hudson Maxim, *Defenseless America* (New York, 1915), pp. 1–21.

Defenseless America

There will be no war in the future, for it has become impossible now that it is clear that war means suicide.
I. S. Bloch, "The Future of War," 1899

What shall we say of the Great War of Europe ever threatening, ever impending, and which never comes? We shall say that it will never come. Humanly speaking, it is impossible.
Dr. David Starr Jordan, "War and Waste," 1913

They who are loudest in their vociferations about the calamities that the warring nations of Europe have brought upon themselves are those peace-palavering persons who have been telling us all along, during the past twenty-five years, that human nature had improved so much lately, and the spirit of international brotherhood had become so dominant, that the fighting spirit was nearly dead in the souls of men.

The peace praters have assured us from time to time that the last great war of the world had been fought; they have told us that no great nations would dare to go to war any more, because war between any of the Great Powers would now mean bankruptcy and national suicide; they have assured us that all international differences would hereafter be settled by jurisprudential procedure, and that law would be substituted for war.

About fifteen years ago, a M. de Bloch "proved" in his book, entitled *The Future of War. Is War Now Possible?* that war had become so deadly and destructive, and, above all, so expensive, as to be impossible. So impressed was the Czar of Russia with de Bloch's arguments that he called a conference of the nations to consider disarmament. Since that time a thousand different persons have, in a thousand different ways, "proved" to us that war on a large scale was not only impossible, but also absolutely unthinkable. Droll, isn't it, that the nations keep right on fighting? We are consoled, however, by the insistence of the peace prophets that this war is truly the last great war. We are assured that this war will be the death of militarism, and then the lamb can safely cuddle up to the lion. Consequently, we have been told that, war on a large scale being now impossible, the United States needs no army and no navy, and that it would be folly to waste the taxpayers' money on such useless things.

Many believe that this country should set the other nations of the world a great moral example by pulling the teeth of our dogs of war, making them lambs, and inviting the lions to lie down with them, unheedful of the lesson of all ages that when the lion does lie down with the lamb, the lamb is always inside the lion.

Furthermore, we have been assured that the mere possession of armaments leads a nation to wage war, because being able to fight makes one want to fight; and that, obviously, the best way to avoid a fight is to be unable to fight.

I quote the following from Theodore Roosevelt's book, "America and the World War":—

> These peace people have persistently and resolutely blinked facts. One of the peace congresses sat in New York at the very time that the feeling in California about the Japanese question gravely threatened the good relations between ourselves and the great empire of Japan. The only thing which at the moment could practically be done for the cause of peace was to secure some proper solution of the question at issue between ourselves and Japan. But this represented real effort, real thought. The peace congress paid not the slightest serious attention to the matter and instead devoted itself to listening to speeches which favored the abolition of the United States Navy and even in one case the prohibiting the use of tin soldiers in nurseries because of the militaristic effect on the minds of the little boys and girls who played with them!

When the prophet Isaiah told the Jews that there were big troubles brewing for them in the East, he spoke to unhearing ears, because unwilling ears. There were in those days, as in our day, the false prophets of peace who said that Isaiah was wrong; that there was no cause for worry about the indignation of Jehovah; that even at the worst His wrath could be appeased at any time, as necessity might arise, by a few burnt offerings and sacrificial mumblings. Their assurances were more pleasing than the warnings of Isaiah, so the Jews listened to the false prophets instead of to Isaiah, and they paid the penalty in Babylonian bondage.

The Isaiahs of true prophecy have long warned the people of this country that there is big trouble brewing for us in the East and in the Far East, and that we need armaments and men trained to arms to safeguard us against that trouble. These Isaiahs have told us that we cannot safeguard ourselves by any sacrifices made upon the altar of international brotherhood, or forefend ourselves against the great red peril of war by a few mumblings written down in arbitration treaties; but that we must have guns and men behind the guns. The Isaiahs who have been telling us these things are our true peace advocates.

Those self-styled peace men who are telling us that the best way to avoid war is to be unable to defend ourselves are not peace men, but war breeders. Though they emulate the dove in their cooing, they are far from being doves of peace. They ought to be styled dubs of peace. Their intentions may be good, yet they are enemies of peace, and betrayers of their country. Those who prevent the building of coast fortifications, which are our modern city gates, by advising against them, betray their country as actually as those who opened the gates of Rome to the hordes of Alaric.

Those who are trying to defeat our Congressional appropriations for a larger navy, for an adequate army, and for sufficient coast fortifications, although they may mean well, are as truly enemies of their country as if they should, in war, contribute to the armament and fighting force of an enemy, for the effect in both cases is identical.

Again I quote from Mr. Roosevelt:

> We object to the actions of those who do most talking about the necessity of peace because we think they are really a menace to the just and honorable peace which alone this country will in the long run support. We object to their actions because we believe they represent a course of conduct which may at any time produce a war in which we and not they would labor and suffer.
>
> In such a war the prime fact to be remembered is that the men really responsible for it would not be those who would pay the penalty. The ultra-pacifiists are rarely men who go to battle. Their fault or their folly would be expiated by the blood of countless thousands of plain and decent American citizens of the stamp of those, North and South alike, who in the Civil War laid down all they had, including life itself, in battling for the right as it was given to them to see the right.

But the false prophets of peace have assured us all along that there is no danger whatever of war between the United States and any other country. They tell us further that our armaments are a menace to other nations; that they evidence suspicion of other nations, and thereby place us under suspicion. According to such philosophy, the college man who becomes an athlete is a trouble-breeder, for the reason that the mere possession of muscle makes him a menace to other men.

Now, if we are in any danger of war, we ought to do the right thing to secure the safety of our country, of our homes and our families, and all things that are dear to us.

If it be true that the possession of armaments is an inducement for those who have them to use them, and if it be true that armaments fret the fighting spirit of other nations as a red rag frets a bull, and thereby lead to war, then, surely, we do not need more armaments, but less. Instead of arming ourselves any more, we should disarm until we are defenseless enough to be perfectly safe. On the other hand, if there be any likelihood that this country may be invaded by a foreign foe, we should be prepared to meet the invaders in the right way, and with the right spirit.

If it be the proper way to go and meet them as the inhabitants of Jerusalem went out to meet Alexander, with the keys to our gates, and with presents and sacrificial offerings, then we should adopt that way of preparing to pave their path with flowers and make them drunk on grape juice and the milk of human kindness.

Dr. David Starr Jordan believes in disarmament. He further believes that armorplate, guns, battleships, and ammunition should not be made by private manufacturers, but that, on the contrary, these things should be made exclusively by the government, for he is of the opinion that manufacturers of war materials foment disorder and promote war in order to bring themselves more business.

Long association with the manufacturers of war materials, especially of explosive materials, has enabled me to know whereof I speak, and I do know that such a belief is the utterest nonsense. The manufacturers of war materials with whom I am acquainted are among the staunchest of peace men, and they would no more be guilty of promoting war to bring themselves business than a reputable surgeon would be likely to string a cord across the street to trip up pedestrians and break their limbs in order to bring himself business.

In the treatment of human physical ailments, we should deem it folly to confound remedy with disease, and to hold the physician responsible for pestilence. No one would think of looking upon our science of sanitation and our quarantine system as breeders and harbingers of pestilence, and no one would think that our laws against crime and our system of police protection tend to foster crime. Yet such is the attitude of many well-intentioned but overzealous persons with respect to our naval and military system and armaments. They consider them breeders and harbingers of war.

An army and navy are merely a mighty quarantine system against the pestilence of war. We must fortify our shores, police our seas with armor-clads, and be prepared to patrol the skies with aeroplanes around our entire national horizon when the need may come.

But it is urged that the people are overburdened with the cost of maintaining armies and navies. Assuming that the burden is great, was it ever less? Was it ever so small as it is now, compared with the numbers and wealth of the people? Again, cannot we well afford to bear a considerable burden of armaments as an insurance against war, and as a further insurance that if war comes, it will be far less deadly than it would be without them?

If Dr. Jordan were better acquainted with the manufacture of war materials, he would know that they can be made more cheaply, with equal excellence, by private concerns, than by the government. Furthermore, he would know that big manufacturers of war materials are obliged to employ a very large force of skilled labor, and that this labor has to be supplied employment when there are no government orders for war materials. For example, the manufacture of armorplate by the United States Steel Corporation is only a small part of the company's business. The manufacture of guns and armorplate by the Bethlehem Steel Company does not keep it constantly occupied, and it has to furnish other employment for its men when government orders are not forthcoming. Consequently, it is obliged to make things besides armorplate and guns and war materials.

The Du Pont explosives companies do a far larger business in high explosives and smokeless powders for commercial purposes than they do for government purposes.

Therefore, if the manufacture of war materials were to be confined entirely to government shops, then the government would truly have to promote war to keep its employees busy. At any rate, the government would have to maintain a large labor force, making war materials alone, for the government could not devote itself to the manufacture of automobiles, chairs, cloth, artificial leather, dynamite, sporting powder, and the like, for commercial purposes, as private manufacturers do.

There is another reason why the private manufacturers of war materials should be encouraged by the government, and it is that, in the event of war, the government would find the large capital and plants of the wealthy Steel Trust, the Bethlehem Steel Company, and the Du Ponts available for the purpose of national defense in addition to the government's own resources. This is very important.

The battle of Lake Erie was quite as much a Du Pont victory as a Perry victory; for the resources, energy, and generalship of the Du Pont Powder Company overcame inconceivable difficulties, carted the powder from Wilmington, Delaware, all the way overland to Lake Erie, and got it there on time.

It is unfortunate that a person's confidence in his knowledge of a subject is often directly proportionate to his ignorance of the subject. It is a psychological truth that ignorance may be taught, just like anything else, and a person may become very erudite in things which are not true, just as he may in things which are true.

Dr. Jordan, in recent public utterances, has said that he would rather the United States should lose its Pacific possessions than that we should go to war; and he has remarked that now, while the world is drunk with war, is a bad time to lay in more liquor. This is an ingenious metaphor, and well designed to trip the intelligence of the unwary. As a matter of fact, when the world is drunk with war, and rapine, murder, and plunder and rife, it is exactly the time to lay in more ammunition.

Had Dr. Jordan been in the position of Captain John Smith in the Virginia colony, when the Indians were on the warpath, he would have advised the settlers to disarm and destroy their stockades and forts. The Indians at that time went on the warpath and got drunk for war because they had a grievance.

When the present war is over and international commerce is reestablished, we are destined to give some other nation a grievance, for the same reason that we then gave those Indians a grievance, and that other nation will go on the warpath, just as those Indians did, and that other nation when it takes up the torch and the sword and gets a taste of blood, is going to be as savage as the men engaged in the present European conflict.

There are two kinds of true prophets: The one kind, like Isaiah, who is directly inspired of God; and the other kind, who judges the future by the lessons of the past. The scientist is a true prophet; but he is not one of the inspired kind. The way he does his predicting is the way of the astronomer, who uses a base line the width of the earth's orbit in order to triangulate the parrallax of a star. So the scientific prophet triangulates the parallax of future events from a base line compassing all human history.

There is no one lesson which history teaches us more plainly than that the possession of wealth by a defenseless nation is a standing *casus belli* to other nations, and that always there has been the nation standing ready to attack and plunder any other nation when there was liekly to be sufficient profit in the enterprise to pay for the trouble. Never have we seen any treaty stand for long in the way of such practices between nations. Treaties have always been mere scraps of paper, which, like the cobweb, ensnare the weak, while they let the strong break through.

It is strange that those who recommend that this country try the experiment of disarmament to secure peace by setting other nations a great moral example, should not have read history to see whether or not the experiment were a new one; and whether or not, judging by past experiments, it were likely to prove a success or a failure. Should these men look back through history, they would find that ancient Egypt tried the experiment, and went down under the sword and torch of fierce invaders from over the desert. They would learn that the Greeks tried the experiment and found it a failure. They would learn that India and China have bled through the ages because of their peaceableness. They would learn that the fall of Carthage was due not so much to the superior military power of Rome, or to the reiterations of Cato that Carthage must be destroyed, as it was to the peace talk of Hanno, which withheld the necessary support of Hannibal in Italy. They would learn that when old Rome lost her vigor and neglected her defenses, she was hewn to pieces by fierce barbarians. They would learn that the fathers of our own country, after the Revolution, tried the same old experiment, with the result that the city of Washington was captured and burned by the British in the war of 1812. They would learn, furthermore, that all prophets who have said that the nations will war no more, have been false prophets.

Four years before the Russo-Japanese war, I wrote an article for a New York magazine, in which I prophesied that war, and predicted Japanese victory. I predicted also at the same time that there would be in the near future a general European conflict. It has come.

The following quotations from that article may be of interest:

By far the greatest probability of imminent war lies in the Far East, between Russia and Japan. Japan feels the sting of the Russian whip that made her drop Port Arthur and withdraw from the continent of Asia, thus relinquishing the chief advantages gained by her victory over China. The whole sum paid Japan by China as a war indemnity has been expended on her navy and on armaments. In the East, in both naval and military strength, she is superior to Russia.

Whether or not we shall soon have war will depend on whether Japan will quietly wait until Russia shall have finished the Trans-Siberian Railway, secured Korea, intrenched and fortified herself along the Asiatic coast, and built a fleet of sufficient strength entirely to overawe the little empire. It is doubtful if Japan will wait for the time when Russia shall be ready to strangle her. She may strike and drive Russia from Korea and secure, as well, a fair share of Chinese territory; or, what amounts to the same thing, a lease of a portion of the Celestial Empire. She will thereafter be better able to protect her interests in Chinese trade and opportunities. Should she strike soon, and she and Russia be left to themselves, Japan ought to win, for she is close at hand and will be able to bring to bear upon the points of collision a much greater force than Russia. She will also be able to act with correspondingly greater celerity.

If we would essay to predict future events, we must draw the lines of divination in the direction that we see the nations grow, and these lines must be parallel with those of great commercial interests—be parallel with those of national self-interests. We then have but one more question to consider, on which to base *a priori* judgment. It is the question of might—of national resources and blood and iron.

What was true on a small scale, with primitive tribes of men, is also true on a large scale, with the great world powers of today. In early times, like the ebb and flow of the tides of the sea, conquest and reconquest, victory and defeat, followed one another. Then destruction succeeded growth and growth destruction.

As the great banyan tree constantly encroaches upon the territory of surrounding flora, to overlap and blight and kill all upon which its shadow falls, so do and so must nations in their growth encroach upon their neighbors.

In recent times, the tremendous strides made in the arts and sciences, and the birth of new industries, and the enormous growth of all, have provided room and occupation for the earth's great dominating peoples. Vast land areas have been reclaimed, and boundless resources developed. Thus far the overflow has been upon the lands of the tameless American Indian—of the lazy African—of the docile Hindoo, and the simple savage of the southern seas. Now it is China's turn, and the wolves of greed, in the guise of trade, are already howling at her gates.

Growth is proceeding with constantly accelerating rapidity, and soon the overflow must be on lands already filled to overflowing—not then with simple savages. It will then be Greek to Greek, over fortresses that frown along the whole frontier. Then there will be a clash. It is coming. Where the storm will first break, and when, is a question. That a great conflict will come, and at no distant date, is certain.—*The Home Magazine,* July 1900.

At the first annual banquet of the Aeronautical Society four years ago, I predicted exactly the use of the aeroplane in war that it has had since that time. President Taft was one of the speakers, and his subject was his pet peace and arbitration treaties. He said that there were not likely to be the requisite wars for testing out the aeroplane, as predicted. He said that there was going to be a shortage of wars.

Since that time, we have had the revolution in China, the Italian war with Tripoli, the Balkan wars, a continuous revolutionary performance in Mexico, and finally, we have the present great European War. Not much of a shortage in wars, truly!

The following quotation from Dr. David Starr Jordan's "War and Waste" is an excellent illustration of the prophetic wisdom that is keeping the United States of America unprepared against war:

What shall we say of the Great War of Europe, ever threatening, ever impending, and which never comes? We shall say that it will never come. Humanly speaking, it is impossible.

Not in the physical sense, of course, for with weak, reckless, and godless men nothing evil is impossible. It may be, of course, that some half-crazed archduke or some harassed minister of state shall half-knowing give the signal for Europe's conflagration. In fact, the agreed signal has been given more than once within the last few months. The tinder is well dried and laid in such a way as to make the worst of this catastrophe. All Europe cherishes is ready for the burning. Yet Europe recoils and will recoil even in the dread stress of spoil-division of the Balkan war. . . .

But accident aside, the Triple Entente lined up against the Triple Alliance, we shall expect no war. . . .

The bankers will not find the money for such a fight, the industries of Europe will not maintain it, the statesmen cannot. So whatever the bluster or apparent provocation, it comes to the same thing at the end. There will be no general war until the masters direct the fighters to fight. The masters have much to gain, but vastly more to lose, and their signal will not be given.

Eight years ago, when the great Peace Conference was held at Carnegie Hall, New York, to discuss the limitation and abolishment of armaments, the most notable of the pacifists represented were invited by the Economic Club of Boston to attend a banquet in that city for the free hot-airing of their views.

There was much sophistical palaver about destroying our old battle flags and leveling our soldiers' monuments and all landmarks and reminders of war. William T. Stead, however, was more rational, and he was annoyed by the silly impracticable nonsense of some of the dubs of peace. Stead's better sense was evidenced by the fact that the following winter he recommended to the British Parliament that England build two battleships to every one built by Germany.

Invited to speak in defense of armaments, I held that we must arm for peace, and not disarm for it. I began my remarks by telling them this story:

In a small paragraph in an obscure place upon the back page of a leading Boston paper, I once saw the announcement that Herbert Spencer, the great philosopher, was very ill, and not expected to live. On the front page of the same paper, under bold headlines, was a three-column article on the physical condition of John L. Sullivan.

John L. Sullivan was a fighter, while Herbert Spencer was only a philosopher; hence the difference in public interest.

John L. Sullivan, in his time, standing on the corner, would deplete the hall and break up any peace meeting in the world, and block the street with massed humanity for a square, jostling for a sight of him.

Several years ago, a reverend gentleman by the name of Charles Edward Jefferson elicited much applause by his public utterances on the blessings and advantages of nonresistance and meekness mild. He made it as clear as the day dawn of June, to the unreasoning, that it is all a mistake to build guns, warships, and coast fortifications; that our war colleges are not institutions of actual learning at all, but are institutions for teaching ignorance. He declared that militarism is squandering the taxpayers' money by the hundreds of millions, and all because the advocates of militarism and the friends of militarism are perverse and wilfully wot not what they do, though wisdom radiant as the rainbow stares them in the face; and because our military men, who have been educated at government expense and who, we have thought, were devoting their lives to the country's service in studying its needs and fighting its battles, are desirous merely of promotion and of widening the sphere of their activities.

According to Dr. Jefferson, these men are not what we have supposed them—a bulwark against trouble, but are troublemakers, ignorant of the primary essential of their profession, namely militant meekness; and instead of being guardians of peace and an assurance against war, they are actual war breeders. He seems to think that there is a real conspiracy to squander the taxpayers' money in the interest of a military clique.

A man may be wrong, and yet be honest. Prejudice is honest. Dr. Jefferson is doubtless honest, and if it should be that he is right, then his doctrine is practicable. If he is right, our military men are wrong. If our army and navy officers, who have been educated at the public expense and in the school of experience, do not know and understand better this country's needs in the respects and particulars for which they have been educated than does this good ecclesiastic, then it is proved that the church is a better military school than Annapolis or West Point. Theology, and not military science, should hereafter be taught in those institutions. The military parade should be called in from the campus and be replaced by knee drill in the chapel, and hereafter, at Annapolis, at West Point, and along the firing-line, the command should be Shoulder Psalms, instead of Shoulder Arms.

Let us lay down our arms and spike our guns, disband the military parade from the campus, as the sentimentalists desire us to do, and we shall very soon, with Kubla Khan, hear "ancestral voices (George Washington's among them) prophesying war."

11. American Intervention—a Pragmatist's View: John Dewey

John Dewey and William James generally are considered the primary contributors to the philosophical system of pragmatism. Dewey also is credited with evolving the most important theories of twentieth century progressive education. He retained an empathy with the mental processes of ordinary Americans which obliges the historian to give respectful attention when presented with Dewey's intuitive essays on public opinion. In this article he suggests that the nation's long hesitation before commiting itself to the European conflict in 1917 was more important than the decision for war itself, indicating a high degree of American independence from Europe.

Were I a poet, this should be, even at the dangerous risk of comparisons invited, an ode. But, alas, the passion as well as the art is lacking. I can but set down a blurred perception of immense masses stirring across great spaces. There is not even the assurance that the fogged outlines mark a thing beheld. They may be only felt, and felt with too much of an observing curiosity to find out what they mean to permit them to kindle into passion.

It is likely that our national hesitation will outwardly have been swallowed up in act before these words appear upon the printed page. But if I read the hesitation aright such a resolution of uncertainty will be but partial. We shall have decided a small thing, what to do, but the great thing, the thing so great as to cause and perpetuate our hesitation, may remain. We may still be uncertain as to our will to be. In the course of doing, we may, it is true, learn something of what we would be. But also it may turn out that even while doing deeds which are imperatively demanded of us our hesitation may grow into a greater doubt. For the hesitation which I see is that of a nation which knows that its time has not come, its hour not struck. The ripening forces have not yet matured, and like all vital processes they are not to be forced. The time of national hesitation is the time of slow and certain growth to an end which is

Source: John Dewey, "In a Time of National Hesitation," *The Seven Arts,* 1 (May 1917): 3–7.

not to be anticipated nor prevented. The day of fate tarries and not till it arrives will the authentic direction be spoken. Meantime suspense.

This is not the usual rendering of our course. The most vocal among us tell us that our hesitation is at best the provincialism of ignorance and at worst a slothful cowardice bred of mammon-serving peace; that we hesitate from inner division and distraction; because we are not a nation, but a boardinghouse of aliens; because we have been corrupted by overmuch prosperity and a sentimentally humanitarian pacifism. Our fiber is gone: we are spineless. We have been told that we are justly the objects of universal scorn and contempt, that our national hesitation is a national humiliation. When a fellow citizen said, after the dismissal of the German ambassador, that now for the first time in two years could he stand straight and look others in the eye, he only said what the more vocal elements have been reiterating day after day, week after week. Such has been the obvious, not to say clamorous, explanation of our prolonged and penetrating hesitation.

Such statements are not material for argument or disproof. One only sees what one sees, and it is hard to tell even that. But these accounts prove too much. We are told that the nation pauses for lack of leadership, when heaven knows our ears have ached from the roarings of those who have told us what to do and who have exhausted the fishwives' vocabulary in scolding us because we have not done it. We have bowed our heads, and allowed the tempest of words to pass over. We have waited listening for something, just what we have not known, but assuredly for something else than what platform and press are dinning into us. Hordes and aggregates of accident do not wait and hesitate in this fashion. They respond with a stampede. The strident tone of our critics in its increasing shrillness is evidence that the inertia, the solidity of a people was there; for only those who are fused into a single being can wait enduringly in the midst of such clamor and world stir. We have continued to be uncertain just because we were certain that our destiny had not declared itself. Those who have offered themselves as prophets have shown that they were rather historians, reminiscent of a colonial age out of which the people, the masses, had slowly grown. Those who lamented the lack of leadership proclaimed by their laments that a fused people had assumed its own leadership and was waiting in silence to issue its directions. Never has the American people so little required apologizing for, because never before has it been in such possession of its senses.

If there has been such impressive unification, why the prolonged hesitation? Because though we have become a single body—hence the inertia which the unknowing have taken to be apathy—and are in possession of our senses, we have not yet found a national mind, a will as to what to be. It is easy to be stampeded; it is easy to be told what one's mind is, and humbly to accept on trust a mind thus made up. It is not easy to make up the mind, for the mind is made up only as the world takes on form. We have hesitated in making up our mind just because we would make it up not arbitrarily but in the light of the confronting situation. And that situation is dark, not light.

This is itself proof that a New World is at last a fact, and not a geographical designation. We no longer can be spoken to in the language of the Old World and respond. We must be spoken to in our own terms. I do not say this in a complacent or congratulatory mood, but record it as a fact. It is a disagreeable fact to many, and especially disagreeable to those with whom we feel most friendly. It cannot fail to be in some measure disagreeable to ourselves that we should have attained a state which is bound to be intellectually and morally unpleasant to those who are our near spiritual kin and who have, as against anybody but ourselves, our warm sympathies and best wishes. That the gallant fight for democracy and civilization fought on the soil of France is not our fight is a thing not to be realized without pangs and qualms. But it is a fact which has slowly disclosed itself as these last long years have disclosed us to ourselves. It was not ours, because for better or for worse we are committed to a fight for another democracy and another civilization. Their nature is not clear to us: all that is sure is that they are different. This is the fact of a New World. The Declaration of Independence is no longer a merely dynastic and political declaration.

For this reason I hold that a termination of hesitation so far as to engage in overt war against Germany will not be of itself a conclusion of our hesitation. There is such a thing as interests being affected vitally without a vital interest being affected. As I write, we seem to be on the point of arriving at the conclusion that we cannot aid, by means of a passive compliance, the triumph of a nation that regards its triumph as the one thing so necessary that all means whatsoever that lead to that triumph are not only legitimate but sacred. Such a future neighbor we do not wish to be developed, certainly not by our aid as passive accomplices. So far our hesitation gives way to action, because so far the situation has declared itself. We but meet a clearly proffered challenge.

But it is vain to suppose that thereby our deeper hesitation is concluded; that on this account we join with full heart and soul even though we join with unreserved energy. Not until the almost impossible happens, not until the Allies are fighting on our terms for our democracy and civilization, will that happen. And so we shall still hesitate, for the huge slow-moving body does not see its goal and path. When the President spoke his words as to the conditions under which the American people would voluntarily cooperate in fixing the terms of future international relationships, something stirred within, but the whole bulk did not respond, not even though the appeal was couched in that combination of legal and sentimental phraseology which is our cherished political dialect. At the Russian revolution there was a more obvious thrill. Perhaps through some convulsion, some rearrangement still to come, there will be a revelation of the conditions under which the world's future may be wrought out in patient labor and fraternal comity, a disclosure so authoritative that in it we shall see and know ourselves and recognize our will. More likely there will be partial events and partial conclusions. But one thing has already happened. The war has shown that we are no longer a colony of any European nation nor of them all collectively. We are a new body and a new spirit in the world. Such at least is the impression which has been forming in me, unbidden and unforeseen, concerning the time of our national hesitation.

12. American Intervention—an Explanation: Woodrow Wilson

THIS ADDRESS *by President Wilson to a joint session of Congress on April 2, 1917, won quick support for a declaration of war from almost every legislator except a few renegades and those from states with large numbers of German-American or Irish-American voters. Wisconsin alone provided almost one-quarter of the votes in the two houses against the war resolution. Wilson expressed the views of a unanimous cabinet, and his speech was greeted enthusiastically by almost every important English language newspaper in the country, even those that had opposed intervention in the past.*

I have called the Congress into extraordinary session because there are serious, very serious, choices of policy to be made, and made immediately, which it was neither right nor constitutionally permissible that I should assume the responsibility of making.

On the third of February last I officially laid before you the extraordinary announcement of the Imperial German Government that on and after the first day of February it was its purpose to put aside all restraints of law or of humanity and use its submarines to sink every vessel that sought to approach either the ports of Great Britain and Ireland or the western coasts of Europe or any of the ports controlled by the enemies of Germany within the Mediterranean. . . . I was for a little while unable to believe that such things would in fact be done by any government that had hitherto subscribed to the humane practices of civilized nations. . . . I am not now thinking of the loss of property involved, immense and serious as that is, but only of the wanton and wholesale destruction of the lives of noncombatants, men, women, and children. . . . Property can be paid for; the lives of peaceful and innocent people cannot be. The present German submarine warfare against commerce is a warfare against mankind.

It is a war against all nations. American ships have been sunk,

SOURCE: R. S. Baker and W. E. Dodd, eds., *The Public Papers of Woodrow Wilson: War and Peace* (New York, 1927), I: 6–16.

American lives taken, in ways which it has stirred ships and people of other neutrals and us very deeply to learn of, but the friendly nations have been sunk and overwhelmed in the waters in the same way. There has been no discrimination. The challenge is to all mankind. Each nation must decide for itself how it will meet it. . . .

When I addressed the Congress on the twenty-sixth of February last I thought that it would suffice to assert our neutral rights with arms, our right to use the seas against unlawful interference, our right to keep our people safe against unlawful violence. But armed neutrality, it now appears, is impracticable. . . . Armed neutrality is ineffectual enough at best; in such circumstances and in the face of such pretensions it is worse than ineffectual: it is likely only to produce what it was meant to prevent; it is practically certain to draw us into the war without either the rights or the effectiveness of belligerents. There is one choice we cannot make, we are incapable of making: we will not choose the path of submission. . . .

With a profound sense of the solemn and even tragic character of the step I am taking and of the grave responsibilities which it involves, but in unhesitating obedience to what I deem my constitutional duty, I advise that the Congress declare the recent course of the Imperial German Government to be in fact nothing less than war against the government and people of the United States; that it formally accept the status of belligerent which has thus been thrust upon it; and that it take immediate steps not only to put the country in a more thorough state of defense but also to exert all its power and employ all its resources to bring the Government of the German Empire to terms and end the war.

What this will involve is clear. It will involve the utmost practicable cooperation in counsel and action with the governments now at war with Germany, and, as incident to that, the extension to those governments of the most liberal financial credits, in order that our resources may so far as possible be added to theirs. It will involve the organization and mobilization of all the material resources of the country. . . . It will involve the immediate full equipment of the navy in all respects but particularly in supplying it with the best means of dealing with the enemy's submarines. It will involve the immediate addition to the armed forces of the United States already provided for by law in case of war at least five hundred thousand men, who should, in my opinion, be chosen upon the principle of universal liability to service. . . .

While we do these things, these deeply momentous things, let us be very clear, and make very clear to all the world what our motives and our objects are. . . . Neutrality is no longer feasible or desirable where the peace of the world is involved and the freedom of its peoples, and the menace to that peace and freedom lies in the existence of autocratic governments backed by organized force which is controlled wholly by their will, not by the will of their people. We have seen the last of neutrality in such circumstances. We are at the beginning of an age in which it will be insisted that the same standards of conduct and of responsibility for wrong done shall be observed among nations and their governments that are observed among the individual citizens of civilized states.

We have no quarrel with the German people. We have no feelings towards them but one of sympathy and friendship. It was not upon their impulse that their government acted in entering this war. . . .

One of the things that has served to convince us that the Prussian autocracy was not and could never be our friend is that from the very outset of the present war it has filled our unsuspecting communities and even our offices of government with spies and set criminal intrigues everywhere afoot against our national unity of counsel, our peace within and without, our industries and our commerce. Indeed, it is now evident that its spies were here even before the war began; and it is unhappily not a matter of conjecture but a fact proved in our courts of justice that the intrigues which have more than once come perilously near to disturbing the peace and dislocating the industries of the country have been carried on at the instigation, with the support, and even under the personal direction of official agents of the Imperial Government accredited to the Government of the United States. . . . That it means to stir up enemies against us at our very doors the intercepted note to the German Minister at Mexico City is eloquent evidence. . . .

We are now about to accept gage of battle with this natural foe to liberty and shall, if necessary, spend the whole force of the Nation to check and nullify its pretensions and its power. We are glad, now that we see the facts with no veil of false pretense about them, to fight thus for the ultimate peace of the world and for the liberation of its peoples, the German peoples included: for the rights of nations great and small and the privilege of men everywhere to choose their way of life and of obedience. The world must be made safe for democracy. Its peace must be planted upon the tested foundations of political liberty. We have no selfish ends to serve. We desire no conquest, no dominion. We seek no indemnities for ourselves, no material compensation for the sacrifices we shall freely make. We are but one of the champions of the rights of mankind. We shall be satisfied when those rights have been made as secure as the faith and the freedom of nations can make them. . . .

It is a distressing and oppressive duty, Gentlemen of the Congress, which I have performed in thus addressing you. There are, it may be, many months of fiery trial and sacrifice ahead of us. It is a fearful thing to lead this great peaceful people into war, into the most terrible and disastrous of all wars, civilization itself seeming to be in the balance. But the right is more precious than peace, and we shall fight for the things which we have always carried nearest our hearts,—for democracy, for the right of those who submit to authority to have a voice in their own Governments, for the rights and liberties of small nations, for a universal dominion of right by such a concert of free peoples as shall bring peace and safety to all nations and make the world itself at last free. To such a task we can dedicate our lives and our fortunes, everything that we are and everything that we have, with the pride of those who know that the day has come when America is privileged to spend her blood and her might for the principles that gave her birth and happiness and the peace which she has treasured. God helping her, she can do no other.

13. A Plea for Peace: Senator George W. Norris

THE MOST *bitter attack on the President's policies toward the belligerents in World War I, including his request for a declaration of war, came from Senator George W. Norris of Nebraska. Norris, one of the acknowledged leaders of congressional progressives, spoke with a moral fervor fully equal to Wilson's. Robert La Follette, another leading progressive, also opposed the war resolution in a four-hour speech. Sections of Norris' attack foreshadowed later investigation, by historians as well as Congressmen, into the possibility that economic commitments by bankers and munitions manufacturers played a crucial role in the decision for war. Note that Norris took the precaution of acknowledging that political and journalistic leaders can be influenced "unconsciously" by the economic interests by their nation.*

Mr. President, . . . The resolution now before the Senate is a declaration of war. Before taking this momentous step, and while standing on the brink of this terrible vortex, we ought to pause and calmly and judiciously consider the terrible consequences of the step we are about to take. We ought to consider likewise the route we have recently traveled and ascertain whether we have reached our present position in a way that is compatible with the neutral position which we claimed to occupy at the beginning and through the various stages of this unholy and unrighteous war.

No close student of recent history will deny that both Great Britain and Germany have, on numerous occasions since the beginning of the war, flagrantly violated in the most serious manner the rights of neutral vessels and neutral nations under existing international law as recognized up to the beginning of this war by the civilized world.

The reason given by the President in asking Congress to declare war against Germany is that the German Government has declared certain war zones, within which, by the use of submarines, she sinks, without notice, American ships and destroys American lives. . . .

SOURCE: *The Congressional Record,* 65th Congress, 1st Session (April 4, 1917), pp. 212–215.

The German Government, by its order declaring its war zone around the south of England, declared that the order would be made effective by the use of submarines.

Thus we have the two declarations of the two Governments, each declaring a military zone and warning neutral shipping from going into the prohibited area. England sought to make her order effective by the use of submerged mines. Germany sought to make her order effective by the use of submarines. Both of these orders were illegal and contrary to all international law as well as the principles of humanity. Under international law no belligerent Government has the right to place submerged mines in the high seas. Neither has it any right to take human life without notice by the use of submarines. If there is any difference on the ground of humanity between these two instrumentalities, it is certainly in favor of the submarines. The submarine can exercise some degree of discretion and judgment. The submerged mine always destroys without notice, friend and foe alike, guilty and innocent the same. In carrying out these two policies, both Great Britain and Germany have sunk American ships and destroyed American lives without provocation and without notice. There have been more ships sunk and more American lives lost from the action of submarines than from English mines in the North Sea; for the simple reason that we finally acquiesced in the British war zone and kept our ships out of it, while in the German war zone we have refused to recognize its legality and have not kept either our ships or our citizens out of its area. If American ships had gone into the British war zone in defiance of Great Britain's order, as they have gone into the German war zone in defiance of the German Government's order, there would have been many more American lives lost and many more American ships sunk by the instrumentality of the mines than the instrumentality of the submarines.

We have in the main complied with the demands made by Great Britain. Our ships have followed the instructions of the British Government in going not only to England but to the neutral nations of the world, and in thus complying with the British order American ships going to Holland, Denmark, Norway, and Sweden have been taken by British officials into British ports, and their cargoes inspected and examined. All the mails we have carried even to neutral countries have been opened and censored, and oftentimes the entire cargo confiscated by the Government.

Nothing has been permitted to pass to even the most neutral nations except after examination and with the permission of the officials of the British Government. . . .

It is unnecessary to cite authority to show that both of these orders declaring military zones were illegal and contrary to international law. It is sufficient to say that our Government has officially declared both of them to be illegal and has officially protested against both of them.

The only difference is that in the case of Germany we have persisted in our protests, while in the case of England we have submitted. What was our duty as a government and what were our rights when we were confronted with these extraordinary orders declaring these military zones? First, we could have defied both of them and could have gone to war against both of these nations for this violation of international law and interference with our neutral rights. Second, we had the technical right to defy one and to acquiesce in the other. Third, we could, while denouncing them both as illegal, have acquiesced in them both and thus remained neutral with both sides, although not agreeing with either as to the righteousness of their respective orders. We could have said to American shipowners that, while these orders are both contrary to international law and are both unjust, we do not believe that the provocation is sufficient to cause us to go to war for the defense of our rights as a neutral nation, and, therefore, American ships and American citizens will go into these zones at their own peril and risk. Fourth, we might have declared an embargo against the shipping from American ports of any merchandise to either one of these Governments that persisted in maintaining its military zone. We might have refused to permit the sailing of any ship from any American port to either of these military zones. In my judgment, if we had pursued this course, the zones would have been of short duration. England would have been compelled to take her mines out of the North Sea in order to get any supplies from our country. When her mines were taken out of the North Sea then the German ports upon the North Sea would have been accessible to American shipping and Germany would have been compelled to cease her submarine warfare in order to get any supplies from our nation into German North Sea ports.

There are a great many American citizens who feel that we owe it as a duty to humanity to take part in this war. Many instances of cruelty and inhumanity can be found on both sides. Men are often biased in their judgment on account of their sympathy and their interests. To my mind, what we ought to have maintained from the beginning was the strictest neutrality. If we had done this I do not believe we would have been on the verge of war at the present time. We had a right as a nation, if we desired, to cease at any time to be neutral. We had a technical right to respect the English war zone and to disregard the German war zone, but we could not do that and be neutral. I have no quarrel to find with the man who does not desire our country to remain neutral. While many such people are moved by selfish motives and hopes of gain, I have no doubt but that in a great many instances, through what I believe to be a misunderstanding of the real condition, there are many honest, patriotic citizens who think we ought to engage in this war and who are behind the President in his demand that we should declare war against Germany. I think such people err in judgment and to a great extent have been misled as to the real history and the true facts by the almost unanimous demand of the great combination of wealth that has a direct financial interest in our participation in the war. We have loaned many hundreds of millions of dollars to the allies in this controversy. While such action was legal and countenanced by international law, there is no doubt in my mind but the enormous amount of money loaned to the allies in this country has been instrumental in bringing about a public sentiment in favor of our country taking a course that would make every bond worth a hundred cents on the dollar and making the payment of every debt certain and sure. Through this instrumentality and also through the instrumentality of others who have not only made millions out of the war in the manufacture of munitions, etc., and who would expect to make millions more if our country can be drawn into the catastrophe, a large number of the great newspapers and news agencies of the country have been controlled and enlisted in the greatest propaganda that the world has ever known, to manufacture sentiment in favor of war. It is now demanded that the American citizens shall be used as insurance policies to guarantee the safe delivery of munitions of war to belligerent nations. The enormous profits of munition manufacturers, stockbrokers, and bond dealers must be still further increased by our entrance into the war. This has brought us to the present moment, when Congress, urged by the President and backed by the artificial sentiment, is about to declare war and engulf our country in the greatest holocaust that the world has ever known.

To whom does war bring prosperity? Not to the soldier who for the munificent compensation of $16 per month shoulders his musket and goes into the trench, there to shed his blood and to die if necessary; not to the broken-hearted widow who waits for the return of the mangled body of her husband; not to the mother who weeps at the death of her brave boy; not to the little children who shiver with cold; not to the babe who suffers from hunger; nor to the millions of mothers and daughters who carry broken hearts to their graves. War brings no prosperity to the great mass of common and patriotic citizens. It increases the cost of living of those who toil and those who already must strain every effort to keep soul and body together. War brings prosperity to the stock gambler on Wall Street—to those who are already in possession of more wealth than can be realized or enjoyed.

Their object in having war and in preparing for war is to make money. Human suffering and the sacrifice of human life are necessary, but Wall Street considers only the dollars and the cents. The men who do the fighting, the people who make the sacrifices, are the ones who will not be counted in the measure of this great prosperity that he depicts. The stockbrokers would not, of course, go to war, because the very object they have in bringing on the war is profit, and therefore they must remain in their Wall Street offices in order to share in that great prosperity which they say war will bring. The volunteer officer, even the drafting officer, will not find them. They will be concealed in their palatial offices on Wall Street, sitting behind mahogany desks, covered up with clipped coupons—coupons soiled with the sweat of honest toil, coupons stained with mothers' tears, coupons dyed in the lifeblood of their fellow men.

We are taking a step today that is fraught with untold danger. We are going into war upon the command of gold. We are going to run the risk of sacrificing millions of our countrymen's lives in order that other countrymen may coin their lifeblood into money. And even if we do not cross the Atlantic and go into the trenches, we are going to pile up a debt that the toiling masses that shall come many generations after us will have to pay. Unborn millions will bend their backs in toil in order to pay for the terrible step we are now about to take. We are about to do the bidding of wealth's terrible mandate. By our act we will make millions of our countrymen suffer, and the consequences of it may well be that millions of our brethren must shed their lifeblood, millions of broken-hearted women must weep, millions of children must suffer with cold, and millions of babes must die from hunger, and all because we want to preserve the commercial right of American citizens to deliver munitions of war to belligerent nations.

Mr. Reed Mr. President——

The president pro tempore Does the Senator from Nebraska yield to the Senator from Missouri?

Mr. Norris I will say to the Senator that I prefer not to yield.

The president pro tempore Does the Senator yield?

Mr. Reed Of course I cannot interrupt under those circumstances.

The president pro tempore The Senator declines to yield.

Mr. Norris I know that I am powerless to stop it. I know that this war madness has taken possession of the financial and political powers of our country. I know that nothing I can say will stay the blow that is soon to fall. I feel that we are committing a sin against humanity and against our countrymen. I would like to say to this war god, You shall not coin into gold the lifeblood of my brethren. I would like to prevent this terrible catastrophe from falling upon my people. I would be willing to surrender my own life if I could cause this awful cup to pass. I charge no man here with a wrong motive, but it seems to me that this war craze has robbed us of our judgment. I wish we might delay our action until reason could again be enthroned in the brain of man. I feel that we are about to put the dollar sign upon the American flag.

I have no sympathy with the military spirit that dominates the Kaiser and his advisers. I do not believe that they represent the heart of the great German people. I have no more sympathy with the submarine policy of Germany than I have with the mine-laying policy of England. I have heard with rejoicing of the overthrow of the Czar of Russia and the movement in that great country toward the establishment of a government where the common people will have their rights, liberty, and freedom respected. I hope and pray that a similar revolution may take place in Germany, that the Kaiser may be overthrown, and that on the ruins of his military despotism may be established a German republic, where the great

German people may work out their world destiny. The working out of that problem is not an American burden. We ought to remember the advice of the father of our country and keep out of entangling alliances. Let Europe solve her problems as we have solved ours. Let Europe bear her burdens as we have borne ours. In the greatest war of our history and at the time it occurred, the greatest war in the world's history, we were engaged in solving an American problem. We settled the question of human slavery and washed our flag clean by the sacrifice of human blood. It was a great problem and a great burden, but we solved it ourselves. Never once did we think of asking Europe to take part in its solution. Never once did any European nation undertake to settle the great question. We solved it, and history has rendered a unanimous verdict that we solved it right. The troubles of Europe ought to be settled by Europe, and wherever our sympathies may lie, disagreeing as we do, we ought to remain absolutely neutral and permit them to settle their questions without our interference. We are now the greatest neutral nation. Upon the passage of this resolution we will have joined Europe in the great catastrophe and taken America into entanglements that will not end with this war, but will live and bring their evil influences upon many generations yet unborn.

Mr. Reed Mr. President, it has been no part of my purpose to participate in this debate, but a statement or series of statements made by the Senator from Nebraska [Mr. Norris] seem to me to demand instant repudiation. I need not say to that Senator or to the members of this body that I hold the Senator from Nebraska in the very highest personal regard and esteem, and because of that regard and esteem I shall not permit myself to characterize his speech as I believe it ought to be characterized. There are men in this world of high intelligence who become so obsessed by certain ideas that they permit them to color all other objects coming within their mental vision. The Senator from Nebraska, I fear, is so obsessed with a fear of "money" and of "profits" and of "fortunes" that all that it is necessary to suggest is that some wealthy concern may have an interest, remote, contingent, or direct, in the subject matter under consideration in order to confuse his mental vision. So we find the Senator here today reading a letter which he says comes from some unnamed Wall Street man. The letter purports to be nothing save a business man's view as to the business outcome in the event of possible hostilities. Because of that letter the

Senator makes the statements which I propose to challenge. He said:

> We are taking a step today that is fraught with untold danger. We are going into war upon the command of gold. We are going to run the risk of sacrificing millions of our countrymen's lives in order that other countrymen may coin their lifeblood into money.

Mr. President, that is an indictment of the President of the United States. That is an indictment of the Congress of the United States. That is an indictment of the American people. That is an indictment of truth, and it is not the truth. The Senator continues:

> By our act we will make millions of our countrymen suffer, and the consequences of it may well be that millions of our brethren must shed their lifeblood, millions of broken-hearted women must weep, millions of children must suffer with cold, and millions of babes must die from hunger, and all because we want to preserve the commercial right of American citizens to deliver munitions of war to belligerent nations.

Mr. President, that is another indictment of the President of the United States, of the Congress of the United States, of the American people, and of truth and fact. The Senator continues:

> I know that I am powerless to stop it. I know that this war madness has taken possession of the financial and political powers of our country.

And he continues:

> I would like to say to this war god, "You shall not coin into gold the lifeblood of my brethren."

Then he adds:

> I feel we are about to put the dollar sign upon the American flag.

Ah, Mr. President, I am sorry from my heart that such a statement should have been made at this time by an American citizen in the highest body of the American Congress. If that be not giving aid and comfort to the enemy on the very eve of the opening of hostilities then I do not know what would bring comfort to the heart of a Hapsburg or a Hohenzollern. If that be not treason it takes on a character and guise that is so near to treason that the enemies of America will gain from it much consolation.

Mr. Williams If it be not treason it grazes the edge of treason.

Mr. Reed As the Senator from Mississippi says with his usual terseness, if it be not treason it grazes the edge of treason.

Sir, this war is not being waged over dollars. It is not being waged over commerce. It is not being waged over profits and losses. It is a war for the maintenance of the sovereign rights of the American Republic and for the preservation of American dignity in the councils of the nations of the earth.

There was a time when Great Britain sought to levy a little tax on tea. The tax amounted to nothing from the dollar-and-cent standpoint. There were men then in old Boston town who said they would not pay that tax. If my friend had been there then I have no doubt he would have said to the Boston tea party, "You are waging war to save a few paltry dollars; you should not wage war for money; you would sacrifice human life to save a little tax." But there were patriots in that day who knew that a great principle was involved. They knew it was not a question of dollars. They knew that liberty was involved. They knew that back of the tax-gatherer stood the power of a great country, that proposed to lay its heavy hand upon the liberties of this people; and so those Boston men went forth not to resist the tax, but to resist tyranny; not to save money, but to pour out their lifeblood that liberty might live on this side of the Atlantic.

And today, as the President of the United States calls our country to arms, he does not do so because of the loss of a few paltry dollars. He calls us to arms because the life of this Republic, its honor and its integrity, have been assailed. He calls us to arms in order that the rights of the American Nation upon the high seas shall not be sacrificed. He calls us to arms to the end that neutral nations, great and small, shall not be crushed beneath the iron heel of that military despotism which today threatens not alone the civilization of Europe but of the world at large.

14. Mobilization of Public Opinion: George Creel

ALTHOUGH *George Creel writes with obvious pride in* How We Advertised America (1920), *about the Committee on Public Information, which he had directed, Creel already was being assigned a role as villain by those who deplored the conformity enforced during the war and during the Red Scare of 1919–1920. Creel's story was read with great interest, however, by those with more material products to sell the nation.*

How We Advertised America

As Secretary Baker points out, the war was not fought in France alone. Back of the firing line, back of armies and navies, back of the great supply depots, another struggle waged with the same intensity and with almost equal significance attaching to its victories and defeats. It was the fight for the *minds* of men, for the "conquest of their convictions," and the battle line ran through every home in every country.

It was in this recognition of Public Opinion as a major force that the Great War differed most essentially from all previous conflicts. The trial of strength was not only between massed bodies of armed men, but between opposed ideals, and moral verdicts took on all the value of military decisions. Other wars went no deeper than the physical aspects, but German *Kultur* raised issues that had to be fought out in the hearts and minds of people as well as on the actual firing line. The approval of the world meant the steady flow of inspiration into the trenches; it meant the strengthened resolve and the renewed determination of the civilian population that is a nation's second line. The condemnation of the world meant the destruction of morale and the surrender of that conviction of justice which is the very heart of courage.

The Committee on Public Information was called into existence

SOURCE: George Creel, *How We Advertised America* (New York, 1920), pp. 3–14, 117–132.

to make this fight for the "verdict of mankind," the voice created to plead the justice of America's cause before the jury of Public Opinion. The fantastic legend that associated gags and muzzles with its work may be likened only to those trees which are evolved out of the air by Hindu magicians and which rise, grow, and flourish in gay disregard of such usual necessities as roots, sap, and sustenance. *In no degree was the Committee an agency of censorship, a machinery of concealment or repression. Its emphasis throughout was on the open and the positive. At no point did it seek or exercise authorities under those war laws that limited the freedom of speech and press.* In all things, from first to last, without halt or change, it was a plain publicity proposition, a vast enterprise in salesmanship, the world's greatest adventure in advertising.

Under the pressure of tremendous necessities an organization grew that not only reached deep into every American community, but that carried to every corner of the civilized globe the full message of America's idealism, unselfishness, and indomitable purpose. We fought prejudice, indifference, and disaffection at home and we fought ignorance and falsehood abroad. We strove for the maintenance of our own morale and the Allied morale by every process of stimulation; every possible expedient was employed to break through the barrage of lies that kept the people of the Central Powers in darkness and delusion; we sought the friendship and support of the neutral nations by continuous presentation of facts. We did not call it propaganda, for that word, in German hands, had come to be associated with deceit and corruption. Our effort was educational and informative throughout, for we had such confidence in our case as to feel that no other argument was needed than the simple, straightforward presentation of facts.

There was no part of the great war machinery that we did not touch, no medium of appeal that we did not employ. The printed word, the spoken word, the motion picture, the telegraph, the cable, the wireless, the poster, the signboard—all these were used in our campaign to make our own people and all other peoples understand the causes that compelled America to take arms. All that was fine and ardent in the civilian population came at our call until more than one hundred and fifty thousand men and women were devoting highly specialized abilities to the work of the Committee, as faithful and devoted in their service as though they wore the khaki.

While America's summons was answered without question by the citizenship as a whole, it is to be remembered that during the three and a half years of our neutrality the land had been torn by a thousand divisive prejudices, stunned by the voices of anger and confusion, and muddled by the pull and haul of opposed interests. These were conditions that could not be permitted to endure. What we had to have was no mere surface unity, but a passionate belief in the justice of America's cause that should weld the people of the United States into one white-hot mass instinct with fraternity, devotion, courage, and deathless determination. The *war will*, the will to win, of a democracy depends upon the degree to which each one of all the people of that democracy can concentrate and consecrate body and soul and spirit in the supreme effort of service and sacrifice. What had to be driven home was that all business was the nation's business, and every task a common task for a single purpose.

Starting with the initial conviction that the war was not the war of an administration, but the war of one hundred million people, and believing that public support was a matter of public understanding, we opened up the activities of government to the inspection of the citizenship. A voluntary censorship agreement safeguarded military information of obvious value to the enemy, but in all else the rights of the press were recognized and furthered. Trained men, at the center of effort in every one of the war-making branches of government, reported on progress and achievement, and in no other belligerent nation was there such absolute frankness with respect to every detail of the national war endeavor.

As swiftly as might be, there were put into pamphlet form America's reasons for entering the war, the meaning of America, the nature of our free institutions, our war aims, likewise analyses of the Prussian system, the purposes of the imperial German government, and full exposure of the enemy's misrepresentations, aggressions, and barbarities. Written by the country's foremost publicists, scholars, and historians, and distinguished for their conciseness, accuracy, and simplicity, these pamphlets blew as a great wind against the clouds of confusion and misrepresentation. Money could not have purchased the volunteer aid that was given freely, the various universities lending their best men and the National Board of Historical Service placing its three thousand members at the complete disposal of the Committee. Some thirty-odd booklets, covering every phase of America's ideals, purposes, and aims, were printed in many languages other than English. Seventy-five millions reached the people of America, and other millions went to every corner of the world, carrying our defense and our attack.

The importance of the spoken word was not underestimated. A speaking division toured great groups like the Blue Devils, Pershing's Veterans, and the Belgians, arranged mass meetings in the communities, conducted forty-five war conferences from coast to coast, coordinated the entire speaking activities of the nation, and assured consideration to the crossroads hamlet as well as to the city.

The Four Minute Men, an organization that will live in history by reason of its originality and effectiveness, commanded the volunteer services of 75,000 speakers, operating in 5,200 communities, and making a total of 755,190 speeches, every one having the carry of shrapnel.

With the aid of a volunteer staff of several hundred translators, the Committee kept in direct touch with the foreign-language press, supplying selected articles designed to combat ignorance and disaffection. It organized and directed twenty-three societies and leagues designed to appeal to certain classes and particular foreign-language groups, each body carrying a specific message of unity and enthusiasm to its section of America's adopted peoples.

It planned war exhibits for the state fairs of the United States, also a great series of interallied war expositions that brought home to our millions the exact nature of the struggle that was being waged in France. In Chicago alone two million people attended in two weeks, and in nineteen cities the receipts aggregated $1,432,261.36.

The Committee mobilized the advertising forces of the country—press, periodical, car, and outdoor—for the patriotic campaign that gave millions of dollars' worth of free space to the national service.

It assembled the artists of America on a volunteer basis for the production of posters, window cards, and similar material of pictorial publicity for the use of various government departments and patriotic societies. A total of 1,438 drawings was used.

It issued an official daily newspaper, serving every department of government, with a circulation of one hundred thousand copies a day. For official use only, its value was such that private citizens ignored the supposedly prohibitive subscription price, subscribing to the amount of $77,622.58.

It organized a bureau of information for all persons who sought direction in volunteer war work, in acquiring knowledge of any administrative activities, or in approaching business dealings with the government. In the ten months of its existence it gave answers to eighty-six thousand requests for specific information.

It gathered together the leading novelists, essayists, and publicists of the land, and these men and women, without payment, worked faithfully in the production of brilliant, comprehensive articles that went to the press as syndicate features.

One division paid particular attention to the rural press and the plate-matter service. Others looked after the specialized needs of the labor press, the religious press, and the periodical press. The Division of Women's War Work prepared and issued the information of peculiar interest to the women of the United States, also aiding in the task of organizing and directing.

Through the medium of the motion picture, America's war progress, as well as the meanings and purposes of democracy, were carried to every community in the United States and to every corner of the world. *Pershing's Crusaders*, *America's Answer*, and *Under Four Flags* were types of feature films by which we drove home America's resources and determinations, while other pictures, showing our social and industrial life, made our free institutions vivid to foreign peoples. From the domestic showings alone, under a fair plan of distribution, the sum of $878,215 was gained, which went to support the cost of the campaigns in foreign countries where the exhibitions were necessarily free.

Another division prepared and distributed still photographs and stereopticon slides to the press and public. Over two hundred thousand of the latter were issued at cost. This division also conceived the idea of the "permit system," that opened up our military and naval activities to civilian camera men, and operated it successfully. It handled, also, the voluntary censorship of still and motion pictures in order that there might be no disclosure of information valuable to the enemy. The number of pictures reviewed averaged seven hundred a day.

Turning away from the United States to the world beyond our borders, a triple task confronted us. First, there were the peoples of the Allied nations that had to be fired by the magnitude of the American effort and the certainty of speedy and effective aid, in order to relieve the war weariness of the civilian population and also to fan the enthusiasm of the firing line to new flame. Second, we had to carry the truth to the neutral nations, poisoned by German lies; and third, we had to get the ideals of America, the determination of America, and the invincibility of America into the Central Powers.

Unlike other countries, the United States had no subsidized press service with which to meet the emergency. As a matter of bitter fact, we had few direct news contacts of our own with the outside world, owing to a scheme of contracts that turned the foreign distribution of American news over to European agencies. The volume of information that went out from our shores was small, and, what was worse, it was concerned only with the violent and unusual in our national life. It was news of strikes and lynchings, riots, murder cases, graft prosecutions, sensational divorces, the bizarre extravagance of "sudden millionaires." Naturally enough, we were looked upon as a race of dollar-mad materialists, a land of cruel monopolists, our real rulers the corporations and our democracy a "fake."

Looking about for some way in which to remedy this evil situation, we saw the government wireless lying comparatively idle, and through the close and generous cooperation of the navy we worked out a news machinery that soon began to pour a steady stream of American information into international channels of communication. Opening an office in every capital of the world outside the Central Powers, a daily service went out from Tuckerton to the Eiffel Tower for use in France and then for relay to our representatives in Berne, Rome, Madrid, and Lisbon. From Tuckerton the service flashed to England, and from England there was relay to Holland, the Scandinavian countries, and Russia. We went into Mexico by cable and land wires; from Darien we sent a service in Spanish to Central and South American countries for distribution by our representatives; the Orient was served by telegraph from

New York to San Diego, and by wireless leaps to Cavite and Shanghai. From Shanghai the news went to Tokio and Peking, and from Peking on to Vladivostok for Siberia. Australia, India, Egypt, and the Balkans were also reached, completing the world chain.

For the first time in history the speeches of a national executive were given universal circulation. The official addresses of President Wilson, setting forth the position of America, were put on the wireless always at the very moment of their delivery, and within twenty-four hours were in every language in every country in the world. Carried in the newspapers initially, they were also printed by the Committee's agents on native presses and circulated by the millions. The swift rush of our war progress, the tremendous resources of the United States, the Acts of Congress, our official deeds and utterances, the laws that showed our devotion to justice, instances of our enthusiasm and unity—all were put on the wireless for the information of the world, Teheran and Tokio getting them as completely as Paris or Rome or London or Madrid.

Through the press of Switzerland, Denmark, and Holland we filtered an enormous amount of truth to the German people, and from our headquarters in Paris went out a direct attack upon Hun censorship. Mortar guns, loaded with "paper bullets," and airplanes, carrying pamphlet matter, bombarded the German front, and at the time of the armistice balloons with a cruising radius of five hundred miles were ready to reach far into the Central Powers with America's message.

This daily news service by wire and radio was supplemented by a mail service of special articles and illustrations that went into foreign newspapers and magazines and technical journals and periodicals of special appeal. We aimed to give in this way a true picture of the American democracy, not only in its war activities, but also in its devotion to the interests of peace. There were, too, series of illustrated articles on our education, our trade and industry, our finance, our labor conditions, our religions, our work in medicine, our agriculture, our women's work, our government, and our ideals.

Reading rooms were opened in foreign countries and furnished with American books, periodicals, and newspapers. Schools and public libraries were similarly supplied. Photographs were sent for display on easels in shop windows abroad. Window hangers and news display sheets went out in English, French, Italian, Swedish,

Portuguese, Spanish, Danish, Norwegian, and Dutch; and display sheets went to Russia, China, Japan, Korea, parts of India and the Orient, to be supplemented with printed reading matter by the Committee's agents there.

To our representatives in foreign capitals went, also, the feature films that showed our military effort—cantonments, shipyards, training stations, warships, and marching thousands—together with other motion pictures expressing our social and industrial progress, all to be retitled in the language of the land, and shown either in theaters, public squares, or open fields. Likewise we supplied pamphlets for translation and distribution, and sent speakers, selected in the United States from among our foreign born, to lecture in the universities and schools, or else to go about among the farmers, to the labor unions, to the merchants, etc.

Every conceivable means was used to reach the foreign mind with America's message, and in addition to our direct approach we hit upon the idea of inviting the foremost newspaper men of other nations to come to the United States to see with their own eyes, to hear with their own ears, in order that they might report truly to their people as to American unity, resolve, and invincibility. The visits of the editors of Mexico, Italy, Switzerland, Denmark, Sweden, and Norway were remarkable in their effect upon these countries, and no less successful were the trips made to the American front in France under our guidance by the newspaper men of Holland and Spain.

Before this flood of publicity the German misrepresentations were swept away in Switzerland, the Scandinavian countries, Italy, Spain, the Far East, Mexico, and Central and South America. From being the most misunderstood nation, America became the most popular. A world that was either inimical, contemptuous, or indifferent was changed into a world of friends and well-wishers. Our policies, America's unselfish aims in the war, the services by which these policies were explained and these aims supported, and the flood of news items and articles about our normal life and our commonplace activities—these combined to give a true picture of the United States to foreign eyes. It is a picture that will be of incalculable value in our future dealings with the world, political and commercial. It was a bit of press agenting that money could not buy, done out of patriotism by men and women whose services no money could have bought.

In no other belligerent nation was there any such degree of centralization as marked our duties. In England and France, for instance, five to ten organizations were intrusted with the tasks that the Committee discharged in the United States. And in one country, in one year, many of the warring nations spent more money than the total expenditure of the Committee on Public Information during the eighteen months of its existence in its varied activities that reached to every community in America and to every corner of the civilized world. From the President's fund we received $5,600,000, and Congress granted us an appropriation of $1,250,000, a total working capital of $6,850,000. From our films, war expositions, and minor sources we earned $2,825,670.23, and at the end were able to return $2,937,447 to the Treasury. Deduct this amount from the original appropriations, and it is seen that the Committee on Public Information cost the taxpayers of the United States just $4,912,553! These figures might well be put in bronze to stand as an enduring monument to the sacrifice and devotion of the one hundred and fifty thousand men and women who were responsible for the results. A world fight for the verdict of mankind—a fight that was won against terrific odds—and all for less than five millions—less than half what Germany spent in Spain alone!

It is the pride of the Committee, as it should be the pride of America, that every activity was at all times open to the sun. No dollar was ever sent on a furtive errand, no paper subsidized, no official bought. From a thousand sources we were told of the wonders of German propaganda, but our original determinations never altered. Always did we try to find out what the Germans were doing and then we *did not do it*.

There is pride, also, in the record of stainless patriotism and unspotted Americanism. In June 1918, after one year of operation—a year clamorous with ugly attack—the Committee submitted itself to the searching examination of the House Committee on Appropriations. Every charge of partisanship, dishonesty, inaccuracy, and inefficiency was investigated, the expenditure of every dollar scrutinized, and the Congressmen even went back as far as 1912 to study my writings and my political thought. At the end of the inquiry the appropriation was voted unanimously, and on the floor of the House the Republican members supported the recommendation as strongly as did the Democrats.

Mr. Gillett of Massachusetts, then acting leader of the Republican minority, and now Speaker, made this declaration in the course of the debate:

> But after examining Mr. Creel and the other members of his bureau I came to the conclusion that as far as any evidence that we could discover it had not been conducted in a partisan spirit.

Mr. Mondel of Wyoming, after expressing his disapproval of Iniative and Referendum editorials written by me in 1912, spoke as follows:

> Having said this much about Mr. Creel and his past utterances, I now want to say that I believe Mr. Creel has endeavored to patriotically do his duty at the head of this bureau. I am of the opinion that, whatever his opinions may have been or may be now, so far as his activities in connection with this work are concerned, they have been, in the main, judicious, and that the work has been carried on for the most part in a businesslike, thoroughgoing, effective, and patriotic way. Mr. Creel has called to his assistance and placed in positions of responsibility men of a variety of political views, some of them Republicans of recognized standing. I do not believe that Mr. Creel has endeavored to influence their activities and I do not believe there have been any activities of the bureau consciously and intentionally partisan. A great work has been done. A great work has been done by the Four Minute Men, forty thousand of them speaking continuously to audiences, ready-made, all over the country. A great work has been done and will be done through the medium of the picture-film. A great work has been done through the medium of the publications of the bureau, which I believe can be commended and approved by every good citizen. Much remains to be done, and I believe the committee has not granted any too much money for this work.

The Battle of the Films

Pershing's Crusaders, *America's Answer*, and *Under Four Flags* are feature films that will live long in the memory of the world, for they reached every country, and were not only the last word in photographic art, but epitomized in thrilling, dramatic sequence the war effort of America. Yet these pictures, important as they were, represented only a small portion of the work of the Division of Films, a work that played a vital part in the world fight for public opinion. A steady output, ranging from one-reel subjects to seven-reel features, and covering every detail of American life, endeavor, and purpose, carried the call of the country to every community in the land, and then, captioned in all the various languages, went over the seas to inform and enthuse the peoples of Allied and neutral nations.

At the very outset, it was obvious that the motion picture had to be placed on the same plane of importance as the written and spoken word. There were, however, many obstacles in the way that prevented straightforward, driving action. In the first place, it was our original hope that we could put our reliance upon commercial producers, thus saving the time and expense that necessarily attended the creation of new machinery. This theory had to be abandoned, for the War Department issued a flat ruling that only the photographers in actual service would be permitted to take pictures of any kind either on the firing line in France or in the cantonments and other branches of the military establishment in the United States. Aside from the unwisdom of allowing individuals in private employ to have free run of aviation fields and munition factories, there was also the physical impossibility of handling the army of individual photographers that equitable representation would have demanded.

Going into the matter fully, we discovered that there was to be a photographic section of the Signal Corps, with first purpose to serve the fighting force and a second purpose to make pictures for the historical record desired by the War College. The Committee then went to the Secretary of War with representations as to the publicity value of much of the material that would be gathered. It was pointed out that since protection of military secrets barred private photographers, it was both wise and proper that we should have the right to go through the Signal Corps photographs, selecting such as were suitable for public exhibition. The contention was granted by Secretary Baker, and the Committee on Public Information was recognized by the War Department as the one authorized medium for the distribution of Signal Corps photographs, still pictures as well as "movies."

All of which seemed encouraging enough until investigation developed the sad news that the Photographic Section of the Signal Corps was a hope rather than a fact. Looking after film matters for the Committee at the time were Kendall Banning, formerly editor of *System*, and Mr. Lawrence E. Rubel, a young Chicago businessman, both of the temperament that found inaction intolerable. The two made a survey of the photographers of the United States, motion and still, and urged selections upon the Signal Corps until an adequate force had been assembled for duty at home and abroad. Mr. Banning accepted a commission as major in the army, and as the distribution of still pictures occupied Mr. Rubel's full time, the motion-picture end was turned over to Mr. Louis B. Mack, a Chicago lawyer, and Mr. Walter Niebuhr, both volunteers. The routine, as finally worked out, was as follows: The negatives of still and motion pictures taken in France and in the United States by the uniformed photographers of the Signal Corps were delivered, undeveloped, to the Chief of Staff for transmission to the War College division. The material was "combed" and such part as was decided to be proper for public exhibition was then turned over to the Committee on Public Information in the form of duplicate negatives. The Committee, out of its own funds, made prints from these negatives.

Our first hope was to avoid all appearance of competition with the commercial producers, and as a consequence the bulk of material was distributed fairly and at a nominal price among the film-news weeklies. Experts were then engaged to put the remainder into feature form, and these pictures were handed over to the State Councils of Defense and to the various patriotic societies. They were not shown in motion-picture theaters, nor was admission charged except in the case of benefits for a particular purpose. Among the early features thus produced were:

The 1917 Recruit, 2 editions (training of the National Army)
The Second Liberty Loan
Ready for the Fight (Artillery and Cavalry maneuvers)
Soldiers of the Sea (Marine Corps in training)
Torpedo Boat Destroyers (naval maneuvers)
Submarines
Army and Navy Sports
The Spirit of 1917 (the largest maneuver staged in America; an attack by the Jackies at Lake Bluff upon Fort Sheridan, Illinois)
In a Southern Camp (general army maneuvers)
The Lumber Jack (showing the growth of the Lumber Jack Regiment for reconstruction work in Europe)
The Medical Officers' Reserve Corps in Action (showing the development of the Medical Corps and training)
Fire and Gas (showing maneuvers of the new Thirtieth Engineer Regiment)
American Ambulances (complete display of ambulance work)

Labor's Part in Democracy's War (labor union activities in the war)
Annapolis (naval officers in the making)
Shipbuilding (construction of all types of ships)
Making of Big Guns
Making of Small Arms
Making of Uniforms for the Soldiers
Activities of the Engineers
Woman's Part in the War
The Conquest of the Air (airplane and balloon maneuvers)

As time went on, however, it was seen that this method of distribution not only put an unnecessary burden of expense upon the government, but that it was failing absolutely to place the pictorial record of America's war progress before more than a small percentage of the motion-picture audiences of the world. The growth of the Signal Corps's great Photographic Section was producing an enormous amount of material, both in the United States and France, possessed of the very highest propaganda value, and the existing arrangement wasted what it did not fritter away. Mr. Charles S. Hart, about to take a commission in the army, was persuaded to assume full charge of the work of reorganization, and too much credit cannot be given him for his accomplishment. He took an idea and a policy, and with courage, imagination, and driving genius he evolved a world machinery and built a business that handled millions, all without a single breakdown at any point.

One of Mr. Hart's first determinations was to take the cream of the material received from the Signal Corps, put it into great seven-reel features designed to set before the people a comprehensive record of war progress both in the United States and in France, and to *have the government itself present the pictures*. In plain, the Committee on Public Information went into the motion-picture business as a producer and exhibitor. The funds received from these sources were not to represent profit in any sense of the word. Every cent was to go to the manufacture and distribution of the huge amount of film that we were compelled to distribute without return in other countries as part of the educational campaign of the United States. Wherever possible this foreign distribution was made through the regular commercial channels, but there were various nations where these channels did not exist and where free showings were a necessity. It was also the case that we were put to heavy expense by the policy that sent all of the Committee's films, free of charge, to the encampments in the United States as well as to the picture shows on the firing line in France. The other belligerent countries all marketed their film. Why, then, was it not proper for the United States to use its own product in an effort to lighten the taxpayers' load, especially when commercial distribution meant 100 percent exhibition?

Our first feature film was *Pershing's Crusaders,* and at intervals of six weeks we produced *America's Answer* and *Under Four Flags.* The policy decided upon was this: first, direct exhibition of the feature by the Committee itself in the larger cities in order to establish value and create demand; second, sale, lease, or rental of the feature to the local exhibitors. This activity was placed in the hands of Mr. George Bowles, an experienced theatrical and motion-picture manager, who had made a name for himself in exploiting *The Birth of a Nation.* Mr. Bowles operated as many as eight road companies in different sections of the country at one time, each with its own advertising, advance sales, and business management. The utmost care was taken with these "official showings," for what we sought was an impressiveness that would lift them out of the class of ordinary motion-picture productions in the minds of the public. L. S. Rothapfel, of the Rialto and Rivoli theaters in New York City, gave us his own aid and that of his experts in the matter of scenic accessories, orchestra, and incidental music, while for "America's Answer" Frank C. Yohn painted a great canvas, so much a thing of beauty and inspiration that it thrilled audiences into enthusiasm for the motion pictures that followed.

Pershing's Crusaders was officially presented in twenty-four cities, *America's Answer* in thirty-four, and *Under Four Flags* in nine. Each of these so-called official showings extended over the period of a week or more and was presented at municipal halls, well-known legitimate or motion-picture theaters centrally located in the respective cities. Wide and intensive publicity and advertising campaigns were conducted by representatives on the spot by means of department-store window and hotel lobby displays, street car cards, and banners and newspaper space donated by local advertisers, etc. This campaign, under the direction of Mr. Marcus A. Beeman, also included circularization and personal interviews with representatives, officials, and leading citizens, clubs, societies, and organizations, including large industrial plants and firms. Churches, schools, chambers of commerce, political and social clubs, Young Men's Christian Association, Red Cross, Liberty Loan, and fraternal organizations were among those included in the lists.

Taking, for example, the official presentations in New York City—*Pershing's Crusaders* was shown at the Lyric Theater; *America's Answer* was shown at the George M. Cohan Theater; *Under Four Flags* was shown simultaneously at the Rivoli and Rialto theaters on Broadway. Each of these showings was preceded by a press campaign of about two weeks, several hundred twenty-four-sheet, three-sheet, and one-sheet posters were posted, and thousands of window cards were displayed, invitations were sent to all local dignitaries, and the showings were attended by representatives of the French, British, and Italian High Commissions. In Washington, members of Congress, the President, his cabinet, and many other officials attended, all of which facts were used extensively in advertising the features for general distribution.

As features did not consume the whole of the Signal Corps material by any means, we decided upon weekly releases, and in order to give this the highest interest as well as to emphasize the fact of partnership, we entered into cooperative arrangements with the representatives of England, France, and Italy. Each of the four nations contributed a fourth of the material and shared in the profits, and the joint product went forth as the Allied War Review.

Not one of the other governments, it may be explained, made free gifts of its pictures to private enterprise, but handled them upon commercial lines entirely, for in the motion-picture world revenue and circulation are synonymous. It was the first contention of the representatives of the English, French, and Italians that the War Review should be offered to the highest bidder, but the Committee on Public Information insisted that the four film-news weeklies of the United States should be given prior consideration. As a consequence, these four companies—the Hearst-Pathé, the Universal, the Mutual, and the Gaumont—were offered a weekly release of 2,000 feet of firing line film at a flat rate of $5,000. The representatives of the Allied governments felt that this price robbed them of fair and demonstrated profits, but the Committee on Public Information gained its point through insistence.

At that period in the negotiations when the largest of the weeklies had accepted the contract, one company addressed a series of letters to various officials of the government, complaining bitterly of the arrangement, not only insisting that the films should be given free of charge, but even hinting at a subsidy. As a consequence of this attitude, the Official War Review was offered to the motion-picture industry as a whole, as was the case with the feature film. Every exchange was given an opportunity to bid, and the Pathé Exchange, Inc., was awarded the contract on these terms: Eighty percent of proceeds and a guaranty of showing in 25,000 theaters as a minimum.

Even after the making of the feature films and the Official War Review there remained a certain amount of material that had as high publicity value as any of the other footage, and we placed this at the disposal of the news weeklies at the nominal cost of one dollar a foot, an equitable arrangement that worked.

With the tremendous advertising gained from these governmental showings in the principal cities we were then able to go direct to the exhibitor in the certainty of his keen interest. Our aim was to secure the widest possible distribution of the government films in the shortest possible time. To this end every effort was made to eliminate the competitive idea from the minds of exhibitors, and wherever possible to secure simultaneous showings in houses which ordinarily competed for pictures.

Mr. Denis Sullivan and his assistant, Mr. George Meeker, who were in charge of domestic distribution through motion-picture houses, inaugurated a proportionate selling plan whereby the rental charged every house was based on the average income derived from that particular house. By this method the small house as well as the large one could afford to run the government films. The result of these efforts to obtain the widest possible showing for government films was amazingly successful, and the showing of *America's Answer* broke all records for range of distribution of any feature of any description ever marketed.

On the basis of twelve thousand motion-picture theaters in the United States, over one-half the total number of theaters in the country exhibited the Official War Review and nearly that portion of *America's Answer*. In the film industry a booking of 40 percent of the theaters is considered as 100 percent distribution because of the close proximity of a great number of theaters, rendering them dependent on the same patronage—that is, theaters are plotted as available in zones rather than as individual theaters; thus three theaters in one zone present but one possible booking because of the identity of clientele. Taking this into consideration, the distribution of government features approximated 80 percent and 90 percent rather than 50 percent distribution, although on *America's Answer*, in certain territories such as New York and Seattle, the percentage of total theaters booked reached over 60 percent and 54 percent, respectively, which on the above basis would equal 100 percent distribution.

The success of the feature-films and the Official War Review are best indicated by the following figures:

Pershing's Crusaders	$181,741 69
America's Answer	185,144 30
Under Four Flags	63,946 48
Official War Review	334,622 35
Our Bridge of Ships	992 41
USA Series	13,864 98
Our Colored Fighters	640 60
News Weekly	15,150 00
Miscellaneous sales	56,641 58
Total sales from films	$852,744 30

It was not only the case that the entire output of the Division of Films was handed over to the Foreign Section for circulation in the various countries of the world, but the Educational Department saw to it that all of the Committee pictures were furnished free of charge to every proper organization in the United States.

The films were loaned to army and navy stations, educational and patriotic institutions, without charge except transportation. Other organizations and individuals were usually charged one dollar per reel for each day used. When it is considered that the average reel costs forty dollars for raw stock and printing, and that the average life of a reel is about two hundred runs, it can be readily seen that this charge of one dollar per reel barely covered cost. For the purpose of comparison the leading motion-picture houses in New York pay as high as three thousand dollars for the use of one picture for one week's run.

On June 1, 1918, the Division of Films formed a scenario department to experiment with an interesting theory. The departments at Washington had been in the habit of contracting for the production of films on propaganda subjects and then making additional contracts to secure a more or less limited circulation of the pictures when produced. The general attitude of motion-picture exhibitors was that propaganda pictures were uninteresting to audiences and could have no regular place in their theaters. The theory of the Division of Films was that the fault lay in the fact that propaganda pictures had never been properly made, and that if skill and care were employed in the preparation of the scenarios the resultant pictures could secure place in regular motion-picture programs. Producers were at first skeptical, but in the end they agreed to undertake the production of one-reel pictures for which the division was to supply the scenario, the list of locations, and permits for filming the same, and to give every possible cooperation, all without charge. The finished picture became the sole property of the producer, who obligated himself merely to give it the widest possible circulation after it had been approved by the Division of Films. Mr. Rufus Steele was given charge of the new venture, and while many difficulties had to be overcome, the theory proved sound.

The following one-reel pictures were produced:

By the Paramount-Bray Pictograph:
- Says Uncle Sam: Keep 'Em Singing and Nothing Can Lick 'Em—the purpose and method of the vocal training of the army and the navy.
- Says Uncle Sam: I Run the Biggest Life-Insurance Company on Earth—story of the War Risk Insurance Bureau.
- Says Uncle Sam: A Girl's a Man for A'That—story of women in war work.
- Says Uncle Sam: I'll Help Every Willing Worker Find a Job—story of the United States Employment Service.

By the Pathé Co.:
- Solving the Farm Problem of the Nation—story of the United States Boys' Working Reserve.
- Feeding the Fighter—how the army was supplied with food.

By the Universal Co.:
- Reclaiming the Soldiers' Duds—the salvage work of the War Department.
- The American Indian Gets into the War Game—how the Indian took his place, both in the military forces and in food production.

By C. L. Chester:
- Schooling Our Fighting Mechanics—work of the Committee on Education and Special Training of the War Department.
- There Shall Be No Cripples—rehabilitation work of the Surgeon-General's Office.
- Colored Americans—activities of the Negroes, both in the military forces and in war work at home.

It's an Engineers' War—work of the Engineers' training camps of the War Department.
Finding and Fixing the Enemy—certain work of the Engineer Corps of the War Department.
Waging War in Washington—the method of government operation.
All the Comforts of Home—methods of War Department in providing necessities and conveniences for soldiers.
Masters for the Merchant Marine—development of both officers and men for the new merchant navy.
The College for Camp Cooks—thorough training given men who were to prepare the food for the soldiers.
Rail-less Railroads—work of the Highway Transport Committee.

The following pictures, of more than one reel in length, were made by private producers from our scenarios and under our supervision:

By C. L. Chester:
The Miracle of the Ships, a six-reel picture covering in detail the construction of the carrier ships at Hog Island and other yards, and showing every detail of construction.
By The W. W. Hodkinson Corporation:
Made in America, an eight-reel picture telling the full story of the Liberty Army. It follows the soldier through every stage of the draft and through every step of his military, physical, and social development and into the actual combat overseas. Such a picture was greatly desired by General Munson, head of the Morale Branch of the War Department, for circulation in the army and among the people of the United States, as well as abroad. As this picture was to show the relation of the home life to the soldier, professional actors and actresses and much studio work were required. The Morale Branch had no funds to pay for such a picture, and the Division of Films was able to work out a scenario of such promise that the Hodkinson Corporation agreed to produce the picture at their own expense, which they did at a cost exceeding forty thousand dollars.

Late in the summer of 1918, our system of production through outside concerns having worked out satisfactorily, it was decided to undertake production on our own account. Accordingly, scenarios were written, and the following six two-reel pictures were produced by the division:

If Your Soldier's Hit, showing the operation of the regimental detachment and field hospital unit in getting wounded men off the front line, giving them first aid, and conveying them safely to recuperation bases. This picture was made in conjunction with the

Surgeon-General's Office at the training camp at Fort Riley, Kansas, and the scenes were supplemented by scenes from overseas.

Our Wings of Victory, showing the complete processes of the manufacture and operation of airplanes for war purposes. The construction scenes were taken in the chief plane factories and were supplemented by extraordinary scenes of flying.

Our Horses of War, showing how the remount depots of the army obtain and train the horses and mules for cavalry and artillery purposes, and the feats performed by the animals so trained under the manipulation of the soldiers.

Making the Nation Fit, showing how new recruits for the great army and the great navy were developed to a stage of physical fitness.

The Storm of Steel, showing how twelve billions of the Liberty Loan money was being expended in the construction of guns and munitions. These scenes were taken in half a dozen of the chief gun plants of the country and on the proving grounds and are the most complete record in the government's possession of this undertaking.

The Bath of Bullets, showing the development and use of machine-guns in this war.

A second series of six two-reel pictures had been laid out and the filming was about to proceed when the armistice caused the division to suspend all new undertakings.

The distribution of still pictures under the direction of Mr. Rubel and Mr. Harold E. Hecht also underwent a process of reorganization as time presented new needs and afforded new opportunities. One of the first of the new plans was the inauguration of the "permit system." While the military authorities were correct in refusing general admission to ordnance and airplane factories, to navy yards and to certain cantonments where secret tests were being made, there was no good reason for barring private photographers from the majority of the camps and factories. Mr. Rubel, therefore, in consultation with the army and the navy, worked out a plan of permits that safeguarded military secrets even while it opened up the military effort to the cameras of civilians. Our procedure investigated each applicant and certified him to the camp commanders, and a "voluntary censorship" agreed to by the commercial photographers protected against indiscretion. Under this system, and as illustrative of its liberal provisions, the division issued more than six thousand permits, the daily applications ranging from ten to twenty-five.

This arrangement took care of domestic photographers, permitting Mr. Rubel to devote all his energy to the distribution of still pictures taken by the Signal Corps in France. In the first days, when the shipments were few, it was a simple matter to spread the photographs among the newspapers, but as great bundles commenced to be received, our simple machinery broke down. To meet the new demand, an arrangement was made with the Photographic Association, including such firms as Underwood & Underwood, International Film Service, Brown Bros., Paul Thompson, Kadel & Herbert, Harris & Ewing, Western Newspaper Union, the Newspaper Enterprise Association, and other firms that syndicated photographs nationally and internationally. Through organized effort these syndicate members placed our photographs in daily newspapers, weekly and monthly magazines, technical publications, and other mediums. To expedite production and delivery, a laboratory was secured in New York City and operated by the Signal Corps Photographic Division in conjunction with Columbia University. The prices fixed were nominal, designed only to cover expenses.

This department also furnished quantities of photographs each week to the Foreign Service Section of the Committee for use in propaganda media in the Allied and neutral nations. Photographs were also furnished for publicity purposes for motion-picture features and we reproduced in hundreds of newspapers reaching millions of circulation. Another means of distribution of war photographs was to private collections, to universities, historical societies, state and municipal libraries, and any organization that could make use of pictures for future reference. Also, individuals who were interested in getting pictures of war activities, more especially those who had members of their families or friends directly connected with the war.

The Department of Slides was next added to the activities of the bureau and supplied a long-felt need for official and authentic photographs in stereopticon form for the use of ministers, lecturers, school teachers, and others. Mr. Rubel and Mr. Hecht succeeded in putting out standard size black and white slides of the finest workmanship at fifteen cents each, which price saved the user from 50 to 80 percent. At first the production of slides was entirely dependent on the laboratory of the Signal Corps in Washington, which, as the orders increased in volume, proved inadequate to turn out sufficient quantity. The Committee on Public Information then built its own laboratory with ample production facilities. Out of this idea came another—that of illustrated war lectures. Taking the "Ruined Churches of France" as a first subject, for the original demand came from ministers for the most part, we prepared 50 slides, and accompanied them with a wonderful little lecture written movingly by Dr. John S. P. Tatlock of Leland Stanford University. Such was its enthusiastic reception that the following lectures were issued in rapid sequence: "Our Boys in France," 100 slides; "Building a Bridge of Ships to Pershing," 50 slides; "To Berlin *via* the Air Route," 50 slides; "Making the American Army," 50 slides. About 700 of these sets were ordered by patriotic organizations and individuals, as well as churches and schools.

The next series of illustrated lectures to be distributed were as follows: "The Call to Arms," 58 slides; "Trenches and Trench Warfare," 73 slides; "Airplanes and How Made," 61 slides; "Flying for America," 54 slides; "The American Navy," 51 slides; "The Navy at Work," 36 slides; "Building a Bridge of Ships," 63 slides; "Transporting the Army to France," 63 slides; "Carrying the Home to the Camp," 61 slides. These sets were prepared and the lectures written by George F. Zook, professor of Modern European History in Pennsylvania State College. A total of 900 were ordered. While the greater number of orders came from various parts of this country, many were received from foreign countries.

In the year of existence the Department of Slides distributed a total of 200,000 slides.

15. Protecting America from the League of Nations: Senator Henry Cabot Lodge

HENRY CABOT LODGE, *Chairman of the Senate Foreign Relations Committee, to which all agreements with foreign nations had to be submitted, took advantage of that position to stall action on the peace treaty submitted by Wilson until public opinion against sections of the treaty could be aroused. Articles and speeches like that reprinted below*

SOURCE: *Congressional Record,* 66th Congress, 1st Session (August 12, 1919), pp. 318–384.

perplexed millions of Americans who, in principle, favored United States participation in a League. Lodge probably would have approved a treaty with reservations that marked it as the work of the Senate as well as the President. His reluctance to take such a position publicly was due in some measure to the necessity of pacifying elements within the Republican party unalterably opposed to American participation in an international organization to protect the peace.

Mr. Lodge Mr. President, in the Essays of Elia, one of the most delightful is that entitled "Popular Fallacies." There is one very popular fallacy, however, which Lamb did not include in his list and that is the common saying that history repeats itself. Universal negatives are always dangerous, but if there is anything which is fairly certain, it is that history never exactly repeats itself. Popular fallacies, nevertheless, generally have some basis, and this saying springs from the undoubted truth that mankind from generation to generation is constantly repeating itself. We have an excellent illustration of this fact in the proposed experiment now before us, of making arrangements to secure the permanent peace of the world. To assure the peace of the world by a combination of the nations is no new idea. Leaving out the leagues of antiquity and of mediaeval times and going back no further than the treaty of Utrecht, at the beginning of the eighteenth century, we find that at that period a project of a treaty to establish perpetual peace was brought forward in 1713 by the Abbé de Saint-Pierre. The treaty of Utrecht was to be the basis of an international system. A European league or Christian republic was to be set up, under which the members were to renounce the right of making war against each other and submit their disputes for arbitration to a central tribunal of the allies, the decisions of which were to be enforced by a common armament. I need not point out the resemblance between this theory and that which underlies the present league of nations. It was widely discussed during the eighteenth century, receiving much support in public opinion; and Voltaire said that the nations of Europe, united by ties of religion, institutions, and culture, were really but a single family. The idea remained in an academic condition until 1791, when under the pressure of the French Revolution Count Kaunitz sent out a circular letter in the name of Leopold, of Austria, urging that it was the duty of all the powers to make common cause for the purpose of "preserving public peace, tranquillity of States, the inviolability of possession, and the faith of treaties," which has a very familiar sound. Napoleon had a scheme of his own for consolidating the great European peoples and establishing a central assembly, but the Napoleonic idea differed from that of the eighteenth century, as one would expect. A single great personality dominated and hovered over all. In 1804 the Emperor Alexander took up the question, and urged a general treaty for the formation of a European confederation. "Why could one not submit to it," the Emperor asked, "the positive rights of nations, assure the privilege of neutrality, insert the obligation of never beginning war until all the resources which the mediation of a third party could offer have been exhausted, until the grievances have by this means been brought to light, and an effort to remove them has been made? On principles such as these one could proceed to a general pacification, and give birth to a league of which the stipulations would form, so to speak, a new code of the law of nations, while those who should try to infringe it would risk bringing upon themselves the forces of the new union."

The Emperor, moved by more immediately alluring visions, put aside this scheme at the treaty of Tilsit and then decided that peace could best be restored to the world by having two all-powerful emperors, one of the east and one of the west. After the Moscow campaign, however, he returned to his early dream. Under the influence of the Baroness von Krudener he became a devotee of a certain mystic pietism which for some time guided his public acts, and I think it may be fairly said that his liberal and popular ideas of that period, however vague and uncertain, were sufficiently genuine. Based upon the treaties of alliance against France, those of Chaumont and of Vienna, was the final treaty of Paris, of November 20, 1815. In the preamble the signatories, who were Great Britain, Austria, Russia, and Prussia, stated that it is the purpose of the ensuing treaty and their desire "to employ all their means to prevent the general tranquillity—the object of the wishes of mankind and the constant end of their efforts—from being again disturbed; desirous, moreover, to draw closer the ties which unite them for the common interests of their people, have resolved to give to the principles solemnly laid down in the treaties of Chaumont of March 1, 1814, and of Vienna of March 25, 1815, the application the most analogous to the present state of affairs, and to fix beforehand by a solemn treaty the principles which they propose to follow, in order to guarantee Europe from dangers by which she may still be menaced."

Then follow five articles which are devoted to an agreement to hold France in control and check, based largely on other more detailed agreements. But in article 6 it is said:

> To facilitate and to secure the execution of the present treaty, and to consolidate the connections which at the present moment so closely unite the four sovereigns for the happiness of the world, the high contracting parties have agreed to renew their meeting at fixed periods either under the immediate auspices of the sovereigns themselves, or by their respective ministers, for the purpose of consulting upon their common interests, and for the consideration of the measures which at each of those periods shall be considered the most salutary for the repose and prosperity of nations and for the maintenance of the peace of Europe.

Certainly nothing could be more ingenuous or more praiseworthy than the purposes of the alliance then formed, and yet it was this very combination of powers which was destined to grow into what has been known, and we might add cursed, throughout history as the Holy Alliance.

As early as 1818 it had become apparent that upon this innocent statement might be built an alliance which was to be used to suppress the rights of nationalities and every attempt of any oppressed people to secure their freedom. Lord Castlereagh was a Tory of the Tories, but at that time, only three years after the treaty of Paris when the representatives of the alliance met at Aix-la-Chapelle he began to suspect that this new European system was wholly inconsistent with the liberties to which Englishmen of all types were devoted. At the succeeding meetings, at Troppau and Laibach, his suspicion was confirmed and England began to draw away from her partners. He had indeed determined to break with the alliance before the Congress of Verona, but his death threw the question into the hands of George Canning, who stands forth as the man who separated Great Britain from the combination of the continental powers. The attitude of England, which was defined in a memorandum where it was said that nothing could be more injurious to the idea of government generally than the belief that their force was collectively to be prostituted to the support of an established power without any consideration of the extent to which it was to be abused, led to a compromise in 1818 in which it was declared that it was the intention of the five powers, France being invited to adhere, "to maintain the intimate union, strengthened by the ties of Christian brotherhood, contracted by the sovereigns; to pronounce the object of this union to be the preservation of peace on the basis of respect for treaties." Admirable and gentle words these, setting forth purposes which all men must approve.

In 1820 the British Government stated that they were prepared to fulfill all treaty obligations, but that if it was desired "to extend the alliance so as to include all objects, present and future, foreseen and unforeseen, it would change its character to such an extent and carry us so far that we should see in it an additional motive for adhering to our course at the risk of seeing the alliance move away from us, without our having quitted it." The Czar Alexander abandoned his Liberal theories and threw himself into the arms of Metternich, as mean a tyrant as history can show, whose sinister designs probably caused as much misery and oppression in the years which followed as have ever been evolved by one man of second-rate abilities. The three powers, Russia, Austria, and Prussia, then put out a famous protocol in which it was said that the "States which have undergone a change of government due to revolution, the results of which threaten other States, ipso facto cease to be members of the European alliance, and remain excluded from it until their situation gives guaranties for legal order and stability. If, owing to such alterations, immediate danger threatens other states, the powers bind themselves, by peaceful means, or if need be by arms, to bring back the guilty State into the bosom of the great alliance." To this point had the innocent and laudable declarations of the treaty of Paris already developed. In 1822 England broke away and Canning made no secret of his pleasure at the breach. In a letter to the British minister at St. Petersburg he said:

> So things are getting back to a wholesome state again. Every nation for itself, and God for us all. The time for Areopagus, and the like of that, is gone by.

He also said, in the same year, 1823:

> What is the influence we have had in the counsels of the alliance, and which Prince Metternich exhorts us to be so careful not to throw away? We protested at Laibach; we remonstrated at Verona. Our protest was treated as waste paper; our remonstrances mingled with the air. Our influence, if it is to be maintained abroad, must be secure in the source of strength at home; and the sources of that

> strength are in the sympathy between the people and the Government; in the union of the public sentiment with the public counsels; in the reciprocal confidence and cooperation of the House of Commons and the Crown.

These words of Canning are as applicable and as weighty now as when they were uttered and as worthy of consideration.

The Holy Alliance, thus developed by the three continental powers and accepted by France under the Bourbons, proceeded to restore the inquisition in Spain, to establish the Neapolitan Bourbons, who for 40 years were to subject the people of southern Italy to one of the most detestable tyrannies ever known, and proposed further to interfere against the colonies in South America which had revolted from Spain and to have their case submitted to a congress of the powers. It was then that Canning made his famous statement, "We have called a new world into existence to redress the balance of the old." It was at this point also that the United States intervened. The famous message of Monroe, sent to Congress on December 2, 1823, put an end to any danger of European influence in the American Continents. A distinguished English historian, Mr. William Alison Phillips, says:

> The attitude of the United States effectually prevented the attempt to extend the dictatorship of the alliance beyond the bounds of Europe, in itself a great service to mankind.

In 1825 Great Britain recognized the South American republics. So far as the New World was concerned the Holy Alliance had failed. It was deprived of the support of France by the revolution of 1830, but it continued to exist under the guidance of Metternich and its last exploit was in 1849, when the Emperor Nicholas sent a Russian army into Hungary to crush out the struggle of Kossuth for freedom and independence.

I have taken the trouble to trace in the merest outline the development of the Holy Alliance, so hostile and dangerous to human freedom, because I think it carries with it a lesson for us at the present moment, showing as it does what may come from general propositions and declarations of purposes in which all the world agrees. Turn to the preamble of the covenant of the league of nations now before us, which states the object of the league. It is formed "in order to promote international cooperation and to achieve international peace and security by the acceptance of obligations not to resort to war, by the prescription of open, just, and honorable relations between nations, by the firm establishment of the understandings of international laws as the actual rule of conduct among governments, and by the maintenance of justice and a scrupulous respect for all treaty obligations in the dealings of organized peoples with one another."

No one would contest the loftiness or the benevolence of these purposes. Brave words, indeed! They do not differ essentially from the preamble of the treaty of Paris, from which sprang the Holy Alliance. But the covenant of this league contains a provision which I do not find in the treaty of Paris, and which is as follows:

> The assembly may deal at its meetings with any matter within the sphere of action of the league or affecting the peace of the world.

There is no such sweeping or far-reaching provision as that in the treaty of Paris, and yet able men developed from that treaty the Holy Alliance, which England, and later France, were forced to abandon and which, for 35 years, was an unmitigated curse to the world. England broke from the Holy Alliance and the breach began three years after it was formed, because English statesmen saw that it was intended to turn the alliance—and this league is an alliance—into a means of repressing internal revolutions or insurrections. There was nothing in the treaty of Paris which warranted such action, but in this covenant of the league of nations the authority is clearly given in the third paragraph of article 3, where it is said:

> The assembly may deal at its meetings with any matter within the sphere of action of the league or affecting the peace of the world.

No revolutionary movement, no internal conflict, of any magnitude can fail to affect the peace of the world. The French Revolution, which was wholly internal at the beginning, affected the peace of the world to such an extent that it brought on a world war which lasted some 25 years. Can anyone say that our Civil War did not affect the peace of the world? At this very moment, who would deny that the condition of Russia, with internal conflicts raging in all parts of that great Empire, does not affect the peace of the world and therefore come properly within the jurisdiction of the league? "Any matter affecting the peace of the world" is a very broad statement which could be made to justify almost any interference on the part of the league with the internal affairs of other countries. That this fair and obvious interpretation is the one given to it abroad is made perfectly apparent in the direct and vigorous statement of M. Clemenceau in his letter to Mr. Paderewski, in which he takes the ground in behalf of the Jews and other nationalities in Poland that they should be protected, and where he says that the associated powers would feel themselves bound to secure guaranties in Poland "of certain essential rights which will afford to the inhabitants the necessary protection, whatever changes may take place in the internal constitution of the Polish Republic," he contemplates and defends interference with the internal affairs of Poland—among other things—in behalf of a complete religious freedom, a purpose with which we all deeply sympathize. These promises of the French prime minister are embodied in effective clauses in the treaties with Germany and with Poland and deal with the internal affairs of nations, and their execution is intrusted to the "principal allied and associated powers"; that is, to the United States, Great Britain, France, Italy, and Japan. This is a practical demonstration of what can be done under article 3 and under article 11 of the league covenant, and the authority which permits interference in behalf of religious freedom—an admirable object—is easily extended to the repression of internal disturbances, which may well prove a less admirable purpose. If Europe desires such an alliance or league with a power of this kind, so be it. I have no objection, provided they do not interfere with the American continents or force us against our will but bound by a moral obligation into all the quarrels of Europe. If England, abandoning the policy of Canning, desires to be a member of a league which has such powers as this, I have not a word to say. But I object in the strongest possible way to having the United States agree, directly or indirectly, to be controlled by a league which may at any time, and perfectly lawfully and in accordance with the terms of the covenant, be drawn in to deal with internal conflicts in other countries, no matter what those conflicts may be. We should never permit the United States to be involved in any internal conflict in another country, except by the will of her people expressed through the Congress which represents them.

With regard to wars of external aggression on a member of the league, the case is perfectly clear. There can be no genuine dispute whatever about the meaning of the first clause of article 10. In the first place, it differs from every other obligation in being individual and placed upon each nation without the intervention of the league. Each nation for itself promises to respect and preserve as against external aggression the boundaries and the political independence of every member of the league. Of the right of the United States to give such a guarantee I have never had the slightest doubt, and the elaborate arguments which have been made here and the learning which has been displayed about our treaty with Granada, now Colombia, and with Panama, were not necessary for me, because, I repeat, there can be no doubt of our right to give a guarantee to another nation that we will protect its boundaries and independence. The point I wish to make is that the pledge is an individual pledge. We have, for example, given guarantees to Panama and for obvious and sufficient reasons. The application of that guarantee would not be in the slightest degree affected by ten or twenty other nations giving the same pledge, if Panama, when in danger, appealed to us to fulfill our obligation. We should be bound to do so without the slightest reference to the other guarantors. In article 10 the United States is bound on the appeal of any member of the league not only to respect but to preserve its independence and its boundaries, and that pledge, if we give it, must be fulfilled.

There is to me no distinction whatever in a treaty between what some persons are pleased to call legal and moral obligations. A treaty rests and must rest, except where it is imposed under duress and securities and hostages are taken for its fulfillment, upon moral obligations. No doubt a great power impossible of coercion can cast aside a moral obligation if it sees fit and escape from the performance of the duty which it promises. The pathway of dishonor is always open. I for one, however, can not conceive of voting for a clause of which I disapprove because I know it can be escaped in that way. Whatever the United States agrees to, by that agreement she must abide. Nothing could so surely destroy all prospects of the world's peace as to have any powerful nation refuse to carry out an obligation, direct or indirect, because it rests only on moral grounds. Whatever we promise we must carry out to the full, "without mental reservation or purpose of evasion." To me any other attitude is inconceivable. Without the most absolute and minute good faith in carrying out a treaty to which we have agreed, without ever resorting to doubtful interpretations or to the plea that it is only a moral obligation, treaties are worthless. The greatest foundation of peace is the scrupulous observance of every promise, express or implied, of every pledge, whether it can be described as legal or moral. No vote should be given to any clause in any treaty or to any treaty except in this spirit and with this understanding.

I return, then, to the first clause of article 10. It is, I repeat, an individual obligation. It requires no action on the part of the league, except that in the second sentence the authorities of the league are to have the power to advise as to the means to be employed in order to fulfill the purpose of the first sentence. But that is a detail of execution, and I consider that we are morally and in honor bound to accept and act upon that advice. The broad fact remains that if any member of the league suffering from external aggression should appeal directly to the United States for support the United States would be bound to give that support in its own capacity and without reference to the action of other powers, because the United States itself is bound, and I hope the day will never come when the United States will not carry out its promises. If that day should come, and the United States or any other great country should refuse, no matter how specious the reasons, to fulfill both in letter and spirit every obligation in this covenant, the United States would be dishonored and the league would crumble into dust, leaving behind it a legacy of wars. If China should rise up and attack Japan in an effort to undo the great wrong of the cession of the control of Shantung to that power, we should be bound under the terms of article 10 to sustain Japan against China, and a guaranty of that sort is never invoked except when the question has passed beyond the stage of negotiation and has become a question for the application of force. I do not like the prospect. It shall not come into existence by any vote of mine.

Article 11 carries this danger still further, for it says:

> Any war or threat of war, whether immediately affecting any of the members of the league or not, is hereby declared a matter of concern to the whole league and the league shall take any action that shall be deemed wise and effectual to safeguard the peace of nations.

"Any war or threat of war" means both external aggression and internal disturbance, as I have already pointed out in dealing with article 3. "Any action" covers military action, because it covers action of any sort or kind. Let me take an example, not an imaginary case, but one which may have been overlooked, because most people have not the slightest idea where or what a King of the Hejaz is. The following dispatch appeared recently in the newspapers:

> HEJAZ AGAINST BEDOUINS
>
> The forces of Emir Abdullah recently suffered a grave defeat, the Wahabis attacking and capturing Kurma, east of Mecca. Ibn Savond is believed to be working in harmony with the Wahabis. A squadron of the royal air force was ordered recently to go to the assistance of King Hussein.

Hussein I take to be the Sultan of Hejaz. He is being attacked by the Bedouins, as they are known to us, although I fancy the general knowledge about the Wahabis and Ibn Savond and Emir Abdullah is slight and the names mean but little to the American people. Nevertheless, here is a case of a member of the league—for the King of the Hejaz is such a member in good and regular standing and signed the treaty by his representatives, Mr. Rustem Haidar and Mr. Abdul Havi Aouni.

Under article 10, if King Hussein appealed to us for aid and protection against external aggression affecting his independence and the boundaries of his kingdom, we should be bound to give that aid and protection and to send American soldiers to Arabia. It is not relevant to say that this is unlikely to occur; that Great Britain is quite able to take care of King Hussein, who is her fair creation, reminding one a little of the Mosquito King, a monarch once developed by Great Britain on the Mosquito Coast of Central America. The fact that we should not be called upon does not alter the right which the King of Hejaz possesses to demand the sending of American troops to Arabia in order to preserve his independence against the assaults of the Wahabis or Bedouins. I am unwilling to give that right to King Hussein, and this illustrates the point which is to me the most objectionable in the league as it stands—the right of other powers to call out American troops and American ships to go to any part of the world, an obligation we are bound to fulfill under the terms of this treaty. I know the answer well—that of course they could not be sent without action by Congress. Congress would have no choice if acting in good faith, and if under article 10 any member of the league summoned us, or if under article 11 the league itself summoned us, we should be bound in honor and morally to obey. There would be no escape except by a breach of faith, and legislation by Congress under those circumstances would be a mockery of independent action. Is it too much to ask that provision should be made that American troops and American ships should never be sent anywhere or ordered to take part in any conflict except after the deliberate action of the American people, expressed according to the Constitution through their chosen representatives in Congress?

Let me now briefly point out the insuperable difficulty which I find in article 15. It begins: "If there should arise between members of the league any dispute likely to lead to a rupture." "Any dispute" covers every possible dispute. It therefore covers a dispute over tariff duties and over immigration. Suppose we have a dispute with Japan or with some European country as to immigration. I put aside tariff duties as less important than immigration. This is not an imaginary case. Of late years there has probably been more international discussion and negotiation about questions growing out of immigration laws than any other one subject. It comes within the definition of "any dispute" at the beginning of article 15. In the eighth paragraph of that article it is said that "if the dispute between the parties is claimed by one of them, and is found by the council to arise out of a matter which, by international law, is solely within the domestic jurisdiction of that party, the council shall so report and shall make no recommendation as to its settlement." That is one of the statements, of which there are several in this treaty, where words are used which it is difficult to believe their authors could have written down in seriousness. They seem to have been put in for the same purpose as what is known in natural history as protective coloring. Protective coloring is intended so to merge the animal, the bird, or the insect in its background that it will be indistinguishable from its surroundings and difficult, if not impossible, to find the elusive and hidden bird, animal, or insect. Protective coloring here is used in the form of words to give an impression that we are perfectly safe upon immigration and tariffs, for example, because questions which international law holds to be solely within domestic jurisdiction are not to have any recommendation from the council, but the dangers are there just the same, like the cunningly colored insect on the tree or the young bird crouching motionless upon the sand. The words and the coloring are alike intended to deceive. I wish somebody would point out to me those provisions of international law which make a list of questions which are hard and fast within the domestic jurisdiction. No such distinction can be applied to tariff duties or immigration nor indeed finally and conclusively to any subject. Have we not seen the school laws of California, most domestic of subjects, rise to the dignity of a grave international dispute? No doubt both import duties and immigration are primarily domestic questions, but they both constantly involve and will continue to involve international effects. Like the protective coloration, this paragraph is wholly worthless unless it is successful in screening from the observer the existence of the animal, insect, or bird which it is desired to conceal. It fails to do so and the real object is detected. But even if this bit of deception was omitted—and so far as the question of immigration or tariff questions are concerned it might as well be—the ninth paragraph brings the important point clearly to the front. Immigration, which is the example I took, can not escape the action of the league by any claim of domestic jurisdiction; it has too many international aspects.

Article 9 says:

> The council may, in any case under this article, refer the dispute to the assembly.

We have our dispute as to immigration with Japan or with one of the Balkan States, let us say. The council has the power to refer the dispute to the assembly. Moreover, the dispute shall be so referred at the request of either party to the dispute, provided that such request be made within 14 days after the submission of the dispute to the council. So that Japan or the Balkan States, for example, with which we may easily have the dispute, ask that it be referred to the assembly, and the immigration question between the United States and Jugoslavia or Japan, as the case may be, goes to the assembly. The United States and Japan or Jugoslavia are excluded from voting, and the provisions of article 12, relating to the action and powers of the council, apply to the action and powers of the assembly, provided, as set forth in article 15, that a report made by the assembly, "if concurred in by the representatives of those members of the league represented on the council and of a majority of the other members of the league, exclusive in each case of the representatives of the parties to the dispute, shall have the same force as a report by the council concurred in by all the members thereof other than the representatives of one or more of the parties to the dispute." This course of procedure having been pursued, we find the question of immigration between the United States and Japan is before the assembly for decision. The representatives of the council, except the delegates of the United States and of Japan or Jugoslavia, must all vote unanimously upon it, as I understand it, but a majority of the entire assembly, where the council will have only seven votes, will decide. Can anyone say beforehand what the decision of that assembly will be, in which the United States and Jugoslavia or Japan will have no vote? The question in one case may affect immigration from every country in Europe, although the dispute exists only for one, and in the other the whole matter of Asiatic immigration is involved. Is it too fanciful to think that it might be decided against us? For my purpose it matters not whether it is decided for or against us. An immigration dispute or a dispute over tariff duties, met by the procedure set forth in article 15, comes before the assembly of delegates for a decision by what is practically a majority vote of the entire assembly. That is something to which I do not find myself able to give my assent. So far as immigration is concerned, and also so far as tariff duties, although less important, are concerned, I deny the jurisdiction. There should be no possibility of other nations deciding who shall come into the United States or under what conditions they shall enter. The right to say who shall come into a country is one of the very highest attributes of sovereignty. If a nation can not say without appeal who shall come within its gates and become a part of its citizenship it has ceased to be a sovereign nation. It has become a tributary and a subject nation, and it makes no difference whether it is subject to a league or to a conqueror.

If other nations are willing to subject themselves to such a domination, the United States, to which many immigrants have come and many more will come, ought never to submit to it for a moment. They tell us that so far as Asiatic emigration is concerned there is not the slightest danger that that will ever be forced upon us by the league, because Australia and Canada and New Zealand are equally opposed to it. I think it highly improbable that it would be forced upon us under those conditions, but it is by no means impossible. It is true the United States has one vote, and that

England, if you count the King of the Hejaz, has seven—in all eight—votes; yet it might not be impossible for Japan and China and Siam to rally enough other votes to defeat us; but whether we are protected in that way or not does not matter. The very offering of that explanation accepts the jurisdiction of the league, and personally I can not consent to putting the protection of my country and of her workingmen against undesirable immigration out of our own hands. We and we alone must say who shall come into the United States and become citizens of this Republic, and no one else should have any power to utter one word in regard to it.

Article 21 says:

> Nothing in this covenant shall be deemed to affect the validity of international engagements, such as treaties of arbitration or regional understandings like the Monroe doctrine for securing the maintenance of peace.

This provision did not appear in the first draft of the covenant, and when the President explained the second draft of the convention to the peace conference he said:

> Article 21 is new.

And that was all he said. No one can question the truth of the remark, but I trust I shall not be considered disrespectful if I say that it was not an illuminating statement. The article was new, but the fact of its novelty, which the President declared, was known to everyone who had taken the trouble to read the two documents. We were not left, however, without a fitting explanation. The British delegation took it upon themselves to explain article 21 at some length, and this is what they said:

> Article 21 makes it clear that the covenant is not intended to abrogate or weaken any other agreements, so long as they are consistent with its own terms, into which members of the league may have entered or may hereafter enter for the assurance of peace. Such agreements would include special treaties for compulsory arbitration and military conventions that are genuinely defensive.
>
> The Monroe doctrine and similar understandings are put in the same category. They have shown themselves in history to be not instruments of national ambition, but guarantees of peace. The origin of the Monroe doctrine is well known. It was proclaimed in 1823 to prevent America from becoming a theater for intrigues of European absolutism. At first a principle of American foreign policy, it has become an international understanding, and it is not illegiti-

mate for the people of the United States to say that the covenant should recognize that fact.

In its essence it is consistent with the spirit of the covenant, and, indeed, the principles of the league, as expressed in article 10, represent the extension to the whole world of the principles of the doctrine while, should any dispute as to the meaning of the latter ever arise between the American and European powers, the league is there to settle it.

The explanation of Great Britain received the assent of France.

It seems to me monumentally paradoxical and a trifle infantile—

Says M. Lausanne, solicitor of the "Treaties" and a chief spokesman for M. Clemenceau—

to pretend the contrary.

When the executive council of the league of nations fixes the "reasonable limits of the armament of Peru"; when it shall demand information concerning the naval program of Brazil (art. 7 of the covenant); when it shall tell Argentina what shall be the measure of the "contribution to the armed forces to protect the signatures of the social covenant" (art. 16); when it shall demand the immediate registration of the treaty between the United States and Canada at the seat of the league, it will control, whether it wills or not, the destinies of America.

And when the American states shall be obliged to take a hand in every war or menace of war in Europe (art. 11), they will necessarily fall afoul of the fundamental principle laid down by Monroe.

* * * If the league takes in the world, then Europe must mix in the affairs of America: if only Europe is included, then America will violate of necessity her own doctrine by intermixing in the affairs of Europe.

It has seemed to me that the British delegation traveled a little out of the precincts of the peace conference when they undertook to explain the Monroe doctrine and tell the United States what it was and what it was not proposed to do with it under the new article. That, however, is merely a matter of taste and judgment. Their statement that the Monroe doctrine under this article, if any question arose in regard to it, would be passed upon and interpreted by the league of nations is absolutely correct. There is no doubt that this is what the article means. Great Britain so stated it, and no American authority, whether friendly or unfriendly to the league, has dared to question it. I have wondered a little why it was left to the British delegation to explain that article, which so nearly concerns the United States, but that was merely a fugitive thought upon which I will not dwell. The statement of M. Lausanne is equally explicit and truthful, but he makes one mistake. He says in substance that if we are to meddle in Europe, Europe can not be excluded from the Americas. He overlooks the fact that the Monroe doctrine also says:

> Our policy in regard to Europe, which was adopted at an early stage of the wars which have so long agitated that quarter of the globe, nevertheless remains the same, which is not to interfere in the internal concerns of any of the powers.

The Monroe doctrine was the corollary of Washington's neutrality policy and of his injunction against permanent alliances. It reiterates and reaffirms the principle. We do not seek to meddle in the affairs of Europe and keep Europe out of the Americas. It is as important to keep the United States out of European affairs as to keep Europe out of the American Continents. Let us maintain the Monroe doctrine, then, in its entirety, and not only preserve our own safety, but in this way best promote the real peace of the world. Whenever the preservation of freedom and civilization and the overthrow of a menacing world conqueror summon us we shall respond fully and nobly, as we did in 1917. He who doubts that we should do so has little faith in America. But let it be our own act, and not done reluctantly by the coercion of other nations, at the bidding or by the permission of other countries.

Let me now deal with the article itself. We have here some protective coloration again. The Monroe doctrine is described as a "regional understanding," whatever that may mean. The boundaries between the States of the Union, I suppose, are "regional understandings," if anyone chooses to apply to them that somewhat swollen phraseology. But the Monroe doctrine is no more a regional understanding than it is an "international engagement." The Monroe doctrine was a policy declared by President Monroe. Its immediate purpose was to shut out Europe from interfering with the South American Republics, which the Holy Alliance designed to do. It was stated broadly, however, as we all know, and went much further than that. It was, as I have just said, the corollary of Washington's declaration against our interfering in European questions. It was so regarded by Jefferson at the time, and by John Quincy Adams, who formulated it, and by President Monroe, who declared it. It rested firmly on the great law of self-preservation, which is the basic principle of every independent State. It is not necessary to trace its history, or to point out the extensions which it has received, or its universal acceptance by all American statesmen without regard to party. All Americans have always been for it. They may not have known its details, or read all the many discussions in regard to it, but they knew that it was an American doctrine, and that, broadly stated, it meant the exclusion of Europe from interference with American affairs and from any attempt to colonize or set up new States within the boundaries of the American continent. I repeat, it was purely an American doctrine, a purely American policy, designed and wisely designed for our defense. It has never been an "international engagement." No nation has ever formally recognized it. It has been the subject of reservation at international conventions by American delegates. It has never been a "regional understanding," or an understanding of any kind with anybody. It was the declaration of the United States of America, in their own behalf, supported by their own power. They brought it into being, and its life was predicated on the force which the United States could place behind it. Unless the United States could sustain it, it would die. The United States has supported it. It has lived—strong, efficient, respected. It is now proposed to kill it by a provision in a treaty for a league of nations.

The instant that the United States, who declared, interpreted, and sustained the doctrine, ceases to be the sole judge of what it means, that instant the Monroe doctrine ceases and disappears from history and from the face of the earth. I think it is just as undesirable to have Europe interfere in American affairs now as Mr. Monroe thought it was in 1823, and equally undesirable that we should be compelled to involve ourselves in all the wars and brawls of Europe. The Monroe doctrine has made for peace. Without the Monroe doctrine we should have had many a struggle with European powers to save ourselves from possible assault and certainly from the necessity of becoming a great military power, always under arms and always ready to resist invasion from States in our near neighborhood. In the interests of the peace of the world it is now proposed to wipe away this American policy, which has been a bulwark and a barrier for peace. With one exception it has always been successful, and then success was only delayed. When we were torn by civil war France saw fit to enter Mexico and endeavored to establish an empire there. When our hands were once free the empire perished, and with it the unhappy tool of the third Napoleon. If the United States had not been rent by civil war no such attempt would have been made, and nothing better illustrates the value to the cause of peace of the Monroe doctrine. Why, in the name of peace, should we extinguish it? Why, in the name of peace, should we be called upon to leave the interpretation of the Monroe doctrine to other nations? It is an American policy. It is our own. It has guarded us well, and I for one can never find consent in my heart to destroy it by a clause in a treaty and hand over its body for dissection to the nations of Europe. If we need authority to demonstrate what the Monroe doctrine has meant to the United States we can not do better than quote the words of Grover Cleveland, who directed Mr. Olney to notify the world that "today the United States is practically sovereign on this continent, and its fiat is law to which it confines its interposition." Theodore Roosevelt, in the last article written before his death, warned us, his countrymen, that we are "in honor bound to keep ourselves so prepared that the Monroe doctrine shall be accepted as immutable international law." Grover Cleveland was a Democrat and Theodore Roosevelt was a Republican, but they were both Americans, and it is the American spirit which has carried this country always to victory and which should govern us today, and not the international spirit, which would in the name of peace hand the United States over bound hand and foot to obey the fiat of other powers.

Another point in this covenant where change must be made in order to protect the safety of the United States in the future is in article 1, where withdrawal is provided for. This provision was an attempt to meet the very general objection to the first draft of the league, that there was no means of getting out of it without denouncing the treaty; that is, there was no arrangement for the withdrawal of any nation. As it now stands it reads that—

> Any member of the league may, after two years' notice of its intention to do so, withdraw from the league, provided that all its international obligations and all its obligations under this covenant shall have been fulfilled at the time of its withdrawal.

The right of withdrawal is given by this clause, although the time for notice, two years, is altogether too long. Six months or a year would be found, I think, in most treaties to be the normal period fixed for notice of withdrawal. But whatever virtue there may be in the right thus conferred is completely nullified by the proviso. The right of withdrawal can not be exercised until all the international obligations and all the obligations of the withdrawing nations have been fulfilled. The league alone can decide whether "all international obligations and all obligations under this covenant" have been fulfilled, and this would require, under the provisions of the league, a unanimous vote, so that any nation desiring to withdraw could not do so, even on the two years' notice, if one nation voted that the obligations had not been fulfilled. Remember that this gives the league not only power to review all our obligations under the covenant but all our treaties with all nations, for every one of those is an "international obligation."

Are we deliberately to put ourselves in fetters and be examined by the league of nations as to whether we have kept faith with Cuba or Panama before we can be permitted to leave the league? This seems to me humiliating, to say the least. The right of withdrawal, if it is to be of any value whatever, must be absolute, because otherwise a nation desiring to withdraw could be held in the league by objections from other nations until the very act which induces the nation to withdraw had been completed, until the withdrawing nation had been forced to send troops to take part in a war with which it had no concern and upon which it did not desire to enter. It seems to me vital to the safety of the United States not only that this provision should be eliminated and the right to withdraw made absolute but that the period of withdrawal should be much reduced. As it stands it is practically no better in this respect than the first league draft, which contained no provision for withdrawal at all, because the proviso here inserted so encumbers it that every nation to all intents and purposes must remain a member of the league indefinitely unless all the other members are willing that it should retire. Such a provision as this, ostensibly framed to meet the objection, has the defect which other similar gestures to give an impression of meeting objections have, that it apparently keeps the promise to the ear but most certainly breaks it to the hope.

I have dwelt only upon those points which seem to me most dangerous. There are, of course, many others, but these points, in the interest not only of the safety of the United States but of the maintenance of the treaty and the peace of the world, should be dealt with here before it is too late. Once in the league the chance of amendment is so slight that it is not worth considering. Any analysis of the provisions of this league covenant, however, brings out in startling relief one great fact. Whatever may be said, it is not a league of peace; it is an alliance, dominated at the present moment by five great powers, really by three, and it has all the marks of an alliance. The development of international law is neglected. The court which is to decide disputes brought before it fills but a small place. The conditions for which this league really provides with the utmost care are political conditions, not judicial questions, to be reached by the executive council and the assembly, purely political bodies without any trace of a judicial character about them. Such being its machinery, the control being in the hands of political appointees whose votes will be controlled by interest and expediency, it exhibits that most marked characteristic of an alliance—that its decisions are to be carried out by force. Those articles upon which the whole structure rests are articles which provide for the use of force; that is, for war. This league to enforce peace does a great deal for enforcement and very little for peace. It makes more essential provisions looking to war than to peace for the settlement of disputes.

Article 10 I have already discussed. There is no question that the preservation of a State against external aggression can contemplate nothing but war. In article 11, again, the league is authorized to take any action which may be necessary to safeguard the peace of the world. "Any action" includes war. We also have specific provisions for a boycott, which is a form of economic warfare. The use of troops might be avoided, but the enforcement of a boycott would require blockades in all probability, and certainly a boycott in its essence is simply an effort to starve a people into submission, to ruin their trade, and, in the case of nations which are not self-supporting, to cut off their food supply. The misery and suffering caused by such a measure as this may easily rival that caused by actual war. Article 16 embodies the boycott and also, in the last paragraph, provides explicitly for war. We are told that the word "recommend" has no binding force; it constitutes a moral obligation; that is all. But it means that if we, for example, should refuse to accept the recommendation we should nullify the operation of article 16 and, to that extent, of the league. It seems to me that to attempt to relieve us of clearly imposed duties by saying that the word "recommend" is not binding is an escape of which no nation regarding the sanctity of treaties and its own honor would care to avail itself. The provisions of article 16 are extended to States outside the league who refuse to obey its command to come in and submit themselves to its jurisdiction—another provision for war.

Taken altogether, these provisions for war present what to my mind is the gravest objection to this league in its present form. We are told that of course nothing will be done in the way of warlike acts without the assent of Congress. If that is true let us say so in the covenant. But as it stands there is no doubt whatever in my mind that American troops and American ships may be ordered to any part of the world by nations other than the United States, and that is a proposition to which I for one can never assent. It must be made perfectly clear that no American soldiers, not even a corporal's guard, that no American sailors, not even the crew of a submarine, can ever be engaged in war or ordered anywhere except by the constitutional authorities of the United States. To Congress is granted by the Constitution the right to declare war, and nothing that would take the troops out of the country at the bidding or demand of other nations should ever be permitted except through congressional action. The lives of Americans must never be sacrificed except by the will of the American people expressed through their chosen Representatives in Congress. This is a point upon which no doubt can be permitted. American soldiers and American sailors have never failed the country when the country called upon them. They went in their hundreds of thousands into the war just closed. They went to die for the great cause of freedom and of civilization. They went at their service. We were late in entering the war. We made no preparation, as we ought to have done, for the ordeal which was clearly coming upon us; but we went and we turned the wavering scale. It was done by the American soldier, the American sailor, and the spirit and energy of the American people. They overrode all obstacles and all shortcomings on the part of the administration or of Congress and gave to their country a great place in the great victory. It was the first time we had been called upon to rescue the civilized world. Did we fail? On the contrary, we succeeded, succeeded largely and nobly, and we did it without any command from any league of nations. When the emergency came we met it, and we were able to meet it because we had built up on this continent the greatest and most powerful Nation in the world, built it up under our own policies, in our own way, and one great element of our strength was the fact that we had held aloof and had not thrust ourselves into European quarrels; that we had no selfish interest to serve. We made great sacrifices. We have done splendid work. I believe that we do not require to be told by foreign nations when we shall do work which freedom and civilization require. I think we can move to victory much better under our own command than under the command of others. Let us unite with the world to promote the peaceable settlement of all international disputes. Let us try to develop international law. Let us associate ourselves with the other nations for these purposes. But let us retain in our own hands and in our own control the lives of the youth of the land. Let no American be sent into battle except by the constituted authorities of his own country and by the will of the people of the United States.

Those of us, Mr. President, who are either wholly opposed to the league, or who are trying to preserve the independence and the safety of the United States by changing the terms of the league, and who are endeavoring to make the league, if we are to be a member of it, less certain to promote war instead of peace have been reproached with selfishness in our outlook and with a desire to keep our country in a state of isolation. So far as the question of isolation goes, it is impossible to isolate the United States. I well remember the time, 20 years ago, when eminent Senators and other distinguished gentlemen who were opposing the Philippines and shrieking about imperialism sneered at the statement made by some of us, that the United States had become a world power. I think no one now would question that the Spanish war marked the entrance of the United States into world affairs to a degree which had never obtained before. It was both an inevitable and an irrevocable step, and our entrance into the war with Germany certainly showed once and for all that the United States was not unmindful of its world responsibilities. We may set aside all this empty talk about isolation. Nobody expects to isolate the United States or to make it a hermit Nation, which is a sheer absurdity. But there is a wide difference between taking a suitable part and bearing a due responsibility in world affairs and plunging the United States into every controversy and conflict on the face of the globe. By meddling in all the differences which may arise among any portion or fragment of humankind we simply fritter away our influence and injure ourselves to no good purpose. We shall be of far more value to the world and its peace by occupying, so far as possible, the situation which we have occupied for the last 20 years and by adhering to the policy of Washington and Hamilton, of Jefferson and Monroe, under which we have risen to our present greatness and prosperity. The fact that we have been separated by our geographical situation and by our consistent policy from the broils of Europe has made us more than any one thing capable of performing the great work which we performed in the war against Germany, and our disinterestedness is of far more value to the world than our eternal meddling in every possible dispute could ever be.

Now as to our selfishness. I have no desire to boast that we are better than our neighbors, but the fact remains that this Nation in making peace with Germany had not a single selfish or individual interest to serve. All we asked was that Germany should be rendered incapable of again breaking forth, with all the horrors incident to German warfare, upon an unoffending world, and that demand was shared by every free nation and indeed by humanity itself. For ourselves we asked absolutely nothing. We have not asked any government or governments to guarantee our boundaries or our political independence. We have no fear in regard to either. We have sought no territory, no privileges, no advantages, for ourselves. That is the fact. It is apparent on the face of the treaty. I do not mean to reflect upon a single one of the powers with which we have been associated in the war against Germany, but there is not one of them which has not sought individual advantages for their own national benefit. I do not criticize their desires at all. The services and sacrifices of England and France and Belgium and Italy are beyond estimate and beyond praise. I am glad they should have what they desire for their own welfare and safety. But they all receive under the peace territorial and commercial benefits. We are asked to give, and we in no way seek to take. Surely it is not too much to insist that when we are offered nothing but the opportunity to give and to aid others we should have the right to say what sacrifices we shall make and what the magnitude of our gifts shall be. In the prosecution of the war we gave unstintedly American lives and American treasure. When the war closed we had 3,000,000 men under arms. We were turning the country into a vast workshop for war. We advanced ten billions to our allies. We refused no assistance that we could possibly render. All the great energy and power of the republic were put at the service of the good cause. We have not been ungenerous. We have been devoted to the cause of freedom, humanity, and civilization everywhere. Now we are asked, in the making of peace, to sacrifice our sovereignty in important respects, to involve ourselves almost without limit in the affairs of other nations and to yield up policies and rights which we have maintained throughout our history. We are asked to incur liabilities to an unlimited extent and furnish assets at the same time which no man can measure. I think it is not only our right but our duty to determine how far we shall go. Not only must we look carefully to see where we are being led into endless disputes and entanglements, but we must not forget that we have in this country millions of people of foreign birth and parentage.

Our one great object is to make all these people Americans so that we may call on them to place America first and serve America as they have done in the war just closed. We can not Americanize them if we are continually thrusting them back into the quarrels and difficulties of the countries from which they came to us. We shall fill this land with political disputes about the troubles and quarrels of other countries. We shall have a large portion of our people voting not on American questions and not on what concerns the United States but dividing on issues which concern foreign countries alone. That is an unwholesome and perilous condition to force upon this country. We must avoid it. We ought to reduce to the lowest possible point the foreign questions in which we involve ourselves. Never forget that this league is primarily—I might say overwhelmingly—a political organization, and I object strongly to having the politics of the United States turn upon disputes where deep feeling is aroused but in which we have no direct interest. It will all tend to delay the Americanization of our great population, and it is more important not only to the United States but to the peace of the world to make all these people good Americans than it is to determine that some piece of territory should belong to one European country rather than to another. For this reason I wish to limit strictly our interference in the affairs of Europe and of Africa. We have interests of our own in Asia and in the Pacific which we must guard upon our own account, but the less we undertake to play the part of umpire and thrust ourselves into European conflicts the better for the United States and for the world.

It has been reiterated here on this floor, and reiterated to the point of weariness, that in every treaty there is some sacrifice of sovereignty. That is not a universal truth by any means, but it is true of some treaties and it is a platitude which does not require reiteration. The question and the only question before us here is how much of our sovereignty we are justified in sacrificing. In what I have already said about other nations putting us into war I have covered one point of sovereignty which ought never to be yielded—the power to send American soldiers and sailors everywhere, which ought never to be taken from the American people or impaired in the slightest degree. Let us beware how we palter with our independence. We have not reached the great position from which we were able to come down into the field of battle and help to save the world from tyranny by being guided by others. Our vast power has all been built up and gathered together by ourselves alone. We forced our way upward from the days of the Revolution, through a world often hostile and always indifferent. We owe no debt to anyone except to France in that Revolution, and those policies and those rights on which our power has been founded should never be lessened or weakened. It will be no service to the world to do so and it will be of intolerable injury to the United States. We will do our share. We are ready and anxious to help in all ways to preserve the world's peace. But we can do it best by not crippling ourselves.

I am as anxious as any human being can be to have the United States render every possible service to the civilization and the peace of mankind, but I am certain we can do it best by not putting ourselves in leading strings or subjecting our policies and our sovereignty to other nations. The independence of the United States is not only more precious to ourselves but to the world than any single possession. Look at the United States today. We have made mistakes in the past. We have had shortcomings. We shall make mistakes in the future and fall short of our own best hopes. But none the less is there any country today on the face of the earth which can compare with this in ordered liberty, in peace, and in the largest freedom? I feel that I can say this without being accused of undue boastfulness, for it is the simple fact, and in making this treaty and taking on these obligations all that we do is in a spirit of unselfishness and in a desire for the good of mankind.

But it is well to remember that we are dealing with nations every one of which has a direct individual interest to serve, and there is grave danger in an unshared idealism. Contrast the United States with any country on the face of the earth today and ask yourself whether the situation of the United States is not the best to be found. I will go as far as anyone in world service, but the first step to world service is the maintenance of the United States. You may call me selfish, if you will, conservative or reactionary, or use any other harsh adjective you see fit to apply, but an American I was born, an American I have remained all my life. I can never be anything else but an American, and I must think of the United States first, and when I think of the United States first in an arrangement like this I am thinking of what is best for the world, for if the United States fails the best hopes of mankind fail with it. I have never had but one allegiance—I can not divide it now. I have loved but one flag and I can not share that devotion and give affection to the mongrel banner invented for a league. Internationalism, illustrated by the Bolshevik and by the men to whom all countries are alike provided they can make money out of them, is to me repulsive. National I must remain, and in that way I like all other Americans can render the amplest service to the world. The United States is the world's best hope, but if you fetter her in the interests and quarrels of other nations, if you tangle her in the intrigues of Europe, you will destroy her power for good and endanger her very existence. Leave her to march freely through the centuries to come as in the years that have gone. Strong, generous, and confident, she has nobly served mankind. Beware how you trifle with your marvelous inheritance, this great land of ordered liberty, for if we stumble and fall freedom and civilization everywhere will go down in ruin.

We are told that we shall "break the heart of the world" if we do not take this league just as it stands. I fear that the hearts of the vast majority of mankind would beat on strongly and steadily and without any quickening if the league were to perish altogether. If it should be effectively and beneficiently changed the people who would lie awake in sorrow for a single night could be easily gathered in one not very large room but those who would draw a long breath of relief would reach to millions.

We hear much of visions and I trust we shall continue to have visions and dream dreams of a fairer future for the race. But visions are one thing and visionaries are another, and the mechanical appliances of the rhetorician designed to give a picture of a present which does not exist and of a future which no man can predict are as unreal and short lived as the steam or canvas clouds, the angels suspended on wires and the artificial lights of the stage. They pass with the moment of effect and are shabby and tawdry in the daylight. Let us at least be real. Washington's entire honesty of mind and his fearless look into the face of all facts are qualities which can never go out of fashion and which we should all do well to imitate.

Ideals have been thrust upon us as an argument for the league until the healthy mind which rejects cant revolts from them. Are ideals confined to this deformed experiment upon a noble purpose, tainted, as it is, with bargains and tied to a peace treaty which might have been disposed of long ago to the great benefit of the world if it had not been compelled to carry this rider on its back? "Post equitem sedet atra cura," Horace tells us, but no blacker care ever sat behind any rider than we shall find in this covenant of doubtful and disputed interpretation as it now perches upon the treaty of peace.

No doubt many excellent and patriotic people see a coming fulfillment of noble ideals in the words "League for Peace." We all respect and share these aspirations and desires, but some of us see no hope, but rather defeat, for them in this murky covenant. For we, too, have our ideals, even if we differ from those who have tried to establish a monopoly of idealism. Our first ideal is our country, and we see her in the future, as in the past, giving service to all her people and to the world. Our ideal of the future is that she should continue to render that service of her own free will. She has great problems of her own to solve, very grim and perilous problems, and a right solution, if we can attain to it, would largely benefit mankind. We would have our country strong to resist a peril from the West, as she has flung back the German menace from the East. We would not have our politics distracted and embittered by the dissensions of other lands. We would not have our country's vigor exhausted, or her moral force abated, by everlasting meddling and muddling in every quarrel, great and small, which afflicts the world. Our ideal is to make her ever stronger and better and finer, because in that way alone, as we believe, can she be of the greatest service to the world's peace and to the welfare of mankind.

16. The Last Great Crusade: Woodrow Wilson

WOODROW WILSON'S *effort to take the League question to the public in 1919 indicated a willlingness if not a desire on the President's part to make the League the chief issue in the 1920 presidential campaign, if the Republican-controlled Senate continued to balk at ratification of the peace treaty. Possibly Wilson planned to run for an unprecedented third term as the League's chief sponsor and leading symbol. Speeches like that below, delivered at Pueblo, Colorado, reveal the force of Wilson's belief in the League. This fervor gave him a power to reach audiences with concise but moving statements which exceeded even the extraordinary prowess as an orator that he already had demonstrated. Even his unfortunate attempts to connect "organized" opposition to the treaty with "disloyalty" and "foreign sympathizers," probably was effective in the nativistic atmosphere of 1919, to which he contributed. Unfortunately for the cause of American participation in the League, a stroke disabled Wilson almost immediately after he completed the Pueblo speech.*

Voting Power in the League

(PUEBLO, COLORADO, SEPTEMBER 25, 1919)

In the President's final address he made a particular point of explaining the six votes of Great Britain and her colonies in the League Assembly. Mr. Wilson said in part:

But you say, "we have heard that we might be at a disadvantage in the League of Nations." Well, whoever told you that either was deliberately falsifying or he had not read the covenant of the League of Nations. I leave him the choice.

I want to give you a very simple account of the organization of the League of Nations and let you judge for yourselves. It is a very simple organization.

The power of the League, or rather the activities of the League, lie in two bodies. The first is a council, which consists of one representative from each of the principal allied and associated powers—that is to say, the United States, Great Britain. France, Italy, and Japan, along with four other representatives of smaller powers, chosen out of the general body of the membership of the League.

The Council is the source of every active policy of the League, and no active policy of the League can be adopted without a unanimous vote of the Council. That is explicitly stated in the covenant itself. Does it not evidently follow that the League of Nations can adopt no policy whatever without the consent of the United States? The affirmative vote of the representative of the United States is necessary in every case.

Now, you have heard of six votes belonging to the British Empire. Those six votes are not in the Council, they are in the Assembly, and the interesting thing is that the Assembly does not vote. I must qualify that statement a little, but essentially it is absolutely true. In every matter in which the Assembly is given a voice, and there are only four or five, its vote does not count unless concurred in by the representatives of all the nations represented on the Council, so that there is no validity to any vote of the Assembly unless in that vote also the representative of the United States concurs. That one vote of the United States is as big as the six votes of the British Empire. I am not jealous for advantage, my fellow citizens, but I think that is a perfectly safe situation. There is not any validity in a vote either by the Council or the Assembly in which we do not concur. So much for the statements about the six votes of the British Empire.

And look at it in another aspect. The Assembly is the talking body. The Assembly was created in order that anybody that purposed anything wrong should be subjected to the awkward circumstances that everybody could talk about it. This is the great Assembly in which all the things that are likely to disturb the peace of the world or the good understanding between nations are to be exposed to the general view, and I want to ask you if you think it was unjust, unjust to the United States, that speaking parts should be assigned to the several portions of the British Empire?

Do you think it unjust that there should be some spokesman in debate for that fine, little, stout republic down in the Pacific, New Zealand? Do you think it was unjust that Australia should be allowed to stand up and take part in the debate, Australia from which we have learned some of the most useful progressive policies of modern times, a little nation of only five million in a great continent, but counting for several times five in its activities and in its interest in liberal reform?

Do you think it unjust that that little republic down in South

Africa whose gallant resistance to being subjected to any outside authority at all we admired for so many months and whose fortunes we followed with such interest should have a speaking part? Great Britain obliged South Africa to submit to her sovereignty, but she immediately after that felt that it was convenient and right to hand the whole self-government of that colony over to the very men whom she had beaten, and among the representatives of South Africa in Paris were two of the most distinguished generals of the Boer army, two of the realest men I ever met, two men that could talk sober counsel and wise advice along with the best statesmen in Europe. To exclude General Botha and General Smuts from the right to stand up in the parliament of the world and say something concerning the affairs of mankind would be absurd.

And what about Canada? Isn't Canada a good neighbor? I ask you, isn't Canada more likely to agree with the United States than with Great Britain? Canada has a speaking part.

And then for the first time in the history of the world that great, voiceless multitude, that throng, hundreds of millions strong, in India, has a voice. And I want to testify that some of the wisest and most dignified figures in the Peace Conference at Paris came from India, men who seemed to carry in their minds an older wisdom than the rest of us had, whose traditions ran back into so many of the unhappy fortunes of mankind that they seemed very useful counselors as to how some ray of hope and some prospect of happiness could be opened to its people.

I for my part have no jealousy whatever of those five speaking parts in the Assembly, and these speaking parts cannot translate themselves into five votes that can in any matter override the voice and purpose of the United States.

Let us sweep aside all this language of jealousy. Let us be big enough to know the facts and to welcome the facts. Because the facts are based upon the principle that America has always fought for, namely, the equality of self-governing peoples, whether they were big or little, not counting men, but counting rights, not counting representation, but counting the purpose of that representation.

When you hear an opinion quoted, you do not count the number of persons who hold it. You ask, "Who said that?" You weigh opinions, you do not count them, and the beauty of all democracies is that every voice can be heard, every voice can have its effect, every voice can contribute to the general judgment that is finally arrived at. That is the object of democracy.

Let us accept what America has always fought for, and accept it with pride that America showed the way and made the proposal. I do not mean that America made the proposal in this particular instance, I mean that the principle was an American principle, proposed by America.

The chief pleasure of my trip has been that it has nothing to do with my personal fortunes. That it has nothing to do with my personal reputation, that it has nothing to do with anything except great principles uttered by Americans of all sorts and of all parties which we are now trying to realize at this crisis of the affairs of the world.

But there have been unpleasant impressions as well as pleasant impressions. My fellow citizens, as I have crossed the continent I have perceived more and more that men have been busy creating an absolutely false impression of what the treaty of peace and the covenant of the League of Nations contain and mean.

I find, moreover, that there is an organized propaganda against the League of Nations and against the treaty, proceeding from the same sources that the organized propaganda proceeded from which threatened this country here and there with disloyalty, and I want to say, I cannot say too often, any man who carries a hyphen about with him carries a dagger that he is ready to plunge into the vitals of this republic whenever he gets ready. If I can catch any man with a hyphen in this great country I will know that I have got an enemy of the republic. For, my fellow citizens, it is only certain bodies of foreign sympathizers, certain bodies in sympathy with foreign nations that are organized against this great document which the American representatives have brought back from Paris.

III

Postwar Reaction

17. The Master Race: Madison Grant

MADISON GRANT'S The Passing of the Great Race *was only one of hundreds of polemical books and articles that appeared with increasing frequency beginning in the 1890s, mingling social Darwinian concepts of race superiority with fears of the massive "new immigration" from Southern and Eastern Europe. These racial attitudes were common throughout Europe; but the "new" immigration and the simultaneous migration of Negroes to urban areas—in the South during the late nineteenth century but gradually shifting to the North early in the twentieth century—were peculiar to the United States. In no other country, therefore, did books like Grant's find such a large and receptive audience during this period.*

Race and Democracy

Failure to recognize the clear distinction between race and nationality and the still greater distinction between race and language and the easy assumption that the one is indicative of the other have been in the past serious impediments to an understanding of racial values. Historians and philologists have approached the subject from the viewpoint of linguistics and as a result we are today burdened with a group of mythical races, such as the Latin, the Aryan, the Indo-Germanic, the Caucasian and, perhaps, most inconsistent of all, the Celtic race.

Man is an animal differing from his fellow inhabitants of the globe not in kind but only in degree of development and an intelligent study of the human species must be preceded by an extended knowledge of other mammals, especially the primates. Instead of such essential training, anthropologists often seek to qualify by research in linguistics, religion or marriage customs or in designs of pottery or blanket weaving, all of which relate to ethnology alone. As a result the influence of environment is often overestimated and overstated at the expense of heredity.

The question of race has been further complicated by the effort of old-fashioned theologians to cramp all mankind into the scant six thousand years of Hebrew chronology as expounded by Archbishop Usher. Religious teachers have also maintained the proposi-

SOURCE: Madison Grant, *The Passing of the Great Race* (New York, 1916), pp. 3–36.

tion not only that man is something fundamentally distinct from other living creatures, but that there are no inherited differences in humanity that cannot be obliterated by education and environment.

It is, therefore, necessary at the outset for the reader to appreciate thoroughly that race, language and nationality are three separate and distinct things and that in Europe these three elements are found only occasionally persisting in combination, as in the Scandinavian nations.

To realize the transitory nature of political boundaries one has but to consider the changes which have occurred during the past century and as to language, here in America we hear daily the English language spoken by many men who possess not one drop of English blood and who, a few years since, knew not one word of Saxon speech.

As a result of certain religious and social doctrines, now happily becoming obsolete, race consciousness has been greatly impaired among civilized nations but in the beginning all differences of class, of caste and of color marked actual lines of race cleavage.

In many countries the existing classes represent races that were once distinct. In the city of New York and elsewhere in the United States there is a native American aristocracy resting upon layer after layer of immigrants of lower races and these native Americans, while, of course, disclaiming the distinction of a patrician class and lacking in class consciousness and class dignity, have, nevertheless, up to this time supplied the leaders in thought and in the control of capital as well as of education and of the religious ideals and altruistic bias of the community.

In the democratic forms of government the operation of universal suffrage tends toward the selection of the average man for public office rather than the man qualified by birth, education and integrity. How this scheme of administration will ultimately work out remains to be seen but from a racial point of view it will inevitably increase the preponderance of the lower types and cause a corresponding loss of efficiency in the community as a whole.

The tendency in a democracy is toward a standardization of type and a diminution of the influence of genius. A majority must of necessity be inferior to a picked minority and it always resents specializations in which it cannot share. In the French Revolution the majority, calling itself "the people," deliberately endeavored to destroy the higher type and something of the same sort was in a measure done after the American Revolution by the expulsion of the Loyalists and the confiscation of their lands, with a resultant loss to the growing nation of good race strains, which were in the next century replaced by immigrants of far lower type.

In America we have nearly succeeded in destroying the privilege of birth; that is, the intellectual and moral advantage a man of good stock brings into the world with him. We are now engaged in destroying the privilege of wealth; that is, the reward of successful intelligence and industry and in some quarters there is developing a tendency to attack the privilege of intellect and to deprive a man of the advantage gained from an early and thorough classical education. Simplified spelling is a step in this direction. Ignorance of English grammar or classic learning must not, forsooth, be held up as a reproach to the political or social aspirant.

Mankind emerged from savagery and barbarism under the leadership of selected individuals whose personal prowess, capacity or wisdom gave them the right to lead and the power to compel obedience. Such leaders have always been a minute fraction of the whole, but as long as the tradition of their predominance persisted they were able to use the brute strength of the unthinking herd as part of their own force and were able to direct at will the blind dynamic impulse of the slaves, peasants or lower classes. Such a despot had an enormous power at his disposal which, if he were benevolent or even intelligent, could be used and most frequently was used for the general uplift of the race. Even those rulers who most abused this power put down with merciless rigor the antisocial elements, such as pirates, brigands or anarchists, which impair the progress of a community, as disease or wounds cripple an individual.

True aristocracy or a true republic is government by the wisest and best, always a small minority in any population. Human society is like a serpent dragging its long body on the ground, but with the head always thrust a little in advance and a little elevated above the earth. The serpent's tail, in human society represented by the antisocial forces, was in the past dragged by sheer strength along the path of progress. Such has been the organization of mankind from the beginning, and such it still is in older communities than ours. What progress humanity can make under the control of universal suffrage, or the rule of the average, may find a further analogy in the habits of certain snakes which wiggle sideways and disregard the head with its brains and eyes. Such serpents, however, are not noted for their ability to make rapid progress.

A true republic, the function of which is administration in the interests of the whole community—in contrast to a pure democracy, which in last analysis is the rule of the demos or a majority in its own interests—should be, and often is, the medium of selection for the technical task of government of those best qualified by antecedents, character and education, in short, of experts.

To use another simile, in an aristocratic as distinguished from a plutocratic or democratic organization the intellectual and talented classes form the point of the lance while the massive shaft represents the body of the population and adds by its bulk and weight to the penetrative impact of the tip. In a democratic system this concentrated force is dispersed throughout the mass. It supplies, to be sure, a certain amount of leaven but in the long run the force and genius of the small minority is dissipated, and its efficiency lost. *Vox populi*, so far from being *Vox Dei*, thus becomes an unending wail for rights and never a chant of duty.

Where a conquering race is imposed on another race the institution of slavery often arises to compel the servient race to work and to introduce it forcibly to a higher form of civilization. As soon as men can be induced to labor to supply their own needs slavery becomes wasteful and tends to vanish. From a material point of view slaves are often more fortunate than freemen when treated with reasonable humanity and when their elemental wants of food, clothing and shelter are supplied.

The Indians around the fur posts in northern Canada were formerly the virtual bond slaves of the Hudson Bay Company, each Indian and his squaw and papoose being adequately supplied with simple food and equipment. He was protected as well against the white man's rum as the red man's scalping parties and in return gave the Company all his peltries—the whole product of his year's work. From an Indian's point of view this was nearly an ideal condition but was to all intents serfdom or slavery. When through the opening up of the country the continuance of such an archaic system became an impossibility, the Indian sold his furs to the highest bidder, received a large price in cash and then wasted the proceeds in trinkets instead of blankets and in rum instead of flour, with the result that he is now gloriously free but is on the highroad to becoming a diseased outcast. In this case of the Hudson Bay

Indian the advantages of the upward step from serfdom to freedom are not altogether clear. A very similar condition of vassalage existed until recently among the peons of Mexico, but without the compensation of the control of an intelligent and provident ruling class.

In the same way serfdom in mediaeval Europe apparently was a device through which the landowners repressed the nomadic instinct in their tenantry which became marked when the fertility of the land declined after the dissolution of the Roman Empire. Years are required to bring land to its highest productivity and agriculture cannot be successfully practised even in well-watered and fertile districts by farmers who continually drift from one locality to another. The serf or villein was, therefore, tied by law to the land and could not leave except with his master's consent. As soon as the nomadic instinct was eliminated serfdom vanished. One has but to read the severe laws against vagrancy in England just before the Reformation to realize how widespread and serious was this nomadic instinct. Here in America we have not yet forgotten the wandering instincts of our Western pioneers, which in that case proved beneficial to every one except the migrants.

While democracy is fatal to progress when two races of unequal value live side by side, an aristocracy may be equally injurious whenever, in order to purchase a few generations of ease and luxury, slaves or immigrants are imported to do the heavy work. It was a form of aristocracy that brought slaves to the American colonies and the West Indies and if there had been an aristocratic form of governmental control in California, Chinese coolies and Japanese laborers would now form the controlling element, so far as numbers are concerned, on the Pacific coast.

It was the upper classes who encouraged the introduction of immigrant labor to work American factories and mines and it is the native American gentleman who builds a palace on the country side and who introduces as servants all manner of foreigners into purely American districts. The farming and artisan classes of America did not take alarm until it was too late and they are now seriously threatened with extermination in many parts of the country. In Rome, also, it was the plebeian, who first went under in the competition with slaves but the patrician followed in his turn a few generations later.

The West Indian sugar planters flourished in the eighteenth

century and produced some strong men; today from the same causes they have vanished from the scene.

During the last century the New England manufacturer imported the Irish and French Canadians and the resultant fall in the New England birthrate at once became ominous. The refusal of the native American to work with his hands when he can hire or import serfs to do manual labor for him is the prelude to his extinction and the immigrant laborers are now breeding out their masters and killing by filth and by crowding as effectively as by the sword.

Thus the American sold his birthright in a continent to solve a labor problem. Instead of retaining political control and making citizenship an honorable and valued privilege, he intrusted the government of his country and the maintenance of his ideals to races who have never yet succeeded in governing themselves, much less any one else.

Associated with this advance of democracy and the transfer of power from the higher to the lower races, from the intellectual to the plebeian class, we find the spread of socialism and the recrudescence of obsolete religious forms. Although these phenomena appear to be contradictory, they are in reality closely related since both represent reactions from the intense individualism which a century ago was eminently characteristic of Americans.

The Physical Basis of Race

In the modern and scientific study of race we have long since discarded the Adamic theory that man is descended from a single pair, created a few thousand years ago in a mythical Garden of Eden somewhere in Asia, to spread later over the earth in successive waves.

It is a fact, however, that Asia was the chief area of evolution and differentiation of man and that the various groups had their main development there and not on the peninsula we call Europe.

Many of the races of Europe, both living and extinct, did come from the East through Asia Minor or by way of the African littoral, but most of the direct ancestors of existing populations have inhabited Europe for many thousands of years. During that time numerous races of men have passed over the scene. Some undoubtedly have utterly vanished and some have left their blood behind them in the Europeans of today.

We now know, since the elaboration of the Mendelian Laws of Inheritance, that certain bodily characters, such as skull shape, stature, eye color, hair color and nose form, some of which are so-called unit characters, are transmitted in accordance with fixed laws, and, further, that various characters which are normally correlated or linked together in pure races may, after a prolonged admixture of races, pass down separately and form what is known as disharmonic combinations. Such disharmonic combinations are, for example, a tall brunet or a short blond; blue eyes associated with brunet hair or brown eyes with blond hair.

The process of intermixture of characters has gone far in existing populations and through the ease of modern methods of transportation this process is going much further in Europe and in America. The results of such mixture are not blends or intermediate types, but rather mosaics of contrasted characters. Such blends, if any, as ultimately occur are too remote to concern us here.

The crossing of an individual or pure brunet race with an individual of pure blond race produces in the first generation offspring which are distinctly dark. In subsequent generations, brunets and blonds appear in various proportions but the former tend to be such the more numerous. The blond is consequently said to be recessive to the brunet because it recedes from view in the first generation. This or any similar recessive or suppressed trait is not lost to the germ plasm, but reappears in later generations of the hybridized stock. A similar rule prevails with other physical characters.

In defining race in Europe it is necessary not only to consider pure groups or pure types but also the distribution of characters belonging to each particular subspecies of man found there. The interbreeding of these populations has progressed to such an extent that in many cases such an analysis of physical characters is necessary to reconstruct the elements which have entered into their ethnic composition. To rely on averages alone leads to misunderstanding and to disregard of the relative proportion of pure, as contrasted with mixed types.

Sometimes we find a character appearing here and there as the sole remnant of a once numerous race, for example, the rare appearance in European populations of a skull of the Neanderthal type, a race widely spread over Europe 40,000 years ago, or of the Cro-Magnon type, the predominant race 16,000 years ago. Before the fossil remains of the Neanderthal and Cro-Magnon races were studied and understood such reversional specimens were considered pathological, instead of being recognized as the reappearance of an ancient and submerged type.

These physical characters are to all intents and purposes immutable and they do not change during the lifetime of a language or an empire. The skull shape of the Egyptian fellaheen, in the unchanging environment of the Nile Valley, is absolutely identical in measurements, proportions and capacity with skulls found in the predynastic tombs dating back more than six thousand years.

There exists today a widespread and fatuous belief in the power of environment, as well as of education and opportunity to alter heredity, which arises from the dogma of the brotherhood of man, derived in its turn from the loose thinkers of the French Revolution and their American mimics. Such beliefs have done much damage in the past and if allowed to go uncontradicted, may do even more serious damage in the future. Thus the view that the Negro slave was an unfortunate cousin of the white man, deeply tanned by the tropic sun and denied the blessings of Christianity and civilization, played no small part with the sentimentalists of the Civil War period and it has taken us fifty years to learn that speaking English, wearing good clothes and going to school and to church do not transform a Negro into a white man. Nor was a Syrian or Egyptian freedman transformed into a Roman by wearing a toga and applauding his favorite gladiator in the amphitheatre. Americans will have a similar experience with the Polish Jew, whose dwarf stature, peculiar mentality and ruthless concentration of self-interest are being engrafted upon the stock of the nation.

Recent attempts have been made in the interest of inferior races among our immigrants to show that the shape of the skull does change, not merely in a century, in a single generation. In 1910, the report of the anthropological expert of the Congressional Immigration Commission gravely declared that a round skull Jew on his way across the Atlantic might and did have a round skull child; but a few years later, in response to the subtle elixir of American institutions as exemplified in an East Side tenement, might and did have a child whose skull was appreciably longer; and that a long skull south Italian, breeding freely, would have precisely the same experience in the reverse direction. In other words the Melting Pot was acting instantly under the influence of a changed environment.

What the Melting Pot actually does in practice can be seen in

Mexico, where the absorption of the blood of the original Spanish conquerors by the native Indian population has produced the racial mixture which we call Mexican and which is now engaged in demonstrating its incapacity for self-government. The world has seen many such mixtures and the character of a mongrel race is only just beginning to be understood at its true value.

It must be borne in mind that the specializations which characterize the higher races are of relatively recent development, are highly unstable and when mixed with generalized or primitive characters tend to disappear. Whether we like to admit it or not, the result of the mixture of two races, in the long run, gives us a race reverting to the more ancient, generalized and lower type. The cross between a white man and an Indian is an Indian; the cross between a white man and a Negro is a Negro; the cross between a white man and a Hindu is a Hindu; and the cross between any of the three European races and a Jew is a Jew.

In the crossing of the blond and brunet elements of a population, the more deeply rooted and ancient dark traits are prepotent or dominant. This is matter of everyday observation and the working of this law of nature is not influenced or affected by democratic institutions or by religious beliefs. Nature cares not for the individual nor how he may be modified by environment. She is concerned only with the perpetuation of the species or type and heredity alone is the medium through which she acts.

As measured in terms of centuries these characters are fixed and rigid and the only benefit to be devised from a changed environment and better food conditions is the opportunity afforded a race which has lived under adverse conditions to achieve its maximum development but the limits of that development are fixed for it by heredity and not by environment.

In dealing with European populations the best method of determining race has been found to lie in a comparison of proportions of the skull, the so-called cephalic index. This is the ratio of maximum *width*, taken at the widest part of the skull above the ears, to maximum *length*. Skulls with an index of 75 or less, that is, those with a width that is three-fourths of the length or less, are considered dolichocephalic or long skulls. Skulls of an index of 80 or over are round or brachycephalic skulls. Intermediate indices, between 75 and 80, are considered mesaticephalic. These are cranial indices. To allow for the flesh on living specimens about two percent is to be added to this index and the result is the cephalic index. In the following pages only long and round skulls are considered and the intermediate forms are assigned to the dolichocephalic group.

This cephalic index, though an extremely important if not the controlling character, is, nevertheless, but a single character and must be checked up with other somatological traits. Normally, a long skull is associated with a long face and a round skull with a round face.

The use of this test, the cephalic index, enables us to divide the great bulk of the European populations into three distinct subspecies of man, one northern and one southern, both dolichocephalic or characterized by a long skull and a central subspecies which is brachycephalic or characterized by a round skull.

The first is the Nordic or Baltic subspecies. This race is long skulled, very tall, fair skinned with blond or brown hair and light colored eyes. The Nordics inhabit the countries around the North and Baltic Seas and include not only the great Scandinavian and Teutonic groups, but also other early peoples who first appear in southern Europe and in Asia as representatives of Aryan language and culture.

The second is the dark Mediterranean or Iberian subspecies, occupying the shores of the inland sea and extending along the Atlantic coast until it reaches the Nordic species. It also spreads far east into southern Asia. It is long skulled like the Nordic race but the absolute size of the skull is less. The eyes and hair are very dark or black and the skin more or less swarthy. The stature is distinctly less than that of the Nordic race and the musculature and bony framework weak.

The third is the Alpine subspecies occupying all central and eastern Europe and extending through Asia Minor to the Hindu Kush and the Pamirs. The Armenoids constitute an Alpine subdivision and may possibly represent the ancestral type of this race which remained in the mountains and high plateaux of Anatolia and western Asia.

The Alpines are round skulled, or medium height and sturdy build both as to skeleton and muscles. The coloration of both hair and eyes was originally very dark and still tends strongly in that direction but many light colored eyes, especially gray, are now common among the Alpine populations of western Europe.

While the inhabitants of Europe betray as a whole their mixed origin, nevertheless, individuals of each of the three main subspecies are found in large numbers and in great purity, as well as sparse remnants of still more ancient races represented by small groups or by individuals and even by single characters.

These three main groups have bodily characters which constitute them distinct subspecies. Each group is a large one and includes several well-marked varieties, which differ even more widely in cultural development than in physical divergence so that when the Mediterranean of England is compared with the Hindu, or the Alpine Savoyard with the Rumanian or Tucoman, a wide gulf is found.

In zoology, related species when grouped together constitute subgenera and genera and the term species implies the existence of a certain definite amount of divergence from the most closely related type but race does not require a similar amount of difference. In man, where all groups are more or less fertile when crossed, so many intermediate or mixed types occur that the word species has at the present day too extended a meaning.

For the sake of clearness the word race and not the word species or subspecies will be used in the following chapters as far as possible.

The old idea that fertility or infertility of races of animals was the measure of species is now abandoned. One of the greatest difficulties in classifying man is his perverse predisposition to mismate. This is a matter of daily observation, especially among the women of the better classes, probably because of their wider range of choice.

There must have existed many subspecies and species, if not genera, of men since the Pliocene and new discoveries of their remains may be expected at any time and in any part of the eastern hemisphere.

The cephalic index is of less value in the classification of Asiatic populations but the distribution of round and long skulls is similar to that in Europe. The vast central plateau of that continent is inhabited by round skulls. In fact, Tibet and the western Himalayas were probably the center of radiation of all the round skulls of the world. In India and Persia south of this central area occurs a long skull race related to Mediterranean man in Europe.

Both skull types occur much intermixed among the American

Indians and the cephalic index is of little value in classifying the Amerinds. No satisfactory explanation of the variability of the skull shape in the western hemisphere has as yet been found, but the total range of variation of physical characters among them, from northern Canada to southern Patagonia, is less than the range of such variation from Normandy to Provence in France.

In Africa the cephalic index is also of small classification value because all of the populations are characterized by a long skull.

The distinction between a long skull and a round skull in mankind probably goes back at least to early Paleolithic times, if not to a period still more remote. It is of such great antiquity that when new species or races appear in Europe at the close of the Paleolithic, between 10,000 and 7,000 years B.C., the skull characters among them are as clearly defined as they are today.

The fact that two distinct species of mankind have long skulls, as have the north European and the African Negro, is no necessary indication of relationship and in that instance is merely a case of parallel specialization, but the fact, however, that the Swede has a long skull and the Savoyard a round skull does prove them to be racially distinct.

The claim that the Nordic race is a mere variation of the Mediterranean race and that the latter is in turn derived from the Ethiopian Negro rests upon a mistaken idea that a dolichocephaly in common must mean identity of origin, as well as upon a failure to take into consideration many somatological characters of almost equal value with the cephalic index. Indeed, the cephalic index, being merely a ratio, may be identical for skulls differing in every other proportion and detail, as well as in absolute size and capacity.

Eye color is of very great importance in race determination because all blue, gray or green eyes in the world today came originally from the same source, namely, the Nordic race of northern Europe. This light colored eye has appeared nowhere else on earth, is a specialization of this subspecies of man only and consequently is of extreme value in the classification of European races. Dark colored eyes are all but universal among wild mammals and entirely so among the primates, man's nearest relatives. It may be taken as an absolute certainty that all the original races of man had dark eyes.

One subspecies of man and one alone specialized in light colored eyes. This same subspecies also evolved light brown or blond hair, a character far less deeply rooted than eye color, as blond children tend to grow darker with advancing years and populations partly of Nordic extraction, such as those of Lombardy, upon admixture with darker races lose their blond hair more readily than their light colored eyes. In short, light colored eyes are far more common than light colored hair. In crosses between Alpines and Nordics, the Alpine stature and the Nordic eye appear to prevail. Light color in eyes is largely due to a greater or less absence of pigment but it is not associated with weak eyesight, as in the case of albinos. In fact, among marksmen, it has been noted that nearly all the great rifle-shots in England or America have had light colored eyes.

Blond hair also comes everywhere from the Nordic subspecies and from nowhere else. Whenever we find blondness among the darker races of the earth we may be sure some Nordic wanderer has passed that way. When individuals of perfect blond type occur, as sometimes in Greek islands, we may suspect a recent visit of sailors from a passing ship but when only single characters remain spread thinly, but widely, over considerable areas, like the blondness of the Atlas Berbers or of the Albanian mountaineers, we must search in the dim past for the origin of these blurred traits of early invaders.

The range of blond hair color in pure Nordic peoples runs from flaxen and red to shades of chestnut and brown. The darker shades may indicate crossing in some cases, but absolutely black hair certainly does mean an ancestral cross with a dark race—in England with the Mediterranean race.

It must be clearly understood that blondness of hair and of eye is not a final test of Nordic race. The Nordics include all the blonds, and also those of darker hair or eye when possessed of a preponderance of other Nordic characters. In this sense the word "blond" means those lighter shades of hair or eye color in contrast to the very dark or black shades which are termed brunet. The meaning of "blond" as now used is therefore not limited to the lighter or flaxen shades as in colloquial speech.

In England among Nordic populations there are large numbers of individuals with hazel brown eyes joined with the light brown or chestnut hair which is the typical hair shade of the English and Americans. This combination is also common in Holland and Westphalia and is frequently associated with a very fair skin. These men are all of "blond" aspect and constitution and consequently are to be classed as members of the Nordic race.

In Nordic populations the women are, in general, lighter haired than the men, a fact which points to a blond past and a darker future for those populations. Women in all human races, as the females among all mammals, tend to exhibit the older, more generalized and primitive traits of the past of the race. The male in his individual development indicates the direction in which the race is tending under the influence of variation and selection.

It is interesting to note in connection with the more primitive physique of the female, that in the spiritual sphere also women retain the ancient and intuitive knowledge that the great mass of mankind is not free and equal but bound and unequal.

The color of the skin is a character of importance but one that is exceedingly hard to measure as the range of variation in Europe between skins of extreme fairness and those that are exceedingly swarthy is almost complete. The Nordic race in its purity has an absolutely fair skin and is consequently the white man par excellence.

Many members of the Nordic race otherwise apparently pure have skins, as well as hair, more or less dark, so that the determinative value of this character is uncertain. There can be no doubt that the quality of the skin and the extreme range of its variation in color from black, brown, red, yellow to ivory-white are excellent measures of the specific or subgeneric distinctions between the larger groups of mankind but in dealing with European populations it is sometimes difficult to correlate the shades of fairness with other physical characters.

In general, hair color and skin color are linked together, but it often happens that an individual with all other Nordic characters in great purity has a skin of an olive or dark tint. Even more frequently we find individuals with absolutely pure brunet traits in possession of a skin of almost ivory whiteness and of great clarity. This last combination is very frequent among the brunets of the British Isles. That these are, to some extent, disharmonic combinations we may be certain but beyond that our knowledge does not lead. Women, however, of fair skin have always been the objects of keen envy by those of the sex whose skins are black, yellow or red.

Stature is another character of greater value than skin color and, perhaps, than hair color and is one of much importance in European classification for on that continent we have the most extreme variations of human height.

Exceedingly adverse economic conditions may inhibit a race from attaining the full measure of its growth and to this extent environment plays its part in determining stature but fundamentally it is race, always race, that sets the limit. The tall Scot and the dwarfed Sardinian owe their respective sizes to race and not to oatmeal or olive oil. It is probable, however, that the fact that the stature of the Irish is, on the average, shorter than that of the Scotch is due partly to economic conditions and partly to the depressive effect of a considerable population of primitive short stock.

The Mediterranean race is everywhere marked by a relatively short stature, sometimes greatly depressed, as in south Italy and in Sardinia, and also by a comparatively light bony framework and feeble muscular development.

The Alpine race is taller than the Mediterranean, although shorter than the Nordic, and is characterized by a stocky and sturdy build. The Alpines rarely, if ever, show the long necks and graceful figures so often found in the other two races.

The Nordic race is nearly everywhere distinguished by great stature. Almost the tallest stature in the world is found among the pure Nordic populations of the Scottish and English borders while the native British of pre-Nordic brunet blood are for the most part relatively short. No one can question the race value of stature who observes on the streets of London the contrast between the Piccadilly gentleman of Nordic race and the cockney costermonger of the old Neolithic type.

In some cases where these three European races have become mixed stature seems to be one of the first Nordic characters to vanish, but wherever in Europe we find great stature in a population otherwise lacking in Nordic characters we may suspect a Nordic crossing, as in the case of a large proportion of the inhabitants of Burgundy, of the Tyrol and of the Dalmatian Alps south to Albania.

These four characters, skull shape, eye color, hair color and stature, are sufficient to enable us to differentiate clearly between the three main subspecies of Europe, but if we wish to discuss the minor variations in each race and mixtures between them, we must go much further and take up other proportions of the skull than the cephalic index, as well as the shape and position of the eyes, the proportions and shape of the jaws, the chin and other features.

The nose is an exceedingly important character. The original human nose was, of course, broad and bridgeless. This trait is shown clearly in new-born infants who recapitulate in their development the various stages of the evolution of the human genus. A bridgeless nose with wide, flaring nostrils is a very primitive character and is still retained by some of the larger divisions of mankind throughout the world. It appears occasionally in white populations of European origin but is everywhere a very ancient, generalized and low character.

The high bridge and long, narrow nose, the so-called Roman, Norman or aquiline nose, is characteristic of the most highly specialized races of mankind. While an apparently unimportant character, this feature is one of the very best clues to racial origin and in the details of its form, and especially in the lateral shape of the nostrils, is a race determinant of the greatest value.

The lips, whether thin or fleshy or whether clean-cut or everted, are race characters. Thick, protruding, everted lips are very ancient traits and are characteristic of many primitive races. A high instep also has long been esteemed an indication of patrician type while the flat foot is often the test of lowly origin.

The absence or abundance of hair and beard and the relative absence or abundance of body hair are characters of no little value in classification. Abundant body hair is, to a large extent, peculiar to populations of the very highest as well as the very lowest species, being characteristic of the north European as well as of the Australian savages. It merely means the retention in both these groups of a very early and primitive trait which has been lost by the Negroes, Mongols and Amerinds.

The Nordic and Alpine races are far better equipped with head and body hair than the Mediterranean, which is throughout its range a glabrous or relatively naked race but among the Nordics the extreme blond types are less equipped with body hair or down than are darker members of the race. A contrast in color between head hair and beard, the latter always being lighter than the former, may be one of the results of an ancient crossing of races.

The so-called red haired branch of the Nordic race has special characters in addition to red hair, such as a greenish cast of eye, a skin of delicate texture tending either to great clarity or to freckles and certain peculiar temperamental traits. This was probably a variety closely related to the blonds and it first appears in history in association with them.

While the three main European races are the subject of this book and while it is not the intention of the author to deal with the other human types, it is desirable in connection with the discussion of this character, hair, to state that the three European subspecies are subdivisions of one of the primary groups or species of the genus *Homo* which, taken together, we may call the Caucasian for lack of a better name.

The existing classification of man must be radically revised, as the differences between the most divergent human types are far greater than are usually deemed sufficient to constitute separate species and even subgenera in the animal kingdom at large. Outside of the three European subspecies the greater portion of the genus *Homo* can be roughly divided into the Negroes and Negroids, and the Mongols and Mongoloids.

The former apparently originated in south Asia and entered Africa by way of the northeastern corner of that continent. Africa south of the Sahara is now the chief home of this race, though remnants of Negroid aborigines are found throughout south Asia from India to the Philippines, while the very distinct black Melanesians and the Australoids lie farther to the east and south.

The Mongoloids include the round skulled Mongols and their derivatives, the Amerinds or American Indians. This group is essentially Asiatic and occupies the center and the eastern half of that continent.

A description of these Negroids and Mongoloids and their derivatives, as well as of certain aberrant species of man, lies outside the scope of this work.

In the structure of the head hair of all races of mankind we find a regular progression from extreme kinkiness to lanky straightness and this straightness or curliness depends on the shape of the cross section of the hair itself. This cross section has three distinct forms, corresponding with the most extreme divergences among human species.

The cross section of the hair of the Negroes is a flat ellipse with the result that they all have kinky hair. This kinkiness of the Negroes' hair is also due somewhat to the acute angle at which the hair is set into the skin and the peppercorn form of hair probably represents an extreme specialization.

The cross section of the hair of the Mongols and their derivatives, the Amerinds, is a complete circle and their hair is perfectly straight and lank.

The cross section of the hair of the so-called Caucasians, including the Mediterranean, Alpine and Nordic subspecies, is an oval ellipse and consequently is intermediate between the cross sections of the Negroes and Mongoloids. Hair of this structure is wavy or curly, never either kinky or absolutely straight and is characteristic of all the European populations almost without exception.

Of these three hair types the straighter forms most closely represent the earliest human form of hair.

We have confined the discussion to the most important characters but there are many other valuable aids to classification to be found in the proportions of the body and the relative length of the limbs. In this latter respect, it is a matter of common knowledge that there occur two distinct types, the one long legged and short bodied, the other long bodied and short legged.

Without going into further physical details, it is probable that all relative proportions in the body, the features, the skeleton and the skull which are fixed and constant and lie outside of the range of individual variation represent dim inheritances from the past. Every generation of human beings carries the blood of thousands of ancestors, stretching back through thousands of years, superimposed upon a prehuman inheritance of still greater antiquity and the face and body of every living man offer an intricate mass of hieroglyphs that science will some day learn to read and interpret.

Only the foregoing main characters will be used as the basis for determining race and attention will be called later to such temperamental and spiritual traits as seem to be associated with distinct physical types.

We shall discuss only European populations and, as said, shall not deal with exotic and alien races scattered among them nor with those quarters of the globe where the races of man are such that other physical characters must be called upon to provide clear definitions.

A fascinating subject would open up if we were to dwell upon the effect of racial combinations and disharmonies, as, for instance, where the mixed Nordic and Alpine populations of Lombardy usually retain the skull shape, hair color and stature of the Alpine race, with the light eye color of the Nordic race, or where the mountain populations along the east coast of the Adriatic from the Tyrol to Albania have the stature of the Nordic race and an Alpine skull and coloration.

18. On Saving the United States from Communism: Attorney General A. Mitchell Palmer

ATTORNEY GENERAL A. *Mitchell Palmer's defense of the assault by the Justice Department against "the Reds" was issued in response to a deluge of criticism that followed disclosure of the unconstitutional actions taken by agents under the authority of Palmer's subordinates. The Attorney General's sensitivity was heightened by his candidacy for the presidency, the success of which fluctuated with popular belief in the idea that Palmer's actions were saving the nation from violent revolution.*

Like a prairie fire, the blaze of revolution was sweeping over every American institution of law and order a year ago. It was eating its way into the homes of the American workman, its sharp tongues of revolutionary heat were licking the altars of the churches, leaping into the belfry of the school bell, crawling into the sacred corners of American homes, seeking to replace marriage vows with libertine laws, burning up the foundations of society.

Robbery, not war, is the ideal of communism. This has been demonstrated in Russia, Germany, and in America. As a foe, the anarchist is fearless of his own life, for his creed is a fanaticism that admits no respect of any other creed. Obviously it is the creed of any criminal mind, which reasons always from motives impossible to clean thought. Crime is the degenerate factor in society.

Upon these two basic certainties, first that the "Reds" were criminal aliens, and secondly that the American Government must prevent crime, it was decided that there could be no nice distinctions drawn between the theoretical ideals of the radicals and their actual violations of our national laws. An assassin may have bril-

SOURCE: A. Mitchell Palmer, "The Case against the 'Reds,'" *The Forum*, 63 (February 1920): 174–185.

liant intellectuality, he may be able to excuse his murder or robbery with fine oratory, but any theory which excuses crime is not wanted in America. This is no place for the criminal to flourish, nor will he do so, so long as the rights of common citizenship can be exerted to prevent him.

Our Government in Jeopardy

It has always been plain to me that when American citizens unite upon any national issue, they are generally right, but it is sometimes difficult to make the issue clear to them. If the Department of Justice could succeed in attracting the attention of our optimistic citizens to the issue of internal revolution in this country, we felt sure there would be no revolution. The Government was in jeopardy. My private information of what was being done by the organization known as the Communist Party of America, with headquarters in Chicago, of what was being done by the Communist Internationale under their manifesto planned at Moscow last March by Trotzky, Lenine and others, addressed "To the Proletariats of All Countries," of what strides the Communist Labor Party was making, removed all doubt. In this conclusion we did not ignore the definite standards of personal liberty, or free speech, which is the very temperament and heart of the people. The evidence was examined with the utmost care, with a personal leaning toward freedom of thought and word on all questions.

The whole mass of evidence, accumulated from all parts of the country, was scrupulously scanned, not merely for the written or spoken differences of viewpoint as to the government of the United States, but, in spite of these things, to see if the hostile declarations might not be sincere in their announced motive to improve our social order. There was no hope of such a thing.

By stealing, murder and lies, Bolshevism has looted Russia not only of its material strength, but of its moral force. A small clique of outcasts from the East Side of New York has attempted this, with what success we all know. Because a disreputable alien—Leon Bronstein, the man who now calls himself Trotzky—can inaugurate a reign of terror from his throne room in the Kremlin; because this lowest of all types known to New York can sleep in the Czar's bed, while hundreds of thousands in Russia are without food or shelter, should Americans be swayed by such doctrines?

Such a question, it would seem, should receive but one answer from America.

My information showed that communism in this country was an organization of thousands of aliens, who were direct allies of Trotzky. Aliens of the same misshapen caste of mind and indecencies of character, and it showed that they were making the same glittering promises of lawlessness, of criminal autocracy to Americans, that they had made to the Russian peasants. How the Department of Justice discovered upwards of 60,000 of these organized agitators of the Trotzky doctrine in the United States, is the confidential information upon which the Government is now sweeping the nation clean of such alien filth. Merely as a part of this review, to make it complete, it must be shown how the Department of Justice proceeds to cause deportations today. For the moment we must go back to my report to the Senate of the United States, on November 4, 1919, in response to the Senate Resolution of October 14, 1919, which is as follows:

> Resolved, that the Attorney-General of the United States is requested to advise and inform the Senate whether or not the Department of Justice has taken the legal proceedings, and if not, why not, and if so, to what extent, for the arrest and punishment of the various persons within the United States, who, during recent days and weeks, and for a considerable time, continuously previous thereto, it is alleged, have attempted to bring about the forcible overthrow of the Government of the United States; who, it is alleged have preached anarchy and perdition, and who it is alleged have advised the defiance of law and authority, both by the printing and circulation of printed newspapers, books, pamphlets, circulars, stickers, and dodgers, and also by spoken word; and who, in like manner it is alleged, have advised and openly advocated the unlawful obstruction of industry and the unlawful and violent destruction of property, in the pursuance of a deliberate plan and purpose to destroy existing property rights and to impede and obstruct the conduct of business essential to the prosperity and life of the community.
>
> Also the Attorney-General is requested to advise and inform the Senate whether or not the Department of Justice has taken legal proceedings for the arrest and deportation of aliens, who, it is alleged, have, within the United States, permitted the acts aforesaid, and if not, why not, and if so, to what extent.

In replying to this request, I found it necessary to divide the subject under three headings as follows:

(1) The Conditions of Our Legislation; (2) The Deportation of Aliens; (3) General Activities of the Bureau of Investigation of the Department of Justice.

Briefly, in this article, the entire surface of the work of the Department of Justice will be surveyed.

Sedition Reached by Espionage Act

It was shown in my report to the Senate that the Espionage Act, approved June 15, 1917, and amended May 16, 1918, was invoked to be used against seditious utterances and acts, although I felt that it was limited to acts and utterances only which tended to weaken the waging of actual hostilities. Evidently there were others who saw my difficulty, however, among them even Senator Poindexter, who introduced the resolution under which I made my report and who subsequently sought to repeal it, by Congressman LaGuardia, Senator La Follette, Senator France, and Mr. Voigt, in House Bill No. 1697. Nevertheless, I caused to be brought several test prosecutions in order to obtain a court ruling on the Espionage Law and its application to seditions committed since the cessation of the armed activity of our forces.

I did this because our general statutes as to treason and rebellion do not apply to the present radical activities, with the exception of Section 6 of the Federal Penal Code of 1910, which says:

> If two or more persons in any State or Territory or in any place subject to the jurisdiction of the United States conspire to overthrow, put down or to destroy by force, the Government of the United States, or to levy war against them, or to oppose by force the authority thereof, or by force to prevent, hinder or delay, the execution of any law of the United States, or by force to seize, take or possess any porperty of the United States, contrary to the authority thereof, they shall each be fined, not more than $5,000 or imprisonment not more than six years, or both.

Although this Act by no means covered individual activities, under this law I prosecuted the El Arieto Society, an anarchistic organization in operation in Buffalo, N.Y., indicting three of its members for circulating a manifesto which was an appeal to the proletariat to arise and destroy the Government of the United States by force, and substitute Bolshevism or anarchy in place thereof. It was printed in Spanish. Phrases such as, "the proletariat of all countries to invite to participate the revolution," "for all others who suffer the evils of servitude must join in the conflict," "to attack the State directly and assail it without hesitation or compunction," were uncompromisingly seditious advice. In threatening the officers of the Government, the manifesto went on to say, presumably addressing the officers themselves:

> Cannibals, your hour of reckoning has arrived. You have fattened before having your throats cut like hogs. You haven't lived and consequently cannot die decently like men. You are at your wits ends and at the prospects of millions of human beings everywhere rising and not only asking, but demanding and executing vengeance for the promotion of your usurpt interests. Yes, they will overwhelm you. We are convinced that rebellion is the noble vindication of slaves, that from generation to generation the shameful reproach of slavery has now come. Make way for Bolshevism, for the Department of Labor, Mines, Railroads, fields, factories, and shops. Let the Soviet be organized promptly. The ideal is not converted into facts until it has come to consciousness after having been acquired by the sacrifice of innumerable voluntary victims.

On motion to dismiss the indictment this case came before Judge Hazel of the Western District Court of New York, July 24, 1919, who, after hearing counsel, dismissed the case and discharged the defendants. In his opinion the Court, after citing Section 6, said:

> I do not believe that the acts and deeds set forth in the indictment and the evidence given in support of it establish an offense such as this Section which I have just read contemplates.

However, the language of this Spanish document was so violent and desperate in its declarations of defiance to the existing Government of the United States, that I, at once, placed the entire record of this case before the Commissioner of Immigration, with a recommendation that the defendants involved be deported as undesirable aliens.

All deportation activities conducted since by the Department of Justice against the "Reds" have been with the cooperation of the Department of Labor, which issued the warrants of arrest and deportation recommended by evidence that meets the conditions of the Federal Penal Code of 1910. I pointed out to the Senate certain classes of radical activities that might come under certain sections of this Penal Code:

1. Those who have "attempted to bring about the forcible overthrow of the Government of the United States have committed no crime unless their acts amount to treason, rebellion or seditious conspiracy." This is defined in Section 1, 4 and 6 of the Criminal Code above quoted.

No Laws against Some "Red" Crimes

There were other activities of the Reds, however, for which there was no legislation. These were:

2. The preaching of anarchy and sedition is not a crime under the general criminal statutes of the United States.

3. Advising the defiance of law is not a crime under the general criminal laws whether the same be done by printing and circulating literature or by the spoken word.

4. Nor is the advising and openly advocating the unlawful obstruction of industry and the unlawful and violent destruction of property a crime under the United States general statutes.

These conclusions were reached after wide consultation with the best criminal lawyers in the country. In my testimony before the subcommittee of the Judiciary Committee of the Senate on July 14, 1919, at its request, I had fully outlined the conditions threatening internal revolution in the nation that confronted us. Legislation which I then recommended to meet this great menace has not been enacted. This is not my fault, for I knew that Congress was fully aware of the "Reds' " activities in this country.

Many States passed certain acts which embodied the basis of my request to Congress for national legislation bearing upon radicalism. California, Indiana, Michigan, New York, Ohio, Pennsylvania, Washington and West Virginia have passed State laws governing the rebellious acts of the "Reds" in their separate territories. These States have infinitely greater legal force at their command against the revolutionary element than the United States Government for detecting and punishing seditious acts. In their equipment of men to carry out their laws, they far surpass the facilities of the Department of Justice. New York City alone has 12,000 policeman charged with the duty of investigation, and the District Attorney of New York County has a force of over fifty prosecuting attorneys.

Under the appropriations granted by Congress to the Department of Justice, the maximum number of men engaged in the preparation of the violation of all United States laws is limited to about 500 for the entire country. Startling as this fact may seem to the reader who discovers it for the first time, it is the highest testimony to the services of these men, that the Department of Justice of the United States, is today, a human net that no outlaw can escape. It has been netted together in spite of congressional indifference, intensified by the individual patriotism of its personnel aroused to the menace of revolution, inspired to superlative action above and beyond private interests.

One of the chief incentives for the present activity of the Department of Justice against the "Reds" has been the hope that American citizens will, themselves, become voluntary agents for us, in a vast organization for mutual defense against the sinister agitation of men and women aliens, who appear to be either in the pay or under the criminal spell of Trotzky and Lenine.

Deportations Under Immigration Laws

Temporary failure to seize the alien criminals in this country who are directly responsible for spreading the unclean doctrines of Bolshevism here, only increased the determination to get rid of them. Obviously, their offenses were related to our immigration laws, and it was finally decided to act upon that principle. Those sections of the Immigration Law applicable to the deportation of aliens committing acts enumerated in the Senate Resolution of October 14, 1919, above quoted, were found in the Act of Congress, approved October 16, 1918, amending the immigration laws of the United States.

By the administration of this law deportations have been made, the law being as follows:

> Be it enacted by the Senate and House of Representatives of the United States of America in Congress assembled:
>
> Sec. 1. That aliens who are anarchists; aliens who believe in or advocate the overthrow by force or violence of the Government of the United States or of all forms of law; aliens who disbelieve in or who are opposed to all organized government; aliens who advocate or teach the assassination of public officials; aliens who advocate or teach the unlawful destruction of property; aliens who are members of or affiliated with any organization that entertains a belief in, teaches, or advocates the overthrow by force or by violence of the Government of the United States or of all forms of law, or that

> entertains or teaches disbelief in or opposition to all organized Government, or that advocates the duty, necessity or property of the unlawful assaulting or killing of any officer or officers, either of specific individuals or of officers generally, of the Government of the United States, or of any other organized Government, because of his or their official character, or that advocates or teaches the unlawful destruction of property, shall be excluded from admission into the United States.
>
> Sec. 2. That any alien who, at any time, after entering the United States, is found to have been at the time of entry, or to become thereafter, a member of any one of the classes of aliens enumerated in Sec. 1 of this Act, shall upon the warrant of the Secretary of Labor, be taken into custody and deported in the manner provided in the Immigration Act of Feb. 5, 1917. The provisions of this Section shall be applicable to the classes of aliens mentioned in this Act irrespective of the time of their entry into the United States.

Although this law is entirely under the jurisdiction of the Department of Labor, it seemed to be the only means at my disposal of attacking the radical movement. To further this plan, as Congress had seen fit to refuse appropriations to the Department of Labor which might have enabled it to act vigorously against the "Reds," I offered to cooperate with the immigration officials to the fullest extent. My appropriation became available July 19, 1919. I then organized what is known as the Radical Division.

Briefly this is a circumstantial statement of the present activities of the Department of Justice, cooperating with the Department of Labor, against the "Reds." They require no defense, nor can I accept as true the counter claims of the "Reds" themselves, who, apparently indifferent to their disgrace, violent in their threats against the United States Government, until they are out of sight and sound of it, betray the characterless ideas and purposes that Trotzky has impressed upon the criminal classes which constitute communism.

Will Deportations Check Bolshevism?

Behind, and underneath, my own determination to drive from our midst the agents of Bolshevism with increasing vigor and with greater speed, until there are no more of them left among us, so long as I have the responsible duty of that task, I have discovered the hysterical methods of these revolutionary humans with increasing amazement and suspicion. In the confused information that sometimes reaches the people, they are compelled to ask questions which involve the reasons for my acts against the "Reds." I have been asked, for instance, to what extent deportation will check radicalism in this country. Why not ask what will become of the United States Government if these alien radicals are permitted to carry out the principles of the Communist Party as embodied in its so-called laws, aims and regulations?

There wouldn't be any such thing left. In place of the United States Government we should have the horror and terrorism of bolsheviki tyranny such as is destroying Russia now. Every scrap of radical literature demands the overthrow of our existing government. All of it demands obedience to the instincts of criminal minds, that is, to the lower appetites, material and moral. The whole purpose of communism appears to be a mass formation of the criminals of the world to overthrow the decencies of private life, to usurp property that they have not earned, to disrupt the present order of life regardless of health, sex or religious rights. By a literature that promises the wildest dreams of such low aspirations, that can occur to only the criminal minds, communism distorts our social law.

The chief appeal communism makes is to "The Worker." If they can lure the wage earner to join their own gang of thieves, if they can show him that he will be rich if he steals, so far they have succeeded in betraying him to their own criminal course.

Read this manifesto issued in Chicago:

The Communist Party Manifesto

The world is on the verge of a new era. Europe is in revolt. The masses of Asia are stirring uneasily. Capitalism is in collapse. The workers of the world are seeing a new light and securing new courage. Out of the night of war is coming a new day.

The spectre of communism haunts the world of capitalism. Communism, the hope of the workers to end misery and oppression.

The workers of Russia smashed the front of international Capitalism and Imperialism. They broke the chains of the terrible war; and in the midst of agony, starvation and the attacks of the Capitalists of the world, they are creating a new social order.

The class war rages fiercely in all nations. Everywhere the workers are in a desperate struggle against their capitalist masters. The call to action has come. The workers must answer the call!

> The Communist Party of America is the party of the working class. The Communist Party proposes to end Capitalism and organize a workers' industrial republic. The workers must control industry and dispose of the product of industry. The Communist Party is a party realizing the limitation of all existing workers' organizations and proposes to develop the revolutionary movement necessary to free the workers from the oppression of Capitalism. The Communist Party insists that the problems of the American worker are identical with the problems of the workers of the world.

These are the revolutionary tenets of Trotzky and the Communist Internationale. Their manifesto further embraces the various organizations in this country of men and women obsessed with discontent, having disorganized relations to American society. These include the IWWs, the most radical socialists, the misguided anarchists, the agitators who oppose the limitations of unionism, the moral perverts and the hysterical neurasthenic women who abound in communism. The phraseology of their manifesto is practically the same wording as was used by the Bolsheviks for their International Communist Congress.

The Communist Absorbs the Socialist Party

Naturally the Communist Party has bored its revolutionary points into the Socialist Party. They managed to split the Socialists, for the so-called Left Wing of the Socialist Party is now the Communist Party, which specifically states that it does not intend to capture the bourgeosie parliamentary state, but to conquer and destroy, and that the final objective, mass action, is the medium intended to be used in the conquest and destruction of the bourgeosie state to annihilate the parliamentary state, and introduce a revolutionary dictatorship of the Proletariat.

The Left Wing Socialists declared themselves when they issued a call for a convention held in Chicago, September 1, 1919, to organize a Communist Party. An effort was made at a convention of the Socialist Party of America in Chicago, August 30, 1919, to harmonize differences. Their first plan in harmonious endeavor was to refuse admission to their convention to members of the Left Wing, on the ground that the latter intended to capture it. At the Communist Convention of Left Wing Socialists on September 1, 1919, 129 delegates, representing 55,000 members, attended. Extensive Communist propaganda followed, including the establishment of a paper, "The Communist."

There is no legislation at present which can reach an American citizen who is discontented with our system of American Government, nor is it necessary. The dangerous fact to us is that the Communist Party of American is actually affiliated and adheres to the teaching program and tactics of the Third Internationale. Consider what this means.

The first congress of the Communist Nationale held March 6, 1919, in Moscow, subscribed to by Trotzky and Lenine, adopted the following:

> This makes necessary the disarming of the bourgeosie at the proper time, the arming of the laborer, and the formation of a communist army as the protectors of the rules of the proletariat and the inviolability of the social structure.

When we realize that each member of the Communist Party of America pledges himself to the principles above, set forth, deportation of men and women bound to such a theory is a very mild reformatory sentence.

Have the "Reds" Betrayed Labor?

If I were asked whether the American Federation of Labor had been betrayed by the "Reds," I should refer the inquiry to the manifesto and constitution of the Communist Party of America, in which, under the heading, "Revolutionary Construction," the following paragraph appears:

> But the American Federation of Labor, as a whole, is hopelessly reactionary. At its recent convention the A. F. of L. approved the Versailles Peace Treaty and the League of Nations, and refused to declare its solidarity with Soviet Russia. It did not even protest the blockade of Russia and Hungary! This convention, moreover, did all in its power to break radical unions. The A. F. of L. is united with the Government, securing a privileged status in the governing system of State Capitalism. A Labor Party is being organized—much more conservative than the British Labor Party.

It has been inferred by the "Reds" that the United States Government, by arresting and deporting them, is returning to the autocracy of Czardom, adopting the system that created the severity of Siberian banishment. My reply to such charges is, that in our determination to maintain our government we are treating our alien enemies with extreme consideration. To deny them the privilege of remaining in a country which they have openly deplored as an unenlightened community, unfit for those who prefer the privileges of Bolshevism, should be no hardship. It strikes me as an odd form of reasoning that these Russian Bolsheviks who extol the Bolshevik rule, should be so unwilling to return to Russia. The nationality of most of the alien "Reds" is Russian and German. There is almost no other nationality represented among them.

It has been impossible in so short a space to review the entire menace of the internal revolution in this country as I know it, but this may serve to arouse the American citizen to its reality, its danger, and the great need of united effort to stamp it out, under our feet, if needs be. It is being done. The Department of Justice will pursue the attack of these "Reds" upon the Government of the United States with vigilance, and no alien, advocating the overthrow of existing law and order in this country, shall escape arrest and prompt deportation.

It is my belief that while they have stirred discontent in our midst, while they have caused irritating strikes, and while they have infected our social ideas with the disease of their own minds and their unclean morals, we can get rid of them! and not until we have done so shall we have removed the menace of Bolshevism for good.

19. Causes of the Steel Strike, 1919: *Report* of the Commission of Inquiry of the Interchurch World Movement

THE ATROCIOUS conditions under which workers were obliged to labor in the steel industry had been public knowledge at least since President Taft authorized his Department of Commerce and Labor to investigate working conditions in the Bethlehem Steel Company in 1910. During the early stages of the 1919 strike, public and newspaper sentiment seemed to support the strikers and their moderate demands. Not until steel corporations launched a concerted campaign linking the strikers to

SOURCE: The Commission of Inquiry of the Interchurch World Movement, *Report on the Steel Strike of 1919* (New York, 1920), pp. 10–19, 245–251. Reprinted by permission of Harcourt Brace Jovanovich, Inc.

a Bolshevik conspiracy did public opinion swing to the employers' side. A congressional investigation obligingly found evidence of Communist activity. The much more thorough Interchurch inquiry demonstrated that the Communists played almost no role in the walkout and were almost completely inept (and rejected by the strikers) when they belatedly attempted to exploit the disturbance. Furthermore, the investigation corroborated almost all the strikers' complaints and justified their demands.

The first half of the inquiry concerned, primarily, conditions of labor.

The second half concerned, primarily, methods for changing the conditions revealed by the first half.

The second line of inquiry was found to stretch back with decisive effect over the first half; in short, the key to the steel industry, both before and during the strike and now was found in following to its furthest implications this question: What means of conference exist in the steel mills? Both sides agreed that the *occasion* of the strike, leaving aside for the moment its relation to any fundamental cause, was the denial of a conference, requested by organized labor and refused by Mr. Gary.

The inquiry into the means of conference was pursued through the three possible forms of conference: (a) through individuals; (b) through shop committee or company unions; (c) through labor unions.

The complete scope of this phase of the inquiry might be restated as follows:

A. Investigation of a system of denial of organization and collective bargaining (the policy of the Steel Corporation).
B. Investigation of a system or systems of nonunion collective bargaining (existent in certain "independent" plants where strikes had once existed or were feared).
C. Investigation of a movement for collective bargaining and organization of the traditional trade union kind (initiated by the American Federation of Labor and fought by the Steel Corporation).

Inquiry B was not sufficiently completed to be presented in this report, except as a sidelight on the main conditions. The plans in operation or attempted in the Pueblo plant of the Colorado Fuel and Iron Company, the Midvale-Cambria Company, the Bethlehem, Inland and International Harvester plants, etc., did not suggest to the dominant factor, the Steel Corporation, any modification of its policy.

Summarized Conclusions

Sufficient data were analyzed to warrant the following main conclusions concisely stated here and discussed at length in this report and the subreports.

1. The conduct of the iron and steel industry was determined by the conditions of labor accepted by the 191,000 employees in the U. S. Steel Corporation's manufacturing plants.
2. These conditions of labor were fixed by the Corporation, without collective bargaining or any functioning means of conference; also without aboveboard means of learning how the decreed conditions affected the workers.
3. Ultimate control of the plants was vested in a small group of financiers whose relation to the producing force was remote. The financial group's machinery of control gave it full knowledge of output and dividends, but negligible information of working and living conditions.
4. The jobs in the five chief departments of the plants were organized in a pyramid divided roughly into thirds; the top third of skilled men, chiefly Americans, resting on a larger third of semiskilled, all based on a fluctuating mass of common labor. Promotion was at pleasure of company representatives.
5. Rates of pay and other principal conditions were based on what was accepted by common labor; the unskilled and semiunskilled force was largely immigrant labor.
6. The causes of the strike lay in the hours, wages and control of jobs and in the manner in which all these were fixed.
7. *Hours:* Approximately one-half the employees were subjected to the twelve-hour day. Approximately one-half of these in turn were subjected to the seven-day week.
   Much less than one-quarter had a working day of less than ten hours (sixty-hour week).
   The average week for all employees was 68.7 hours; these employees generally believed that a week of over sixty hours ceased to be a standard in other industries fifteen to twenty years ago.
   Schedules of hours for the chief classes of steel workers were from twelve to forty hours longer per week than in other basic industries near steel communities; the American steel average was over twenty hours longer than the British, which ran between forty-seven to forty-eight hours in 1919.
   Steel jobs were largely classed as heavy labor and hazardous.
   The steel companies professed to have restored practically prewar conditions; the hours nevertheless were longer than in 1914

or 1910. Since 1910 the Steel Corporation has increased the percentage of its twelve-hour workers.

The only reasons for the twelve-hour day, furnished by the companies, were found to be without adequate basis in fact. The increased hours were found to be a natural development of large-scale production, which was not restricted by public sentiment or by organization among employees. The twelve-hour day made any attempt at "Americanization" or other civic or individual development for one-half of all immigrant steel workers arithmetically impossible.

8. *Wages:* The annual earnings of over one-third of all productive iron and steel workers were, and had been for years, below the level set by government experts as the *minimum of subsistence* standard for families of five.

   The annual earnings of 72 percent of all workers were, and had been for years, below the level set by government experts as the *minimum of comfort* level for families of five.

   This second standard being the lowest which scientists are willing to term an "American standard of living," it follows that nearly three-quarters of the steel workers could not earn enough for an American standard of living.

   The bulk of unskilled steel labor earned less than enough for the average family's minimum subsistence; the bulk of semi-skilled labor earned less than enough for the average family's minimum comfort.

   Skilled steel labor was paid wages disproportionate to the earnings of the other two-thirds, thus binding the skilled class to the companies and creating divisions between the upper third and the rest of the force.

   Wage rates in the iron and steel industry as a whole are determined by the rates of the U. S. Steel Corporation. The Steel Corporation sets its wage rates, the same as its hour schedules, without conference (or collective bargaining), with its employees.

   Concerning the financial ability of the Corporation to pay higher wages the following must be noted (with the understanding that the Commission's investigation did not include analysis of the Corporation's financial organization): the Corporation vastly increased its undistributed financial reserves during the Great War. In 1914 the Corporation's total undivided surplus was $135,204,471.90. In 1919 this total undivided surplus had been increased to $493,048,201.93. Compared with the wage budgets, in 1918, the Corporation's final surplus after paying dividends of $96,382,027 and setting aside $274,277,835 for Federal taxes payable in 1919, was $466,888,421—a sum large enough to have paid a second time the total wage and salary budget for 1918 ($452,663,524), and to have left a surplus of

> over $14,000,000. In 1919 the undivided surplus was $493,048,-201.93, or $13,000,000 more than the total wage and salary expenditures.[1]

This report does not go into the long dispute over the Corporation's financing, a controversy which blazed up during the strike but not as a part of the issue. A typical criticism printed about this time was the following from the *Searchlight*, commenting on Basil Manly's analysis of Senate Document 259, (a report from the Secretary of the Treasury):

"On the basis of the Steel Corporation's public reports, its net profits for the two years 1916 and 1917, 'after the payment of interest on bonds, and other allowances for all charges growing out of the installation of special war facilities,' amounted, according to Mr. Manly, to $888,931,511. The bonds of the corporation represent all the money actually invested in the concern, for the common stock is 'nothing but water.'

"Of course out of the net income the Steel Corporation had to pay its taxes to the federal government, but the hundreds of millions that remained represented earnings on 'shadow dollars.' "

> Increases in wages during the war in no case were at a sacrifice of stockholders' dividends.
>
> Extreme congestion and unsanitary living conditions, prevalent in most Pennsylvania steel communities, were largely due to underpayment of semi-skilled and common labor.

9. *Grievances:* The Steel Corporation's arbitrary control of hours and wages extended to everything in individual steel jobs, resulting in daily grievances.

   The Corporation, committed to a nonunion system, was as helpless as the workers to anticipate these grievances.

   The grievances, since there existed no working machinery of redress, weighed heavily in the industry, because they incessantly reminded the worker that he had no "say" whatever in steel.

   Discrimination against immigrant workers, based on rivalry of economic interests, was furthered by the present system of control and resulted in race divisions within the community.

10. *Control:* The arbitrary control of the Steel Corporation extended outside the plants, affecting the workers as citizens and the social institutions in the communities.

    The steel industry was under the domination of a policy whose

1. Detailed figures on the Corporation's surpluses, accumulation of which was begun in 1901, are:

1913–Total undivided surplus	$151,798,428.89
1914–Total undivided surplus	135,204,471.90
1915–Total undivided surplus	180,025,328.74
1916–Total undivided surplus	381,360,913.37
1917–Total undivided surplus	431,660,803.63
1918–Total undivided surplus	466,888,421.38
1919–Total undivided surplus	493,048,201.93

aim was to keep out labor unions. In pursuit of this policy, blacklists were used, workmen were discharged for union affiliation, "undercover men" and "labor detectives" were employed and efforts were made to influence the local press, pulpit and police authorities.

In Western Pennsylvania the civil rights of free speech and assembly were abrogated without just cause, both for individuals and labor organizations. Personal rights of strikers were violated by the State Constabulary and sheriff's deputies.

Federal authorities, in some cases, acted against groups of workmen on the instigation of employees of steel companies. In many places in Western Pennsylvania, community authorities and institutions were subservient to the maintenance of one corporation's antiunion policies.

11. The organizing campaign of the workers and the strike were for the purpose of forcing a conference in an industry where no means of conference existed; this specific conference to set up trade union collective bargaining, particularly to abolish the twelve-hour day and arbitrary methods of handling employees.
12. No interpretation of the movement as a plot or conspiracy fits the facts; that is, it was a mass movement, in which leadership became of secondary importance.
13. Charges of Bolshevism or of industrial radicalism in the conduct of the strike were without foundation.
14. The chief cause of the defeat of the strike was the size of the Steel Corporation, together with the strength of its active opposition and the support accorded it by employers generally, by governmental agencies and by organs of public opinion.
15. Causes of defeat, second in importance only to the fight waged by the Steel Corporation, lay in the organization and leadership, not so much of the strike itself, as of the American labor movement.
16. The immigrant steel worker was led to expect more from the twenty-four International Unions of the A. F. of L. conducting the strike than they, through indifference, selfishness or narrow habit, were willing to give.
17. Racial differences among steel workers and an immigrant tendency toward industrial unionism, which was combated by the strike leadership, contributed to the disunity of the strikers.
18. The end of the strike was marked by slowly increasing disruption of the new unions; by bitterness between the "American" and "foreign" worker and by bitterness against the employer, such as to diminish production.

The following question was definitely placed before the Commission of Inquiry: Were the strikers justified? The investigation's data seem to make impossible any other than this conclusion:

The causes of the strike lay in grievances which gave the workers just cause for complaint and for action. These unredressed grievances still exist in the steel industry.

Recommendations

I. Inasmuch as—

a. conditions in the iron and steel industry depend on the conditions holding good among the workers of the U. S. Steel Corporation, and—
b. past experience has proved that the industrial policies of large-scale producing concerns are basically influenced by (1) public opinion expressed in governmental action, (2) labor unions, which in this case have failed, or (3) by both, and—
c. permanent solutions for the industry can only be reached by the Steel Corporation in free cooperation with its employees, therefore—

It is recommended—

a. that the Federal Government be requested to initiate the immediate undertaking of such settlement by bringing together both sides;
b. that the Federal Government, by presidential order or by congressional resolution, set up a commission representing both sides and the public, similar to the Commission resulting from the coal strike; such Commission to—
1. inaugurate immediate conferences between the Steel Corporation and its employees for the elimination of the 12-hour day and the 7-day week, and for the readjustment of wage rates;
2. devise with both sides and establish an adequate plan of permanent free conference to regulate the conduct of the industry in the future;
3. continue and make nationwide and exhaustive this inquiry into basic conditions in the industry.

II. Inasmuch as—

a. the administration of civil law and police power in Western Pennsylvania has created many injustices which persist, and—
b. no local influence has succeeded in redressing this condition, therefore—

It is recommended—

a. that the Federal Government inaugurate full inquiry into the past and present state of civil liberties in Western Pennsylvania and publish the same.

III. Inasmuch as——

a. the conduct and activities of "labor detective" agencies do not seem to serve the best interests of the country, and—
b. the Federal Department of Justice seems to have placed undue reliance on cooperation with corporations' secret services, therefore—

It is recommended—

a. that the Federal Government institute investigation for the purpose of regulating labor detective agencies; and for the purpose of publishing what government departments or public moneys are utilized to cooperate with company "undercover men."

IV. It is recommended that the proper Federal authorities be requested to make public two reports of recent investigations of conditions in the steel industry, in making which public money was spent, and to explain why these and similar reports have not hitherto been made public, and why reports which were printed have been limited to extremely small editions.

(Reference is made specifically to Mr. Ethelbert Stewart's report on civil liberties in Western Pennsylvania, made to the Secretary of Labor; to Mr. George P. West's report made to the War Labor Board; to the Testimony of the Senate Committee's strike investigation, 2 vols., printed in an edition of 1,000 only; and to Senate Document 259.)

V. It is recommended that the Industrial Relations Department of the Interchurch World Movement continue and supplement the present inquiry into the iron and steel industry with particular reference to——
1. Company unions and shop committees;
2. Social, political and industrial beliefs of the immigrant worker;
3. Present aims of production in the industry.
4. Conduct of trade unions with reference to democracy and to responsibility.

VI. It is recommended that immediate publication, in the most effective forms possible, be obtained for this report with its sub-reports.

Concluding

The Summarized Conclusions and Recommendations of the Report have been transferred for convenience to pages 11–19 in Chapter I (Introduction) from the end of the book, where they belong naturally, inasmuch as they were formulated after all the foregoing analyses and discussion had been drafted.

The gist of the Conclusions is that conditions in the steel industry "gave the workers just cause for complaint and for action" and that "these unredressed grievances still exist."

The gist of the Recommendations is that the Federal Government set up a commission for the industry, in order to initiate free, open conference between those who must always be chiefly responsible for settlement of the industry's problems:—its owners and its workers. To this is added recommendation for persistent investigation and publicity.

In pursuit of its recommendations and in concluding its immediate task, the Commission put this report before the American people and the American people's government, in the person of President Wilson. The action of the Commission virtually raised this question of fundamental importance:

> Is the nation helpless before conditions in a basic industry which promise a future crisis? Can our democratic society be moved to do industrial justice without the pressure of crisis itself?

As a part of the task of publishing the facts and as a means of expressing their judgment as Christians, the Commissioners requested a committee to draw up, for separate free distribution, if possible, a compact form of General Findings based on the Conclusions of the Report. Necessarily they are in part repetitious, but they were designed to include expressions of moral judgment, such as were not the first concern of the Report. A subcommittee, of which Dr. Alva W. Taylor was chairman, drafted these findings, which were presented to the Executive Committee of the Interchurch Movement with the Report on May 10, 1920, as adopted by the Commission.

Findings

1. The fundamental grievances were found to be:
   a. Excessive hours
   b. The "boss system"
   c. No right to organize or to representation.

2. The remedies desired were:
   a. Shorter day and week with a living wage
   b. Representation and conference, and an end to the "boss system" which so often subjects common labor to petty tyrannies

c. Right to unionize and a substitution of industrial democracy for industrial autocracy.

3. These grievances were of long standing, but had found no expression because:
   a. They were limited largely to foreigners of many races and languages without industrial tradition, education or leadership to organize
   b. Race prejudice effectually kept the more skilled, more intelligent and better paid American workmen from taking up the cause of the foreign-speaking workmen
   c. Labor unions have been accustomed to look upon the foreigner as an actual or potential strike breaker
   d. The steel companies have most effectively deterred men from joining labor organizations.

4. These long-standing grievances were brought to expression by:
   a. The part these workingmen played in the war and the treatment afforded them for the sake of war production which gave them a new sense of worth and independence
   b. The fight for democracy and news of a larger workingmen's freedom in their native lands together with a growing sense of real Americanism, which brought a spirit of democracy to their ranks
   c. The decision of the American Federation of Labor to organize them and its actual work of organizing them into Craft Unions.

5. We found:
   a. That the strike was regularly conducted in orthodox fashion according to the A. F. of L. rules and principles
   b. That while radicals sympathized with the strikers, as was natural, they were effectually debarred by the strike leaders and that far from having influence in it, they often denounced and opposed those who conducted the strike.

6. We find the grievances to have been real:
   a. The average week of 68.7 hours, the twelve-hour day, whether on a straight twelve-hour shift or on a broken division of 11-13 or 10-14 hours, the unbroken 24-hour work period at the turn of a shift and the underpayment of unskilled labor, are all inhuman
   b. It is entirely practicable to put all processes requiring continuous operation on a straight eight-hour basis as is illustrated by the Colorado Fuel and Iron Company. These processes require the services of only a fraction of the workers
   c. The "boss system" is bad, the plant organization is military and the control autocratic. The companies' claims, that they accord the right to join unions and the opportunity of con-

ference, are theoretical; neither is allowed in practice

d. The use of "undercover" men is severely condemned. It breeds distrust, breaks down morals and stimulates ill will; it is undemocratic and un-American

e. The refusal of the United States Steel Corporation to confer, to accept mediation and its attitude of hauteur as shown by its refusal to follow the recommendations of the War Labor Board incited labor strife and because of the strength and influence of this Corporation, forms one of the greatest obstacles to a just settlement of industrial grievances and unrest at this time.

7. The Strike was defeated by:

a. The strike-breaking methods of the steel companies and their effective mobilization of public opinion against the strikers through the charges of radicalism, bolshevism, and the closed shop, none of which were justified by the facts; and by the suppression of civil rights

b. The hostility of the press giving biased and colored news and the silence of both press and pulpit on the actual question of justice involved; which attitudes of press and pulpit helped to break the strikers' morale

c. Public fear of a general labor war, to the coincidence of the coal strike and threat of the railroad strike, together with labor's failure to formulate and explain its purposes with regard to public service

d. The prevailing prejudice in the steel towns and in the general public mind and among the English-speaking workingmen against the foreigners who constituted the overwhelming number of the strikers

e. The ineffective support given the strike by most of the twenty-four affiliated Craft Unions through which it was organized, and by the A. F. of L.

8. Recommendations:

1. The adoption of the eight-hour shift on all continuous processes

2. Limiting of the day to not more than ten hours on duty, with not more than a six-day and a fifty-four-hour week, with at least a minimum comfort wage

3. Recognition of right to join regular Craft Unions or any other freely chosen form of labor organization; recognition of right to open conference, either through shop committees or union representatives; recognition of right of collective bargaining

4. A vast extension of house building—by the communities where possible; by the steel companies where community building is inadequate or impossible.

5. That organized labor:

a. Democratize and control the unions, especially in regard to the calling, conduct and settlement of strikes
b. Reorganize unions with a view of sharing in responsibility for production and in control of production processes; to this end:
    1. Repudiating restriction of production as a doctrine
    2. Formulating contracts which can be lived up to
    3. Finding a substitute for the closed shop wherever it is a union practice
c. Scrupulously avoid all advocates of violence
d. Accept all possible proffers of publicity and conciliation
e. Promote Americanization in all possible ways and insist upon an American standard of living for all workingmen
f. Prepare more adequate technical information for the public in regard to all conditions bearing upon the calling and the conduct of a strike.
g. Seek alliance and council from the salaried class known as brain workers.

6. That the President's Industrial Conference's plan for standing tribunals of conciliation and publicity be given a fair trial. We believe that the most effective step to be taken for the obtaining of justice in a strike situation is through publicity, conciliation and a voluntary system of arbitration; and as a beginning we recommend the fullest publication of these findings and of our more complete reports
7. That minimum wage commissions be established and laws enacted providing for an American standard of living through the labor of the natural breadwinner permitting the mother to keep up a good home and the children to obtain at least a high school education
8. That the Federal Government investigate the relations of Federal authorities to private corporations' "undercover" men and to "labor detective agencies."
9. That the eight-hour day be accepted by labor, capital and the public as the immediate goal for the working day and that government provide by law against working days that bring over-fatigue and deprive the individual, his home and his community of that minimum of time which gives him an opportunity to discharge all his obligations as a social being in a democratic society.

We recommend to the press that it free itself of the all too well-founded charge of bias, favoring capital as against labor and redeem its power as a promoter of truth and a formulator of public opinion by searching out all the facts in regard to industrial questions and publishing them without fear or favor.

We plead with the pulpit that it be diligent to discharge its legitimate prophetic role as an advocate of justice, righteousness and humanity in all such conflicts of human interest as those involved in industrial strife.

We condemn unsparingly those authorities who suspended the right of free speech and peaceful assemblage before, during and after the steel strike.

We recommend that the Industrial Department of the Interchurch World Movement and the Social Service Commission of the Federal Council of Churches continue this type of impartial investigation of industrial strife and unrest and extend it to studies of general conditions in industry affecting the life, peace, and welfare of all concerned and that their findings be published as a means of enlightening public opinion, begetting impartial judgment, and promoting industrial justice and peace.

Conclusion

All the conditions that caused the steel strike continue to exist. We feel that unless changes are made approximating in some degree the findings here presented, further unrest is inevitable and another strike must come. In the measure that workingmen become intelligent and Americanized, will they refuse to labor under such conditions.

20. Cultural Pluralism—an Alternative to the Melting Pot: Horace Meyer Kallen

A GROUP *of Jewish, Catholic, and Negro intellectuals led a counterattack against demands by 100 percenters that minority ethnic groups must be "melted down" into true Americans and that meanwhile free immigration must cease and Negroes must remain subordinate. Horace Kallen's theory of cultural pluralism, though not influential during the 1920s, later received recognition as an original contribution to disputes about the ultimate nature of American civilization. Actually, Kallen's arguments elaborated those presented in the journals of the National Catholic Welfare Conference and the NAACP and in some foreign language newspapers like New York's Jewish Daily Forward.*

"Americanization" and the Cultural Prospect

That the image of these United States as a "melting pot" might be a delusion and its imputed harmony with democracy a snare was not an idea which, prior to the Great War, seemed even possible to Americans, whether of the philanthropic or the academic or the business community. The spontaneous invincible egotism of the group was too impenetrable and the absorption in the autochthonous interests of the national enterprise—evangelism, industrial expansion, finance and the struggle of political parties—was too complete, either for self-observation or for comparison with others. The admitted, and lamented, cultural inferiority to Europe was held to be more than compensated for by the claim of political superiority. The patriotic sentiment, the appreciation of national character, was concentrated in the word "democracy," and in democracy the United States was still felt to be the nonpareil among the nations, the paragon and avatar of a state of literally free and equal citizens, or at least, if not equal in fact, equal in opportunity for every man to become the same as his betters. The traits of these betters were envisaged as the traits of the essential American, and personified as Uncle Sam. The current leaders of the community were accepted as variants of him, and each in his turn—Bryan or Roosevelt, for example—was hailed as the "typical" American. Whoever failed to acknowledge and to conform to this type was somehow alien, a different order of being, not admissible to the benefits of democracy, and fit at best to be a hewer of wood and a drawer of water to the true Americans.

The historic name for this attitude and sentiment is Know-Nothingism. Know-Nothingism is not, of course, an American but a human trait. What differs from ourselves we spontaneously set upon a different level of value. If it seems to be strong it is called wicked and is feared; if it is regarded as weak, it is called brutish and exploited. Sometimes, as in the attitude toward the negro, the emotions interpenetrate and become a sentiment focalizing the worst qualities of each. Only watchful discipline, much suffering or rare sophistication enables us to acknowledge the equality in nature and peerage in the community of that which is different and strange, enables us to give its individuality understanding and its character respect. Otherwise, these are won from us by conflict, not yielded by good will, and most completely so among peoples, nations, states.

That the paragon and avatar of democracy should be an exception to this rule would have been morally proper but naturally impossible. The newcomers in the United States figured significantly, therefore, only as so much cheap labor power, not as sentient men and women with temperaments, histories and hungers, settling down as neighbors in the house next door, to make a life as well as a living. As neighbors they were "undesirable," and over the barriers raised against them only a few of them could pass into the free intimacies of the neighborly life. On the whole and in the long run, they remained in their own communities, with their churches as the focus of the common life, and their "Americanization" consisted of their compenetration into the country's economic and political pattern, and of that alone. The residue of their being, where they were freest and most at home, remained continuous with their own old-worldly inheritance. As this inheritance did not enter into the overt contacts of economics and politics, it was ignored. Such attention as was given it, was given it as only an aspect of the struggles and rivalries in those fields of the national life, and then only to suit the occasion. Defeated parties had always the traditional animadversions to make on the political corruption and economic obstreperousness due to depraved aliens.

So, as in the new world the aliens grew in mass, number and articulation, they changed in the form and in the intensity of their consciousness. When, at last, interest was directed upon their peculiar status in the cultural complex of American life, and upon the qualities and implications of their communities for excellence and evil in American society, Europe was at war, and the hateful passions of that unhappy continent were echoing and swelling across the waters. Social intelligence, never too keen in America, got beclouded by sharp partisanship and vague fears. Anxiety over the economic significance of the immigrant was reenforced by anxiety over his social significance. A turmoil of organization and fulmination ensued, with the late Colonel Roosevelt in his usual role of drum major and prophet. Protecting the immigrant; restraining him; keeping him out; compelling him to conform to ourselves; doing at least something to the immigrant and especially talking all sorts of phantasies about him, became the order of the day. Only in very rare instances was any fundamental attempt made to discern the forces in American social life with which the immigrant was involved, and to analyze out their behavior and relationships.

And even in those cases the philosophical preconceptions and national eventualities of the ethnic, economic and cultural differences of the communities composing the complex and vivid pattern of American nationhood could not fail of contagion from the burning issues underlying the civil war in Europe. One publicist,[1] grown up in the tradition that equality and similarity were synonymous, had, in the course of his own reflection upon the character of civilization in the United States, come to the realization of the democratic significance and necessity of free diversification for groups no less than for individuals. He had grown distrustful of the uniformity and monotony imposed by the material conditions of modern life, and had reached the conclusion that diversity was not a menace to but a promise for democracy. Another, the late Randolph Bourne, saw his country over against the melee of national rivalries in Europe as a "transnational America." The currents of modern life, he thought, rendered impossible tight geographical groupings of nationality. The world's population was once more adrift. Labor had been rendered unprecedentedly mobile. Groups were involved in temporary as well as permanent mixings, mixings in such wise that they could maintain their distinctive cultural individualities without special territorial sovereignties or political institutions. Thus, the great North American republic, with its free institutions and continental spaces, was a wonderful promise of the reconciliation without the destruction of the diverse races of Europe, one nation of many peoples. John Dewey, regarding the same situation in the light of the problems of education, came, although his sense of the solidity and continuity of the ethnic groups was much weaker than Bourne's, to very much the same conclusion. "Such terms as Irish-American or Hebrew-American or German-American," he wrote in 1916, "are false terms because they seem to assume something which is already in exis-

1. Cf. Norman Hapgood in the *Menorah Journal.*

tence called America, to which the other factors may be externally hitched on. The fact is, the genuine American, the typical American, is himself a hyphenated character. This does not mean that he is part American and that some foreign ingredient is then added. It means that . . . he is international and interracial in his makeup. He is not American plus Pole or German. But the American is himself Pole-German-English-French-Spanish-Italian-Greek-Irish-Scandinavian-Bohemian-Jew—and so on. The point is to see to it that the hyphen connects instead of separates. And this means at least that our public schools shall teach each factor to respect every other, and shall take pains to enlighten all as to the great past contributions of every strain in our composite makeup. . . . I wish our teaching of American history in the schools would take more account of the great waves of migration by which our land for over three centuries has been continuously built up, and make every pupil conscious of the rich breadth of our national makeup. When every pupil recognizes all the factors which have gone into our being, he will continue to prize and reverence that coming from his own past, but he will think of it as honored in being simply one factor in forming a whole nobler and finer than itself. In short, unless our education is nationalized in a way which recognizes that the peculiarity of our nationalism is its internationalism, we shall breed enmity and division in our frantic efforts to secure unity. . . . Since as a nation we are composed of the representatives of all nations who have come here to live in peace with one another and to escape the enmities and jealousies which characterize old-world nations, to nationalize our education means to make it an instrument in the active and constant suppression of the war spirit and in the positive cultivation of sentiments of respect and friendship for all men and women, wherever they live."

Dewey, Hapgood, Bourne, could not but be the exceptions. Public opinion as a whole responded with the customary clamor of blind fear. It echoed almost to a man Roosevelt's demand that immigrants should be required at once to forget their past and cut themselves off from their present connections, learn English and be naturalized or expelled from the country. In the interval between America's participation in the war and the making of the peace, this sentiment grew. Its animus was not then, however, directed against the total complex of European heritages upon American soil. It was directed only against the enemy, not the friendly alien. The former was the true, the divisive hyphenate, and his language, his civilization, and his cooking[2] were equally anathema. In the beginning he was almost exclusively the German-speaking immigrant from the Central Empires; toward the end the person of any speech having origin in or acknowledging sympathy with the revolutionary All Russian Soviet Republic was joined to him. Other former denizens of these Empires, and after the Revolution in Russia, Czarist émigrés, in their societies and groupings, became to the government objects of special appreciative regard, while the magnification of the unique ethnic and cultural virtues of the Allies was a paean of advertising beyond words. All these appreciations, all these emphatic hyphenations, were of course, to a large degree war phenomena, instruments and engines in the warfare of propaganda and morale abroad, devices and agencies in the business of financing and espionage at home. The Poles, the Jews, the Czechs, the Italians, the Greeks, every nationality represented in appreciable numbers on these shores, became the subjects of intriguing consideration to their brethren abroad, and of solicitous interest to their government at home. Indeed, the departments of government changed toward these nationalities, as it were, overnight, from an attitude of *laissez faire* to an attitude of hysterical interference and manipulation. From the Postmaster General, from the Secretary of Labor, of State, of the Treasury, and from the Attorney General, there came upon them a flood of concerned and confusing attention. On the one hand, their publications were coerced, controlled or suppressed; on the other, they were invited to fill their columns with items of public information fabricated *ad hoc*. On the one hand, their racial and national associations were used to effect American policies in Austria-Hungary, in Germany, in Russia; on the other their meetings were raided and their members unlawfully arrested and jailed. On the other hand their social organizations and linguistic facilities were being drafted to sell liberty bonds and thrift stamps; on the other, their members were being defrauded and reduced to penury by the Office of the Alien Property Custodian. On the one hand their brethren abroad were declared the cherished beneficiaries of the American program of democracy and self-determination; on the

2. On the menus of restaurants "German-fried potatoes" became "American-fried" and sauerkraut became "liberty cabbage."

other, they themselves were filled with "undercover" agents of Mr. Palmer's Department of Justice and denounced for the slightest deviation from conventional opinion by one or more of the 250,000-odd members of its voluntary spy system, the "Citizens' Protective Association."

Among the legion of unconscious comedies which the officers of government perpetrated, none was so comic—or so pitiful—as the confusion of public policy and the aggravation of alien terrors they so successfully accomplished during the war. The defense of the most trivial "rights" of nationality abroad, the violation of the most basic rights of man at home; collusion with nationalist organizations in foreign policy, suppression of even the religious use of their national speech in domestic policy; a draft army one third of whose numbers is foreign born; persecution of the brothers, the wives, the fathers and mothers and uncles and cousins of this soldiery because they are foreign born—such is the wartime behavior of the government, preparing for a long war. Then, suddenly, the armistice: the rising and unexhausted tide of propaganda-drunk, warlike emotion unexpectedly deprived of its object; its projection upon the "reds" in place of the Germans; its elaboration by the Attorney General's Okhrana into the witch-hunting red hysteria; illegal seizures; frame-ups; persecutions; third degrees; deportations; on all sides great groups of people thrown back upon themselves, rendered fearful of their neighbors, fearful of each other, fearful of the government; on all sides driven into a state of feeling that must, undispelled, progressively insulate them against any sort of assimilation into the American community.

This feeling, which was an induction from the mass feeling, continually whipped to new intensity by the reptile press, of the more or less native Americans, impelled immigrants to seize the first opportunity to flee the country. They preferred the security of Europe in destruction to the insecurity of the "law-and-order" lynching bees of government departments, newspapers and 100 percent Americanist mobs. Four hundred thousand of them left for the countries of their origin in the second year of the armistice, the governments of some of these countries, like Poland, stimulating and facilitating the return of their nationals; the governments of all, even of Britain, exhibiting a hitherto nonexistent concern about their movements, cultural development and social destiny.

The mass feeling of the more or less native Americans found another and far more significant pattern of self-expression than that of government confusion and mob turmoil. Like all deep and wide-ranging public emotion, it came to rest in an ideology, an orthodoxy of dogma to which all were to conform, whether freely or under compulsion. This orthodoxy was integrated and focalized in the term "Americanization." By means of it feeling was articulated in formula and restlessness drawn into a channel wherein it became policy. Between the indefinitely distensible formulae of Americanization and the restricted channels of possible execution there was a Rabelaisian contrast. For the formulae, being purely discharges of feeling unrestrained by fact, only served to make conspicuous the irrationality, the extravagance, and hysteria usual in such phenomena; while action, being, when it is sincere and not either politic or mad, of necessity relevant to fact, tended, wherever it really occurred, to deflate the formulae to dimensions of sanity and to convert them from devices for the salvation of the panic-stricken into descriptions of the machinery of group adjustment for the reasonable. The formulae were monstrous birth cries for the parturition of such a mouse of real action. Thus, the Superintendent of the Public Schools of New York City, describing in August 1918, what must be meant by Americanization, called it "broadly speaking . . . an appreciation of the institutions of this country, absolute forgetfulness of all obligations or connections with other countries because of descent or birth."[3] This commandment expressed the tension and temper of innumerable traders, manufacturers and bankers and their derivative economic groups, such as newspaper writers, clerks, congressmen, and other politicians, school committees and their superintendents or shop managers, and all others who were and who knew they were in a relation of organic dependence on the first group. "The institutions of this country" had a special signification for them: they were not the institutions in the totality of their diversified function and import in the national life; they were the institutions in so far and only in so far as they served to maintain the privileged classes in America secure in their privileges. These classes have no direct apprehension of the psyche of any social or ethnic group other than their own.

3. Reported in the *New York Evening Post*, August 9, 1918.

They are proverbially timid, and they act and talk on fear far more than on need, and on need far oftener than on understanding. What they knew about the immigrant was neither seen, nor heard, nor encountered; it was transmitted in words by a specious press,[4] anxious about its advertising, an oratorical rotary club, a scared chamber of commerce, social club, or defense society organized *ad hoc*. Most frequently it was the broadside of a sinister economic or political interest.

That time—he, the notorious healer of all hurt—will put a period to the public sentiment underlying the Americanization hysteria and shift the approval of public opinion from the coercive to the persuasive conception of public policy regarding the integration of immigrant groups and native society, is by no means a foregone conclusion. The causes of disturbance are as varied as they are lasting. Their repression on one side leads most of the time only to their protrusion on another. Alone the coincidence of ethnic differences with economic stratification is enough to exacerbate a condition which, with the pressure of immigration removed, must of necessity tend toward fixation. One need only cast an eye over the negro-white relations in the South to realize the limit that such a condition would, unchecked, engender. And even checked, with all the healing that time might bring, the current of public sentiment would still have left institutional deposits, have set up interests and organizations whose pattern of behavior and endeavor to survive would be postulated upon his sentiment. The Ameri-

4. The most illuminating record for the period in article, story and cartoon is that of the *Saturday Evening Post*—one of the largest and most expensive advertising sheets in America. To these may be added the utterances of such organizations as the industrial department of the Young Men's Christian Association and its head, Dr. Peter Roberts; the industrial committee of the North American Civic League for Immigrants; the latter's subsidiary, Order and Liberty Alliance; the National Security League; the United Americans; the Ku Klux Klan; the Loyal American League; the National American Council, whose president is David Jayne Hill; whose vice-presidents are Charles D. Orth of the National Security League, F .W. Galbraith of the American Legion, Albert E. Shiels of the Inter-Racial Council, and whose constituent organizations are the Constitutional League of America, the Inter-Racial Council, the American Legion, the Veterans of Foreign Wars, the Sons of the American Revolution, the Daughters of the American Revolution, the Daughters of 1812, the American Defense Society, the Constitutional Defense League, the National Security League, the Chamber of Commerce of the United States.

canizers and the Americanization agencies are themselves such interests and organizations. Such, also, the immigrant institutions, now reenforced and sustained by the solicitude of the new and old governments abroad, have been compelled to become. These, and the protective reactions which they express against the assault of the public sentiment to which they are in part a reply, form the mutually sustaining halves of a circle; a complete, a closed circle. Only a stronger sentiment of another nature can break this circle, break it either by displacing the original mood as the power sustaining the interests and organizations, or by diverting the nourishing energy of opinion into the generation and sanction of other vocations and institutions. The likelihood of such an eventuality, however, seems at present too remote. Unless it happens soon, it will happen too late.

For the Americanization emotion of 1919 was no eccentric or isolated phenomenon, no idiosyncratic aspect of war psychology. The moods of war were added unto it, but did not create it; they intensified it, but its original force did not come from them. Nor was its source—as some, following the current fashion of interpreters of social behavior, opine—in the conflict of economic interests. Organized labor's attitude toward immigration might be so envisaged, and the passing complication of the immigrant with economic radicalism might be so envisaged. But the classes in whom the Americanization psychosis was most compulsive and outstanding were the classes whose economic interests are most fully served by un-Americanized, that is, by cheap, ignorant and slavish immigrant labor, such as Judge Gary's liberalism toward the immigrant specifically calls for. The more intelligent among these classes, such as the Inter-Racial Council, recognized this, and set themselves hard at the task of persuading their peers of it—with doubtful success. The mood of 1919 has an authenticated ancestry in the story of the persistent temper of public sentiment in the United States. It is the old Know-Nothingism in contemporary dress. This Know-Nothingism was not postulated on either economic rivalry or war anxiety. It was postulated on something more protean and more enduring, on something taboo to law and intelligence, something that even derision strengthens and scorn confirms. The something is religious tradition, the prejudice of cultus. Its language is various, but its mood is the same. It is transmitted through one of the most basic and intimate of community groupings and it goes on, from the Massachusetts colonials to their offspring in the fourth, and even the forty and fourth, generation. It has, of course, its peaks and its valleys, its cycles of mania and depression. The postarmistice manifestations were a period of mania. The witch hunting of the Quaker Attorney General, Palmer, the czaristically inspired Jew-baiting of the Baptist automobile maker, Ford, the malevolent mass mummery of the Ku Klux Klan, the racial rumblings[5] of Mr. Madison Grant, Mrs. Gertrude Atherton, the *Saturday Evening Post*, are all, ultimately, manifestations of this Know-Nothingism. The economic process has, on the whole, tended to reenforce rather than to subdue it. There is the possibility that it might, by shifting the balance of social power, drain it, and finally dry it up. But this is only a possibility, and at best, a possibility of the far future. The testimony of history favors rather the cumulative integration and enhanced rate of explosion of the emotions underlying this Know-Nothingism.

Intellectuals dealing with the process and qualities of group adjustment in the United States have altogether overlooked the psychological substructure of American Know-Nothingism, its patterns and periods. As it is the non-British, not the native community, that is being thereby challenged as a menace, the attention of the intellectuals has been devoted to the analysis and dissipation of this imputed menace, and to the restoration of that complacency of conduct which is the crown of unruffled feelings. They have been content to pass by the prior question regarding the specific nature and social significance of that which the non-British communities are said to be a menace to, and which would have to absorb them and digest them, converting them into flesh of its flesh and soul of its soul, if it is to be forever inviolate and safe. Assimilation, declares the Carnegie Study, is as inevitable as it is desirable. But of what, to what? How is assimilation to be understood? As a cooperative harmony, which is the outcome of mutual respect, understanding and adjustment, on the rule of one for all and all for one, or as the dissolution and absorption of diversities, on the rule of all for one and all in one? The very language of the

5. Directly derivative from the race mythology imagined in Germany and elaborated for pan-Germans by Houston Stewart Chamberlain, a renegade Englishman.

Study, written about "foreigners" from the standpoint of the American native insecure in their presence, shows how impossible it is for the best will in the world to avoid sharing the native emotion and the native assumption that alien heritages, which are "methods of valuation," are inferior to the native and must give way to the native. This assumption of superiority is, of course, automatic, universal, and endemic. It is to be found everywhere that individual or group diversities confront one another. It is everywhere a defense against and an evasion of the intolerable alternative which challenges every student of civilization—the alternative, namely, that the heritage which is his, is at least not better than and perhaps not as good as the heritage which confronts his. Yet intelligence cannot be honest or effective in this field, cannot *be* intelligence, until it has learned not only to tolerate but to feel at home with this intolerable thing. Until it does, it will at bottom, like the Carnegie Study, knowingly or unknowingly, condone conformity and approve submission.

And conformity and submission are what will seem to come. But only seem. For the adaptability of life is wonderful, and communities, like persons, suffer much and surrender more, only to save their souls alive. The compulsion of native mores is a stimulus to which the American of non-British stock makes appropriate response. But the response is far from determined by this stimulus alone. In one way or another, that inward half of his being, the "methods of valuation," the group patternings, the consuetudinous rhythms and symbols of custom and speech that are his heritage, the springs of his character, will color and direct his response. This inward half necessarily and automatically behaves in such a way as to maintain itself and grow, and if it is prevented from doing so directly, openly, in free interplay with its social milieu—then, necessarily and automatically, it will do so obliquely, hiddenly, in conflict with its milieu. The milieu may exterminate it, but the milieu will not assimilate it. It will fight like the Irish, or recede behind the church like the Poles, or intrench itself in cult like the Pennsylvania Dutch or generate protective adaptations like the Jews. But it will not of its own will give up the ghost. It will automatically defend itself from day to day, and to gain strength concede its own failure, justify itself by the ideology of its opponents, and carry on; all with the deepest, naïvest sincerity, the greatest piety, to the ineffables of the ruling society, the utmost deference toward this society's taboos.[6] All the valuations of the majority, its idols from cave, market place, forum, closet and altar, are automatically and unconsciously used as agencies to conserve the integrity of the minority's values. . . . Conceivably, a newborn Chinese child, brought up from its first cry in a loving Yankee family, might for all practical purposes be a Yankee. The patterns of its behavior and the contents of its mind would certainly be Yankee. And if enough such infants could be so brought up, they might compose a race of Mongolian Yankees. The thing would seem far easier, less unnatural, with children of the non-Yankee European stocks. If America be a melting pot, this is the thing that is done.

Only, the United States is no more, and no less, a melting pot than any other country in the world. In the nature of things, none can be, for the particular condition—just exemplified—which might make it one is precisely the condition which can never obtain. Birth, which we do not choose, carries with it simultaneously certain cultural acquirements of a nature so basic, so primary, as to be indistinguishable from inheritance. The acquirements are, in fact, the infant's immediate social inheritance. They are the aboriginal impressions from the familial milieu. This, with its predominantly ethnic elements, tone and rhythms, is more than any other continuous with the past. The present substance of the past may be rich, elaborated and various, or thin and threadbare, but certain indefinable essentials endure. They set the infant's mind and predetermine the direction of its larger reactions in many more and socially more significant ways than the purely sexual with which Freud and his school concern themselves. Particularly, they establish the lines of association, the preferences of the herd type in which the individual feels freest and most at ease, in which he can feel relaxed and be at play. These appear to be prevailingly ethnic. Italians and Jews and Yankees and Irishmen may have become people of a single culture, tradition, aspiration and public behavior, yet they will regularly associate with people of their own racial and familial tone, and their marriages will not so very largely

6. Cf. Mr. Ludwig Lewisohn's "wealthy Jewish physician who had turned Methodist in his boyhood, avoided all questionable subjects, prayed at love feasts in the church, and, though he surreptitiously distributed alms among the poor Jews of the city, achieved a complete conformity of demeanor." He has his comrades in every race.

overflow the boundaries set by these factors and by their churches. The United States is conspicuously marked by groupings of this kind. . . .

The social story, in sum, is the story of both the persistence and diversification of individual temperament and familial tradition. The persistent ones get integrated and emphasized in larger forms of association. Of these the religious has been the most continuous and the most important. But all of them have constituted communities tending to preserve and to sustain the continuity of the physical stock. Empirically, race is nothing more than this continuity confirmed and enchanneled in basic social inheritances. It is hardly distinguishable from nationality.

As to "democracy":

The confusion about Democracy is greater and more passionate than the confusion about race. Race, when all is said and done, remains an academic conception, a residual issue in the social life of the European peoples of the world. It is invoked as an accessory to the strengthening and justification of other issues which are nearer, more momentous, more "practical." Democracy, however, is itself an issue of practice, invoked in every crisis of economy or politics that arises between the societies which make up the conflict and community of the national life. It is a eulogium applied variously—to an article of political faith, abstract and metaphysically grounded; to an attitude of mind; to a program of reform. It is simultaneously and successively an engine accessory to class struggles; a process of social conflict and readjustment; and a formulary sanctification of the *status quo*. The numerous items to which it is applied are often in fact mutually contradictory and exclusive of one another, according to the efficacious interests they conceal or propound. But they all have the same ideological root which is laid bare whenever some protagonist of democracy, crowded in argument, feels himself against the ropes. This root is the conception of thought ceased, only to be replaced by legalism. The political premises went unquestioned; issues came to crisis only about their implications. Political thinking ceased to be reflection and became scholasticism with the Supreme Court in the role of the Benedictines and Franciscans, and the Constitution for a Summa Theologiae.

Hope was strong that the declaration of political independence which was consummated by the acknowledgment of the British colonies as free and sovereign states would have further consummation in esthetic and cultural sovereignty. Aspiring patriots hungered for independence and freedom in the spiritual life. Culturally, America was to be an autonomous creative whole, self-sufficient and self-sufficing, with its own sovereign painting, sculpture, architecture, music and literature, literature particularly, the peer of any, with a claim equal to any on international recognition and regard. That these did not exist was acknowledged, but the sense of cultural inferiority and the feeling of esthetic insufficiency was more than compensated for by the cultural hope. Of course the United States was a raw country, of course it was a young country, undeveloped, unadorned. Was it not also, however, a free country, and a good country, with an empty past, and therefore, inevitably, a uniquely noble future? Sooner or later, probably sooner, the great American artist would appear, to captivate and astound. Irving, Poe, Emerson, Whitman, Howells, and their literary descendants of this day and generation issued the same challenge and uttered the same prophecy. They called many, and never a one was chosen. Whitman's "literatus" is still a hope deferred, and that hope deferred turns to despair is not a maxim for nothing. It is exemplified in at least the yearning distress of the "younger intellectuals."

Also eager and declarant of literary and cultural independence, and more so, than their forbears, the young ones cry aloud that the young country and the good country and the free country has failed to keep its promise. It has produced pigs instead of poets, machines and money instead of men, bunk instead of beauty. It is a country evangelical, superficial, afraid of ideas, gullible and smart; starved in its intellectual and esthetic life, coarse in its pleasures, vulgar in its tastes, surrendering all things pertaining to the spirit into the hands of the female of the species. Of its artists it makes merchants, of its thinkers, preachers. Demanding, above all, conformity, it stifles genius and prostitutes talent. How, unendowed with an autonomous cultural past, can it have a cultural future? It is still merely colonial, "an English colonial possession," says Mr. Mencken, "intellectually and spiritually." The American author who would be American is, staying at home, condemned to "a sort of social and intellectual vacuum"; if he would find comradeship, he must wander. "Whenever one encounters a novel that rises superior . . . the thing takes on a subtle but unmistakable air of foreignness . . . in part grounded soundly enough on the facts.

The native author of any genuine force and originality is almost invariably found to be under strong foreign influences, either English or continental. It was so in the earliest days. Freneau, the poet of the Revolution, was thoroughly French in blood and traditions. Irving, as H. R. Heweis has said, "took to England as a duck takes to water," and was in exile seventeen years. Cooper, with the great success of *The Last of the Mohicans* behind him, left the country in disgust and was gone for seven years. Emerson, Bryant, Lowell, Hawthorne, and even Longfellow kept their eyes turned across the water; Emerson, in fact, was little more than an importer and popularizer of German and French ideas. Bancroft studied in Germany; Prescott like Irving, was enchanted by Spain. Poe, unable to follow the fashion, invented mythical travels to save his face—to France, to Germany, to the Greek Isles. The Civil War revived the national consciousness enormously, but it did not halt the movement of the émigrés. Henry James, in the seventies, went to England, Bierce and Bret Harte followed him, and even Mark Twain, absolutely American though he was, was forever pulling up stakes and setting out for Vienna, Florence and London. Only poverty tied Whitman to the soil; his audience, for many years, was chiefly beyond the water, and there, too, he often longed to be. This distaste for the national scene is often based upon a genuine alienness. The more, indeed, one investigates the ancestry of Americans who have won distinction in the fine arts, the more one discovers tempting game for the critical Know-Nothings. Whitman was half Dutch, Harte was half Jew, Poe was partly German, James had an Irish grandfather, Howells was largely Irish and German, Dreiser is German, and Hergesheimer is Pennsylvania Dutch. Fully a half of the painters discussed in John C. Van Dyke's *American Painting and Its Tradition* were of mixed blood, with the Anglo-Saxon plainly recessive. And of the five poets singled out for encomium by Miss Lowell in *Tendencies in Modern American Poetry* one is a Swede, two are partly German, one was educated in the German language, and three of the five exiled themselves to England as soon as they got out of their nonage. The exiles are of all sorts: Frank Harris, Vincent O'Sullivan, Ezra Pound, Herman Scheffauer, T. S. Eliot, Henry B. Fuller, Stuart Merrill, Edith Wharton. They go to England, France, Germany, Italy—anywhere to escape. Even at home the literatus is perceptibly foreign in his mien. If he lies under the New England tradition he is furiously colonial—more English than the English. If he turns to revolt, he is apt to put on a French hat and a Russian red blouse. . . . This tendency of American literature, the moment it begins to show enterprise, novelty and significance, to radiate a foreign smell is not an isolated phenomenon. . . . Whenever one hears that a new political theory is in circulation, or a scientific heresy, or a movement toward rationalism in religion, it is safe to guess that some discontented stranger or other has a hand in it . . . intellectual experimentation is chiefly left to immigrants of the later migrations, and the small sections of the native population that have been enriched with their blood. . . . All the arts in America are thoroughly exotic. Music is almost wholly German or Italian, painting is French, architecture . . . is a maddening phantasmagoria of borrowings. . . ."[7] In sum, the United States is culturally naked, wearing an esthetic barrel of foreign make. We are a comfortable, but not a cultivated community.

Need it be pointed out that it is the intellectual attitude, not the facts toward which the attitude is taken that is the course of the despair? What literature has not had its exiles and lonely souls, or otherwise come under foreign influence? Of how many artists can it be said that their blood is pure? All that Mr. Mencken's rhodomontade attests is that creation comes from the impact of diversities, a truism which nobody will deny. Mr. Mencken converts the truism into an indictment because he is a romantic protestant, a reactionary Utopian. His theory of life and letters requires that culture shall be sustained by a "civilized aristocracy, secure in its position, animated by an intelligent curiosity, skeptical of all facile generalizations, superior to the sentimentality of the mob, and delighting in the battle of ideas for its own sake." Such an aristocracy is, like Plato's philosopher-king, a figment of its author's imagination. It has no ground either in psychology or in history. The qualities of mind it is to be endowed with have never been a function of security but of insecurity, and of insecurity in the presence of whatever aristocracy there happened to be challenging them. Vested interests of the body invest the mind with their own partisanship, as the history of aristocracies shows. The play and progress of ideas have been the outcome of other conflicts than those of ideas, and their future has been contingent upon the

7. H. L. Mencken: *Prejudices*, Second Series, pp. 44 seq.

clash of classes, the confrontation of communities,[8] the free association and collaboration of thereby uprooted individuals coming out of all kinds of corporate unities into a sort of no-class land where the distinction between lord and yokel is obliterated and the distinction between master craftsman and amateur becomes coercive. From Plato to Darwin and beyond, this has been the case, and the recorded role of aristocracies in this stretch of intellectual and cultural history is a complete repudiation of Mr. Mencken's ideal so far as it purports to derive from the facts in the case. Where these are concerned, this brave and well-read critic does not seem to know what he is talking about.

Cultural values arise upon the confrontation, impact, and consequent disintegration and readjustment of different orders, with the emergence therefrom of new harmonies carrying unprecedented things in their heart. They have not had a different origin in the United States, as Mr. Mencken attests, nor are their future springs likely to be of a different kind. Their quality will necessarily vary with the variety, pitch and timbre of the forces whose interplay and reverberation they so largely are. The cultural prospect can be indicated in the cultural retrospect, although it cannot, so changeful is the constellation of influences in the American scene, be predicted. . . .

It is within the unifying, all-enveloping atmosphere of science and industry that a man today must come to himself. Against the architectonic and regimentation of the latter, the logical oneness of the former, the deep-lying cultural diversities of the ethnic groups are the strongest shield, the chief defense. They are the reservoirs of individuality, the springs of difference on which freedom and creative imagination depend. Those, let it be remembered, do not come into play through the uninterrupted flow of a single tradition and habit of life. Where that is isolated, uninterrupted, unchallenged, no thought is born, nothing of high order, as the critics of American civilization complain of America, is created. Freedom and creative imagination crown only the confrontation of traditions and habits of life; the assimilation of one culture but not of one people, into the body and soul of another. New England went to Europe, the Middle West to New England, Europe, a low and

8. Cf. Petrie: *The Revolutions of Civilization:* "Every civilization of a settled population tends to incessant decay from its maximum position. . . ."

peasant Europe perhaps, but the subsoil which aristocratic Europe grew and fed on, to the Middle West. If what comes of this clash and compenetration is not so very high, it is none the less a growth of the soil, a portent and promise of the country's future.

The races of Europe have now for a generation been grouped upon the American continent, among Americans, in patterns not so unlike those they brought home. The generation is at its first flowering in things of the spirit, in works of art and of science. Can it be that the freshness, the candor, the poignancy and beauty as well as the strangeness of this flowering have no relation to the contrasted doctrines and disciplines of the communities living in the land, nourishing one another's spirits through mutual contagion? Surely, the more cohesive and flexible, the more adjustable and self-sustaining are these communities, the more certain it is that the men and women they intimately breed shall bring a richer, a more sustained and masterlike endowment into the wider ranges of the national life and the national letters. The Jewish community, the most cohesive and the most adaptable of the non-British communities in America, is said not only to have contributed largely to the fine arts of the nation, but to have in its own existence been already stimulated to new forms of life and growth. "In our examination of the Jewish type of organization," Messrs. Parks and Miller declare, "we gain an impression that the experiments of this community upon its own problems contain an interest not limited to the Jewish community, but extending to American society as a whole. . . . In the case of the Jewish groups we find spontaneous, intelligent and highly organized experiments in democratic control which may assume the character of a permanent contribution to the organization of the American State."

If then cultural history and the American present are any index, the cultural prospect has been enriched, not depleted by the immigration, settlement, and self-maintenance in communities of the peoples of all Europe upon the North American continent. The pioneer Puritan and the puritan Pioneer have thereby received their foils. Color and import have been added to life in the United States, and if the spirit of a cooperative liberty can be poured into the folkways of the British stock and insured in continuance among others, the national fellowship of cultural diversities should eventually come to fulfillment in a truly "transnational America," a new and happy form of associative harmony. But—can such a spirit be poured into such bottles, and can such bottles hold such a spirit?

21. On Patriots: H. L. Mencken

HENRY L. MENCKEN, *born in 1880, during his long career demonstrated a memorable talent for ridiculing the most flagrant absurdities in American civilization and a unique ability to promote the careers of writers who violated genteel good taste. He wrote first as a columnist for the* Baltimore Sun, *then as editor of* The Smart Set *and, beginning in 1923, as editor of* The American Mercury. *Despite the disparity in age between Mencken and the young literary radicals of the 1920s, he served as the youthful intelligentsia's favorite critic of conventional morality, popular values, and national idols. Walter Lippmann described Mencken as "the most powerful personal influence on this whole generation of educated people." In the selection below Mencken joyfully assaults the reputations of national heroes from George Washington to the World War I American Army commander in France, superpatriot General John J. Pershing.*

Star-Spangled Men

I open the memoirs of General Grant, Volume II, at the place where he is describing the surrender of General Lee, and find the following:

> I was without a sword, as I usually was when on horseback on (*sic*) the field, and wore a soldier's blouse for a coat, with the shoulder straps of my rank to indicate to the army who I was.

Anno 1865. I look out of my window and observe an officer of the United States Army passing down the street. Anno 1922. Like General Grant, he is without a sword. Like General Grant, he wears a sort of soldier's blouse for a coat. Like General Grant, he employs shoulder straps to indicate to the army who he is. But there is something more. On the left breast of this officer, apparently a major, there blazes so brilliant a mass of color that, as the

SOURCE: H. L. Mencken, *Prejudices: Third Series* (New York, 1922), pp. 133–145.

sun strikes it and the flash bangs my eyes, I wink, catch my breath and sneeze. There are two long strips, each starting at the sternum and disappearing into the shadows of the axillia—every hue in the rainbow, the spectroscope, the kaleidoscope—imperial purples, *sforzando* reds, wild Irish greens, romantic blues, loud yellows and oranges, rich maroons, sentimental pinks, all the half-tones from ultraviolet to infrared, all the vibrations from the impalpable to the unendurable. A gallant *Soldat*, indeed! How he would shame a circus ticketwagon if he wore all the medals and badges, the stars and crosses, the pendants and lavallières, that go with those ribbons! . . . A glance at his sleeves. A simple golden stripe on the one—six months beyond the raging main. None on the other—the Kaiser's cannon missed him.

Just what all these ribbons signify I am sure I don't know; probably they belong to campaign medals and tell the tale of butcheries in foreign and domestic parts—mountains of dead Filipinos, Mexicans, Haitians, Dominicans, West Virginia miners, perhaps even Prussians. But in addition to campaign medals and the Distinguished Service Medal there are now certainly enough foreign orders in the United States to give a distinct brilliance to the national scene, viewed, say, from Mars. The Frederician tradition, borrowed by the ragged Continentals and embodied in Article 1, Section 9, of the Constitution, lasted until 1918, and then suddenly blew up; to mention it today is a sort of indecorum, and tomorrow, no doubt, will be a species of treason. Down with Frederick; up with John Philip Sousa! Imagine what General Pershing would look like at a state banquet of his favorite American order, the Benevolent and Protective one of Elks, in all the Byzantine splendor of his casket of ribbons, badges, stars, garters, sunbursts and cockades—the lordly Bath of the grateful motherland, with its somewhat disconcerting "Ich dien"; the gorgeous tricolor baldrics, sashes and festoons of the Légion d'Honneur; the grand cross of SS. Maurizio e Lazzaro of Italy; the sinister Danilo of Montenegro, with its cabalistic monogram of Danilo I and its sinister hieroglyphics; the breastplate of the Paulownia of Japan, with its rising sun of thirty-two white rays, its blood-red heart, its background of green leaves and its white ribbon edged with red; the mystical St. Saviour of Greece, with its Greek motto and its brilliantly enameled figure of Christ; above all, the Croix de Guerre of Czechoslovakia, a new one and hence not listed in the books, but surely no shrinking violet! Alas, Pershing was on the wrong side—that is, for one with a fancy for gauds of that sort. The most blinding of all known orders is the Medijie of Turkey, which not only entitles the holder to four wives, but also absolutely requires him to wear a red fez and a frozen star covering his whole façade. I was offered this order by Turkish spies during the war, and it wabbled me a good deal. The Alexander of Bulgaria is almost as seductive. The badge consists of an eight-pointed white cross, with crossed swords between the arms and a red Bulgarian lion over the swords. The motto is "Za Chrabrost!" Then there are the Prussian orders—the Red and Black Eagles, the Pour le Mérite, the Prussian Crown, the Hohenzollern and the rest. And the Golden Fleece of Austria—the noblest of them all. Think of the Golden Fleece on a man born in Linn County, Missouri! . . . I begin to doubt that the General would have got it, even supposing him to have taken the other side. The Japs, I note, gave him only the grand cordon of the Paulownia, and the Belgians and Montenegrins were similarly cautious. There are higher classes. The highest of the Paulownia is only for princes, which is to say, only for non-Missourians.

Pershing is the champion, with General March a bad second. March is a K. C. M. G., and entitled to wear a large cross of white enamel bearing a lithograph of the Archangel Michael and the motto, "Auspicium Melioris Aevi," but he is not a K. C. B. Admirals Benson and Sims are also grand crosses of Michael and George, and like most other respectable Americans, members of the Legion of Honor, but they seem to have been forgotten by the Greeks, the Montenegrins, the Italians and the Belgians. The British-born and extremely Anglomaniacal Sims refused the Distinguished Service Medal of his adopted country, but is careful to mention in "Who's Who in America" that his grand cross of Michael and George was conferred upon him, not by some servile gold-stick, but by "King George of England"; Benson omits mention of His Majesty, as do Pershing and March. It would be hard to think of any other American officer, real or bogus, who would refuse the D. S. M., or, failing it, the grand decoration of chivalry of the Independent Order of Odd Fellows. I once saw the latter hung, with ceremonies of the utmost magnificence, upon a bald-headed tinner who had served the fraternity long and faithfully; as he marched down the hall toward the throne of the Supreme Exalted Pishposh a score of little girls, the issue of other tinners, strewed his pathway with roses, and around the stem of each rose was a piece of glittering tinfoil. The band meanwhile played "The Rosary," and, at the conclusion of the spectacle, as fried oysters were served, "Wien Bleibt Wien."

It was, I suspect, by way of the Odd Fellows and other such gaudy heirs to the Deutsche Ritter and Rosicrucians that the lust to gleam and jingle got into the arteries of the American people. For years the austere tradition of Washington's day served to keep the military bosom bare of spangles, but all the while a weakness for them was growing in the civil population. Rank by rank, they became Knights of Pythias, Odd Fellows, Red Men, Nobles of the Mystic Shrine, Knights Templar, Patriarchs Militant, Elks, Moose, Woodmen of the World, Foresters, Hoo-Hoos, Ku Kluxers—and in every new order there were thirty-two degrees, and for every degree there was a badge, and for every badge there was a yard of ribbon. The Nobles of the Mystic Shrine, chiefly paunchy wholesalers of the Rotary Club species, are not content with swords, baldrics, stars, garters and jewels; they also wear red fezes. The Elks run to rubies. The Red Men array themselves like Sitting Bull. The patriotic ice-wagon drivers and Methodist deacons of the Ku Klux Klan carry crosses set with incandescent lights. An American who is forced by his profession to belong to many such orders—say a life insurance solicitor, a bootlegger or a dealer in Oklahoma oil stock—accumulates a trunk full of decorations, many of them weighing a pound. There is an undertaker in Hagerstown, Md., who has been initiated eighteen times. When he robes himself to plant a fellow joiner he weighs three hundred pounds and sparkles and flashes like the mouth of hell itself. He is entitled to bear seven swords, all jeweled, and to hang his watch chain with the golden busts of nine wild animals, all with precious stones for eyes. Put beside this lowly washer of the dead, Pershing newly polished would seem almost like a Trappist.

But even so the civil arm is robbed of its just dues in the department of gauds and radioactivity, no doubt by the direct operation of military vanity and jealousy. Despite a million proofs (and perhaps a billion eloquent arguments) to the contrary, it is still the theory at the official ribbon counter that the only man who serves in a war is the man who serves in uniform. This is soft for the Bevo officer, who at least has his service stripes and the spurs that gnawed into his desk, but it is hard upon his brother Irving, the dollar-a-year man, who worked twenty hours a day for fourteen months buying soap powder, canned asparagus and raincoats for the army of God. Irving not only labored with inconceivable diligence; he also faced hazards of no mean order, for on the one hand was his natural prejudice in favor of a very liberal rewarding of commercial enterprise, and on the other hand were his patriotism and his fear of Atlanta Penitentiary. I daresay that many and many a time, after working his twenty hours, he found it difficult to sleep the remaining four hours. I know, in fact, survivors of that obscure service who are far worse wrecks today than Pershing is. Their reward is—what? Winks, sniffs, innuendos. If they would indulge themselves in the now almost universal American yearning to go adorned, they must join the Knights of Pythias. Even the American Legion fails them, for though it certainly does not bar noncombatants, it insists that they shall have done their noncombatting in uniform.

What I propose is a variety of the Distinguished Service Medal for civilians,—perhaps, better still, a distinct order for civilians, closed to the military and with badges of different colors and areas, to mark off varying services to democracy. Let it run, like the Japanese Paulownia, from high to low—the lowest class for the patriot who sacrificed only time, money and a few nights' sleep; the highest for the great martyr who hung his country's altar with his dignity, his decency and his sacred honor. For Irving and his nervous insomnia, a simple rosette, with an iron badge bearing the national motto, "Safety First"; for the university president who prohibited the teaching of the enemy language in his learned grove, heaved the works of Goethe out of the university library, cashiered every professor unwilling to support Woodrow for the first vacancy in the Trinity, took to the stump for the National Security League, and made two hundred speeches in moving picture theaters—for this giant of loyal endeavor let no 100 percent American speak of anything less than the grand cross of the order, with a gold badge in polychrome enamel and stained glass, a baldric of the national colors, a violet plug hat with a sunburst on the side, the privilege of the floor of Congress, and a pension of $10,000 a year. After all, the cost would not be excessive; there are not many of them. Such prodigies of patriotism are possible only to rare and gifted men. For the grand cordons of the order, e.g., college professors who spied upon and reported the seditions of their associates, state presidents of the American Protective League, alien property custodians, judges whose sentences of conscientious objectors mounted to more than 50,000 years, members of Dr. Creel's herd of 2,000 American historians, the authors of the Sisson documents, etc.—pensions of $10 a day would be enough, with silver badges and no plug hats. For the lower ranks, bronze badges and the legal right to the title of "the Hon.," already every true American's by courtesy.

Not, of course, that I am insensitive to the services of the gentlemen of those lower ranks, but in such matters one must go by rarity rather than by intrinsic value. If the grand cordon or even the nickelplated eagle of the third class were given to every patriot who bored a hole through the floor of his flat to get evidence against his neighbors, the Krausmeyers, and to every one who visited the Hofbräuhaus nightly, denounced the Kaiser in searing terms, and demanded assent from Emil and Otto, the waiters, and to every one who notified the catchpolls of the Department of Justice when the wireless plant was open in the garret of the Arion Liedertafel, and to all who took a brave and forward part in slacker raids, and to all who lent their stenographers funds at 6 percent to buy Liberty bonds at 4¼ percent, and to all who sold out at 99 and then bought in again at 83.56 and to all who served as jurors or perjurers in cases against members and ex-members of the IWW, and to the German-American members of the League for German Democracy, and to all the Irish who snitched upon the Irish—if decorations were thrown about with any such lavishness, then there would be no nickel left for our bathrooms. On the civilian side as on the military side the great rewards of war go, not to mere dogged industry and fidelity, but to originality—to the unprecedented, the arresting, the bizarre. The New York *Tribune* liar who invented the story about the German plant for converting the corpses of the slain into soap did more for democracy and the Wilsonian idealism, and hence deserves a more brilliant recognition, than a thousand uninspired hawkers of atrocity stories supplied by Viscount Bryce and his associates. For that great servant of righteousness the grand cordon, with two silver badges and the chair of history at Columbia, would be scarcely enough; for the ordinary hawkers any precious metal would be too much.

Whether or not the YMCA has decorated its chocolate pedlars and soul-snatchers I do not know; since the chief YMCA lamassary in my town of Baltimore became the scene of a homosexual scandal I have ceased to frequent evangelical society. If not, then there should be some governmental recognition of those highly characteristic heroes of the war for democracy. The veterans of the line, true enough, dislike them excessively, and have a habit of denouncing them obscenely when the corn-juice flows. They charged too much for cigarettes; they tried to discourage the amiability of the ladies of France; they had a habit of being absent when the shells burst in air. Well, some say this and some say that. A few, at least, of the pale and oleaginous brethren must have gone into the Master's work because they thirsted to save souls, and not simply because they desired to escape the trenches. And a few, I am told, were anything but unpleasantly righteous, as a round of Wassermanns would show. If, as may be plausibly argued, these Soldiers of the Double Cross deserve to live at all, then they surely deserve to be hung with white enameled stars of the third class, with gilt dollar marks superimposed. Motto: "Glory, glory, hallelujah!"

But what of the vaudeville actors, the cheer leaders, the doughnut fryers, the camp librarians, the press agents? I am not forgetting them. Let them be distributed among all the classes from the seventh to the eighth, according to their sufferings for the holy cause. And the agitators against Beethoven, Bach, Brahms, Wagner, Richard Strauss, all the rest of the cacophonous Huns? And the specialists in the crimes of the German professors? And the collectors for the Belgians, with their generous renunciation of all commissions above 80 percent? And the pathologists who denounced Johannes Müller as a fraud, Karl Ludwig as an imbecile, and Ehrlich as a thief? And the patriotic chemists who discovered arsenic in dill pickles, ground glass in pumpernickel, bichloride tablets in Bismarck herring, pathogenic organisms in aniline dyes? And the inspired editorial writers of the New York *Times* and *Tribune*, the Boston *Transcript*, the Philadelphia *Ledger*, the Mobile *Register*, the Jones Corners *Eagle?* And the headline writers? And the Columbia, Yale and Princeton professors? And the authors of books describing how the Kaiser told them the whole plot in 1913, while they were pulling his teeth or shining his shoes? And the ex-ambassadors? And the *Nietzschefresser?* And the chautauqua orators? And the four-minute men? And the Methodist pulpit pornographers who switched so facilely from vice crusading to German atrocities? And Dr. Newell Dwight

Hillis? And Dr. Henry van Dyke? And the master minds of the *New Republic?* And Tumulty? And the Vigilantes? Let no grateful heart forget them!

Palmer and Burleson I leave for special legislation. If mere university presidents, such as Nicholas Murray Butler, are to have the grand cross, then Palmer deserves to be rolled in malleable gold from head to foot, and polished until he blinds the cosmos—then Burleson must be hung with diamonds like Mrs. Warren and bathed in spotlights like Gaby Deslys. . . . Finally, I reserve a special decoration, to be conferred in camera and worn only in secret chapter, for husbands who took chances and refused to read anonymous letters from Paris: the somber badge of the Ordre de la Cuculus Canorus, first and only class.

IV

United States Civilization during the 1920s

22. The Ku Klux Klan: Hiram Evans

FOUNDED IN 1915 by William J. Simmons, an itinerant Georgia minister, salesman, and organizer for fraternal organizations, the modern Ku Klux Klan fell into the hands of a couple of unscrupulous experts at sales and public relations campaigns in 1920. These merchandisers saw enormous possibilities in an organization that could take advantage of fears connected with the contemporary Red scare. The original inspiration of returning to the days of the Reconstruction Klan—of complete white supremacy and old-fashioned Southern ideals—soon gave way to more modern crusades against Catholics, Jews, radicals, foreigners in general, and the widespread breakdown in conventional morality. The new Klan organizers also gave a more dashing flavor to the Klan ceremonies, titles, and even the uniform. Before long the impractical Simmons was obliged to sell his share in the thriving enterprise, and was replaced by an energetic Dallas dentist, Hiram Wesley Evans, who described himself without suffering contradiction as "the most average man in America." As the selection below indicates, Evans, like most Klansmen, thought of his organization as the most thoroughly American association in the country—100 percent American.

The elimination of private profit for officers of the Klan came next and with it went a democratizing of the order. The Klan, being chiefly an organized crusade, cannot operate efficiently on a purely democratic basis, but the autocracy of the early years has been replaced by a system approximating that of the American Government in its early years; final power in the hands of the rank and file, but full power of leadership in the officers they choose.

Another most important reform was a complete change in the method of "propagation"—of recruiting and spreading our gospel. In the early days this had been done very secretively, a high percentage of money had gone to the kleagles—the "sales agents"—there had been a high-pressure appeal to sentimentality, hatred and the invisible government idea, and a tendency to emphasize numbers rather than quality of recruits. Today, instead, the evangelistic emphasis is put on Americanism, Protestant Christianity, and action through government machinery; an increasing number of

SOURCE: Hiram Evans, "The Klan's Fight for Americanism," *The North American Review* 223 (March 1926): pp. 33–63. Reprinted by permission of the University of Northern Iowa.

the field agents are on salary, lists of possible members are carefully weeded out before any are approached, and those found worth while are won by personal work, backed by open discussion. This has, to be sure, cut down the number of new members accepted, but has greatly increased quality and loyalty, and it has brought amazing gains in strength, particularly in the Midwest and North.

Most important of all has been the formulation of the true Klan purposes into definite principles. This has been a gradual process. We in the lead found ourselves with a following inspired in many ways beyond our understanding, with beliefs and purposes which they themselves only vaguely understood and could not express, but for the fulfillment of which they depended on us. We found ourselves, too, at the head of any army with unguessable influence to produce results for which responsibility would rest on us—the leaders—but which we had not foreseen and for which we were not prepared. As the solemn responsibility to give right leadership to these millions, and to make right use of this influence, was brought home to us, we were compelled to analyze, put into definite words, and give purpose to these half conscious impulses.

The Klan, therefore, has now come to speak for the great mass of Americans of the old pioneer stock. We believe that it does fairly and faithfully represent them, and our proof lies in their support. To understand the Klan, it is necessary to understand the character and present mind of the mass of old-stock Americans. The mass, it must be remembered, as distinguished from the intellectually mongrelized "Liberals."

These are, in the first place, a blend of various peoples of the so-called Nordic race, the race which, with all its faults, has given the world almost the whole of modern civilization. The Klan does not try to represent any people but these.

There is no need to recount the virtues of the American pioneers; but it is too often forgotten that in the pioneer period a selective process of intense rigor went on. From the first only hardy, adventurous and strong men and women dared the pioneer dangers; from among these all but the best died swifetly, so that the new Nordic blend which became the American race was bred up to a point probably the highest in history. This remarkable race character, along with the new-won continent and the new-created nation, made the inheritance of the old-stock Americans the richest ever given to a generation of men.

In spite of it, however, these Nordic Americans for the last generation have found themselves increasingly uncomfortable, and finally deeply distressed. There appeared first confusion in thought and opinion, a groping and hesitancy about national affairs and private life alike, in sharp contrast to the clear, straightforward purposes of our earlier years. There was futility in religion, too, which was in many ways even more distressing. Presently we began to find that we were dealing with strange ideas; policies that always sounded well, but somehow always made us still more uncomfortable.

Finally came the moral breakdown that has been going on for two decades. One by one all our traditional moral standards went by the boards, or were so disregarded that they ceased to be binding. The sacredness of our Sabbath, of our homes, of chastity, and finally even of our right to teach our own children in our own schools fundamental facts and truths were torn away from us. Those who maintained the old standards did so only in the face of constant ridicule.

Along with this went economic distress. The assurance for the future of our children dwindled. We found our great cities and the control of much of our industry and commerce taken over by strangers, who stacked the cards of success and prosperity against us. Shortly they came to dominate our government. The *bloc* system by which this was done is now familiar to all. Every kind of inhabitant except the Americans gathered in groups which operated as units in politics, under orders of corrupt, self-seeking and un-American leaders, who both by purchase and threat enforced their demands on politicians. Thus it came about that the interests of Americans were always the last to be considered by either national or city governments, and that the native Americans were constantly discriminated against, in business, in legislation and in administrative government.

So the Nordic American today is a stranger in large parts of the land his fathers gave him. Moreover, he is a most unwelcome stranger, one much spit upon, and one to whom even the right to have his own opinions and to work for his own interests is now denied with jeers and revilings. "We must Americanize the Americans," a distinguished immigrant said recently. Can anything more clearly show the state to which the real American has fallen in this country which was once his own?

Our falling birth rate, the result of all this, is proof of our distress. We no longer feel that we can be fair to children we bring into the world, unless we can make sure from the start that they shall have capital or education or both, so that they need never compete with those who now fill the lower rungs of the ladder of success. We dare no longer risk letting our youth "make its own way" in the conditions under which we live. So even our unborn children are being crowded out of their birthright!

All this has been true for years, but it was the World War that gave us our first hint of the real cause of our troubles, and began to crystallize our ideas. The war revealed that millions whom we had allowed to share our heritage and prosperity, and whom we had assumed had become part of us, were in fact not wholly so. They had other loyalties: each was willing—anxious!—to sacrifice the interests of the country that had given him shelter to the interests of the one he was supposed to have cast off; each in fact did use the freedom and political power we had given him against ourselves whenever he could see any profit for his older loyalty.

This, of course, was chiefly in international affairs, and the excitement caused by the discovery of disloyalty subsided rapidly after the war ended. But it was not forgotten by the Nordic Americans. They had been awakened and alarmed; they began to suspect that the hyphenism which had been shown was only a part of what existed; their quiet was not that of renewed sleep, but of strong men waiting very watchfully. And presently they began to form decisions about all those aliens who were Americans for profit only.

They decided that even the crossing of salt water did not dim a single spot on a leopard; that an alien usually remains an alien no matter what is done to him, what veneer of education he gets, what oaths he takes, nor what public attitudes he adopts. They decided that the melting pot was a ghastly failure, and remembered that the very name was coined by a member of one of the races—the Jews—which most determinedly refuses to melt. They decided that in every way, as well as in politics, the alien in the vast majority of cases is unalterably fixed in his instincts, character, thought and interests by centuries of racial selection and development, that he thinks first for his own people, works only with and for them, cares entirely for their interests, considers himself always one of them, and never an American. They decided that in character, instincts, thought, and purposes—in his whole soul—an alien remains fixedly alien to America and all it means.

They saw, too, that the alien was tearing down the American standard of living, especially in the lower walks. It became clear that while the American can out-work the alien, the alien can so far under-live the American as to force him out of all competitive labor. So they came to realize that the Nordic can easily survive and rule and increase if he holds for himself the advantages won by strength and daring of his ancestors in times of stress and peril, but that if he surrenders those advantages to the peoples who could not share the stress, he will soon be driven below the level at which he can exist by their low standards, low living and fast breeding. And they saw that the low standard aliens of Eastern and Southern Europe were doing just that thing to us.

They learned, though more slowly, that alien ideas are just as dangerous to us as the aliens themselves, no matter how plausible such ideas may sound. With most of the plain people this conclusion is based simply on the fact that the alien ideas do not work well for them. Others went deeper and came to understand that the differences in racial background, in breeding, instinct, character and emotional point of view are more important than logic. So ideas which may be perfectly healthy for an alien may also be poisonous for Americans.

Finally they learned the great secret of the propagandists; that success in corrupting public opinion depends on putting out the subversive ideas without revealing their source. They came to suspect that "prejudice" against foreign ideas is really a protective device of nature against mental food that may be indigestible. They saw, finally, that the alien leaders in America act on this theory, and that there is a steady flood of alien ideas being spread over the country, always carefully disguised as American.

As they learned all this the Nordic Americans have been gradually arousing themselves to defend their homes and their own kind of civilization. They have not known just how to go about it; the idealist philanthropy and good-natured generosity which led to the philosophy of the melting pot have died hard. Resistance to the peaceful invasion of the immigrant is no such simple matter as snatching up weapons and defending frontiers nor has it much spectacular emotionalism to draw men to the colors.

The old-stock Americans are learning, however. They have begun to arm themselves for this new type of warfare. Most important, they have broken away from the fetters of the false ideals and philanthropy which puts aliens ahead of their own children and their own race.

To do this they have had to reject completely—and perhaps for the moment the rejection is a bit too complete—the whole body of "Liberal" ideas which they had followed with such simple, unquestioning faith. The first and immediate cause of the break with Liberalism was that it had provided no defense against the alien invasion, but instead had excused it—even defended it against Americanism. Liberalism is today charged in the mind of most Americans with nothing less than national, racial and spiritual treason.

But this is only the last of many causes of distrust. The plain people now see that Liberalism has come completely under the dominance of weaklings and parasites whose alien "idealism" reaches its logical peak in the Bolshevist platform of "produce as little as you can, beg or steal from those who do produce, and kill the producer for thinking he is better than you." Not that all Liberalism goes so far, but it all seems to be on that road. The average Liberal idea is apparently that those who can produce should carry the unfit, and let the unfit rule them.

This aberration would have been impossible, of course, if American Liberalism had kept its feet on the ground. Instead it became wholly academic, lost all touch with the plain people, disowned its instincts and common sense, and lived in a world of pure, high, groundless logic.

Worse yet, this became a world without moral standards. Our forefathers had standards—the Liberals today say they were narrow!—and they had consciences and knew that Liberalism must be kept within fixed bounds. They knew that tolerance of things that touch the foundations of the home, of decency, of patriotism or of race loyalty is not lovely but deadly. Modern American Liberalism has no such bounds. If it has a conscience it hides it shamefacedly; if it has any standards it conceals them well. If it has any convictions—but why be absurd? Its boast is that it has none except conviction in its own decadent religion of Liberalism toward everything; toward the right of every man to make a fool or degenerate of himself and to try to corrupt others; in the right of any one to pull the foundations from under the house or poison the wells; in the right of children to play with matches in a powdermill!

The old-stock Americans believe in Liberalism, but not in this thing. It has undermined their Constitution and their national customs and institutions, it has corrupted the morals of their children, it has vitiated their thought, it has degenerated and perverted their education, it has tried to destroy their God. They want no more of it. They are trying to get back to decency and common sense. . . .

The old-stock "plain people" are no longer alone in their belief as to the nature of the dangers, their causes, and the folly of Liberal thought. Recently men of great education and mind, students of wide reputation, have come to see all this as the plain Americans saw it years before. This was stated by Madison Grant:

> The Nordic race . . . if it takes warning in time, may face the future with assurance. Fight it must, but let the fight be not a civil war against its own blood kindred but against the dangerous foreign races, whether they advance sword in hand or in the more insidious guise of beggars at our gates, pleading for admittance to share our prosperity. If we continue to allow them to enter they will in time drive us out of our own land by the mere force of breeding.
>
> The great hope of the future here in America lies in the realization of the working classes that competition of the Nordic with the alien is fatal, whether the latter be the lowly immigrant from Southern or Eastern Europe, or the more obviously dangerous Oriental, against whose standards of living the white man cannot compete. In this country we must look to such of our people—our farmers and artisans—as are still of American blood, to recognize and meet this danger.
>
> Our present condition is the result of following the leadership of idealists and philanthropic doctrinaires.

The chief of Mr. Grant's demands, that the un-American alien be barred out, has already been partly accomplished. It is established as our national policy by overwhelming vote of Congress, after years of delay won by the aliens already here through the political power we gave them. The Klan is proud that it was able to aid this work, which was vital.

But the plain people realize also that merely stopping the alien flood does not restore Americanism, nor even secure us against final utter defeat. America must also defend herself against the enemy within, or we shall be corrupted and conquered by those to whom we have already given shelter.

The first danger is that we shall be overwhelmed, as Mr. Grant forecasts, by the aliens' "mere force of breeding." With the present birthrate, the Nordic stock will have become a hopeless minority within fifty years, and will within two hundred have been choked to death, like grain among weeds. Unless some means is found of making the Nordic feel safe in having children we are already doomed.

An equal danger is from disunity, so strikingly shown during the war, and from a mongrelization of thought and purpose. It is not merely foreign policy that is involved; it is all our thought at home, our morals, education, social conduct—everything. We are already confused and disunited in every way; the alien groups themselves, and the skilful alien propaganda, are both tearing steadily at all that makes for unity in nationhood, or for the soul of Americanism. If the word "integrity" can still be used in its original meaning of singleness of purpose or thought, then we as a nation have lost all integrity. Yet our old American motto includes the words ". . . divided we fall!"

One more point about the present attitude of the old-stock American: he has revived and increased his long-standing distrust of the Roman Catholic Church. It is for this that the native Americans, and the Klan as their leader, are most often denounced as intolerant and prejudiced. This is not because we oppose the Catholic more than we do the alien, but because our enemies recognize that patriotism and race loyalty cannot safely be denounced, while our own tradition of religious freedom gives them an opening here, if they can sufficiently confuse the issue.

The fact is, of course, that our quarrel with the Catholics is not religious but political. The Nordic race is, as is well known, almost entirely Protestant, and there remains in its mental heritage an anti-Catholic attitude based on lack of sympathy with the Catholic psychology, on the historic opposition of the Roman Church to the Nordics' struggle for freedom and achievement, and on the memories of persecutions. But this strictly religious prejudice is not now active in America, and so far as I can learn, never has been. I do not know of a single manifestation in recent times of hostility to any Catholic because of his religion, nor to the Catholic Church because of its beliefs. Certainly the American has always granted to the Catholic not only full religious liberty, without interference or abuse either public or private, but also every civil, social and political equality. Neither the present day Protestant nor the Klan wishes to change this in any degree. . . .

The real indictment against the Roman Church is that it is, fundamentally and irredeemably, in its leadership, in politics, in thought, and largely in membership, actually and actively alien, un-American and usually anti-American. The old-stock Americans, with the exception of the few such of Catholic faith—who are in a class by themselves, standing tragically torn between their faith and their racial and national patriotism—see in the Roman Church today the chief leader of alienism, and the most dangerous alien power with a foothold inside our boundaries. It is this and nothing else that has revived hostility to Catholicism. By no stretch of the imagination can it fairly be called religious prejudice, though, now that the hostility has become active, it does derive some strength from the religious schism.

We Americans see many evidences of Catholic alienism. We believe that its official position and its dogma, its theocratic autocracy and its claim to full authority in temporal as well as spiritual matters, all make it impossible for it as a church, or for its members if they obey it, to cooperate in a free democcracy in which Church and State have been separated. It is true that in this country the Roman Church speaks very softly on these points, so that many Catholics do not know them. It is also true that the Roman priests preach Americanism, subject to their own conception of Americanism, of course. But the Roman Church itself makes a point of the divine and unalterable character of its dogma, it has never seen fit to abandon officially any of these un-American attitudes, and it still teaches them in other countries. Until it does renounce them, we cannot believe anything except that they all remain in force, ready to be called into action whenever feasible, and temporarily hushed up only for expediency.

The hierarchical government of the Roman Church is equally at odds with Americanism. The Pope and the whole hierarchy have been for centuries almost wholly Italian. It is nonsense to suppose that a man, by entering a church, loses his race or national loyalties. The Roman Church today, therefore, is just what its name says—Roman; and it is impossible for its hierarchy or the policies they dictate to be in real sympathy with Americanism. Worse, the Italians have proven to be one of the least assimilable of people. The autocratic nature of the Catholic Church organization, and its suppression of free conscience or free decision, need not be discussed; they are unquestioned. Thus it is fundamental to the Roman Church to demand a supreme loyalty, overshadowing national or race loyalty, to a power that is inevitably alien, and which at the best must inevitably inculcate ideals un-American if not actively anti-American. . . .

The facts are that almost everywhere, and especially in the great industrial centers where the Catholics are strongest, they vote almost as a unit, under control of leaders of their own faith, always in support of the interests of the Catholic Church and of Catholic candidates without regard to other interests, and always also in support of alienism whenever their is an issue raised. They vote, in short, not as American citizens, but as aliens and Catholics! They form the biggest, strongest, most cohesive of all the alien *blocs*. On many occasions they form alliances with other alien *blocs* against American interests, as with the Jews in New York today, and with others in the case of the recent opposition to immigrant restriction. Incidentally they have been responsible for some of the worst abuses in American politics, and today are the chief support of such machines as that of Brennan in Chicago, Curley in Boston and Tammany in New York. . . .

We are a movement of the plain people, very weak in the matter of culture, intellectual support, and trained leadership. We are demanding, and we expect to win, a return of power into the hands of the everyday, not highly cultured, not overly intellectualized, but entirely unspoiled and not de-Americanized, average citizen of the old stock. Our members and leaders are all of this class—the opposition of the intellectuals and liberals who held the leadership, betrayed Americanism, and from whom we expect to wrest control, is almost automatic.

This is undoubtedly a weakness. It lays us open to the charge of being "hicks" and "rubes" and "drivers of second hand Fords." We admit it. Far worse, it makes it hard for us to state our case and advocate our crusade in the most effective way, for most of us lack skill in language. Worst of all, the need of trained leaders constantly hampers our progress and leads to serious blunders and internal troubles. If the Klan ever should fail it would be from this cause. All this we on the inside know far better than our critics, and regret more. Our leadership is improving, but for many years the Klan will be seeking better leaders, and the leaders praying for greater wisdom.

Serious as this is, and strange though our attitude may seem to the intellectuals, it does not worry us greatly. Every popular movement has suffered from just this handicap, yet the popular movements have been the mainsprings of progress, and have usually had to win against the "best people" of their time. Moreover, we can depend on getting this intellectual backing shortly. It is notable that when the plain people begin to win with one of their movements, such as the Klan, the very intellectuals who have scoffed and fought most bitterly presently begin to dig up sound—at the least well-sounding!—logic in support of the success. The movement, so far as can be judged, is neither hurt nor helped by this process.

Another weakness is that we have not been able, as yet, to bring home to the whole membership the need of continuous work on organization programs both local and national. They are too prone to work only at times of crisis and excitement, and then to feel they can let down. Partly, of course, this is inherent in the evangelistic quality of our crusade. It is "strong medicine," highly emotional, and presently brings on a period of reaction and lethargy. All crusaders and evangelists know this: the whole country saw it after the war. The Klan will not be fully entrenched till it has passed this reaction period, and steadied down for the long pull. That time is only beginning for most of the Klan, which really is hardly three years old.

But we have no fear of the outcome. Since we indulge ourselves in convictions, we are not frightened by our weaknesses. We hold the conviction that right will win if backed with vigor and consecration. We are increasing our consecration and learning to make better use of our vigor. We are sure of the fundamental rightness of our cause, as it concerns both ourselves and the progress of the world. We believe that there can be no question of the right of the children of the men who made America to own and control America. We believe that when we allowed others to share our heritage, it was by our own generosity and by no right of theirs. We believe that therefore we have every right to protect ourselves when we find that they are betraying our trust and endangering us. We believe, in short, that we have the right to make America *American* and for Americans.

We believe also that only through this kind of a nation, and through development along these lines, can we best serve America, the whole world today, and the greater world yet unborn. We believe the hand of God was in the creation of the American stock and nation. We believe, too, in the right and duty of every man to fight for himself, his own children, his own nation and race. We believe in the parable of the talents, and mean to keep and use those entrusted to us—the race, spirit and nationhood of America!

Finally we believe in the validity and driving power of our race: a faith based on the record of the Nordics throughout all history, and especially in America. J. P. Morgan had a motto which said, in effect, "Never bet against the future of America." We believe it is equally unsafe to bet against the future of any stock of the Nordic race, especially so finely blended and highly bred a stock as that of the sons of the pioneers. Handicaps, weaknesses, enemies and all, we will win!

Our critics have accused us of being merely a "protest movement," of being frightened; they say we fear alien competition, are in a panic because we cannot hold our own against the foreigners. That is partly true. We are a protest movement—protesting against being robbed. We are afraid of competition with peoples who would destroy our standard of living. We are suffering in many ways, we have been betrayed by our trusted leaders, we are half beaten already. But we are not frightened nor in a panic. We have merely awakened to the fact that we must fight for our own. We are going to fight—and win!

The Klan does not believe that the fact that it is emotional and instinctive, rather than coldly intellectual, is a weakness. All action comes from emotion, rather than from ratiocination. Our emotions and the instincts on which they are based have been bred into us for thousands of years; far longer than reason has had a place in the human brain. They are the many-times distilled product of experience; they still operate much more surely and promptly than reason can. For centuries those who obeyed them have lived and carried on the race; those in whom they were weak, or who failed to obey, have died. They are the foundations of our American civilization, even more than our great historic documents; they can be trusted where the fine-haired reasoning of the denatured intellectuals cannot.

Thus the Klan goes back to the American racial instincts, and to the common sense which is their first product, as the basis of its beliefs and methods. The fundamentals of our thought are convictions, not mere opinions. We are pleased that modern research is finding scientific backing for these convictions. We do not need them ourselves; we know that we are right in the same sense that a good Christian knows that he has been saved and that Christ lives—a thing which the intellectual can never understand. These convictions are no more to be argued about than is our love for our children; we are merely willing to state them for the enlightenment and conversion of others.

There are three of these great racial instincts, vital elements in both the historic and the present attempts to build an America which shall fulfill the aspirations and justify the heroism of the men who made the nation. These are the instincts of loyalty to the white race, to the traditions of America, and to the spirit of Protestantism, which has been an essential part of Americanism every since the days of Roanoke and Plymouth Rock. They are condensed into the Klan slogan: "Native, white, Protestant supremacy."

First in the Klansman's mind is patriotism—America for Americans. He believes religiously that a betrayal of Americanism or the American race is treason to the most sacred of trusts, a trust from his fathers and a trust from God. He believes, too, that Americanism can only be achieved if the pioneer stock is kept pure. . . .

Americanism, to the Klansman, is a thing of the spirit, a purpose and a point of view, that can only come through instinctive racial understanding. It has, to be sure, certain defined principles, but he does not believe that many aliens understand those principles, even when they use our words in talking about them. Democracy is one, fair dealing, impartial justice, equal opportunity, religious liberty, independence, self-reliance, courage, endurance, acceptance of individual responsibility as well as individual rewards for effort, willingness to sacrifice for the good of his family, his nation and his race before anything else but God, dependence on enlightened conscience for guidance, the right to unhampered development—these are fundamental. But within the bounds they fix there must be the utmost freedom, tolerance, liberalism. In short, the Klansman believes in the greatest possible diversity and individualism within the limits of the American spirit. But he believes also that few aliens can understand that spirit, that fewer try to, and that there must be resistance, intolerance even, toward anything that threatens it, or the fundamental national unity based upon it.

The second word in the Klansman's trilogy is "white." The

white race must be supreme, not only in America but in the world. This is equally undebatable, except on the ground that the races might live together, each with full regard for the rights and interests of others, and that those rights and interests would never conflict. Such an idea, of course, is absurd; the colored races today, such as Japan, are clamoring not for equality but for their supremacy. The whole history of the world, on its broader lines, has been one of race conflicts, wars, subjugation or extinction. This is not pretty, and certainly disagrees with the maudlin theories of cosmopolitanism. But it is truth. The world has been so made that each race must fight for its life, must conquer, accept slavery or die. The Klansman believes that the whites will not become slaves, and he does not intend to die before his time.

Moreover, the future of progress and civilization depends on the continued supremacy of the white race. The forward movement of the world for centuries has come entirely from it. Other races each had its chance and either failed or stuck fast, while white civilization shows no sign of having reached its limit. Until the whites falter, or some colored civilization has a miracle of awakening, there is not a single colored stock that can claim even equality with the white; much less supremacy.

The third of the Klan principles is that Protestantism must be supreme; that Rome shall not rule America. The Klansman believes this not merely because he is a Protestant, nor even because the Colonies that are now our nation were settled for the purpose of wresting America from the control of Rome and establishing a land of free conscience. He believes it also because Protestantism is an essential part of Americanism; without it America could never have been created and without it she cannot go forward. Roman rule would kill it.

Protestantism contains more than religion. It is the expression in religion of the same spirit of independence, self-reliance and freedom which are the highest achievements of the Nordic race. It sprang into being automatically at the time of the great "upsurgence" of strength in the Nordic peoples that opened the spurt of civilization in the fifteenth century. It has been a distinctly Nordic religion, and it has been through this religion that the Nordics have found strength to take leadership of all whites and the supremacy of the earth. Its destruction is the deepest purpose of all other peoples, as that would mean the end of Nordic rule. . . .

The Negro, the Klan considers a special duty and problem of the white American. He is among us through no wish of his; we owe it to him and to ourselves to give him full protection and opportunity. But his limitations are evident; we will not permit him to gain sufficient power to control our civilization. Neither will we delude him with promises of social equality which we know can never be realized. The Klan looks forward to the day when the Negro problem will have been solved on some much saner basis than miscegenation, and when every State will enforce laws making any sex relations between a white and a colored person a crime.

For the alien in general we have sympathy, opportunity, justice, but no permanent welcome unless he becomes truly American. It is our duty to see that he has every chance for this, and we shall be glad to accept him if he does. We hold no rancor against him; his race, instincts, training, mentality and whole outlook of life are usually widely different from ours. We cannot blame him if he adheres to them and attempts to convert us to them, even by force. But we must see that he can never succeed.

The Jew is a more complex problem. His abilities are great, he contributes much to any country where he lives. This is particularly true of the Western Jew, those of the stocks we have known so long. Their separation from us is more religious than racial. When freed from persecution these Jews have shown a tendency to disintegrate and amalgamate. We may hope that shortly, in the free atmosphere of America, Jews of this class will cease to be a problem. Quite different are the Eastern Jews of recent immigration, the Jews known as the Askhenasim. It is interesting to note that anthropologists now tell us that these are not true Jews, but only Judaized Mongols—Chazars. These, unlike the true Hebrew, show a divergence from the American type so great that there seems little hope of their assimilation. . . .

One of the outstanding principles of the Klan is secrecy. We have been much criticized for it, and accused of cowardice, though how any sane person can allege cowardice against men who stood unarmed while rioters beat and shot them down, as Klansmen were beaten and shot at Carnegie and other places, we cannot understand. Our secrecy is, in fact, necessary for our protection so long as the bitter intolerance and fanatic persecution lasts. Until the Klan becomes strong in a community, individual members have often found themselves in danger of loss of work, business, property and even life. There is also the advantage in secrecy that it gives us greater driving force, since our enemies are handicapped in not knowing just what, where or how great is the strength we can exert.

Both these reasons for secrecy will grow less in time, but it can safely be predicted that the Klan will never officially abandon its secrecy. The mask, by the way, is not a part of our secrecy at all, but of our ritual, and can never be abandoned. . . .

The future of the Klan we believe in, though it is still in the hands of God and of our own abilities and consecration as individuals and as a race. Previous movements of the kind have been short-lived, killed by internal jealousies and personal ambitions, and partly, too, by partial accomplishment of their purposes. If the Klan falls away from its mission, or fails in it, perhaps even if it succeeds—certainly whenever the time comes that it is not doing needed work—it will become a mere derelict, without purpose or force. If it fulfills its mission, its future power and service are beyond calculation so long as America has any part of her destiny unfulfilled. Meantime we of the Klan will continue, as best we know and as best we can, the crusade for Americanism to which we have been providentially called.

23. Intellectual Evolution of a Small-Town American, 1916: Jane Mander

DURING THE *height of the progressive era, the* New Republic *served as the leading journal of politicially-oriented intellectuals—and of intellectually-oriented politicians. Although this fictional diary of a small-town pseudointellectual by Jane Mander was intended to be a spoof, it is not of the Mencken variety. As a brief representation of a typical case, it contains more accuracy than exaggeration and much more sympathy than contempt. The intellectual revolt was not limited to the big-city bohemias, although most of the important books were written and the magazines edited there. During the 1920s, especially, editors of the avant-garde journals were surprised to discover how high a proportion of the stories, poems, and essays they received and published—sometimes a*

SOURCE: Jane Mander, "A Diary of Evolution," *The New Republic* 6, No. 73 (March 25, 1916), pp. 211–212.

majority—were sent from small cities and towns, especially in the Middle West. Possibly the many fine writers who were raised in such communities, authors like Lewis, Hemingway, and Faulkner, left behind counterparts who for one reason or another were unwilling or unable to leave and develop their talents fully in the cosmopolitan centers.

A Diary of Evolution

In a Small Country Town

AGE

5–12 Accept Bible as written, God, Christ, and The Angels in toto, Fixed Heaven and Hell, the Good and the Bad.

12–14 Believe Bible "inspired," but not all "literal." Shed Fixed Hell. See Satan as Force of Evil. Doubt Divinity of Christ.

14–16 Read Bible as history and legend. Shed Divinity of Christ, and The Angels. Keep God as Love, Justice, and Father of Mankind. Have fixed ideas of Right and Wrong, but become interested in the Bad.

16–18 Browning stage. Frame "God's in His Heaven, All's Right With the World." Parade aggressive Optimism. Accept "World as it is." Preach Duty of Cheerfulness, etc. Orthodox as to Poverty and the Working Classes.

18–19 Honest Doubt. Learn Omar Khayyam by heart. Shed Heaven. Question Personal God. Put away "God's in His Heaven." More liberal as to Sin.

19–22 General mental tangle. Study Theosophy and Reincarnation, Spiritualism and Christian Science. Shed Personal God. Call Him Force, the First Cause, the Guiding Principle, Universal Law, etc. Believe in Mind Over Matter, and Love as Constructive Force. Shed fixed ideas of Right and Wrong. See Sin as Defective Education. Morality the new religion. Frame Henley's "Invictus." Exalt The Self. Believe in Human Nature. Get first glimmer of Evolution. Hear vaguely of Socialism. Realize The Brotherhood of Man with due regard for Classes and Types.

In New York

22–23 Discover Bernard Shaw. Shed everything else.

23–25 Plunge into psychology, biology, history. Doubt everything but Scientific Facts. Shed God in any form. Learn the Relativity of Truth. Meet Socialists. Investigate Sex War and Wage War. Have Temperament. Exalt the Intellect. Despise the Average Person. Put "Invictus" away in a drawer.

25–26 Begin again. The new religion—socialism; the new god—humanity; the new Christ—the man, the carpenter; the new devils—poverty, capitalism; the new heaven and hell—the earth; the new Bible—Marx, Wells, The Fabian Society, The Economists; the new sins—ignorance, indifference; the new temples—the street corner, the lecture hall; the new idealism—*liberté, égalité, fraternité*; the new words—Individualism, Communism, Humanitarianism.

26–28 Preach Radicalism, Anarchism, Agitation, and No Compromise. Despise Laws, Ceremonies, Traditions, and Precedents. Believe in Free Love. Exalt Sincerity. Proclaim The Facts of Life. Lose Temperament in the flurry of general destruction. Tolerate all Comrades in the March of Progress. Believe in The People and the Natural Rights of Man.

28–30 Doubt adequacy of Anarchism. Begin to suspect The People. Consider Organization, Cooperation, and Education. Study Unions and Statistics. See need for Some Compromise. Shed Anarchism and Agitation.

30–32 Join a union. Believe in the Wage War. Preach Unity and Sacrifice for the Good of All. Lead Strikes.

32–33 Doubt possibility of Unity. Suspect motives of leaders. Question effectiveness of Sacrifice. Hazy as to definition of The Good of All. Lose illusions about The People. See hope in Political Action. Shed Unions and The Working Man.

33–34 Go into politics. Learn the value of Compromise. Suspect the wisdom of Sincerity. Drop Free Love. Uphold Laws and Ceremonies. Hide The Facts of Life. Try Merit and Reason upon the politician. Suspect the power of Merit and Reason. Try Money and Influence upon the politician. Perceive their immediate and decisive effect. Suspect possibility of Democracy as defined by Lincoln. Suspect the politician. Suspect myself. Begin to feel tired.

34–35 Shed politics and the politician. Turn to Social Service. Join four Clubs and three Movements. Boost the Feminists and Suffragists. Talk, and listen to talk. Begin to suspect Movements. Suspect all Human Nature. Get more tired.

35–36 A great weariness. Sick of Action. Sick of Words. Sick of Humanity. No illusions left. Shed everything. Do nothing. Turn to Art.

36–37 Believe in Art. Recover Temperament, but don't mention it. Fall in love with an artist. Believe in love. Believe in the artist. Get married.

37 Have a child, who will begin it all over again.

24. Organized Crime in Chicago: John Ladesco

As THIS *contemporary study of Chicago gangster Frank Torrio indicates, organized crime in America antedated prohibition. The passage of legislation so easily violated, with huge numbers of eager drinkers congregated in cities where distribution was easy, enormously increased the profits available to suppliers of illegal beverages. Previously, smuggling of tax-free liquor had provided only a minor share of the income that flowed to organized criminal groups—gambling and prostitution, for example, had been far more important sources of funds. Torrio's career did not differ significantly from those of criminal leaders in almost every large metropolitan area in the country. His successor, "Scarface" Al Capone, now a legend of movies and television, expanded and refined the activities of his organization to such an extent that the story of his career is much more unusual. When this selection was written, however, Capone still was consolidating his position as leader of Torrio's operations.*

1. Brewing and Beer Running, the Golden Future

John Torrio, the protege and successor of Colosimo was born in Italy, in 1877, and is now fifty-one years of age. The organization of large scale illegal business in vice, supported by political influence, bribery, and violence, had been a matter of lifelong training for

SOURCE: John Landesco, "Organized Crime in Chicago," *The Illinois Crime Survey* (Chicago, 1929), pp. 909–919. Reprinted by permission of the Chicago Crime Commission.

Torrio when, upon the death of Colosimo, the mantle fell upon his shoulders.

Torrio already was known both by politicians and gangsters as safe and level headed. At the funeral of Colosimo, conspicuous in the throng, which included judges, politicians, city officials, cabaret singers, gamblers, and waiters, were members of the Colosimo vice ring, and Torrio was an honorary pallbearer. At this time Torrio was known as boss of the suburban town of Burnham, where he owned the Burnham Inn in a community of resorts and gambling dens. Ike Bloom owned the Arrowhead Inn, a suburban resort which he later sold to Colosimo before the latter's death. Jakie Adler and the Cusicks, and others of the Twenty-second Street Levee had moved to the southern and western suburbs as early as 1916.

The death of Colosimo occurred in the same year that the Eighteenth Amendment and the Volstead Act came into effect; and Torrio turned his attention to the organization of the contraband business of manufacturing beer and of distributing it by convoy through the streets of the city. In connection with his organization of metropolitan beer running, he extended direct rulership over the other west suburban towns.

2. *The Occupation of Cicero*

Torrio took possession of Cicero, a western suburb, in 1923.

In addition to the vice and gambling houses in Burnham he had established several resorts in Stickney. Then he originated the scheme of making the town of Cicero a base for the operations of beer distribution and gambling. In the fall of 1923 he installed a vice resort on Roosevelt Road in Cicero. But Torrio was not without competition in his occupation of Cicero. Eddie Tanel, a Bohemian who was born and bred in the old Pilsen district, had risen to popularity as a prize fighter and because of his many acts of charity among poor Bohemians was very poopular in Cicero at this time, and was conducting a cafe there. Tanel was killed by James Doherty, a Torrio gangster.

Torrio opened his resort without protection. The Cicero police raided it. Torrio moved the same resort to Ogden and Fifty-second Avenues, and the police wrecked it.

Through the influence of Torrio, Sheriff Hoffman ordered a raid on all slot machines in the suburb. Thus Torrio made it known that if he couldn't import prostitutes others couldn't have slot machines. After a few days the slot machines started going again and Torrio, Capone, and their followers moved into Cicero. Somewhere an understanding had been reached. The "mob" came in strong. They opened gambling houses, peddled beer, but did not bring prostitutes into Cicero again. Stickney and Forest Park and other places in the country were utilized for vice operations which were developed on a large scale. In the suburbs, Torrio, Capone, his first lieutenant, La Cava brothers, and Mondi assisted by Frankie Pope, Joey Miller (Italian), Jimmie Murphy, the Cusicks, and Charlie Carr managed a business which included vice, beer, and gambling.

Torrio and his lieutenants used intrigue and bribery and succeeded in controlling elections. The officials were actually under their thumbs—not only the village president, but every official, including the chief of police. Lauterbach's "The Ship" and "The Hawthorne Smoke Shop" operated apparently without opposition from Joseph Klenha, the village president, or his police chief, Theodore Svoboda, Sheriff Hoffman, or State's Attorney Crowe.

Federal officials, intent upon raiding the saloon concessions, always found the places "tipped off."

3. *The Metropolitan Operations*

The *Daily News*, commenting on this situation, said:

> Under the graft system that flourished while Thompson was mayor of Chicago, Torrio's power increased. He had a finger in the gambling pie and his beer running business was organized in those pleasant times. He was reputed owner of several breweries when Mayor Dever up-ended everything with his beer crusade.

In his city-wide operations in beer, Torrio is first heard of as the real beer boss of the south side. He took over the big West Hammond Brewery (known also as the Puro Products Company) and began running beer at regular rates of fifty dollars a barrel, including protection. He had a monopoly in Woodlawn and all precincts south to the Indiana State line, and enjoyed official favor in the Stockyards and the New City districts. In Englewood, where Captain Allman, Commander of the Police, did not touch graft,

Torrio had an even chance. Allman could not be transferred because he was in high favor with the Englewood business men.

In Englewood, and to some extent the Stockyards and the New City districts, the O'Donnells were developing a small but growing beer running business. This is not the same family as the O'Donnells who figured in the McSwiggin killing in Cicero. For brevity we will designate this family of Steve, Walter, Thomas and Spike as the "South Side O'Donnells," and the others as the "West Side O'Donnells."

4. The O'Donnells Intrude

The South Side O'Donnells were not, however, in a position to challenge Torrio successfully. Thus matters stood when the city administration changed and the old Thompson machine went out in 1923. The transfer of authority caused a revolution in the underworld; the old system of protection was destroyed. None could be sure he was "in" anywhere; therefore competition was free and easy.

The South Side O'Donnells made use of their opportunity. They sold a better beer than did Torrio and began to "cut in" heavily in the Stockyards and the New City districts. Torrio, seeing his business wane, retaliated by cutting prices. He put out his beer at ten dollars less a barrel. The O'Donnells retaliated by terrorizing saloon keepers who bought other beer than theirs.

Torrio's rise invited envy and competition but he knew how to deal with them. On September 7, 1923, Jerry O'Connor, tough young south side gangster, was shot dead. O'Connor was a "pal" and agent of the four O'Donnells. On the fatal night he was with Steve, Walter, and Tommy O'Donnell threatening and slugging saloon keepers for buying beer from John Torrio. At the saloon of Joseph Kepka, 5358 South Loncoln Street, they encountered a Torrio gang. The lights went out; pistols roared; everyone scattered. When police arrived they could find no one who knew about the shooting. Two were arrested, but lawyers started habeas corpus proceedings which were entirely unnecessary, because Chief Morgan Collins had no reason for holding them and freed them instantly. Many people knew the story, more especially the saloon keepers and bartenders, but they would not tell.

On September 17, 1923, George Meegan, 5620 Laflin Street, and George Bucher, 5611 Marshfield Avenue, were killed. Both men were considered dangerous because they threatened to reveal the murderers of Jerry O'Connor. Crowe began a "relentless investigation of the beer war." Torrio was now reputed as the "brains" of the biggest beer running syndicate in the country. He surrendered, in company with his attorney, Michael Igoe, to the State's Attorney and was to be grilled concerning beer running in general.

5. *"Hi-Jacking" and Gang Warfare*

Morrie Keane and William Egan, invaders of Torrio territory, one night in December 1923, started from Joliet at midnight to drive three truckloads of beer to Chicago. At a lonesome stretch of the road, called "The Sag," they were stopped, it was later charged, by McErlane, Torrio gunman, and his "hi-jackers." After the beer had been turned over to some highway policemen, Keane and Egan were forced into McErlane's car. Their bodies, filled with bullets, were later found by the road side.

McErlane was arrested, held by the state's attorney in the Sherman Hotel, and then released.

Under pressure, State's Attorney Crowe laid the case before the grand jury. An indictment was voted. Long delays followed. Months afterward, an assistant state's attorney went into court and nolle prossed the case. McErlane left town a free man.

In this investigation it emerged that Walter Stevens, Daniel McFall, and Frank McErlane were leading Torrio's armed forces in the disputed territory. Walter Stevens, the dean of Chicago gunmen, at this moment was wanted for the killing of an Aurora policeman. He had served time in Joliet. It was known that he was a favorite of Governor Small for services rendered to him in his trial at Waukegan. McFall and McErlane were indicted in 1923 for the double killing of gangsters Meegan and Bucher, but the indictments were later nolle prossed. McFall and Red Golden were associates of Stevens and were also wanted for the murder. Torrio had developed powerful influence, as illustrated by his success in securing the pardon from Governor Small of Harry Cusick and his wife, Alma, convicted panderers. He was high in the esteem of the

Thompson-Lundin machine. Frank McErlane is still in power in that district and recently, with Joe Saltis and Tim Murphy,[1] succeeded in nominating John "Dingbat" Oberta state senator and electing him ward committeeman.

6. *Police Persecution of the Enemies of Torrio*

Torrio's enemies, the O'Donnells, had all been jailed at one time or another during this beer investigation, and two of them were indicted. Torrio had been unmolested and the police professed to be unable to find Stevens. The O'Connor killing was laid to Dan McFall, a Torrio man. McFall was arrested, but released on bail and became a fugitive. Red Golden, named as McFall's accomplice, was released after questioning and disappeared.

7. *Brewery Ownership*

Torrio, owner of the West Hammond Brewery, later purchased the Manhattan Brewery, and was said to be worth millions. He boasted that he "owned" police captains and other officials.

Harry Cusick was serving as downtown "pay-off" man for Torrio and had an office in the "Loop," where he paid Torrio money to police officials who were protecting the vice ring.

The operations of the Torrio syndicate on the south side were disclosed in the investigation into the deaths of Jerry O'Connor, Meegan, and Bucher, which showed the dealings with the retailer and the war for terriroty.

On October 19, 1923, just a few weeks after these killings, the Puro Products Company (The West Hammond Brewery) was on trial in the Federal Court in proceedings to close it for one year under injunction. From this trial we learn more about Torrio's expanding ownership of breweries. Testimony revealed W. R. Strook, a former United States Deputy Marshal, as one-half owner of the concern, and Timothy J. Mullen, an attorney, as holder of one share of the stock. Mullen, according to the Federal agents, was attorney with an interest in the Bielfeldt Brewery at Thornton.

The Puro Products Company was bankrupt in 1915. Then came prohibition and a turn in its financial tide, when Joseph Stenson acquired it in October 1920. In October 1922, Torrio bought it,

1. Later killed by gangsters.

and seven days later turned the lease over to the Puro Products Company. The presence of Stenson, a brewer in the days before prohibition, and these transfers of ownership prior to the hearing on the injunction, should be noted as a feature in our examination of brewery ownership later. Torrio and Strook pleaded guilty and were fined $2,000 and $1,000, respectively; and the company $2,000.

Torrio departed with his family on a European sightseeing jaunt that was to end in Italy, where he had purchased a villa for his mother. It was intimated that he took with him more than a million dollars' worth of negotiable securities and letters of credit. He was reported to have the beer concession to all syndicate resorts; to own West Hammond, Manhattan, and Best Breweries; to be a silent partner in several others. His payroll during the fall of 1923, when beer running was at its then zenith, was said to be twenty-five thousand dollars a week. He carried a gun when he felt like it, but never, as far as is known in Chicago, did Torrio use that gun. When trouble came, those who took care of Torrio were in turn taken care of when their cases came to court.

8. *Controlling of Elections*

Six months later Torrio came back to Chicago. He slipped unostentatiously into the city and summoned his veteran adherents to meet him in a south side rendezvous.

County Judge Edmund K. Jarecki, conducting an investigation of bloodshed and riots in the April 1924, election in Cicero, was interested in Torrio's return. Up to the day of the election, 123 saloons in Cicero had been serving beer put out by Torrio's breweries. For six years the same faction had been in control of Cicero's politics and its saloons. The election brought no change in administration. Democrats charged that the breweries sent into Cicero scores of gunmen who cast ballots and manipulated revolvers. During one of the gun-play episodes, Frank Capone, one of Torrio's closest lieutenants, was shot to death by Sergeant William Cusick's squad from the detective bureau. The night before election there was a Torrio clan gathering. Frank Capone and his brother, Scarface Al, better known as Al Brown, owner of the notorious "Four Deuces" Saloon at 2222 South Wabash Avenue, were present. Judge Jerecki thought that Torrio had instructed the

Capone brothers to act as his emissaries in directing the riots in Cicero.

After Frank Capone's killing, Torrio met Scarface Al in the Capone home. Probably others of the gang were present. The meeting or sessions following the shooting of a Torrio lieutenant usually have to do with matters of vengeance. Every saloon in Cicero was directed to pull down the blinds and to remain in a quasi-closed condition until after the excitement had passed. At the inquest over the body of his brother, Scarface Al testified. After a glance had passed between Capone and Charles Frischetti, a companion of Frank when he was killed, Capone announced that he had nothing to say.

9. *Metropolitan Beer King*

The Sieben Brewery raid, a month later, was the complete disclosure of Torrio's power as the metropolitan beer king, flanked on one side by the mobilized gangster chiefs of the entire city and on the other by business partners, who were pre-Volstead brewers, by public officials, and the police.

On the morning of May 19, 1924, after a carefully planned campaign, a police squad under the direct command of Chief Morgan Collins and Captain Matthew Zimmer (without a betrayal in advance of an intention of immediate action) swooped down upon the Sieben Brewery and found thirteen truckloads of beer ready to be convoyed through the streets of the city; the convoy, composed of gang leaders, was arriving in touring cars. As each car arrived the police placed the gangsters under arrest.

While all of the captured gave aliases, the leaders were recognized, of course. John Torrio, Dion O'Banion, and Louis Alterie were among them, and probably Hymie Weiss. Dion O'Banion was then prince of the north side gang, composed of safe-crackers and gunmen of note. Louie Alterie was the chief of the Valley Gang, which under the leadership of Paddy the Bear Ryan had thrived for a quarter of a century. Alterie had succeeded Terry Druggan and Frankie Lake, who were in turn the successors of Paddy the Bear Ryan.

Chief of Police Collins did not turn the prisoners over to Robert E. Crowe, Prosecutor. He announced that other raids would be made if this one failed to frighten the beer runners out of business.

Asked why he turned these prisoners over to the Federal Government, he answered: "District Attorney Olson has promised us prompt cooperation. That is why the case was turned over to him for prosecution. It was a police raid, pure and simple, but the prosecution will be handled by the Government."

Torrio obtained freedom soon after his arrival at the Federal Building, by peeling $7,500 off a roll he carried. The same roll brought freedom, at five thousand dollars, for James Casey. O'Banion did not have the "five grand" demanded of him as bail, nor could Alterie produce one thousand dollars; the others, at one thousand dollars also, each had to wait for bondsmen to appear. Curiously enough, Torrio did not bail them out, but William Skidmore and Ike Roderick, professional bondsmen, whose names have been associated both with gambling and vice, came to release them.

At this time Thomas Nash was attorney for the O'Banion gang. Later he was attorney for its enemies, the Genna gang, in the memorable Anselmi-Scalise case.

The chief of police, himself, tore the insignia from officers who were supposed to have been on duty at the brewery beat and were absent during the raid.

O'Banion, lieutenant of Torrio, had proved his power when he wriggled out of three tight legal holes that same year, prior to the Sieben Brewery raid,—the shooting of Dave Miller, chief of the Jewish gangsters; the "hijacking" of a truckload of whiskey and Dapper Dan McCarthy; and the Carmen Avenue murders in which Two Gun Doherty was killed. All these cases had been nolle prossed by the State's Attorney, Mr. Crowe.

Torrio, O'Banion, Alterie, Nick Juffra who was among the earliest bootleggers to be prosecuted and already had a record as a bootlegger, and thirty-four others, including four policemen, were indicted. Torrio, himself, was a second offender, and would be subject to a sentence of five years on a conspiracy charge alone.

10. The Gold Coast Brewer and the Underworld Chief

It was the general understanding of city and government officials that Torrio and O'Banion were the real operators of the Sieben plant, with a politician and a "fixer" back of them sharing in the profits and distributing the graft, but that in this case, as in the

Puro Products case, a pre-Volstead brewer was involved in the ownership. It seems that pre-Volstead brewers, who remained in the business, had called these gangsters in to do their convoying and to "front"[2] for them in case of a "fall."[3]

2. Take the brunt of the law if discovered.
3. Charles Gregston analyzes this alliance between pre-Volstead brewers and their new gangster partners as follows:

"John Torrio and a Chicago brewer are the twin kings of commercialized crime in Cook County today. They are the men back of the O'Banions and Druggans, the guns and the gangs. They are the organizers, the directors, the 'fixers' and the profit-takers. Torrio is absolute in the field of vice and gambling; the brewer is king of the 'beer-racket.' They work together and the others, with a few exceptions, work for them.

"A strange pair: Torrio is a native of Italy, a Tammany graduate, a post-graduate pupil of the late 'Big Jim' Colosimo. His colleague is the youngest of four brothers who were rich brewers before prohibition. While Torrio was learning the tricks of ward politics in New York and the rewards of sin in the old Twenty-second Street district, and later in Burnham, his twin king of crime was living pleasantly on what is called the 'Gold Coast,' the son of a wealthy and established family. A common genius for organization brought them together soon after prohibition had ushered in the new era of crime through which Chicago is passing.

"They have made organized crime pay tremendous dividends. The brewer's earnings, from the syndicated beer 'racket' he works under political protection, have been reckoned at $12,000,000 a year since 1920. Nobody has ever risked a guess at the clearings of the many-sided Torrio.

"They are joint rulers of the underworld today. No one can run beer in Chicago without first seeing and paying the beer king. No one can cut in on the gambling 'racket' without Torrio's sanction. Immune from prosecution themselves, the two kings of crime can count on the law as well as their own gunmen when they want an intruder driven out. And they have the power to protect their henchmen from prosecution when murder becomes necessary, as it sometimes does. And the brewer is so completely above the law, so thoroughly protected from prosecution, that it is unsafe to mention his name, though the police and the prosecutors of crime know quite well who he is.

"Beer running offered Torrio a splendid opportunity. He had developed a machinery for 'fixing' the law and he had gangsters at his service; stepping up from vice and gambling to beer was easy and natural. Simultaneously the brewer was dabbling in violation of the Eighteenth Amendment. His brothers are said to have been frowning on his ventures, but their warnings weren't heeded.

"Natural attraction brought the pair together and their dovetailing abilities put crime on its new basis. Gunmen were lured away from the risks of highway robbery and safe-blowing to get into the far more lucrative business of peddling beer and driving out competitors. Breweries were leased from their

Torrio brought O'Banion, the most daring and brilliant of the Combine's gunmen, from safe-blowing to liquor leadership. O'Banion soon earned a sizable "split" for himself. He had eyes "on better things" when he was killed, November 10, 1924.

Walter Stevens, Dan McFall, Dan McCarthy, Louis Alterie, Earl Weiss, scarface Al Capone—all are, or were, subordinates in the crime syndicate, some of them important enough to be profit sharers, some mere hired men. They all danced when Torrio and his colleagues moved the strings—gangsters, gangleaders, and politicians.

Somehow, Torrio had found a way to keep the forces of the state's attorney's office away from his gunmen, and the raiding squads of Sheriff Hoffman out of his dives. Under public pressure sporadic raids were made, resulting in temporary and often momentary stoppage of operations.

11. The Outcome of the Sieben Case

A retrospect of the Sieben Brewery case three years after the indictment shows that thirty-eight men were indicted, including pre-Volstead owners, brewmasters, and brewery workers, laborers, and truck drivers, and policemen as well as gangsters. Four months after the raid, pleas of guilty were entered for eleven of the defendants, and the O'Banion case was dismissed on account of his death by murder. John Torrio was sentenced to nine months in the Du Page County Jail and five thousand dollar fine; Ed O'Donnell, eight months in the Kane County Jail and two thousand dollar fine; Nick Juffra, six months in the De Kalb County Jail and two thousand dollar fine; Joseph Warszynski, three months in the De

---

despairing owners and reopened. Cheating saloon-keepers, thousands of them, found it easy to sell beer profitably after paying the syndicate $50 a barrel or more, and $35 easily covered the cost of production and the expense of 'fixing' the public officials, policemen and prohibition agents.

"The brewer knew the methods of modern business and applied them to syndicated beer running. Torrio knew gangsters and recruited them. Thus Druggan and Lake were drawn away from the hoodlum activities of the Valley Gang into a 'racket' that made both of them rich beyond all their dreams. Working breweries for the combine, they soon were riding in expensive cars, dressing like millionaires and living in fashionable neighborhoods." —*Daily News*, November 17, 1924.

Kalb County Jail; Joseph Lanenfeld, three months in the Kane County Jail; Richard Wilson, two hundred dollar fine; George J. Murphy, two hundred dollar fine; Arthur Barrett, two hundred dollar fine, and Jack Heinan, two hundred dollar fine. Warszynski and Lanenfeld were two of three negligent policemen assigned to the Sieben Brewery. District Attorney Edward A. Olson on the same day dismissed the cases of twenty-one other defendants. Among these were minor gangsters, two policemen, one politician, and the pre-Volstead owners.

On January 31, 1925, the judgment against Nick Juffra was vacated. Juffra was the most persistent offender of all the early beer runners. He had been arrested twenty-four times between the advent of prohibition and the Sieben Brewery case. The case of George Frank, the brewmaster, was not heard until March 20, 1925. He then entered a plea of guilty and received a sentence of three months in the Lake County Jail and a three thousand dollar fine. The case of Louie Alterie still stands undismissed and unprosecuted, three years after.

12. *Immunity and Political Connections*

Dion O'Banion enjoyed an amazing immunity from prosecution, although Police Chief Collins had accused him of responsibility for twenty-five murders. He was a Torrio man.

Terry Druggan and Frankie Lake were immune until they later became entangled in the toils of the Federal Government.

Frankie McErlane, the most brutal gunman who ever pulled a trigger in Chicago, went scot free when, in the interests of Torrio he and Dapper Dan McCarthy had exercised their talents for murder.

13. *Qualities of Leadership*

The story of a midnight "hi-jacking" not only illustrates the level headedness which made it possible for Torrio to command the allied gun chiefs of Chicago, but also throws some light on the elements of the continuous warfare which resulted when Torrio's prestige was destroyed through the unwillingness of Mayor Dever and Chief of Police Collins to deal with him. It is a contrast of the expediency of the seasoned leader against the childish irresponsibility of his young lieutenant.

Two policemen held up a Torrio beer squad on a west side street one night and demanded money. By telephone, over a wire which had been tapped by the police, the convoy gangsters reported this to Dion O'Banion. O'Banion replied, "Three hundred dollars? To them bums? Why say, I can get 'em knocked off for half that much." Scenting trouble, police headquarters sent rifle squads to prevent murder if O'Banion should send killers after the "hi-jacking" policemen, but in the meantime the beer runner went over O'Banion's head and put the problem up to Torrio, "The Big Boss." He was back on the wire in a little while with a new message for O'Banion: "Say Dionie, I just been talking to Johnny and he said to let them cops have the three hundred. He says he don't want no trouble."

Such was the difference in temper that made Torrio all-powerful and O'Banion just a superior sort of "plug-ugly." Torrio was shrewd enough to keep out of needless trouble. When murder must be done it was done deftly and thoroughly, as in the case of O'Banion himself, who was shot in his florist shop on November 10, 1924, supposedly by the Gennas, Torrio followers; and of Big Jim Colosimo, Meegan, and Bucher. O'Banion, on the other hand, learned his methods from such practitioners as Gene Geary, convicted slayer, who was sent to Chester as insane, and Louis Alterie and Nails Morton, his "pal."

O'Banion first became friendly with them when he was Gimpy O'Banion, a singing waiter in the old McGovern place at North Clark and West Erie Streets. O'Banion had been a choir boy at the Holy Name Cathedral. The singing of songs, especially Irish sentimental songs, always won over the brutal Geary.

O'Banion, Alterie, Yankee Schwartz, Earl (Hymie) Weiss, and others of the Torrio following, had techniques unlike Torrio's quieter, "brainier" methods which made him boss.

14. The Waning of Torrio's Prestige

To bear out the statement that the armed forces of Torrio were composed of the alliance of gun chiefs of Chicago, we list below some of the names:

Dion O'Banion	Dan McFall
Terry Druggan	Louie Alterie
Frankie Lake	Hymie Weiss
Frank McErlane	Scarface Al Capone
Dapper Dan McCarthy	The Genna Brothers
Walter Stevens	The West Side O'Donnells

In the Sieben Brewery case the prestige of Torrio was injured, because it was conclusive evidence that Mayor Dever and Chief of Police Collins were not under his control. Likewise, there was a concurrent weakening of his power over his gangs when the Genna and O'Banion feud began with the murder of O'Banion. Then Torrio himself was wounded by gunfire; when he recovered he actually welcomed the jail sentence, and safety. The Dever onslaughts upset the underworld regime and destroyed the equilibrium. The beer wars followed.

15. Conclusion

The career of John Torrio epitomizes an important stage in the development of organized crime in Chicago. Trained as a lieutenant of Colosimo, he was thoroughly versed in the technique of dealing with gangsters and politicians. As a manager of resorts under Colosimo he had survived all the crusades against vice and had learned how to utilize to full advantage the control of suburban villages like Burnham as open and unmolested centers for outlawed enterprises.

The four years following Colosimo's death (1920–1924) witnessed the steady rise of Torrio to a position of dominant leadership in the underworld of organized crime, a leadership which came to a sudden end with his arrest and conviction in the Sieben Brewery case. In this short period, which coincided with the introduction of constitutional prohibition, Torrio applied all that he had learned in his years of apprenticeship, to the organization on a city and country-wide basis of the new business of bootlegging. The general plan of conducting criminal business enterprises as outlined by Torrio, and which with modifications made by Capone still persists, may be summarized as follows:

1. The operation of pre-prohibition breweries was engineered by Torrio with the connivance of officials and sometimes with the participation of brewery owners. With the improvement of prohibition enforcement the old-time brewery now plays a minor role in the illegal manufacture of alcohol.
2. Criminal business enterprises, like vice, gambling, and bootlegging, were carried on under adequate political protection. Torrio's power rested, in large part, on his ability to insure protection to his fellow gangsters. Immunity from punishment appears to be an almost indispensable element in maintaining the prestige and control

of a gangster chief, as indicated by Torrio's retirement after serving his prison sentence.

3. Torrio was unusually successful in securing agreements among gangsters by the method of an orderly assignment of territory for bootlegging operations. Yet certain gangsters, like the South Side O'Donnells, were not included in these arrangements, and some gangster chiefs, like O'Banion, chafed under Torrio's generalship. Torrio's victory over open enemies like the O'Donnells was in part due to ruthless warfare and in part to police activity against his rivals to which his own gangsters were largely immune.

4. The scheme of orderly cooperation between gangsters engaged in bootlegging which came into existence during the Torrio regime, was disrupted before his retirement by the incoming of the Dever administration which destroyed the previous arrangements for political protection.

5. Bootlegging, because of its enormous profits, naturally became the main illegal business enterprise promoted by Torrio and his fellow gangsters. But with political protection they continued to carry on and to extend the field of operation of vice and gambling enterprises.

6. Torrio was quick to perceive the importance of taking advantage of the fact that the metropolitan region of Chicago falls under many different municipal governments. He not only utilized the suburban villages which he already controlled in the metropolitan region of Chicago as centers for bootlegging, gambling, and vice, but he extended his control over other outlying communities. Cicero, as well as Burnham, River Forest, and Stickney, became notorious as completely controlled for the purposes of organized crime.

With the retirement of Torrio, Al Capone, his chief lieutenant, became the principal contender for the position of leadership of the forces of organized crime. While Capone has not as yet succeeded in securing the position of uncontended supremacy held by Torrio, he has profited by the experience of the latter. He has, for example, endeavored to detach himself from first-hand participation both in criminal activities and in gangster feuds. He has taken extraordinary precautions to protect himself by an armed force of bodyguards against attacks by enemy gangsters. Capone has entered new fields of organized crime like business "racketeering" and has even attempted something like an inter-city federation of the activities of organized crime. And finally, he has adjusted the operations of his criminal enterprises more carefully than did Torrio to meet the exigencies of changes in the political situation.

25. Black Nationalism: Marcus Garvey

MARCUS GARVEY'S United Negro Improvement Association faded from prominence after Garvey's imprisonment for mail fraud in 1925, and his deportation in 1927. At the height of its power in 1922–25, however, it commanded more influence among American Negroes than any militant black nationalist organization in the country's history. The secret of Garvey's ability to win the devotion of millions seems to have eluded even the cleverest among his would-be successors; although Malcolm X appeared to be making significant headway before his murder in a Harlem auditorium. In contrast to the imposing Malcolm, Garvey was short and squat. Witnesses attest, however, to Garvey's magnificent oratorical skills, and to the near-hypnotic magnetism he exercised when delivering messages like that below, which is taken from two of Garvey's editorials in his newspaper, The Negro World.

Once again I desire to sound a warning to those of the race who still profess not to see the stark necessity for striking out along lines of nationhood for Negroes and building for themselves power and independence in our God-given land, Africa. Living as Negroes are in environments of studied hostility. . . , it is difficult to conceive what holds these super-optimists back. By optimistic, if you must, but in Heaven's name, prepare now against the day when your optimism shall be forced to take wings.

The program of "Africa for the Africans, those at home and those abroad," of the Universal Negro Improvement Association is not meant to dump all Negroes in Africa, but to encourage all Negroes to help in the building up of Africa as a great Negro nation. . . . Never forget that our success educationally, industrially, and politically is based upon the protection of a nation founded by ourselves on the continent of Africa. Prejudice against the Negro will only die out when the Negro himself becomes a power sufficiently strong to command fear and respect.

Many of our people argue that the Negro can use his industrial wealth and his ballot to force the government to recognize him.

SOURCE: Marcus Garvey, *The Negro World* (August 9, 1924), p. 14; (November 28, 1925), p. 1.

But we must understand that the government is the people and that the majority of the people dictate the policy of the government. If the majority of the people are against a measure, a thing, or a race, then the government is impotent to protect that measure, that thing, or that race. If the Negro were to live in this western world for another five hundred years he would still find himself outnumbered by superior numbers of other races. . . .

I am here tonight not to blame the white man for what happened to me or the Universal Negro Improvement Association. It was the white man's duty to put Marcus Garvey in jail. It was the white man's duty to get rid of Marcus Garvey. It was the white man's duty to send Marcus Garvey to hell as quickly as they could get him there because it was a fight for existance between peoples. . . . And I don't blame them for doing it. If I were a white man I would send everything to hell that did not look like me that stood in the path of my progress. . . . I am going to send everything to hell that stands in the way of 400,000,000 Negroes.

We are living in a highly strung, or, I may say, barbarous age, when men grapple for that which they want just as the lion would go out and devour the sheep or goat to satisfy its appetite. That is why we were slaves for 300 years; that is why now we are industrial and economic slaves. . . . With the rest of the members of the UNIA I repeat the historic words of Patrick Henry: "I care not what others may say, but as for me, give me liberty or give me death."

26. The Harlem Renaissance: W. E. B. Du Bois

W. E. B. Du Bois, *the most prominent Negro intellectual in America, proclaimed in 1920 in the NAACP journal,* The Crisis, *which he edited, "We have today all too few writers. . . . A renaissance of American Negro literature is due." Partly because of Du Bois's encouragement and aid, by the mid-1920s scores of black authors were publishing poems, short stories, and novels. Some reached an extremely high level of excellence* (see Selection 27). *Du Bois continued to act as the chief inspiration of the Negro cultural revival, outlining below his plans for broadening his journal's influence on black culture.*

Source: W. E. B. Du Bois, "Opinion of W. E. B. Du Bois," *The Crisis*, 30, No. 1 (May 1925) pp. 1, 8–9.

The New Crisis

We have assumed, with the spring, with the beginning of our 30th semi-annual volume, with our 175th number and with the closing of a fateful quarter century, something of a new dress and a certain renewal of spirit.

How long may a *Crisis* last? one might ask, sensing between our name and age some contradiction. To which we answer: What is long? 15 or 5000 years? But even in 15 years we see curious and suggestive change. In November 1910, we wrote:

> The object of this publication is to set forth those facts and arguments which show the danger of race prejudice, particularly as manifested today toward colored people. It takes its name from the fact that the editors believe that this is a critical time in the history of the advancement of men. Catholicity and tolerance, reason and forbearance can today make the world-old dream of human brotherhood approach realization; while bigotry and prejudice emphasized race consciousness and force can repeat the awful history of the contact of nations and groups in the past. We strive for this higher and broader vision of Peace and Good Will.

Then we set forth the plan to make *The Crisis* (1) a newspaper, (2) a review of opinion, (3) a magazine with "a few short articles."

This initial program has unfolded itself, changed and developed. There is no longer need of a monthly newspaper for colored folk. Colored weeklies have arisen with an efficiency and scope in news-gathering that was not dreamed of in 1910. Our news therefore has transformed itself into a sort of permanent record of a few matters of widespread and historic importance. Our review of opinion continues in both "Opinion" and "Looking Glass," but rather as interpretation than as mere quotation. Particularly has our policy changed as to articles. They have increased in number, length and authority. And above all, out of the broad vagueness of our general policy have emerged certain definite matters which we shall pursue with increased earnestness. We name them in something like the order in which they appeal to us now:

1. Economic Development

At Philadelphia, the NAACP made a suggestion of alliance among the laboring people of the United States across the color line. The American Federation of Labor has as yet made no active response to our overtures. Meantime, however, we are not waiting and we propose to make a crusade in *The Crisis* covering the next three years and taking up in succession the history and significance of the Labor Movement in the modern world, the present actual relations of Negroes to labor unions and a practical plan of future cooperation.

2. Political Independence

We shall stress as never before political independence. No longer must Negroes be born into the Republican Party. If they vote the Republican ticket or any other ticket it must be because the candidates of that party in any given election make the best promises for the future and show the best record in the past. Above all we shall urge all Negroes, male and female, to register and vote and to study political ethics and machinery.

3. Education and Talent

We shall stress the education of Negro youth and the discovery of Negro talent. Our schools must be emancipated from the secret domination of the Bourbon white South. Teachers, white or black, in Negro schools who cannot receive and treat their pupils as social equals must go. We must develop brains, ambition, efficiency and ideals without limit or circumscription. If our own Southern colleges will not do this, and whether they do it or not, we must continue to force our way into Northern colleges in larger and larger numbers and to club their doors open with our votes. We must provide larger scholarship funds to support Negroes of talent here and abroad.

4. Art

We shall stress Beauty—all Beauty, but especially the beauty of Negro life and character; its music, its dancing, its drawing and painting and the new birth of its literature. This growth which *The Crisis* long since predicted is sprouting and coming to flower. We shall encourage it in every way—by reproduction, by publication, by personal mention—keeping the while a high standard of merit and stooping never to cheap flattery and misspent kindliness.

5. Peace and International Understanding

Through the Pan-African movement we shall press for better knowledge of each other by groups of the peoples of African descent; we shall seek wider understanding with the brown and yellow peoples of the world and thus, by the combined impact of an appeal to decency and humanity from the oppressed and insulted to those fairer races who today accidentally rule the world, we shall seek universal peace by abolishing the rivalries and hatreds and economic competition that lead to organized murder.

6. The Church

We shall recognize and stress the fact that the American Negro church is doing the greatest work in social uplift of any present agency. We criticise our churches bitterly and in these plaints *The Crisis* has often joined. At the same time we know that without the help of the Negro church neither the NAACP nor *The Crisis* could have come into being nor could they for a single day continue to exist. Despite an outworn creed and ancient methods of worship the black church is leading the religious world in real human brotherhood, in personal charity, in social uplift and in economic teaching. No such tremendous force can be neglected or ignored by a journal which seeks to portray and expound the truth. We shall essay, then, the contradictory task of showing month by month the accomplishment of black religious organization in America and at the same time seeking to free the minds of our people from the futile dogma that makes for unreason and intolerance.

7. Self-criticism

The Crisis is going to be more frankly critical of the Negro group. In our fight for the sheer crumbs of decent treatment we have become habituated to regarding ourselves as always right and resenting criticism from whites and furiously opposing self-criticism from within. We are seriously crippling Negro art and literature by refusing to contemplate any but handsome heroes, unblemished heroines and flawless defenders; we insist on being always and everywhere all right and often we ruin our cause by claiming too much and admitting no fault. Here *The Crisis* has sinned with its group and it purposes hereafter to examine from time to time judicially the extraordinary number of very human faults among us—both those common to mankind and those born of our extraordinary history and experiences.

8. Criticism

This does not mean that we propose for a single issue to cease playing the gadfly to the Bourbon South and the Copperhead North, to hypocritical Philanthropy and fraudulent Science, to race hate and human degradation.

27. The New Negro: Alain Locke

Alain Locke, *like Du Bois, a Harvard Ph.D., edited in 1925 what he called "the first fruits of the Negro Renaissance." These book chapters, stories, essays, poems, and extracts from plays had been published by America's foremost magazines and publishing houses, as well as in Negro journals like* The Crisis. *In the foreword to his book Locke explains why he chose as its title* The New Negro.

In the last decade something beyond the watch and guard of statistics has happened in the life of the American Negro and the three norns who have traditionally presided over the Negro problem have a changeling in their laps. The Sociologist, the Philanthropist, the Race leader are not unaware of the New Negro, but they are at a loss to account for him. He simply cannot be swathed in their formulae. For the younger generation is vibrant with a new psychology; the new spirit is awake in the masses, and under the very eyes of the professional observers in transforming what has been a perennial problem into the progressive phases of contemporary Negro life.

Could such a metamorphosis have taken place as suddenly as it has appeared to? The answer is no; not because the New Negro is not here, but because the Old Negro had long become more of a myth than a man. The Old Negro, we must remember, was a

Source: Alain Locke, "The New Negro" in *The New Negro: An Interpretation* (New York, 1925), pp. 3–16.

creature of moral debate and historical controversy. His has been a stock figure perpetuated as an historical fiction partly in innocent sentimentalism, partly in deliberate reactionism. The Negro himself has contributed his share to this through a sort of protective social mimicry forced upon him by the adverse circumstances of dependence. So for generations in the mind of America, the Negro has been more of a formula than a human being—a something to be argued about, condemned or defended, to be "kept down," or "in his place," or "helped up," to be worried with or worried over, harassed or patronized, a social bogey or a social burden. The thinking Negro even has been induced to share this same general attitude, to focus his attention on controversial issues, to see himself in the distorted perspective of a social problem. His shadow, so to speak, has been more real to him than his personality. Through having had to appeal from the unjust stereotypes of his oppressors and traducers to those of his liberators, friends and benefactors he has had to subscribe to the traditional positions from which his case has been viewed. Little true social or self-understanding has or could come from such a situation.

But while the minds of most of us, black and white, have thus burrowed in the trenches of the Civil War and Reconstruction, the actual march of development has simply flanked these positions, necessitating a sudden reorientation of view. We have not been watching in the right direction; set North and South on a sectional axis, we have not noticed the East till the sun has us blinking.

Recall how suddenly the Negro spirituals revealed themselves; suppressed for generations under the stereotypes of Wesleyan hymn harmony, secretive, half-ashamed, until the courage of being natural brought them out—and behold, there was folk music. Similarly the mind of the Negro seems suddenly to have slipped from under the tyranny of social intimidation and to be shaking off the psychology of imitation and implied inferiority. By shedding the old chrysalis of the Negro problem we are achieving something like a spiritual emancipation. Until recently, lacking self-understanding, we have been almost as much of a problem to ourselves as we still are to others. But the decade that found us with a problem has left us with only a task. The multitude perhaps feels as yet only a strange relief and a new vague urge, but the thinking few know that in the reaction the vital inner grip of prejudice has been broken.

With this renewed self-respect and self-dependence, the life of the Negro community is bound to enter a new dynamic phase, the buoyancy from within compensating for whatever pressure there may be of conditions from without. The migrant masses, shifting from countryside to city, hurdle several generations of experience at a leap, but more important, the same thing happens spiritually in the life attitudes and self-expression of the Young Negro, in his poetry, his art, his education and his new outlook, with the additional advantage, of course, of the poise and greater certainty of knowing what it is all about. From this comes the promise and warrant of a new leadership. As one of them has discerningly put it:

We have tomorrow
Bright before us
Like a flame.

Yesterday, a night-gone thing
A sun-down name.

And dawn today
Broad arch above the road we came.
We march!

This is what, even more than any "most creditable record of fifty years of freedom," requires that the Negro of today be seen through other than the dusty spectacles of past controversy. The day of "aunties," "uncles" and "mammies" is equally gone. Uncle Tom and Sambo have passed on, and even the "Colonel" and "George" play barnstorm roles from which they escape with relief when the public spotlight is off. The popular melodrama has about played itself out, and it is time to scrap the fictions, garret the bogeys and settle down to a realistic facing of facts.

First we must observe some of the changes which since the traditional lines of opinion were drawn have rendered these quite obsolete. A main change has been, of course, that shifting of the Negro population which has made the Negro problem no longer exclusively or even predominantly Southern. Why should our minds remain sectionalized, when the problem itself no longer is? Then the trend of migration has not only been toward the North and the Central Midwest, but cityward and to the great centers of industry—the problems of adjustment are new, practical, local and not peculiarly racial. Rather they are an integral part of the large industrial and social problems of our present-day democracy. And finally, with the Negro rapidly in process of class differentiation, if it ever was warrantable to regard and treat the Negro *en masse* it is becoming with every day less possible, more unjust and more ridiculous.

In the very process of being transplanted, the Negro is becoming transformed.

The tide of Negro migration, northward and cityward, is not to be fully explained as a blind flood started by the demands of war industry coupled with the shutting off of foreign migration, or by the pressure of poor crops coupled with increasing social terrorism in certain sections of the South and Southwest. Neither labor demand, the boll weevil nor the Ku Klux Klan is a basic factor, however contributory any of all of them may have been. The wash and rush of this human tide on the beach line of the northern city centers is to be explained primarily in terms of a new vision of opportunity, of social and economic freedom, of a spirit to seize, even in the face of an extortionate and heavy toll, a chance for the improvement of conditions. With each successive wave of it, the movement of the Negro becomes more and more a mass movement toward the larger and the more democratic chance—in the Negro's case a deliberate flight not only from countryside to city, but from medieval America to modern.

Take Harlem as an instance of this. Here in Manhattan is not merely the largest Negro community in the world, but the first concentration in history of so many diverse elements of Negro life. It has attracted the African, the West Indian, the Negro American; has brought together the Negro of the North and the Negro of the South; the man from the city and the man from the town and village; the peasant, the student, the business man, the professional man, artist, poet, musician, adventurer and worker, preacher and criminal, exploiter and social outcast. Each group has come with its own separate motives and for its own special ends, but their greatest experience has been the finding of one another. Proscription and prejudice have thrown these dissimilar elements into a common area of contact and interaction. Within this area, race sympathy and unity have determined a further fusing of sentiment and experience. So what began in terms of segregation becomes more and more, as its elements mix and react, the laboratory of a great race-welding. Hitherto, it must be admitted that American Negroes have been a race more in name than in fact, or to be exact, more in sentiment than in experience. The chief bond between them has been that of a common condition rather than a common consciousness; a problem in common rather than a life in common. In Harlem, Negro life is seizing upon its first chances for group expression and self-determination. It is—or promises at least to be—a race capital. That is why our comparison is taken with those nascent centers of folk expression and self-determination which are playing a creative part in the world today. Without pretense to their political significance, Harlem has the same role to play for the New Negro as Dublin has had for the New Ireland or Prague for the New Czechoslovakia.

Harlem, I grant you, isn't typical—but it is significant, it is prophetic. No sane observer, however sympathetic to the new trend, would contend that the great masses are articulate as yet, but they stir, they move, they are more than physically restless. The challenge of the new intellectuals among them is clear enough —the "race radicals" and realists who have broken with the old epoch of philanthropic guidance, sentimental appeal and protest. But are we after all only reading into the stirrings of a sleeping giant the dreams of an agitator? The answer is in the migrating peasant. It is the "man farthest down" who is most active in getting up. One of the most characteristic symptoms of this is the professional man himself migrating to recapture his constituency after a vain effort to maintain in some Southern corner what for years back seemed an established living and clientele. The clergyman following his errant flock, the physician or lawyer trailing his clients, supply the true clues. In a real sense it is the rank and file who are leading, and the leaders who are following. A transformed and transforming psychology permeates the masses.

When the racial leaders of twenty years ago spoke of developing race pride and stimulating race consciousness, and of the desirability of race solidarity, they could not in any accurate degree have anticipated the abrupt feeling that has surged up and now pervades the awakened centers. Some of the recognized Negro leaders and a powerful section of white opinion identified with "race work" of the older order have indeed attempted to discount this feeling as a "passing phase," an attack of "race nerves" so to speak, an "aftermath of the war," and the like. It has not abated, however, if we are to gauge by the present tone and temper of the Negro press, or by the shift in popular support from the officially recognized and orthodox spokesmen to those of the independent, popular, and often radical type who are unmistakable symptoms of a new order. It is a social disservice to blunt the fact that the Negro of the Northern centers has reached a stage where tutelage, even of the most interested and well-intentioned sort, must give place to new relationships, where positive self-direction must be reckoned with in every increasing measure. The American mind must reckon with a fundamentally changed Negro.

The Negro too, for his part, has idols of the tribe to smash. If on the one hand the white man has erred in making the Negro appear to be that which would excuse or extenuate his treatment of him, the Negro, in turn, has too often unnecessarily excused himself because of the way he has been treated. The intelligent Negro of today is resolved not to make discrimination an extenuation for his shortcomings in performance, individual or collective; he is trying to hold himself at par, neither inflated by sentimental allowances nor depreciated by current social discounts. For this he must know himself and be known for precisely what he is, and for that reason he welcomes the new scientific rather than the old sentimental interest. Sentimental interest in the Negro has ebbed. We used to lament this as the falling off of our friends; now we rejoice and pray to be delivered both from self-pity and condescension. The mind of each racial group has had a bitter weaning, apathy or hatred on one side matching disillusionment or resentment on the other; but they face each other today with the possibility at least of entirely new mutual attitudes.

It does not follow that if the Negro were better known, he would be better liked or better treated. But mutual understanding is basic for any subsequent cooperation and adjustment. The effort toward this will at least have the effect of remedying in large part what has been the most unsatisfactory feature of our present stage of race relationships in America, namely the fact that the more intelligent and representative elements of the two race groups have at so many points got quite out of vital touch with one another.

The fiction is that the life of the races is separate, and increasingly so. The fact is that they have touched too closely at the unfavorable and too lightly at the favorable levels.

While interracial councils have sprung up in the South, drawing on forward elements of both races, in the Northern cities manual laborers may brush elbows in their everyday work, but the community and business leaders have experienced no such interplay or far too little of it. These segments must achieve contact or the race situation in America becomes desperate. Fortunately this is happening. There is a growing realization that in social effort the cooperative basis must supplant long-distance philanthropy, and that the only safeguard for mass relations in the future must be provided in the carefully maintained contacts of the enlightened minorities of both race groups. In the intellectual realm a renewed and keen curiosity is replacing the recent apathy; the Negro is being carefully studied, not just talked about and discussed. In art and letters, instead of being wholly caricatured, he is being seriously portrayed and painted.

To all of this the New Negro is keenly responsive as an augury of a new democracy in American culture. He is contributing his share to the new social understanding. But the desire to be understood would never in itself have been sufficient to have opened so completely the protectively closed portals of the thinking Negro's mind. There is still too much possibility of being snubbed or patronized for that. It was rather the necessity for fuller, truer self-expression, the realization of the unwisdom of allowing social discrimination to segregate him mentally, and a counter-attitude to cramp and fetter his own living—and so the "spite wall" that the intellectuals built over the "color line" has happily been taken down. Much of this reopening of intellectual contacts has centered in New York and has been richly fruitful not merely in the enlarging of personal experience, but in the definite enrichment of American art and letters and in the clarifying of our common vision of the social tasks ahead.

The particular significance in the reestablishment of contact between the more advanced and representative classes is that it promises to offset some of the unfavorable reactions of the past, or at least to re-surface race contacts somewhat for the future. Subtly the conditions that are molding a New Negro are molding a new American attitude.

However, this new phase of things is delicate; it will call for less charity but more justice; less help, but infinitely closer understanding. This is indeed a critical stage of race relationships because of the likelihood, if the new temper is not understood, of engendering sharp group antagonism and a second crop of more calculated prejudice. In some quarters, it has already done so. Having weaned the Negro, public opinion cannot continue to paternalize. The Negro today is inevitably moving forward under the control largely of his own objectives. What are these objectives? Those of his outer life are happily already well and finally formulated, for they are none other than the ideals of American institutions and democracy. Those of his inner life are yet in process of formation, for the new psychology at present is more of a consensus of feeling than of opinion, of attitude rather than of program. Still some points seem to have crystallized.

Up to the present one may adequately describe the Negro's "inner objectives" as an attempt to repair a damaged group psychology and reshape a warped social perspective. Their realization has required a new mentality for the American Negro. And as it matures we begin to see its effects; at first, negative, iconoclastic, and then positive and constructive. In this new group psychology we note the lapse of sentimental appeal, then the development of a more positive self-respect and self-reliance; the repudiation of social dependence, and then the gradual recovery from hypersensitiveness and "touchy" nerves, the repudiation of the double standard of judgment with its special philanthropic allowances and then the sturdier desire for objective and scientific appraisal; and finally the rise from social disillusionment to race pride, from the sense of social debt to the responsibilities of social contribution, and offsetting the necessary working and commonsense acceptance of restricted conditions, the belief in ultimate esteem and recognition. Therefore the Negro today wishes to be known for what he is, even in his faults and shortcomings, and scorns a craven and precarious survival at the price of seeming to be what he is not. He resents being spoken of as a social ward or minor, even by his own, and to being regarded a chronic patient for the sociological clinic, the sick man of American democracy. For the same reasons, he himself is through with those social nostrums and panaceas, the so-called solutions of his problem, with which he and the country have been so liberally dosed in the past. Religion, freedom, education, money —in turn, he has ardently hoped for and peculiarly trusted these things; he still believes in them, but not in blind trust that they alone will solve his life problem.

Each generation, however, will have its creed, and that of the present is the belief in the efficacy of collective effort, in race cooperation. This deep feeling of race is at present the mainspring of

Negro life. It seems to be the outcome of the reaction to proscription and prejudice; an attempt, fairly successful on the whole, to convert a defensive into an offensive position, a handicap into an incentive. It is radical in tone, but not in purpose and only the most stupid forms of opposition, misunderstanding or persecution could make it otherwise. Of course, the thinking Negro has shifted a little toward the left with the world trend, and there is an increasing group who affiliate with radical and liberal movements. But fundamentally for the present the Negro is radical on race matters, conservative on others, in other words, a "forced radical," a social protestant rather than a genuine radical. Yet under further pressure and injustice iconoclastic thought and motives will inevitably increase. Harlem's quixotic radicalisms call for their ounce of democracy today lest tomorrow they be beyond cure.

The Negro mind reaches out as yet to nothing but American wants, American ideas. But this forced attempt to build his Americanism on race values is a unique social experiment, and its ultimate success is impossible except through the fullest sharing of American culture and institutions. There should be no delusion about this. American nerves in sections unstrung with race hysteria are often fed the opiate that the trend of Negro advance is wholly separatist, and that the effect of its operation will be to encyst the Negro as a benign foreign body in the body politic. This cannot be—even if it were desirable. The racialism of the Negro is no limitation or reservation with respect to American life; it is only a constructive effort to build the obstructions in the stream of his progress into an efficient dam of social energy and power. Democracy itself is obstructed and stagnated to the extent that any of its channels are closed. Indeed they cannot be selectively closed. So the choice is not between one way for the Negro and another way for the rest, but between American institutions frustrated on the one hand and American ideals progressively fulfilled and realized on the other.

There is, of course, a warrantably comfortable feeling in being on the right side of the country's professed ideals. We realize that we cannot be undone without America's undoing. It is within the gamut of this attitude that the thinking Negro faces America, but with variations of mood that are if anything more significant than the attitude itself. Sometimes we have it taken with the defiant ironic challenge of McKay:

Mine is the future grinding down today
Like a great landslip moving to the sea,
Bearing its freight of debris far away
Where the green hungry waters restlessly
Heave mammoth pyramids, and break and roar
Their eerie challenge to the crumbling shore.

Sometimes, perhaps more frequently as yet, it is taken in the fervent and almost filial appeal and counsel of Weldon Johnson's:

O Southland, dear Southland!
Then why do you still cling
To an idle age and a musty page,
To a dead and useless thing?

But between defiance and appeal, midway almost between cynicism and hope, the prevailing mind stands in the mood of the same author's *To America*, an attitude of sober query and stoical challenge:

How would you have us, as we are?
Or sinking 'neath the load we bear,
Our eyes fixed forward on a star,
Or gazing empty at despair?

Rising or falling? Men or things?
With dragging pace or footsteps fleet?
Strong, willing sinews in your wings,
Or tightening chains about your feet?

More and more, however, an intelligent realization of the great discrepancy between the American social creed and the American social practice forces upon the Negro the taking of the moral advantage that is his. Only the steadying and sobering effect of a truly characteristic gentleness of spirit prevents the rapid rise of a definite cynicism and counter-hate and a defiant superiority feeling. Human as this reaction would be, the majority still deprecate its advent, and would gladly see it forestalled by the speedy amelioration of its causes. We wish our race pride to be a healthier, more positive achievement than a feeling based upon a realization of the shortcomings of others. But all paths toward the attainment of a sound social attitude have been difficult; only a relatively few enlightened minds have been able as the phrase puts it "to rise above" prejudice. The ordinary man has had until recently only a hard choice between the alternatives of supine and humiliating submission and stimulating but hurtful counter-prejudice. Fortunately from some inner, desperate resourcefulness has recently sprung up the simple expedient of fighting prejudice by mental passive resistance, in other words by trying to ignore it. For the few, this manna may perhaps be effective, but the masses cannot thrive upon it.

Fortunately there are constructive channels opening out into which the balked social feelings of the American Negro can flow freely.

Without them there would be much more pressure and danger than there is. These compensating interests are racial but in a new and enlarged way. One is the consciousness of acting as the advance-guard of the African peoples in their contact with Twentieth Century civilization; the other, the sense of a mission of rehabilitating the race in world esteem from that loss of prestige for which the fate and conditions of slavery have so largely been responsible. Harlem, as we shall see, is the center of both these movements; she is the home of the Negro's "Zionism." The pulse of the Negro world has begun to beat in Harlem. A Negro newspaper carrying news material in English, French and Spanish, gathered from all quarters of America, the West Indies and Africa has maintained itself in Harlem for over five years. Two important magazines, both edited from New York, maintain their news and circulation consistently on a cosmopolitan scale. Under American auspices and backing, three pan-African congresses have been held abroad for the discussion of common interests, colonial questions and the future cooperative development of Africa. In terms of the race question as a world problem, the Negro mind has leapt, so to speak, upon the parapets of prejudice and extended its cramped horizons. In so doing it has linked up with the growing group consciousness of the dark peoples and is gradually learning their common interests. As one of our writers has recently put it: "It is imperative that we understand the white world in its relations to the nonwhite world." As with the Jew, persecution is making the Negro international.

As a world phenomenon this wider race consciousness is a different thing from the much asserted rising tide of color. Its inevitable causes are not of our making. The consequences are not necessarily damaging to the best interests of civilization. Whether it actually brings into being new Armadas of conflict or argosies of cultural exchange and enlightenment can only be decided by the attitude of the dominant races in an era of critical change. With the American Negro, his new internationalism is primarily an effort to recapture contact with the scattered peoples of African derivation. Garveyism may be a transient, if spectacular, phenomenon, but the possible role of the American Negro in the future development of Africa is one of the most constructive and universally helpful missions that any modern people can lay claim to.

Constructive participation in such causes cannot help giving the Negro valuable group incentives, as well as increased prestige at home and abroad. Our greatest rehabilitation may possibly come through such channels, but for the present, more immediate hope rests in the revaluation by white and black alike of the Negro in terms of his artistic endowments and cultural contributions, past and prospective. It must be increasingly recognized that the Negro has already made very substantial contributions, not only in his folk art, music especially, which has always found appreciation, but in larger, though humbler and less acknowledged ways. For generations the Negro has been the peasant matrix of that section of America which has most undervalued him, and here he has contributed not only materially in labor and in social patience, but spiritually as well. The South has unconsciously absorbed the gift of his folk temperament. In less than half a generation it will be easier to recognize this, but the fact remains that a leaven of humor, sentiment, imagination and tropic nonchalance has gone into the making of the South from a humble, unacknowledged source. A second crop of the Negro's gifts promises still more largely. He now becomes a conscious contributor and lays aside the status of a beneficiary and ward for that of a collaborator and participant in American civilization. The great social gain in this is the releasing of our talented group from the arid fields of controversy and debate to the productive fields of creative expression. The especially cultural recognition they win should in turn prove the key to that revaluation of the Negro which must precede or accompany any considerable further betterment of race relationships. But whatever the general effect, the present generation will have added the motives of self-expression and spiritual development to the old and still unfinished task of making material headway and progress. No one who understandingly faces the situation with its substantial accomplishment or views the new scene with its still more abundant promise can be entirely without hope. And certainly, if in our lifetime the Negro should not be able to celebrate his full initiation into American democracy, he can at least, on the warrant of these things, celebrate the attainment of a significant and satisfying new phase of group development, and with it a spiritual Coming of Age.

28. The Quiet Revolution: Sophia P. Breckinridge

WHILE THE woman suffrage movement won headlines and inspired countless speeches, books, articles, and pamphlets about the drastic changes in American society that success for the movement would bring in its wake, a quiet revolution involving American women actually was taking place. Quantitatively it can be measured by the fact that the number of women sixteen years of age and over gainfully employed outside the home rose from 1,701,000 in 1870 to 10,546,000 in 1930. This six-fold increase was about 50 percent larger than the increase in the female population aged sixteen or more. Most of these women worked because their families required the additional income; studies indicate that even in large metropolitan areas, less than 10 percent of the wives of professional men or business executives worked after marriage. On the other hand, women in that category were increasingly likely to have attended college, suggesting that the more ambitious and talented among them might demonstrate increasing dissatisfaction as the home lost its central place in the culture. The possibility that this dissatisfaction could lie far in the future, however, is suggested by Sophia Breckinridge's admission in 1932 that the proportion of women in the more prestigious professions had been declining, at least since the mid-1920s. Breckinridge's essay was prepared for the comprehensive study of American society commissioned by President Hoover and published as Recent Social Trends.

Women's role in the American community has undergone redefinition during the past thirty years. As delineated in the preceding chapter on the family, the development of mechanical power,

SOURCE: S. P. Breckinridge, "The Activities of Women Outside the Home," *Recent Social Trends in the United States, Report of the President's Committee on Social Trends* (New York, 1932), pp. 709–750. Reprinted by permission of McGraw-Hill Book Company.

the introduction of new inventions, the rise of specialized services outside the home, the changing manner of living and the decreasing size of the family have altered or eliminated many of women's earlier household activities. The chapters on the family, on the people as consumers and on labor groups make it clear that the occupations of women in the home have been of fundamental importance in helping to produce the sum of commodities or services available and likewise in determining the ways in which those commodities and services should be enjoyed. With the departure of many productive activities from the home, however, large numbers of women through necessity or choice are seeking a new place in the economic system and the shift is not being made without revolutionary changes in attitudes with regard to women's responsibilities under the changed surroundings of their lives. Their new position, together with the granting of suffrage, is giving women a share in the entire life of the community. This chapter is concerned then with the activities of women outside the home: their employment for wages, their position in government and their organizations.

No comment is needed at this point on the subject of the activities of women in their own organizations or in government, both of which will be considered at length in later sections. With reference to women's employment, however, a few preliminary remarks will facilitate the later presentation. It should be remembered that there have always been women whose support was not derived from family attachments. There have been and still are four ways in which women obtain a living: (1) in the traditional relationship of marriage, which still implies an obligation on the part of the husband to provide those things suitable to the standard of life in which he places a woman and in return for which there is still the obligation to give marital companionship and to perform domestic services; (2) in the less frequent support of single women by relatives; (3) in the increasing legitimate employment for wages; and finally (4) in prostitution.

Some of these methods of obtaining a livelihood are discussed in other chapters. In the chapter on shifting occupational patterns an attempt is made to estimate the number of single women not economically self-sufficient, and reference is made in the chapter on the family to the changing proportion of married women. With regard to prostitution, the absence of reliable data has made it impossible to present satisfactory conclusions. The present chapter will discuss the third method listed, namely that of women's increasing legitimate employment for wages outside of the home, together with the attendant problems of training, choice of occupation and reward in wages or salaries.[1]

Although attention is called in the chapter on the family to the changes that have occurred with reference to the law of the family group, there are several aspects of this subject, in its relation to the employment of women, on which it is worthwhile to add further comment. Under the older family organization the services of both the wife and the daughter, or their wages if they were gainfully employed, belonged to the husband and father. Whether work was done within or outside the home, the goods, services or earnings accrued to the composite income. Services rendered in the home by the wife or minor children were without any other compensation than provision of support.

This eighteenth and early nineteenth century economy rested on economic and social bases which became radically altered during the course of the nineteenth century. The dissatisfaction produced by the anomalies in the code of the older order made apparent the need for legislative or judicial action directed toward removing the claims on the services of women. By the beginning of the twentieth century nearly all the states had enacted laws giving to married women the right to collect and control their earnings. The fact that, in general, the husband's domicile determines the wife's affects the mobility and hence the opportunities of the married woman who would earn, but there is, nevertheless, abundant evidence that attitudes toward women's role in society are changing and that women are succeeding in establishing their right "as individual human beings to realize their varied interests and capacities in an atmosphere of freedom from the barriers of assumed sex differences."[2]

A final prefatory remark will explain the statements to follow. No evidence is given to the effect that women are capable of doing the various tasks which they have chosen. It is assumed that such

1. For a fuller treatment of the activities of women, see the monograph in this series entitled *Political, Social and Economic Activities of Women*.
2. Hutchinson, Emilie J., "The Economic Problems of Women," *Annals of the American Academy of Political and Social Science*, special number on *Women in the Modern World*, May 1929, vol. 143, p. 132.

material would be superfluous, although at the beginning of the century there was still questioning as to women's capacity for the higher ranks of academic life. The attempt is therefore made to set out only the evidence as to how women are selecting and being selected to carry on the work found socially, economically or industrially profitable. In that connection an underlying assumption may perhaps be brought to the surface of the discussion. It is the assumption that, in general, in finding ways of accomplishing the work of the community a widening of the range from which choice of workers can be made and an increasing selection of workers in accordance with objective tests of qualification will mean raising the level of performance and therefore benefit the community. If a marginal person suffers from this rise in the level of competence his loss is part of the cost which the community might have to pay, but his claim should properly be met by other adjustments than the exclusion of workers more competent than he.[3]

It will be noticed that the statistics which have been used do not cover the same periods in all cases. An effort has been made to cover as much as possible of the period between 1900 and 1930 and in a few cases it has seemed desirable to cite even earlier figures. It has not always been possible, however, to get data for the entire period.

I. The Women Who Work

There are several questions to be considered in connection with the number and status of the women who are gainfully employed. Is the proportion of working women becoming larger in relation to the total number of women, and if so, is it at an increasing rate? Are women becoming an increasing part of the working population? What are the trends in the employment of married women? What are the trends according to age and according to race and nativity among working women? These questions are discussed in this section on the basis of the material available.[4]

3. Nicholson, Joseph Shield, *Principles of Political Economy*, New York, 1897–1901, vol. III, p. 164.

4. Most of the data on which this section is based are from the Population volumes of the United States Bureau of the Census. In many cases, however, the figures cited will not be found in the census reports. The reason for this is that the census classifications are changed from time to time, and in order

Women Workers in Relation to the Total Number of Women

The number of gainfully employed women, 16 years of age and over, has increased from 1,701,000 in 1870, the first year for which the Bureau of the Census collected these data, to 10,546,000 in 1930. This increase of nearly six-fold in sixty years assumes greater significance when it is compared with the somewhat less than four-fold increase in the female population 16 years of age and over.

The increase by decades in the number of women gainfully employed gives clearer evidence of trends, particularly when compared with the increase in the female population. The greatest increase during a ten-year period since 1900 was 47 percent during the first decade, when the female population 16 years of age and over increased only 24 percent. Between 1910 and 1920 the increase in female employment dropped to 16 percent, very close to the 17 percent increase in the female population. The retardation is accounted for, in part at least, by the virtual cessation of immigration. During the third decade, however, the increase in female employment rose to 29 percent while the increase in the female population was 22 percent. These figures are based on all gainfully occupied women although there is some question concerning the accuracy of the enumeration of women in agriculture at the time of the census of 1910 and again in 1920.[5]

---

to secure comparable data over an extended period it was necessary to reclassify certain occupations and to make some estimates. These adjustments were made by Ralph Hurlin for Chapter VI, and the reader is referred to the tables in that chapter, particularly Table 5, and in the monograph on the same subject. Attention is called also to the fact that nearly all of the data are for the age period 16 years of age and over rather than the customary period, 10 years of age and over. The adoption of the older age period more nearly confines the discussion to women and has the additional advantages of eliminating from consideration the somewhat doubtful figures on the occupational status of children less than 16 years of age.

5. The figures for farm laborers in 1910 are adjusted for supposed over-enumeration of women and children in agriculture, but they are still probably too high. The 1920 figures were not adjusted for females although there is probably some inaccuracy due to the fact that the 1920 census was taken as of January 1, whereas the preceding enumeration was made as of April 15, and the 1930 census is as of April 1. Because of the seasonal character of farming it is believed that some persons who would have been enumerated

The growth in the proportion of women who are gainfully employed in comparison with the total female population 16 years of age and over has increased since 1880, save for one year which is uncertain, but the rate of increase has been by no means uniform. With women in agriculture included, 160 out of every 1,000 females 16 years of age and over in 1880 were engaged in a gainful occupation. By 1890 the number had increased to 190; in 1900 it was 206; in 1910, 243; in 1920, 240; and by 1930, 253 out of every 1,000 women were at work for pay. When similar ratios are calculated with the figures for women in agriculture omitted the apparent decline in 1920 disappears. The numbers of employed women per 1,000 for the last four decades then become 172, 202, 213, and 234 respectively, once more indicating a greater change during the ten years 1920 to 1930 than during the preceding decade. It should perhaps be said that had it not been for the retardation of business activity which was well under way at the time of the 1930 census, probably even more women would have reported themselves as occupied. While the occupation census did attempt to include all who usually worked at a gainful occupation even though they might have been unemployed at the time, it sought to avoid the inclusion of those potential accretions to the occupied class, namely young persons, who had not yet found employment because of the temporary conditions.

Women Workers in Relation to the Total Number of Workers

The growing importance of women in occupations outside of the home is strikingly shown by the figures indicating the proportion which they constitute of all occupied persons. In 1930 of all gainfully occupied persons 21.9 percent, or 1 in 5, were women. This is an increase of 50 percent over 1880 when women were but 14.5 percent of the occupied. In 1900 the proportion was 17.7 percent,

---

as agricultural laborers were omitted in 1920 because they were not so employed during the winter months when the census was taken. See U.S. Bureau of the Census, *Fourteenth Census of the United States, Population,* 1920, vol. IV, pp. 22–23, and Chapter VI of this report. With agriculture omitted the figures representing the increase in female employment for the decades ending 1910, 1920, and 1930 are 49 percent, 21 percent, and 34 percent respectively.

in 1910 it was 19.8 and in 1920 it was 20.1 percent. It is apparent from these figures that women are assuming a greater share of the responsibility for carrying on the work of the country.

Age, Race and Nativity of Women Workers

Young women predominate among gainfully employed females, although the tendency is for the age periods of greatest employment to shift upward. In 1920, 20.6 percent of the employed women were less than 20 years of age while in 1930 only 15.5 percent were under that age. The figures in the following list, giving the proportion employed in each age period, indicate declines up to the age of twenty and then increases up to the older ages, 65 and over, where the number remained stationary.

Age period	Percentage of women in each age period who are gainfully occupied		Age period	Percentage of women in each age period who are gainfully occupied	
	1920	1930		1920	1930
Under 16 years	5.6	2.9	25–44 years	22.4	25.4
16–17 years	31.6	22.1	45–64 years	17.1	18.7
18–19 years	42.3	40.5	65 years and over	8.0	8.0
20–24 years	38.1	42.4			

There are several possible interpretations of these figures. The marked decline in the proportion of girls under 20 who are employed may be due, in part at least, to the spread of limitations on child labor and the growing sentiment for giving every child a high school education. Part of the difference may be due to the somewhat doubtful character of the occupation figures for children. It is interesting to note, however, that the figures indicate a drop of from 5.6 percent to 2.9 percent between 1920 and 1930 (from 10.2 percent in 1900) in the proportion of children 10 through 15 years of age who are gainfully employed. It has been suggested that the increase in the percentage of women employed between 20 and 45 years of age may be associated with the increase in the number of married women workers, particularly since the proportion of the population married in these age periods is increasing. And finally, the increase of 13 percent in the proportion of the women 25–44 years of age who are occupied gainfully is interesting in view of the belief that older women find it increasingly difficult to find employment. It is possible that as the supply of young women available for employment is further reduced through the decline in immigration and the decline in the birth rate, older women will find increasing opportunity to work, although this is by no means certain.

Another change already apparent is that native women are making up the ranks of the employed to a greater extent now than at the beginning of the century. In 1900, 58 percent of all employed women were native whites, while 71 percent came under this classification in 1930. In 1900, 15 percent of the native white women were gainfully occupied and this proportion increased to 21 percent, or more than a third, by 1930. The other two major population groups have shown a lesser tendency to vary. The foreign born white women did not vary at all, 19 percent of them having been employed in 1900 and the same proportion in 1930. The reason for this may easily be the shifting age distribution, which is not accounted for in these figures. The Negro group, contrary to expectation, declined from 41 percent employed in 1900 to 39 percent in 1930.

Married Women Workers

The problem of the married woman wage earner took on new aspects during the first thirty years of the twentieth century. Formerly it was assumed that married women with children worked chiefly because they were separated from their husbands or because their husbands did not support them, but a better understanding of the extent to which the household in its earlier form was a productive organization and of the resulting composite character of the family income has made it clear that with the changes in the economics of the family it becomes necessary that either the wife and mother must earn, or the income of the husband and father must in some way be rendered more adequate.

The impression is widespread today that growing numbers of married women are seeking employment and that employed women who marry are more and more endeavoring to remain at work after marriage. Even twenty years ago the married woman was held to be "a considerable factor in the industrial world."[6] A recent study of Chicago families[7] showed that in 23,373 families investigated 61 percent of the married men were the only wage earners in the family, 17.6 percent of the married women were employed and more than half of them had wage earning husbands. Fewer than 10 percent had husbands in the professions or in executive positions. It seems probable then that at least three-fourths had husbands in low income groups. The proportions of wives gainfully employed were, however, similar in the different occupational groups into which the author classifies the family. The data with reference to the contributions of fathers and mothers are interesting but the contributions of sons and daughters are not distinguished. The likelihood of the older children contributing is discussed as though the wage earning of the daughters was as much to be taken for granted as that of the sons.[8]

The numbers of married women in employment have grown greatly, as is shown by the census figures. In 1900 there were 769,000 married women at work, in 1910 the number had increased to 1,891,000, and in 1930 it had reached 3,071,000. Between 1900 and 1930 the total number of employed women doubled but the number of employed married women increased four-fold. Moreover the ratio of married women who work to the total number of married women has more than doubled, the figures showing that 5.6 percent of all married women were gainfully occupied in 1900 and 11.7 percent in 1930. This increase is six times that for single women of the same age period, 15 years and over, during the same thirty years. In 1900, 43.5 percent of the single women were gainfully employed and 50.5 percent in 1930, an increase of only 16 percent as compared with 100 percent for married women. The proportion of all working women who are married has also shown a striking increase since the beginning of the century. In 1900 the married constituted 15 percent of all working women. In 1930 the proportion had increased to 29 percent or twice that of the earlier date.

Another point that has interesting implications but which can

6. U.S. Bureau of Labor Statistics, *Summary of the Report on Women and Child Wage Earners in the United States*, Bulletin no. 175, 1916, p. 18.
7. Monroe, Day, *Chicago Families: A Study of Unpublished Census Data*, Chicago, 1932.
8. *Ibid.*

only be mentioned in passing is brought out by the new census tabulation of families. How many women have placed themselves under the two-fold obligation of caring for a family and pursuing a gainful occupation? Data are available at this time for only 7 states[9] but they indicate that from 1 in 10 to more than 1 in 7 homemakers are gainfully employed. And between 80 and 90 percent of these employed homemakers find their work away from home. Of even greater significance will be the data now under preparation by the Bureau of the Census showing the proportion of married women workers who are also homemakers.

The right of the married woman to work is at issue when an employer raises the question of the marital status of women, as he seldom would do in the case of men. Employers differ greatly in their attitude toward this question, some asking only for competent workers, others having definite views as to whether or not married women should work. Obviously there is still strong opposition to married women on the part of some employers. Whether or not this opposition has increased or lessened during the postwar period can only be a matter of opinion.

In 1930–1931 the National Education Association made a study in nearly 1,500 cities of the general policy of each school system with respect to the employment of married women as new teachers and the retention of single women teachers who marry. Of the cities reporting, in all population groups, about 77 percent do not employ married women as new teachers. Only 37 percent of all cities reporting permit teachers to continue teaching after marriage, and a number of these permit it only in the case of teachers who have been elected for permanent service. As to the legal aspects of the question, apparently no state has passed any legislation with respect to married women as teachers. In at least six states and the District of Columbia, however, decisions on the question have been handed down by the courts, the chief state school officials or the state board of education. Two authorities conclude from their analyses of these decisions that in these states marriage is not in itself a valid cause for dismissing a teacher who is under contract or who is teaching under a tenure law which permits dismissal only for specified causes. It is, of course, unsafe to assume that similar decisions would be made in the other states if

9. Delaware, Maine, New Hampshire, Utah, Vermont, Wisconsin and Wyoming.

cases of this kind should come up for adjudication. The most recent decision on the subject was handed down on December 21, 1931, by the Maryland State Board of Education in response to an appeal from Wicomico County. The board ruled that a woman teacher in the public schools of Maryland cannot be dismissed because she marries. It also stated that a clause in a teacher's contract reading, "If a female teacher marries in any school year she will be expected to resign at the close of the school year," is in plain conflict with the state tenure law. This law provides no basis for discrimination on account of sex or marital status.[10]

II. The Kind of Work Women Do

The Broad Occupational Divisions

Women are represented in relatively large numbers in seven of the ten major occupational classifications employed by the Bureau of the Census. The greatest number, 3,438,000, are in domestic and personal service. There are 1,970,000 in clerical occupations, 1,860,000 in manufacturing and mechanical industries and 1,226,000 in the professions. Trade and agriculture each claim somewhat less than a million female workers, while transportation and communication include something over a quarter of a million.

It is more significant in a study of trends, however, to compare the differentials over the long period from 1870 to 1930. Figure 1 shows the changing relative importance of the major occupation groups for all gainfully employed women 16 years of age and over. In 1870 agriculture claimed 21 percent of the employed women but by 1930 it claimed only 7 percent. In 1870, 20 percent of all working women were engaged in manufacturing, but the proportion fell to 18 percent in 1930. The domestic and personal service group shows a drop of from 53 percent in 1870 to 28 percent in 1920 and then a slight rise to 33 percent in 1930. The remaining occupations show relative increases in the number of women attracted to them. Between 1870 and 1930 the proportion of all gainfully occupied women 16 years of age and over who were in the professions increased from 6 percent to 12 percent. The clerical group increased from 0.4 percent to 19 percent, while trade and

10. National Education Association, *Practices Affecting Classroom Teachers*, Research Bulletin, January, 1932, p. 20.

transportation rose from 1 percent to 12 percent over the same period. These data seem to show a continuous shift in women's employment away from the older agricultural and industrial pursuits toward office, store and professional work with domestic and personal service somewhat more stable.

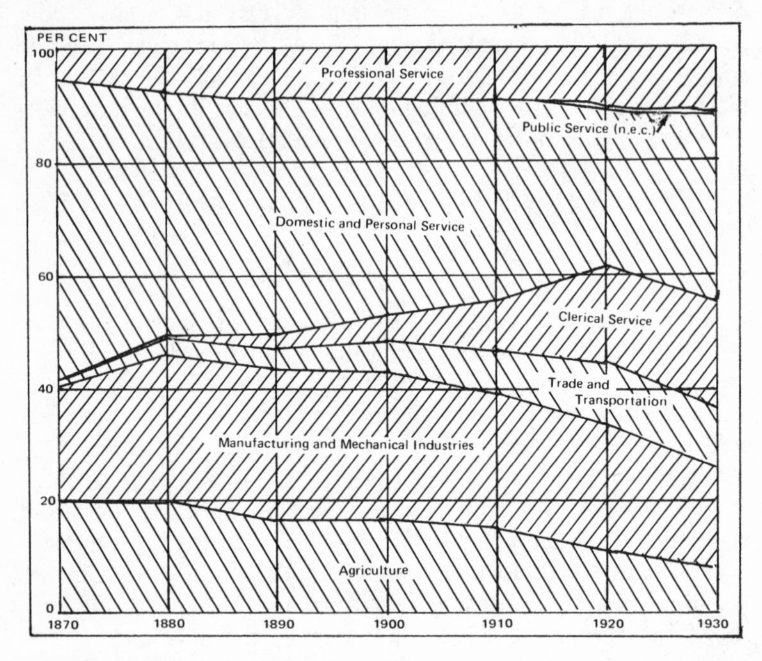

FIG. 1 Distribution of gainfully occupied women, 16 years of age and over, 1870–1930

The tendency is shown more clearly by the numerical increases indicated in Figure 2 and through the comparison of numerical increases among working women with the increases among all occupied persons. In the figure, the very great increases of trade and transportation, clerical and professional occupations between 1870 and 1930 are contrasted with the smaller increases in agriculture, manufacturing and domestic and personal service.

The more recent trends are perhaps a better indication of the immediate situation. Between 1910 and 1930 there was a decline of 6 percent in the total number of persons 16 years of age and over engaged in agriculture, but women in agriculture fell off 26 percent in the same period. Almost as striking is the situation with regard

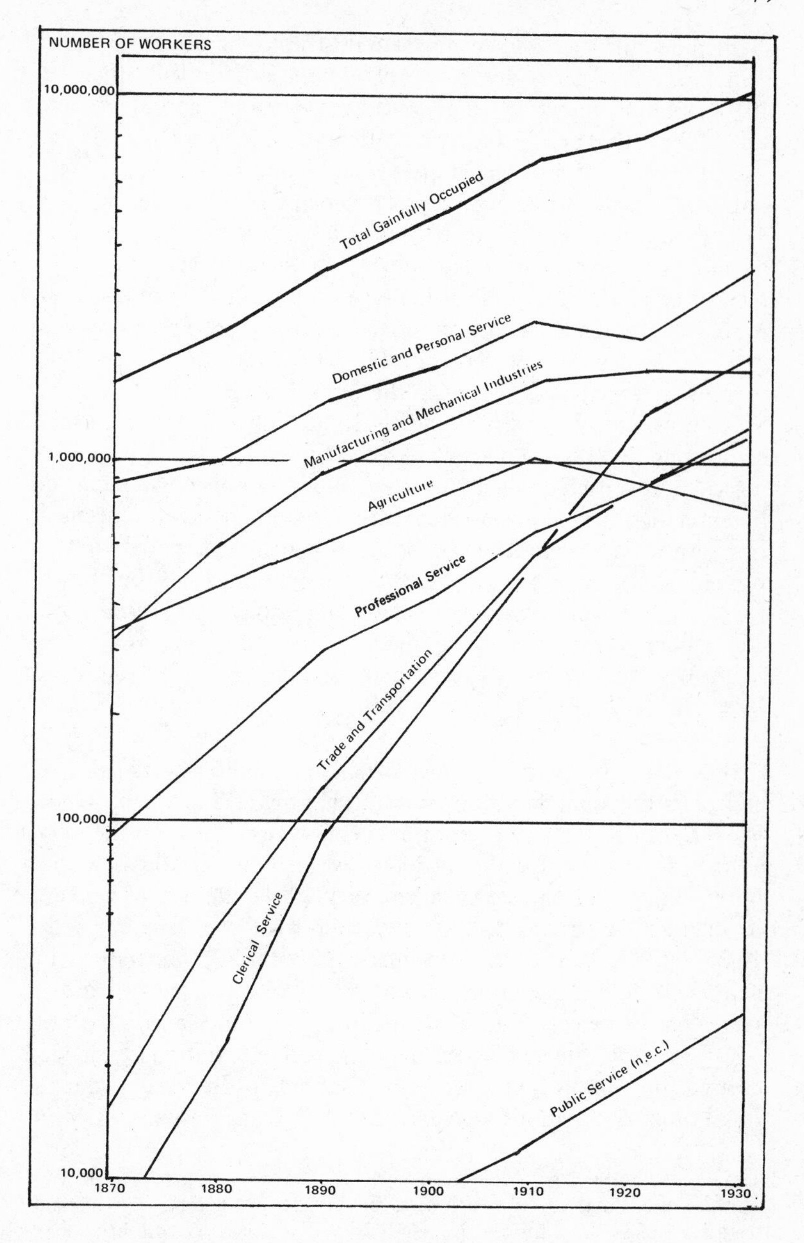

FIG. 2 Women in major occupational groups, 1870–1930.

to manufacturing and mechanical industries. There were 34 percent more persons in this group of occupations in 1930 than in 1910, but the numerical increase among women was only 9 percent. The number of women in domestic and personal service increased 36 percent or only a little more than the increase for both sexes, 43 percent. The increase of women in transportation and communication was 156 percent, or just four times the 39 percent increase for men and women combined. In clerical occupations the total number of employees is 141 percent higher now than it was in 1910, but women are 244 percent more numerous. The two sexes together increased 77 percent in trade, while women advanced 110 percent. For professional service the figures are not very different, 80 percent and 87 percent respectively. In public service, a group comprising less than 2 percent of all occupied persons and including such governmental employees as officials, police, firemen, laborers and others not classified with other industries or occupations, the general increase has been 79 percent compared to 129 percent increase for women. In this section trends will be shown for certain specific occupations and data will be presented with regard to opportunities and training for work.

Women in Manufacturing

Between 1900 and 1930 more than 6.2 million workers were added to the manufacturing and mechanical industries but only 584,000, or less than 10 percent of them, were women. In the later years of this period the proportion of women among the additions to this industry group was even less. In 1930 the number of workers in manufacturing was 1,365,000 greater than in 1920, but only 10,000 of this increase were women. As semiskilled operatives in manufacturing, the number of women 10 years of age and over[11] increased 34 percent, but in virtually every skilled occupation of significant size their number remained about stationary or decreased, thus indicating a tendency contrary to the great increases in all other occupations save agriculture. The greatest decreases in

11. In a few instances comparable data are not available for occupied persons 16 years of age and over. In such cases the broader age period, 10 years and over, is employed and the fact is so indicated. The differences are in no case large, for the number of employed children in 1930 was less than 1.4 percent of all gainfully occupied persons.

the skilled occupations were in dressmaking, tailoring and millinery, and are accounted for largely by the general shift of these industries from hand to factory production. Dressmaking and millinery, as handicraft industries virtually dominated by women, have fallen off numerically by two thirds since 1910. The number of women (10 years of age and over) in tailoring decreased 47 percent over the same twenty year period although the number of men decreased only 10 percent. In contrast to these figures for the skilled workers, the number of women operatives (10 years and over) in the clothing industries increased 46 percent, while the number of men showed a decrease of 5 percent. In three managerial groups women are increasing. As foremen and overseers in manufacturing (10 years and over) they are 44 percent more numerous than in 1910 compared with an increase of 92 percent for the sexes combined. While the total number of proprietors (10 years and over) decreased by 12 percent, women increased by 33 percent. The greatest change, however, has come in the group known as managers and officials in manufacturing. Here women (10 years and over) have increased 459 percent while the group as a whole shows a growth of 149 percent (the number, however, is small, only 10,400). Thus it appears that during this period of rapidly changing methods of production, women as well as men have been called upon to make many new adjustments to the changing situation, and while many have gone into semiskilled jobs others have found opportunity to manage and to direct.

Women in Domestic and Personal Service

In this general occupation group, as in manufacturing, there has been a drift away from pursuits carried on more or less independently to similar work found in factories and other establishments. In 1910, 25 percent, or 514,000, of the women found in domestic and personal service were laundresses outside of laundries. By 1930, however, the proportion in this category of female workers in domestic and personal service had declined to 10 percent; their number in 1930 was 355,000, representing a numerical decrease of 31 percent. Over the same period women laundry operatives, mainly in power laundries, increased 117 percent. Women workers in cleaning and dyeing shops increased 739 percent during these two decades. Women boarding and lodging house keepers declined 11 percent, while hotel keepers and managers increased 22 percent, a trend which indicates, perhaps, a change in the type of housing. Another great increase has been among barbers, manicurists and hairdressers, mainly in beauty parlors. Women's increase of 412 percent in this group, compared with an increase of only 93 percent for both sexes combined, represents the opening of what is almost a new occupational field for women.

Other great increases are found in the numbers of women restaurant keepers and waitresses, two occupations in which the trends are indicative of modern urban dwelling. In the former women are nearly four times as numerous as in 1910, while men increased but two and a half times. In the latter occupation the combined sexes doubled and the women alone increased 175 percent. Women as cleaners, janitors and housekeepers also increased, as they did in the occupations of cook and other servants. More than one third of the women in domestic and personal service are listed as servants, a proportion which has changed little over the twenty-year period. There is, however, one shift in this occupation that is not apparent in the data presented: the decline in the practice of "living in." It was found through special analysis of census data that in 1920 almost one half, 49.6 percent, of servants lived in their own homes, while only one third had lived at home in 1900.[12]

It may be said in summary that in the census classification of domestic and personal service women are increasing, but in the period from 1910 to 1930 they have increased only 36 percent as compared with a rise of 56 percent for men. Moreover, several major changes are taking place among the individual occupations within the larger group.

Women in Business

Of the 265,000 women classified under transportation and communication by the census, 94 percent are telephone operators. Among the 973,000 in trade 83 percent are accounted for by the two groups of occupations, salespersons and clerks in stores, and retail dealers. In the clerical group, numbering almost 2,000,000 women, 39 percent are stenographers and typists, 36 percent are clerks, and 24 percent are listed as bookkeepers and cashiers.

In trade the greatest apparent advance was made in the group of

12. U.S. Bureau of the Census, Hill, Joseph A., *Women in Gainful Occupations, 1870–1920*, Census Monograph IX, p. 138.

decorators and window dressers, which was still numerically small in 1900 and claimed but 439 women in 1910. In this occupation women advanced 1,321 percent as compared with the advance of 277 percent for the occupation as a whole. In the category of real estate agents, a group which increased 91 percent between 1910 and 1930, women increased 986 percent (from 2,927 to 31,787), making them now 13 percent of all real estate agents. Among insurance agents and officials there were 452 percent more women in 1930 than there were in 1910, while the increase of the occupation as a whole was 192 percent. Women bankers are 249 percent more numerous now than they were twenty years ago, while all bankers increased but 109 percent. The more important of the other trade occupations in which women have advanced more quickly than the occupation as a whole are those of inspectors and samplers (230 percent increase), retail dealers (64 percent increase), and store laborers (126 percent increase). It would be noted that saleswomen and store clerks, who are numerically the most important in the trade group, increased only 100 percent, while salespersons and store clerks in general increased 93 percent.

In the clerical occupations women are by far the most numerous in the categories of stenographers and typists (of whom over 95 percent are women), bookkeepers and cashiers (52 percent women) and clerks (34 percent women). Between 1910 and 1930 women stenographers and typists increased 196 percent, while the occupation as a whole increased 156 percent; women bookkeepers and cashiers increased 160 and the occupation 92 percent; and women clerks increased 489 percent and the occupation but 170 percent.

Many of the business and clerical occupations into which women are going demand little more than general ability and experience for their successful performance. Others, such as stenography, accounting and bookkeeping, demand a formal preparation in commercial or business education. In this connection it is interesting to note the growth of attendance at schools offering this type of curriculum. Between 1914 and 1930 the number of girls enrolled in commercial and business schools increased from 183,000 to 653,000. The figures for selected years are shown in the following list. Public high schools are listed separately to indicate the increasingly dominant role publicly provided education is playing in the preparation of girls for occupational adjustment. In addition to the

Year	Girls enrolled in commercial and business courses: Public high schools	Total	Year	Girls enrolled in commercial and business courses: Public high schools	Total
1914[a]	92,650	183,021	1924[a]	286,984	419,141
1915[a]	116,379	213,141	1929–1930[b]	513,964	652,942
1918[a]	173,857	381,631			

[a] U.S. Office of Education, *Biennial Survey of Education*, 1924–1926, Bulletin, 1928, no. 4, p. 252.

[b] Compiled by J. O. Malott of the U.S. Office of Education. Public high schools includes 86,000 in junior high schools in 1929, and 417,964 in senior high schools in 1930.

high schools and business schools, 132 colleges, were in 1928 providing commercial training for almost 12,000 young women.

Women in the Professions

In 1930 women constituted 39 percent of all persons enumerated by the census as professional or semiprofessional workers. Despite this very high proportion of women, their distribution in the individual professional occupations is very different from that of men. The greatest proportions of men are in the categories of teachers (13 percent of all professional men) and technical engineers (12 percent), while the smallest proportion is in the category of trained nurses (0.3 percent). Of women, however, more than nine tenths of those in the professions are in the two categories of teachers (72 percent of all professional women) and trained nurses (23 percent), while the number of those occupied as technical engineers is so slight as to be negligible. Women constitute 78 percent of all teachers and 98 percent of all trained nurses. In five other groups, although they are relatively small numerically, women constitute high proportions of the total number. Women are 48 percent of all musicians and music teachers, 38 percent of all artists and art teachers, 28 percent of all actors and showmen, 27 percent of all authors, editors and reporters, and 21 percent of all photographers. Among physicians, chemists, clergymen, lawyers, dentists and architects the proportion of women varies from 5.2 percent to 1.7 percent. They are 9 percent of all draftsmen and designers.

Despite the small representation of women in a number of these occupations, it will be remembered that between 1910 and 1930 the increase of women in all the professions was 87 percent and that of men and women together but 80 percent. Between 1920 and 1930, however, the increases were almost equal, 40.6 percent for women and 41.4 percent for men. Women authors, chemists, clergymen, designers, lawyers and college teachers increased much more rapidly than the two sexes together. Authors increased 185 percent between 1910 and 1930, but women authors increased 207 percent. Clergymen increased 26 percent in that period but the number of women clergymen increased 378 percent. Designers increased 117 percent but women designers rose 206 percent. Women lawyers (558 in 1910) increased 507 percent while the increase of all lawyers was but 40 percent. There are more than 20,000 women teachers in colleges, representing an increase of 581 percent compared with 295 percent for both sexes. Women actors, artists, photographers, elementary and high school teachers and women in "other professional pursuits" increased at rates similar to those of the combined sexes. Women dentists have not become numerous and their rate of increase is low compared with that of the two sexes. Only among physicians and musicians have women shown a decrease in the period under discussion. The 79,500 women musicians and music teachers is 6 percent less than the number enumerated in 1910, as contrasted with a 19 percent increase in that occupation for men and women together. In medicine and surgery the situation is somewhat different. The 7 percent decline of women is here compared with an increase of only 2 percent in twenty years for the occupation as a whole.

Thus women have made striking advances in winning places for themselves in the professions, but, as has been noted, their numbers are still relatively small except in the groups of teachers and nurses. It must be borne in mind, however, that the professions require longer and more costly preparation, that the work is often more exacting, and that they are surrounded by attitudes rooted much deeper than is the case with most of the other occupations in which women are finding a place. For all of these reasons progress will probably be slow until women have developed a prestige in professional activities and have further overcome the prejudices which in some fields are still a handicap.

The number of women enrolled in law schools has increased without interruption from 170 in 1900 to 2,216 in 1928, but the proportion of law students who are women, although it rose from 1 percent at the beginning of the period to 7 percent in 1918, decreased to 6 percent in 1928.[13] While the number of women lawyers remains small, they are finding increasing opportunities on the bench and in connection with the administration of justice. The appointment of a woman Assistant Attorney General with the rank of assistant secretary was one of the acts by which President Wilson recognized the new political status of women. Since 1920 a woman has been promoted by election from the Common Pleas bench in Cuyahoga County, Ohio, to the Supreme Court of the state, and eighteen other women in the country have been elected or appointed to judgeships, some of them, as in Cook County, Illinois, in great metropolitan centers. At least four women have been chosen clerks of the supreme courts in their states; one has been made a reporter; two of the most highly paid women in the federal service are judges, one appointed for life to serve as judge of the Customs Court in New York, where complicated financial and legal issues are adjudicated, and another sitting on the Board of Tax Appeals. Since judges are elected in most jurisdictions the pathway to recognition is usually by way of partisan political organization. The practice of the law requires no such adjustment, but the obstacle in the shape of prejudice is widespread and obdurate. Although the cases are increasing on which women are given positions of responsibility and authority, a large proportion of the women lawyers are pursuing routine occupations in the offices of others, often with little hope of advancement in their profession.

The registration of women in medical schools has shown a considerable degree of variation since the beginning of the century. Women's registration in 1900 was 1,219, and from then through 1928, the last year for which figures are available, it did not reach that figure again. It showed a general decline until after the war, reached 1,184 in 1924 and then again declined. In 1928 the proportion of women among the total number of medical students was 4

13. The data on enrollment in the professional schools are compiled from the U.S. Office of Education, *Annual Reports of the Commissioner of Education* for the years 1911 through 1916, and from the *Biennial Survey of Education* for the years 1916 through 1928.

percent, or 1 percent less than it was in 1900.[14] Special interest attaches to opportunities in medical schools because for several years there was a certain reticence on their part with reference to the number of women applicants for admission. It was a period when medical education was being reorganized and it seemed important that selection of candidates for the professional opportunities should be based on objective tests and that there should be complete publicity. Nevertheless the figures with reference to the applications for admission and the admissions of women to medical schools were not published by the authorities of those schools and there was a widespread belief that the dice were loaded against women. In 1929–1930 figures were published with reference to the number applying and the number admitted which seemed to show discrimination in favor of women rather than against them.[15] When these figures are more closely examined, however, or are supplemented by independent inquiry they still give the impartial inquirer occasion for doubt. Another problem is presented in the matter of internships. There are at present 660 hospitals in the United States approved for internships, offering a total of 6,119 opportunities. Among these, 5, having a total of 37 internships, are restricted to women, but only 231, maintaining 2,939 or 48.6 percent of the internships, are open to women and many of them appoint women only very rarely.[16]

There is, of course, no question as to women's ability as practitioners or as research workers. Women doctors have attained positions enabling them to make professional contributions of a high order. Six women physicians are members of the American College of Surgeons. In at least eleven states women physicians are directors of a bureau or division in the state public health department. These bureaus are usually concerned with child hygiene and sometimes, in addition, with maternity or public health nursing. A

14. See preceding footnote.

15. Myers, Burton D., *Journal of the Association of American Medical Colleges*, March, 1929, vol. V, p. 65. The results of further study will shortly be available from researches being pursued by Mrs. B. R. Bartlett in cooperation with the U.S. Women's Bureau.

16. Data from the Council on Medical Education and Hospitals of the American Medical Association.

woman was formerly Director of Child Hygiene in the Department of Health in New York City, and there are a few other cases in which women physicians have official positions in local boards of health. In a number of cases women physicians are division chiefs or in other responsible positions in hospitals.

In divinity schools women increased from 181 or 2 percent of all registrations in 1900 to 1,177 or 14 percent in 1922.[17] Between 1922 and 1926 the proportion fell to 11 percent, although numerically the registration of women continued to increase. In 1928 there was a slight decline both in numbers and in percentage. The question of women in the ministry, however, is only one aspect of the activity of women in the church; the position of women in church government and administration should also be considered. Some churches grant no participation, except perhaps certain restricted rights of voting; some grant equal rights; and there are some which grant certain rights, perhaps a great many, but no equality in the administration of the government of the church. The great denominations which have resisted the demands of women are gradually yielding (as the Presbyterians did in 1930[18] and 1932[19] and the Episcopalians[20] in 1931) a share of control in the affairs of the church which women are asking on the basis of ability rather than sex.

Although in 1930 there were 83 percent more women teachers than there were in 1910, the proportion of teachers who were women remained the same, 78 percent, in spite of a rise to 82 percent for 1920. The proportion of professional women who were teachers remained about the same during this period, 73 percent in 1910 and 72 percent in 1930. In 1930 there were 79 percent more women in elementary and high school teaching than there were in 1910 but the proportion of elementary and high school teachers who were women maintained a fairly steady average of 82 percent during this period. Among college teachers and presidents women were 581 percent more numerous in 1930 than in 1910, and the proportion who were women increased steadily from 19 percent in

17. See footnote 15.
18. *Woman's Pulpit*, November–December, 1931.
19. *Cf.* The metropolitan press, June 8–10, 1932.
20. *Ibid.*, September 22, 1931.

1910 to 33 percent in 1930.[21] It is clear, then, that the pressure on teaching is lightened, and that women are also finding opportunities in the other professional categories.

The circulars of information for 1929–1930 concerning the colleges and universities approved by the American Association of Universities show that women constitute only 18 percent of the faculties of these institutions. Of the 226 institutions in the list, 47 were schools for men, 36 were schools for women and the remaining 143 were coeducational. Women constituted 1 percent of the faculty in the men's schools, 16 percent in the coeducational schools and 68.5 percent in the women's schools, in each case the proportion increasing inversely to the rank of the position. In the men's schools 73 percent of the women on the faculties were in the two lower ranks of assistant professor and instructor while only 49 percent of the men were in these ranks; in the coeducational schools 79 percent of the women and 49 percent of the men; and in the women's schools 59 percent of the women and 36 percent of the men. Of the 47 institutions for men there were 40 with no women on their faculties and 6 with only 1 woman. Of the 36 schools for women, there was but 1 whose faculty was composed entirely of women. The 143 coeducational institutions showed 2 with no women and 2 with 1 woman.

The situation with reference to women in the land grant colleges is briefly described in a publication recently issued by the United States Office of Education.[22] In 1930–1931 women constituted 16 percent of the faculties. The two lower ranks held 75 percent of the women, while only 46 percent of the men were in these groups. These figures are similar to those for the other colleges and universities.

In the higher administrative positions in the general school system the proportion of women is also small. The teacher training institutions did not, until recently, include administration in the field of instruction. Although women are not at present executives of school systems in great metropolitan areas, there are six states[23]

21. Note the figures showing the proportion of women receiving the Ph.D. degree in 1900 and 1930.

22. U.S. Office of Education, John H. McNeeley, *Salaries in Land Grant Colleges*, Pamphlet no. 24, 1931, pp. 2, 3.

23. U.S. Office of Education, *Educational Directory*, Bulletin 1931 no. 1.

in which women were listed as heads of the state departments of education in 1931. Out of 3,499 county superintendents 909 (26 percent) are women and out of the 2,841 communities of 2,500 population or over, 38 have women superintendents of school systems. In the National Education Association the election of the first woman president was an epoch making event; now alternate elections see a woman president. The United States Office of Education now has four women specialists on its staff in the field of elementary education or specialized education, all of them selected by civil service examinations.

Women in the Civil Service

Women have been employed in the federal departments since 1862 although even in the 1850s a few women, of whom Clara Barton was probably the first, were in the employ of the government. Until 1919 a bureau chief wishing to fill a position for which there was no eligible list would express a preference for either a man or a woman and an examination would be given admitting only persons of the sex preferred, notwithstanding the fact that the list so compiled would also be used for filling other positions for which the appointing authority had no preference as to sex. In 1919, largely as a result of a study made by the Women's Bureau (then the Women in Industry Service), the Civil Service Commission opened all examinations to both sexes.

Despite the effect which the earlier practice had of preventing women in the civil service from qualifying for many positions similar to those in which they were proving themselves capable in private employment, the war years effected a great increase in the numbers of women in government employment and a considerable widening of the range of their work. After the close of the war the numbers were reduced but in recent years the number of women employees has shown an increase. In 1931 there were 91,196 as compared with 82,180 in 1925, an increase of 11 percent. The proportion of women in the civil service, however, has remained fairly constant. They constitute about two-fifths of the District service and about one-tenth of the field service.

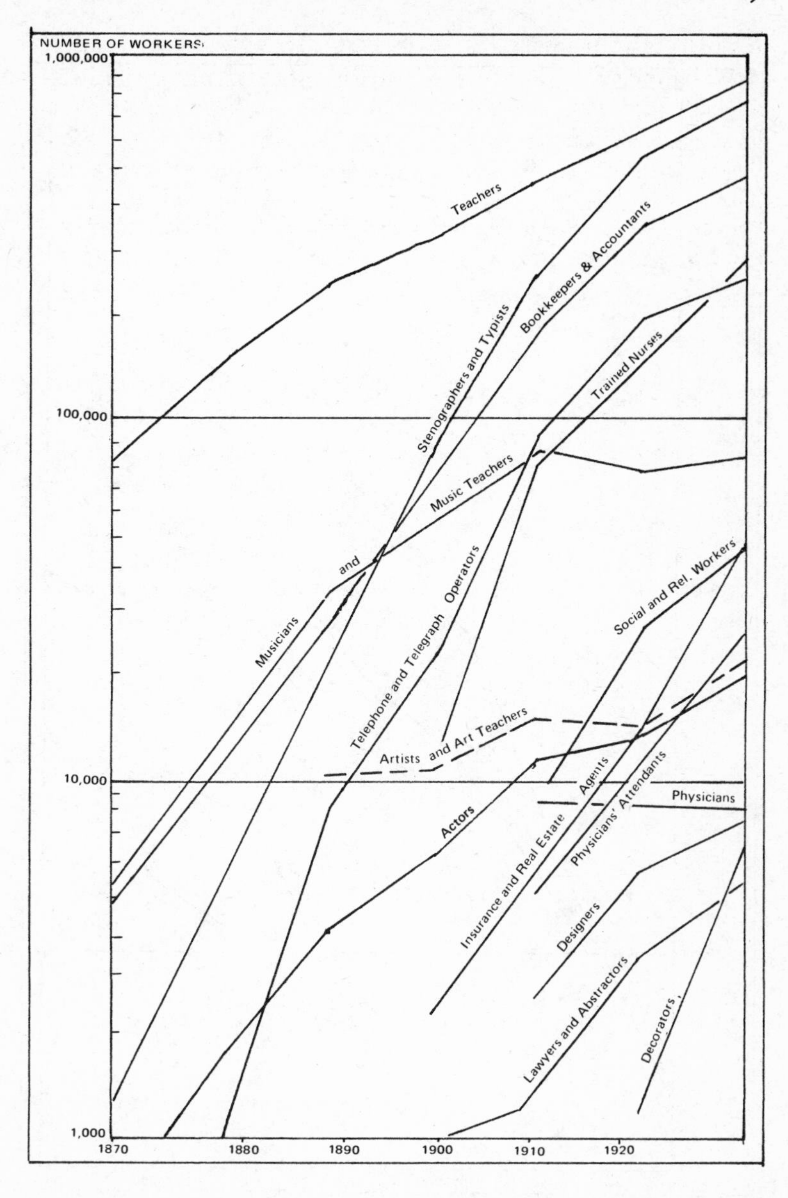

FIG. 3 Women in selected occupational groups, 1870–1930.

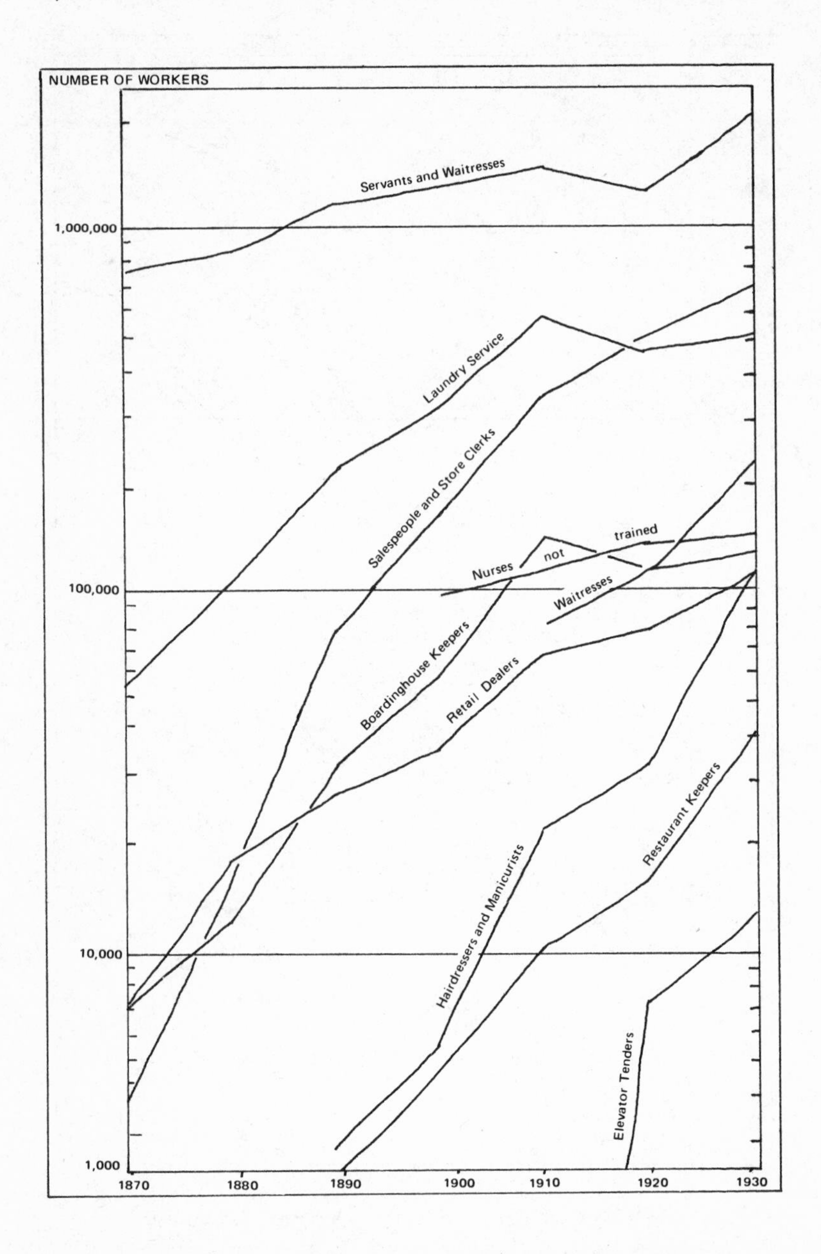

FIG. 4 Women in selected occupational groups, 1870–1930.

The Range of Women's Employment

While it is clear that women have assumed a much larger place among the gainfully employed during the past three decades, the tendency to concentrate in a few large occupations is apparently as marked now as it was in 1900. In 1900 women were found in 295 or 97.4 percent of the occupations listed in the census, but in 1930 they were in only 527 or 93.9 percent of the 557 occupational classifications. In the earlier year one percent or more of the employed women were found in each of 18 occupations; and these 18 accounted for 86.4 percent of all working women. In 1930 a little over 83 percent of the gainfully occupied women are found in the 24 occupations that claim at least one percent of the total. Thus in 1900 this concentration was to be found in 6 percent of the occupations but by 1930 it covered only 4 percent of the total number of categories. It is possible, however, that some doubt may be cast on these figures, for the census changes its classification frequently in such a way that the groups are not comparable. It may be said, too, that the new occupational groups of the census do not, as a rule, represent new occupations, but breakdowns of the old ones.

In 1900 the groups in which women showed the greatest numerical importance were, in order: servants and waitresses, agricultural workers, dressmakers, laundresses, teachers and farmers. In 1930, however, a similar list shows a different ranking: servants, teachers, stenographers, clerks, agricultural laborers, slaeswomen and bookkeepers. The tendency of the business and clerical groups to supplant some of the more domestic and personal occupations is apparent. Figures 3 and 4 show the trends of numerical increases among women in selected occupations.

III. Legislation Concerning Women's Work

Trade union organization among women to gain working status has been very difficult to effect. Men, on the other hand, seem to prefer to rely on unionism and collective bargaining rather than on legislation in securing improved working conditions. Their organizations maintain influential lobbies in Washington and in many state capitols, but they do not seek laws regulating hours of work, night work or minimum wages. This is due partly to the uncertainty as to the attitude of the courts but it is also due to the reluctance of men to rely on legislative protection. The situation with regard to women has been summarized in the words: "In spite of the fact that the increasing number of women workers constitutes a permanent wage earning group, as is indicated by the increasing proportion of married women in industry, and the increasing age limit of working women, there is nevertheless a mental attitude of impermanency among the women workers themselves which constitutes a serious handicap to organization."[24]

The publication of the volume on occupations of the *Twelfth Census* (1900) attracted the attention of students to the conspicuous increase in the number of women gainfully employed and questions were raised as to whether changes were taking place in the amount and character of the work of women and whether women were invading men's field of employment and causing disastrous changes in the home. Examination of the figures showed that in the major industrial occupations women were not displacing men[25] and were probably doing no more work than they had always done, but that in the new occupations which were being developed, especially in the group characterized by the census as "trade and transportation," now subdivided into trade, transportation and clerical occupations, both men and women were finding employment and the older agricultural and domestic occupations were declining relatively. The figures likewise revealed the relative youth of the great majority of women workers as compared with the men, and the large proportion of workers in a small number of occupations. Another important factor in revealing the conditions under which women worked was the appropriation by Congress in 1907 of a special sum to enable the Secretary of Commerce and Labor "to investigate and report on the industrial, social, moral, educational and physical condition of women and child wage workers in the United States wherever employed, with special reference to their age, hours of labor, term of employment, health, illiteracy, sanitary and other conditions surrounding their occupation, and

24. Wolfson, Theresa, "Trade Union Activities of Women," *Women in the Modern World, op. cit.*, p. 120.
25. See Edith Abbott and S. P. Breckinridge, "The Employment of Women in Industries, Twelfth Census Statistics," *Journal of Political Economy*, 1906, vol. XIV, p. 26; see also vol. XIV, p. 614; vol. XVI, pp. 335, 619; vol. XXXI, p. 521.

the means employed for the protection of their health, persons, and morals."[26] The result of this appropriation was the publication between 1910 and 1913 of a series of nineteen volumes and a supplementary volume in 1916.[27] The restricted occupational opportunity, the youth and immaturity of women workers and the resulting lack of bargaining skill as well as bargaining power, as compared with the employer and with men workers, had resulted in the same conditions that had been produced in other countries—excessively long hours, night work, lack of Sunday rest and general working conditions that were often neither safe nor decent.

The problem of women's hours of work had been met by Massachusetts in the 1870's by the enactment of a ten hour law which was upheld by the state Supreme Court as a legitimate exercise of the police power,[28] but when Illinois attempted an eight hour law for women workers the Supreme Court of that state in 1895 held that it was prohibited by the Illinois, and perhaps by the United States constitution.[29] The early years of the new century brought renewed efforts at legislative control with the result that in 1908 an Oregon law limiting the working day of women to ten hours was upheld by the United States Supreme Court[30] and similar laws were later upheld by the highest courts of other states, including Illinois. These statutes followed the general pattern of the English factory acts. By 1930, 44 states had laws limiting the length of the working day, 16 states prohibited night work, 18 states required one day's rest in seven,[31] and 10 states had established special bureaus to deal with the problems of women and children's work.[32]

The Oregon case, in which the exercise of the police power in regulating the work of women was upheld, was important from several points of view. The participation of Louis D. Brandeis, now

26. U.S. *Statutes at Large*, XXXIV, pt. 1, pp. 866, 1330.
27. U.S. Bureau of Labor Statistics, Bulletin no. 175.
28. *Hamilton Manufacturing Co. v. Massachusetts*, 1876, 120 Mass. 383.
29. *Ritchie v. the People*, 1895, 155 Ill. 98.
30. *Muller v. Oregon*, 1908, 208 U.S. 412.
31. See U.S. Women's Bureau, *State Laws Affecting Working Women*, Bulletin no. 63, and summaries in *Annual Reports*.
32. In eight of these states, the director of the bureau was a woman.

Mr. Justice Brandeis of the United States Supreme Court, gave dignity and prestige to the plea that social and other scientific data bearing on the importance of the subject from the point of view of public well being should have weight with the courts. The court took notice of different bases of classification in accordance with which a legislative program for the protection of women different from that affecting men became possible. The resulting decision rested more upon physiological limitations, especially in relation to childbearing, than was perhaps justified or necessary, and failed to take notice of the industrial and occupational inequality from which it appeared that women suffered. This point was not ignored by commentators on the decision[33] for the doctrine of physiological limitations was being urged in many places for purposes not of protection but of exclusion and restriction. Legislation regulating the work of women is vigorously opposed by many women who desire the widening of women's opportunity. An influential organization, the Woman's Party, opposes any legislation affecting the conditions of women's work unless it applies also to men's work. The same position is taken by similar groups in European countries, which are organized on an international basis, as the *Open Door International*.[34] There have been few enactments during the recent sessions of state legislatures dealing with hours of work or prohibition of night work by women. Interesting administrative advances have been made, however, under the leadership of women state officials whenever a favorable state administration has given the opportunity. The administrations in California, Massachusetts, New Jersey, New York and Pennsylvania at different periods during the past decade have indicated an increasing acquiescence in the treatment of the labor administration as an instrument for social readjustment of the productive process and in spite of the opposition to which reference has been made protective legislation for women is slowly but increasingly being developed in

33. See, for example, Ernst Freund, "Constitutional Limitation and Labor Legislation," *Illinois Law Review*, 1909–1910, vol. IV, p. 609.

34. This organization met in Stockholm, August 17–21, 1931. It has branches in nine European countries, with headquarters in London. For the views of these groups see *Women in the Modern World, op. cit.*, articles by E. F. Baker, p. 265; M. N. Winslow, p. 280; and F. Kelley and M. Marsh, p. 286.

the United States for the purpose of setting limits about the wage bargain so that too disastrous an advantage may not be taken of the relative weakness of women in bargaining.

A solution for the problem of women's inadequate pay was sought by the enactment of a minimum wage law in Massachusetts in 1912.[35] This example was followed within a short period by fourteen other states and by Puerto Rico and the District of Columbia. As Mr. Justice Holmes pointed out, similar laws had already been tried in New Zealand and Australia since the early 1890s and in England since 1909. Thirteen of these state enactments were of the so-called flexible type and four—those of Arizona, Puerto Rico, South Dakota and Utah—were inflexible, fixing a minimum sum below which wages should not fall. The question of the constitutionality of these statutes was raised in eleven states and was uniformly upheld until 1923, when the District of Columbia act was held unconstitutional by a vote of five to three,[36] with Mr. Justice Brandeis not taking part because before being appointed to the bench he had argued the case in behalf of the constitutionality of the act. If the decision had affected only the District of Columbia it would not have been so serious, but the law was held to violate the fifth amendment of the United States Constitution. This decision was accepted as authoritative everywhere except in California and Massachusetts, and activity for minimum wage rulings has of course greatly slowed down as a result of adverse court decisions. The California act has been upheld by a superior court and the opinion acquiesced in by the plaintiff before the higher court had passed upon it, so that the act is still administered in that state.[37] In Massachusetts, where the law was largely advisory, it is still in operation and interesting proposals for strengthening it have recently been laid before the Massachusetts legislature.[38] As to the effect of the statutes while they were in operation, the Women's Bureau has stated, "After all, the purpose of minimum-wage laws is not to raise rates in general but to help the most depressed group. Interestingly enough, the

35. U.S. Women's Bureau, *Development of Minimum Wage Laws in the U.S., 1912–1927*, Bulletin no. 61, 1928.

36. *Children's Hospital, etc. v. Atkins*, 1923, 261 U.S. 525 at 542.

37. The subject is admirably set out in the U.S. Women's Bureau, Bulletin 61, *sup. cit.*

38. Release of the U.S. Women's Bureau, April 1, 1932.

few rates that seem high enough to raise the entire depressed group to the cost-of-living level seem to have raised rates in general . . . There is no magic in minimum-wage laws to raise all rates."[39] There is interesting evidence in a recently published report of the Minimum Wage Board of Ontario to the effect that women's wages in that province have not declined during the years 1929–1931 at anything like the same rate as in such industrial states as Illinois and New York, and it is suggested that the minimum wage legislation of the province is to a considerable extent responsible for the difference.[40]

IV. The Earnings of Women

Since the beginning of the century the subject of the earnings of women has been closely connected with the problem of the adequate wage and with the problem of the equal wage. Attention was first directed to the subject of the adequate wage by the United States Industrial Commission in 1899, when it revealed that girls did not earn enough to meet what their living expenses were known to be. Shortly thereafter, in a report on employees and wages, prepared for the census of 1900, it was estimated that one-fourth of the women workers sixteen years of age and over received less than $4.49 a week, and only one-fourth more than $6.86, the median being $5.64. These figures were given wide publicity and toward the end of the decade 1900–1910 the data from the study of woman and child wage earners[41] began to be made available and confirmed the earlier estimates of wage scales below any level of "health, comfort, or safety." In response to these revelations efforts were made to secure the enactment of laws which would establish minimum wages based on carefully estimated costs of planned expenditures including only the most essential elements. Adverse court decisions prevented the movement from attaining any great success. The subject is discussed more extensively in the section on legislation above.

With reference to the problem of the equal wage, Sidney Webb pointed out in the early nineties that: "The inferiority of women's wages is to be gathered not so much from a comparison of the rates

39. U.S. Women's Bureau, Bulletin no. 61, *op. cit.*, pp. 370–1.
40. *United States Daily*, July 14, 1932.
41. U.S. Bureau of Labor Statistics, Bulletin no. 175, *op. cit.*, p. 22.

for identical work, for few such cases exist, but rather from a comparison of the standards of remuneration in men's and women's occupations respectively."[42] As a matter of fact, perhaps the major principle on which the wages of both men and women were determined was the same—the bargaining weakness of the worker as opposed to the bargaining strength of the employer, subject to the limitations set by the public opinion of the community. But the use of economic power, like the use of other forms of power, had to be rationalized, and the fiction of men's responsibility for dependents and of women's freedom from such responsibility[43] served to justify the unequal wage.

During the World War the principle of equal pay received widespread support in the statements of public officials and in the orders issued by the War Labor Policies Board, the Railway Administration and other authorities; it seemed necessary to induce women to try work they had always been taught to think of as men's work and to persuade men that since the scales of pay would not be affected[44] their occupational status would not be damaged by admitting women. When an attempt is made to review the extent to which these orders were actually followed it is found that where the use of women was novel the principle was fairly generally applied but that in the older industries it was applied to a lesser degree.[45]

The census figures reveal that in factory occupations the wages of women have been and continue to be low and that they have been and continue to be lower than those of men. Factory wages tend to rise but the gap between men's and women's wages remains surprisingly constant. Women's hourly earnings and annual earnings remain something less than 55 percent of men's hourly

42. Webb, "Alleged Differences in the Wages Paid to Men and Women for Similar Work," *Economic Journal*, December 1891, vol. I, p. 659. See also analysis by Emilie Hutchinson, *Women in the Modern World, op. cit.*, p. 133.

43. See, for example, John A. Ryan, *Social Reconstruction*, New York, 1920, p. 43.

44. See U.S. Bureau of Labor Statistics, *Monthly Labor Review*, vol. IX, p. 192; see also vol. VIII, pp. 203–205, 205–208, 262–263; New York State Department of Labor, *Annual Report*, 1919, pp. 22–23; A. B. Wolfe and Helen Olsen, "War-Time Industrial Employment of Women in the United States," *Journal of Political Economy*, 1919, vol. XXVII, pp. 639, 658.

45. Wolfe and Olsen, *op. cit.*, p. 661.

and annual earnings,[46] and even the sum of the average earnings for women and for children does not equal the average for men. There are, however, wide differences among the various manufacturing occupations in the disparity between men's and women's earnings. In cotton, the average wage for men in 1925 was $1,015 and for women $793, a disparity of 28 percent when calculated in the women's wage; in tobacco, men averaged $978 and women $543, a disparity of 80 percent; and in glass, the disparity was 206 percent, men averaging $1,650 and women $540. Whether the gap between the earnings of men and of women workers in industry will gradually widen or will become narrower cannot now be foretold; if women are drawn to industrial work from older groups the disparity in earnings between men and women may become gradually narrower. It must be remembered, however, in interpreting these figures that it is almost impossible to secure wage data for both men and women doing precisely the same tasks, even within the limits of a single occupation.

A study by the Association of Business and Professional Women published in 1930 makes data available concerning the earnings of women in these fields. The research covered 14,071 experienced full time workers. Their occupations were grouped in eight fields of employment and twenty classes determined by the nature of the work done. Seventy percent were, in 1927, in clerical, teaching or publicity work. One-fourth of the total number earned less than $1,213; one-half less than $1,548; and three-fourths less than $2,004. Those women who were independently engaged earned more than those who were on a salary basis. Their median was $503 above the median for the salaried workers and one in three of them earned $3,000 or more, while of the salaried workers the earnings of only one in twenty was in that upper level. Of the whole group, only 174 earned $5,000 or more, but there were 25 who were in the $9,000 level or above.

There were wide differences in the range of earnings in the different groups. Median earnings varied from $682 for 23 telephone operators to $3,088 for 55 physicians in private practice. There were also, of course, great differences in the proportions of workers in the different occupational groups who earned $3,000 or more. Only 2.6 percent of the clerical workers, 4 percent of the

46. U.S. Bureau of the Census, Brissenden, Paul F., *Earnings of Factory Workers, 1899–1927*, Census Monograph X, pp. 122, 123, 128, 129.

teachers and 7 percent of the whole group earned that much, while 13.7 percent of the welfare group, 14 percent of the health group, 18 percent of the legal and protective group and 21.6 percent of the personnel group earned $3,000 or more. These figures say nothing of the relation between men's and women's earnings but the evidence is clear that although some women are receiving incomes in the higher levels, on the whole the rewards are low in comparison with a reasonable standard of self-support.

The report on the land grant colleges for 1930–1931, which has already been referred to, gives a fairly indicative view of the salaries of women in college teaching. The author of this report comments on the situation as follows: "Women staff members receive a lower median salary than men staff members in every academic rank . . . The greatest discrepancy is found in the case of deans, women holding this rank being paid a median salary $1,260 less than men. In both the rank of professor and associate professor the difference between the median salaries of the two sexes is fairly large, being $558 for professors and $402 for associate professors. Only an insignificant difference exists between the median salaries of men and women instructors." The median salary for all men teachers in the land grant colleges, irrespective of rank, is $3,169, while that for women is $2,309.

In connection with the earnings of women in the civil service, the Personnel Reclassification Act of 1923 stated the principle of equal pay for the sexes as well as among departments. Until this time there had been very few women in the civil service who received more than $1,800 a year and the greatest numbers were in the $1,100 to $1,200 group. In 1925, after the passage of the Act, a study by the Women's Bureau showed that 10 percent of the women employees received salaries of $1,860 or more at that time.[47] In 1930, of the women in the professional services of the various state departments, 36 percent received salaries of $3,000 or more, but this group is so specialized that it is scarcely indicative of the general salary level.

Figures are likewise available for 1,025 women holding the degree of Doctor of Philosophy,[48] for 3,521 students who have

47. U.S. Women's Bureau, *The Status of Women in Government Service in 1925*, Bulletin no. 53, 1925, p. 4.

48. Hutchinson, Emilie J., *Women and the Ph.D.*, Bulletin no. 2 of the Institute of Women's Professional Relations, published by the North Carolina College for Women.

gone out from the land grant colleges,[49] and for a group of 844 university women.[50] The ranges of these groups are naturally very similar and bear out the conclusion not only that women's earnings are low but also that they are generally less than the earnings of men.

Thus, although detailed information concerning the earnings of women is in most cases not available, from the data which exists it seems clear that not only are women's earnings low but they are also conspicuously less than the earnings of men.

VI. Women in Government

Women as Voters

The ratification of the Nineteenth Amendment to the United States Constitution in 1920—after 56 campaigns for the ratification of amendments to state constitutions, nearly 500 organized efforts with legislatures, 277 appearances at state party conventions, 30 appeals before national political conventions and 19 campaigns with successive congresses—meant the admission of women in all the states to the right to vote and the closing of one era in the movement toward equality of the sexes. Women have now voted in three presidential elections, participated in local, state and national campaigns, been candidates for office and assumed responsibility in high official positions. The direction of women's political activities, however, and the use they will make of their political power are difficult to ascertain. There are some who believe that women must, as women, be politically strong enough to offer to those in control of party organizations such inducements of support, or punishment for failure to support measures in which they are interested, as men evidently thought in the years before 1920 they would be able to offer, and that therefore they must preserve a certain independence with regard to existing party organization. Others believe that what is to be done must be done within the parties. There is perhaps no objective test at the moment as to which view will prove correct. One criticism of

49. *After College What?*, Bulletin no. 4, Institute of Women's Professional Relations, published by the North Carolina College for Women.

50. Hawthorn, Marion O., "Women as College Teachers," *Women in the Modern World, op. cit.*, p. 146.

women, expressed by a leader whose words always command respect, is based on the failure of women who asked freedom to tell what they would do with it after they had secured it.[51] Certainly it cannot be claimed that they have as yet shown clearly all the ways in which they would use it.

When the election of 1920 was over it was found that only 53 percent of the total number of eligible voters had cast their ballots. This led the League of Women Voters to undertake what was known as the Get Out the Vote Campaign. To what extent their work was effective no one can say, but the vote in 1928 increased to 61 percent. This was low, however, when compared with the figures of the earlier decades—71 percent in 1908, 63 percent in 1912 and 71 percent in 1916. The figures with reference to voters are not as a rule reported by sex. There are a few exceptions, however. In Pennsylvania[52] the figures are available for a few years. In 1925, for example, 41.8 percent of the voters were women, while in 1931, they were 44 percent. The percentage increase of women voters was 21, of men 13. In Rhode Island,[53] the percentage of voters who were women was 40.16 in 1922, 44.12 in 1924, 42.79 in 1926, 45.16 in 1928 and 45.37 in 1930. At no time have they been half the voting population, but there has been a percentage increase of 56 in the number of women voting during the decade, while the increase in the number of men voting has been less than twenty percent.

There are also some data with reference to registration by sex. In Chicago the proportion of women among the total number of registrants for voting rose from 32 percent in 1914 to 42 percent in 1931; during this period the number of women registrants increased 173 percent while the number of men registrants increased only 80 percent. In Louisiana the proportion of women rose from 18 percent in 1920 to 30 percent in 1928;[54] the number of women registrants increased during these years 144 percent while the number of men increased only 23 percent. These examples are

51. Howes, Ethel Puffer, "The Meaning of Progress in the Woman Movement," *Women in the Modern World*, *op. cit.*, p. 14.
52. Figures supplied by the Secretray of State of Pennsylvania.
53. Figures supplied by the Secretary of State of Rhode Island.
54. Louisiana, Secretary of State to His Excellency the Governor, *Report*, January 1, 1921, pp. 336–7, and January 1, 1929, pp. 328, 330.

fairly typical of general conditions. There are more men than women who register to vote but on the whole the number of women who make use of their franchise is increasing.

Women as Lobbyists

Women began their work as lobbyists long before they were granted the vote. Antislavery agitation, suffrage, temperance, less cruel treatment of the insane, international agreements for mitigating the horrors of war, were causes to which women devoted their efforts, seeking definite and important community gains without the power of the ballot. What could not be done directly had to be done indirectly. Women had neither funds nor political backing but they had a great belief that legislators who understood would eventually respond to the facts which they presented and the conclusions to be drawn from those facts. In 1900, for example, the General Federation of Women's Clubs resolved "to work for legislation for women and children so that the law of every state will equal the best already enacted," and the technique of this work with legislatures was elaborately described. Speeches on methods of lobbying occupied a place on the programs of meetings and in 1914 and 1916 conferences were held at which the successful methods were discussed, apart from the subject matter of the measures to be advanced.

Table 1 Registration of Men and Women Voters in Chicago, 1914–1932[a]

Year	Number		Percent distribution	
	Men	Women	Men	Women
1914	455,283	217,614	67.7	32.3
1916	470,029	261,172	64.3	35.7
1918	493,578	286,634	63.3	36.7
1920	550,060	334,060	62.2	37.8
1922	511,284	293,364	63.5	36.5
1924	654,640	410,255	61.5	38.5
1926	556,735	318,546	63.6	36.4
1928	787,498	599,133	56.8	43.2
1930	736,343	527,891	58.3	41.7
1931	817,703	594,432	57.9	42.1

[a] Figures obtained from Chicago *Daily News Almanac*, 1915–1932.

The coming of suffrage stimulated further interest in lobbying because of the apparently changed attitudes of persons in positions of power. Since 1920, lobbying in Congress for the special interests of women has been chiefly in the hands of two groups of women. The first of these, representing a very large number of women and known as the Women's Joint Congressional Committee, was organized in 1921 for the purpose of keeping Congress informed as to measures in which women were interested and letting women at home know of ways in which they could help. Since 1923 it has been composed of representatives of seventeen national organizations among which are the American Association of University Women, the American Home Economics Association, the several Federations of Women's Clubs, the National Congress of Mothers and Parent Teachers Associations, the National Council of Women, the National Consumers' League, the National Federation of Business and Professional Women, the National League of Women Voters, the National Women's Trade Union League, the National Women's Christian Union and the Service Star Legion. The second group is the Woman's party, still pushing the fight for the amendment of the United States Constitution by the adoption of the so-called Equal Rights Amendment which reads: *Men and women shall have equal rights throughout the United States and every place subject to its jurisdiction . . . Congress shall have power to enforce this article by appropriate legislation.*

Two successes rewarded women's efforts, directed by the Women's Joint Congressional Committee, during the first years of their new power: the Maternity and Infancy Law of 1921[55] and in the following year the so-called Cable Act, giving independent citizenship to married women.[56] In 1923 they had much to do with the enactment of the Personnel Reclassification Act, with legislation regulating interstate and foreign commerce in livestock and other agricultural or dairy products and prohibiting commerce in "filled" or adulterated milk, and with the measure creating the new federal prison for women offenders. In 1924 they assisted in obtaining submission to the states of the proposed amendment giving Congress power to regulate the labor of young persons, although up to the present time this has been ratified by only six states. In 1930, looking back a decade, a total of 436 state and local

55. U.S. Children's Bureau, *Promotion of the Welfare and Hygiene of Maternity and Infancy*, Publication no. 203, 1931, reviews the history of that act.
56. U.S. *Statutes at Large*, 1922, vol. 42, p. 1021.

laws enacted with the support of this committee can be listed.[57] There have been 61 dealing with child welfare, 130 removing limitations on the rights of women, 75 on social hygiene, 69 in the field of education, 76 dealing with efficiency in government and several on living costs. Sixty measures violating the principle of efficiency in government have been opposed and failed of passage. But the two great measures protecting maternity, infancy and childhood had failed (the act of 1921 was allowed to expire in 1929) and the greatest number of apparent successes had been in the years immediately after 1920. Thus after the granting of suffrage women's interests widened but after the first few years of victory their obvious achievements seemed to diminish.

In general, social welfare legislation and the quest for equal rights have been their primary interests. That it might be possible to secure public resources adequate to meet the costs of the projects they urged, the committee has laid great stress on problems in taxation, finance and general governmental efficiency. Throughout the country mothers' pensions laws exist, child labor standards have been improved, and educational opportunities have been advanced, in part at least because of the activities of the women's lobbies.

Women in Party Organizations

Only brief mention can be made of women in the party organizations and reference will be made only to the two great parties. It is at present impossible to estimate the influence of women in these organizations. Women have official titles and sit on party committees. Both parties have adopted a rule calling for an equal number of men and women in the state committees, and the Republican and the Democratic National Committees consist of 53 men and 53 women each. Of the 26 members of the Republican executive committee in 1930, 11 were women and, of the 9 offices, 2 were held by women. Each state, too, has a director of women's activities. Women's participation in national conventions is an interesting story but has as yet too much of the ceremonial to be of great significance. The experience in party organization is like that in legislation. The year 1924 witnessed a high level in the participa-

57. See publications of the League of Women Voters. See also *Equal Rights*, published by the Woman's party.

tion of women in national conventions, which, as shown in Table 2, declined somewhat in 1928, but rose again in 1932.

TABLE 2 PARTICIPATION OF WOMEN IN NATIONAL CONVENTIONS, 1912–1932[a]

	1912		1916		1920		1924		1928		1932	
Party	Delagates	Alternates	Delagates	Alternates	Delagates	Alternates	Delagates	Alternates	Delagates	Alternates	Delagates	Alternates
Republican	2	..	5	9	27	129	120	277	70	264	88	307
Democrat	2	1	11	11	93	206	199	310	152	263	208	270

[a] Compiled from Republican and Democratic National Conventions *Proceedings* for the various years.

WOMEN IN CONGRESS

Except for an aged lady from Georgia who held office for one ceremonial day, no woman had been either appointed or elected to the United States Senate until the autumn of 1931, when Arkansas elected the widow of a statesman from that commonwealth to succeed her husband for the unexpired term. This is a clue to the attitude of many citizens toward offices supposed to require high degrees of statesmanship and long experience. In the lower house, of the 14 women who have been elected, 7 have been chosen, as it were, by virtue of their deceased husband's "selective ability." Some of these women members have justified the practice and have been subsequently elected in their own right so often that the accidental origin of their elevation to office is forgotten. In 1932 there were six women in the House of Representatives and one in the Senate.

The first woman in the House of Representatives, a Congresswoman at large from Montana, 1916–1918, antedated the suffrage amendment; she did not seek reelection. The first woman after the amendment, a member from Oklahoma, was an antisuffragist, hostile to all the measures in which organized women had been interested. She, too, did not return. In 1922 a representative from an Illinois district filled out her father's unexpired term. In January, 1923, a representative from California won her deceased husband's chair and in December, 1923, she was the only woman member. She did not seek reelection. In December, 1925, a representative from California and one from Massachusetts succeeded to their deceased husbands' places and a newly elected member from New Jersey came in as the first Democratic woman. A member from Kentucky succeeded a husband who was not physically but civilly dead in that he was sentenced to the federal penitentiary for violation of the Volstead Act. She was reelected for the seventy-first Congress, but was defeated in the autumn of 1930. The seventy-first Congress, with nine women, marked the peak of woman membership in the House. Four had been there before and five new ones were added, two by virture of their husbands' deaths. Of the fourteen women who have sat in the House, four did not try for renomination and three were defeated in primaries for reelection. Of the six in the House at present, only one is there by virtue of marital succession. The others are representatives whose constituents have cast one or more votes of confidence in them in their own capacity.

Space does not permit a discussion of women's committee assignments, except to point out that they are varied in interest. The Senator from Arkansas serves on the committees on Agriculture, Forestry, Enrolled Bills and the Library. Two Congresswomen are on the Committee on Foreign Affairs, one on Military Affairs, one on Civil Service, two on the World War Veterans' Legislation Committee, one is on the committees on Labor and on Memorials and is chairman of the Committee on the District of Columbia, one is on the committees on Education and the Library.[58]

Women in Federal Office

Women in federal office are in two groups—those who hold a political office and those who have entered the service through the civil service examinations. The latter have already been discussed. Women's experience in federal political office has been like that in legislative effort. The years just before and after the ratification of the Nineteenth Amendment were the most promising. During the decade prior to the ratification women were recognized by the federal administration in various ways. Reference should be made to the establishment of the United States Children's Bureau in 1912, and to the appointment as Chief of a leader in the field of social reform whose qualifications for the position were of the highest. A woman was later appointed Judge of the Juvenile Court in the District of Columbia; in 1920 a woman was appointed on

58. These data are obtained from the *Congressional Directory*.

the United States Civil Service Commission and a few women were sent into the foreign field by the Department of Commerce. The diplomatic service was technically open to women and there were three bureau chiefs. There were women members of federal commissions, one woman succeeded another as assistant attorney general, women were appointed in the offices of commissioner of internal revenue, collector of customs, immigration commissioner, superintendent of the institution for women offenders and a member of the woman's advisory board of that institution. There are three women officers, all exercising functions judicial in character, who receive $10,000 a year for their services. One other woman magistrate has been appointed to the municipal bench in the District of Columbia. The figures, however, show that relatively few women are admitted to the higher salary levels.

Women in State and Local Office

Holding office under the state or local jurisdiction was not novel in 1920. Clara Barton had been head of the Woman's Reformatory in Massachusetts in the early 1880s; there were women on the early state boards of charities and corrections; women were state factory inspectors and served on state health boards and similar bodies. But only after 1920 were women elected to the highest offices. Two have served as chief executive, one in Wyoming and one in Texas. In twelve states women have been elected secretary of state. They have been state treasurers in three states. In some states, as in California, North Carolina and Pennsylvania, women are getting something of a prescriptive claim to the directorship of the department of public welfare. Reference has been made to their positions in the educational organization and in the courts. A woman director of a state labor department has succeeded in placing the administration in a position of constructive leadership.

The participation of women in state legislation seemed sufficiently interesting to warrant special investigation. Letters were written to all women legislators whose addresses could be obtained—320 in all—and replies from 126 were received. No special type predominates among them. The legislators were pioneering women whose other work seemed done; college graduates who have gone almost directly from the quadrangle to the capitol; some who were against suffrage and about half who were in the old movement. Some had a definite purpose, others did not want to be tarred with the feminist pitch. As to vocational experience, 26 had been teachers, 9 lawyers, 2 doctors, 6 business women, 3 social workers. Twenty-six had held office before. Most of them spoke of their experience as interesting and happy and many spoke of the courtesies of the men.

It is in the local jurisdictions that the evidence of women's activity is most conspicuous and there has perhaps been more substantial advance in the local than in any other jurisdictions. There have been women mayors; women have sat on boards of aldermen or city councils; they have been comptrollers and city clerks; and they are on boards of county commissioners. The facts are difficult to assemble in their entirety and the report of investigations concerning women in state and local office made in four states by the Leagues of Women Voters[59] of those states summarizes what appears to be the only available study of comparable offices over a period of years. It indicates that the woman in politics progresses faster at home than in the larger political units and it shows that women have had what might be thought to be a surprising concern with fiscal responsibilities.

In Connecticut the number of women in local office increased from 134 in 1925 to 652 in 1929, the great majority of them having been appointed rather than elected. In Michigan, Minnesota and Wisconsin, however, there were many more women selected for local office by election than by appointment. In Michigan the numbers increased from 367 in 1927 to 793 in 1929 and in Minnesota they rose from 227 in 1926 to 348 in 1930. The trend in Wisconsin is more difficult to determine as the basis of enumeration did not remain constant throughout the period studied. There were 62 women in local office in that state in 1926 and 171 in 1929, but the earlier figure did not include women in city, village and township offices. Of the 171 in 1929, 80 were in county and state offices.

VII. Women's Organizations

Women's organizations have to do with activities which are frequently outside the exercise of domestic responsibilities, but

59. These can be obtained from the National League of Women Voters, 352 17th Street, Washington, D.C.

they have been, and still are in many cases, concerned with matters which were domestic responsibilities but have become subjects of general interest and of important public policy.

The relationship of women to the granges and to the agricultural associations has been almost the reverse of that of women in other social or occupational groups. Those organizations were made up of men and women and after 1867, when women were admitted on equal terms and even elected master farmers, the men were charged with submitting to "petticoat government." In 1930, in a roster of 128 major state offices, women were listed as holding 26. The farmers' institutes were a form of adult extension education in which the women had their part. In 1898 domestic science associations began to be formed in Illinois. By 1912 there were 720 women's institutes in 8 states with 78,776 women attending. In 1914 the enactment of the so-called Smith-Lever bill gave federal aid to this important aspect of education. Federal funds, matched by state funds, provided an educational program carried out by home demonstration agents, which meant trained leadership. In 1915, county agents had enrolled 6,871 women and organized 250 community clubs in 15 southern states. In 1920 the Farm Bureau Federation was formed; in 1922, 210,560 groups of women and in 1929, 403,602 groups of women had been enrolled under the leadership provided from this source.

Many organizations of women seem to have sprung from a sense of a wrong to be righted, from the experiences connected with war, from a sense of educational, occupational or social need, or from some such special stumulus as was given by the Chicago World's Fair. The process has been, in general, the organization of a small local group, then the federation of the local groups into district or state wide organizations and centralization on a wider, possibly a national basis, then cooperation among national organizations and then a return to specialization in purpose. Women who work are inclined to ally themselves with others in their occupations, or with other grups of women who work. Women of leisure and education are likely to join with others to promote some special program.

It is impossible to make exact comparisons with former years, because the organizations have estimated rather than actually recorded membership figures. One example of the difficulty of exact statement is found in the General Federation of Women's Clubs, of which the total membership is estimated at "over two million."

The Federation is, however, composed of various clubs, and one woman may be a member of several federated clubs.

In spite of these difficulties in the way of exact statement, certain facts may be noted. Women's clubs, both urgan and rural, go back to the eighteen fifties, sixties and seventies. In the early 1890s the men of the labor movement decided that women should be "brought into the stream of associated effort" and, in 1903, the National Woman's Trade Union League was formed. In 1898 the National Consumers' League had already put its hand to the task of bringing consumption, for which women's responsibility was being recognized, under intelligent control. The patriotic motive and the racial bases of association should also be noted. In 1890 the Daughters of the American Revolution was organized; in 1891, the Daughters of the Revolution, the Colonial Dames and the United States Daughters of 1812; in 1894, the Daughters of the Confederacy; in 1917, the War Mothers of America organized in Indiana; in 1919, the Service Star Legion in Baltimore and the American War Mothers; in 1920, the American Auxiliary to the American Legion; in 1931, the Women's Auxiliary of the Veterans of Foreign Wars, the American Legion Auxiliary and the Women's Overseas Service League. They present varied points of view with reference to peace and war and to economic readjustment, some being conservative and militaristic, other liberal and seeking another way out, but all devoted to commenorating those who risked their lives for their country. It is not possible to give exact figures of membership for all of them, but the Daughters of the American Revolution in 1930 were organized in 2,377 chapters with 170,299 members; the Overseas Service League had 2,500 members in 50 units; and the American Legion Auxiliary had 9,130 units and 368,049 members.

Responding to the motive of racial loyalty, sometimes strengthened by the sectarian interest, are organizations among the Negro women and the Jewish women. The Women's Convention (Negro Baptist) was one of the very early organizations. In 1930, 2,000 representatives of their convention attended a conference in Chicago. The National Association of Colored Women was formed in 1896 and in 1930 there were branches in forty-two states which claimed a total of 50,000 members. The Jewish Women's Congress is one of the organizations growing out of the Chicago World's Fair and remains a factor in the life of that important racial community.

In 1930 it counted more than 50,000 members; it owned buildings and institutions valued at more than a million and a quarter dollars and provided aid to immigrants and supported scholarships and schools, in addition to providing opportunities for social intercourse and for study and recreation. The National Council of Catholic Women represents the national organization, 50 diocene councils organized under the general direction of the Ordinary, 6 state and 1,700 local organizations.

For the professions, there are three organizations of nurses, one concerned with educational problems, one with questions of public health nursing and one with service to practicing nurses. The last maintains scholarships ($34,000), a loan fund ($5,500) and a relief fund ($146,404). In 1921 the graduate nurses gave a new school building in memory of nurses who died in the World War to L'École Florence Nightingale, which is part of the Maison de la Santé at Bordeaux. The Medical Women's National Association requires membership in the American Medical Association and, in 1930, numbered only about 600. There are also the Women's Homeopathic and the Osteopathic Medical Women's Associations, both small in membership and both supplying opportunities for social intercourse and providing scholarships for promising women students. Teachers are organized in the National Education Association with about 175,000 members and in the Federation with 40,000 members.

The Association of Collegiate Alumnae organized in 1881 is now the American Association of University Women, with 40,000 members as compared to 18,400 in 1924. They are organized in 586 branches and maintain headquarters in Washington, publishing a quarterly *Journal*, handling funds in the award of fellowships amounting to $15,800 and participating in international efforts to secure for women wider opportunities for research and freer exercise of their intellectual powers. The National Association of College Women (colored) has 300 members in eight branches; the Parent Teachers Association in 1930 counted a million and a half members in branches in fifteen states.

Although the Association of Business and Professional Women is only thirteen years old, it already has state federations in forty-six states, approximately 1,100 local clubs, and about 50,000 members. Its slogan is "at least a high school education for every business girl," and its researches in the field of vocational aptitudes and of pecuniary rewards are important contributions to the existing vocational literature.[60]

The Association of Junior Leagues of America, Inc., has 109 branches and 22,000 members; it maintains national headquarters in New York City. The Women's Luncheon Clubs came in toward the end of the second decade of the century. They provide good fellowship and friendship. Altrusa (1917) boasted 109 clubs in thirty-four states and 3,000 members in 1931; Quota International (1918–1919), 30 clubs and 3,000 members in 1931; Zonta, 108 clubs and 3,000 members; and Soroptomist 4,200 members in 1930.

The sorority system in the colleges and universities began between 1870 and 1880. Twenty chapters organized before 1900 are still active. In 1927 there were 44 national organizations, of which 26 were academic and 18 professional; the academic sororities had 32,000 members in 150 institutions. In 1905, 7 chapters reported owning their houses while in 1927 there were 385 houses valued at $10,602,550. The sororities do not accumulate such funds as the fraternities accumulated in the past, but both in local chapters and as part of their national activity they maintain scholarships.

Women's organizations have tended toward cooperative relationships within the United States and also toward alliances with groups in other countries. The early form taken by the cooperative effort was the National Council of Women, which was and is a branch of an International Council. In 1928 there were 38 state organizations of the National Council. Cooperation sometimes takes the form of regular periodic conferences among organizations on some important subject. The Conference on the Cause and Cure of War, in which there were eleven participating organizations, and a similar Patriotic Conference on National Defense are illustrations of this tendency.

The practice of owning and maintaining clubhouses, although not a novel one, has developed rapidly in the past years. These houses are not only meeting places and refectories, but they also provide residential accommodations and make possible many activities appropriate to the membership. Some of these houses are valued at over $1,000,000.

60. University of Michigan, Elliott and Manson, *Earnings of Business and Professional Women*, Michigan Business Studies, vol. III, no. 1, 1930; and Grace E. Manson, *Occupational Interests and Personality Requirements of Women in Business*, *ibid.*, vol. III, no. 3, 1931.

Few of these organizations are self-supporting in that the dues of members alone enable them to carry on their work. Some, like the Young Women's Christian Association, are part of the social welfare program; or, like the Women's Trade Union League, are to an extent in the social reform movement. Others, like the Home Economics Association, look to foundations for special funds; and still others, like the General Federation of Women's Clubs or the National League of Women Voters, rely on a sort of annual drive. The totals are amazingly large considering the general scale of dues and the modest scale of pay received by most of the workers.

First federation and centralization, then cooperation, and finally specialization seems to be the changing emphasis in women's organizations. The new groups which appear and the older ones which grow are more restricted in the field they cover than the clubs which have been united in the Federation. It seems unlikely that the General Federation is growing now at anything like the pace of former years. Its very size and proud diversity militate against it.

VIII. Conclusion

The material supplied in the preceding pages justifies certain statements with reference to the changing conditions of women's employment.

It is clear that an increasing number of women are joining the wage earning group. The rate at which they pass from the non-gainfully employed to the gainfully employed is not rapid, but it has been increasing. This rate varies with women in different social positions and in different sections of the country, and it is higher for married women than for single women. It also seems to be true that the gainfully employed are coming from a higher age level than before and perhaps more definitely from the native group. Domestic and personal service claims the greatest number of women, with the clerical occupations, the manufacturing and mechanical industries, professional service and trade, and agriculture following in the order named. It is also clear that women are forming a steadily increasing proportion of the gainfully employed. The increase is not great—68 in 1,000 in fifty years—but it seems to be continuous. The proportion of women in the wage earning group and the rate of increase vary considerably in the different occupational classifications. The tendency seems to be away from the older agricultural and industrial pursuits, in the direction of office, store and professional work.

In what is generally known as the business world, described in the census by the terms, "Transportation," "Trade" and "Clerical" occupations, women are increasing steadily. The greatest proportion of the women in these fields are office workers, saleswomen, store clerks, retail dealers and telephone operators. In connection with these occupations the demand for educational opportunities has also grown steadily. There is some evidence that women in these fields are finding their way into positions of greater responsibility and higher pay.

In the professional field the proportion of women is still small in law, medicine and the ministry. By far the greatest number of professional women are teachers or nurses. Women are conspicuously increasing, however, in all professional occupations except those of physicians and musicians.

Women in the semi-skilled divisions of the manufacturing and mechanical industries are increasing somewhat, but in the skilled occupations they are for the most part declining or remaining about stationary. A notable exception to this is in the managerial positions, where women have shown considerable advances. In domestic and personal service, as in manufacturing, there have been changes in alignment reflecting the mechanical trend of contemporary living. The proportion of women in the civil service has not, except during the abnormal conditions of the war years, shown any great variation, in spite of the fact that the number of women entering the service has slightly increased.

As to women's participation in government, figures are not available which would show definite trends, either in the success of lobbying efforts or in the results of party activity. In legislative assemblies, whether federal or state, the numbers rise and fall. Such evidence with reference to voters as is available in certain figures recorded in the registration and in the poll lists by sex indicates an increase in the interest on the part of women voters rather more rapid than that shown by the increase in the men in the same jurisdiction and during the same period.

The changes occurring among women's organizations hardly lend themselves to statistical formulations. Their development, however, becomes more obvious in an objective account of the energy which goes into these organizations. They arose from a volume of interest in religion, social reform and education, and the ratification of the Nineteenth Amendment found a multiplicity of organizations active and occupying the attention of women. With the increase in the number of self-supporting women for whose leisure time the home no longer makes adequate provision, the club and the club house furnish shelter, food and opportunity for friendly association and the exercise of hospitality.

These are the conclusions which lie on the surface of the figures and facts presented in the foregoing pages. For a complete understanding of their significance, it is again necessary to recall the connection of this material with that supplied in other chapters, especially those on the family and labor. Such opportunities for women as have been opened up have often been secured under difficulties and against resistance of which these figures take no note. Those difficulties are suggested in the section referring to the necessity of securing legislative changes and of removing barriers by which women's occupational desires have been blocked. As long as women's relation to industry is discussed with that on "aliens, Mexicans, and Negroes," all acknowledged to be seriously disadvantaged groups, it is probably evident that industry, or the occupational world, is not making full use of the variety of abilities and capacities possessed by women, and that some limitations which were characteristic of the position of women in the earlier order of family organization still persist.

29. What Happened to the Feminist Movement?
Ethel Puffer Howes

Ethel Puffer Howes, a graduate of Smith College who received her Ph.D. from Radcliffe in 1902, taught psychology and mathematics at Smith, Radcliffe, Wellesley, and Simmons. In 1929, when she wrote the article below, Dr. Howes was Director of the Institute for the Coordination of Women's Interests of Smith College. This position and her own

SOURCE: Ethel Puffer Howes, "The Meaning of Progress in The Woman Movement," *The Annals of the American Academy of Political and Social Science*, 143 (May 1929): 14–20. Reprinted by permission of the publisher.

experience gave her a superior overview of women's achievements, their career objectives, and the obstacles in their paths. Clearly, she had devoted many years to considering possible solutions to the dilemmas she described.

It is altogether fitting that there should be at this time a stock-taking of what is known as the woman movement. The last ten years have seen an extraordinary flux in the position, the activities, and most of all in the inner attitudes of women. A natural impulse is to conjure with the word progress; to tell over the new legal freedoms and powers, and the new occupations of women, and to expound the achievements of outstanding individuals. But if this survey is to be a serious reckoning, it must first ask in what sense the quality of progress may be ascribed to these multitudinous changes, or, pressing further, in what progress in the woman movement may rightly be held to consist.

What *is* progress? No concept in the field of social thought has been more eagerly disputed. A recent listing of variant definitions of social progress topped the hundred in number. Nevertheless, for application to a special movement within the social field, the dictionary definition (Webster's) gives a fair clue: "A moving or going forward; an advance toward better or ideal knowledge or condition or that conceived of as better." In the words of a sociologist, "We shall be unable to define concepts of progress . . . except in relation to standards of value."[1] Progress, then, in postwar phrase, is an advance toward an objective, which objective is some ideal condition.

Has the woman movement an objective in this sense? Is there an ideal condition of womankind, clearly envisaged, which is to be sought as a goal, an end? The first answer of most women to this question is likely to be an indignant affirmative. But it is one that must, I believe, be qualified.

Freedom from Legal and Political Disabilities

The great spokesmen of the woman movement have demanded freedom from disabilities. Women have rebelled against their chains, and all that they have currently asked is to be allowed to cast them off. When their condition was something less than

1. H. Odum, *The Quest for Social Guidance* (1928).

human—without legal right in their own persons or their children, without the privilege of mental or any systematic training—they demanded the redress of these manifest injustices. It was a negative aspiration, cast in a negative form. As expressed by Mary Wollstonecraft in the opening of her *Vindication of the Rights of Women* (1798):

> Contending for the rights of woman, my main argument is built on this simple principle, that if she be not prepared by education to become the companion of man, she will stop the progress of knowledge and virtue.

The *Vindication* is in fact a brilliant presentation of the fundamentals of education, illustrated by women's disabilities. Freedom from the ban on rational thinking was what was sought for women.

The negative aspect is still more marked in the next great women's manifesto, put forth by the first Woman's Rights Convention of 1848. It is primarily a declaration of woman's wrongs at the hands of men, wrongs which called for redress. The fact that the demand for the vote was only included as an afterthought at this convention is a well-known bit of suffrage history; but the way in which that first convention was precipitated is also significant. The moment came through Elizabeth Cady Stanton's sudden denunciation of the wretched conditions of daily life for all women, wives and mothers, as she had seen them among poor women in her remote country dwelling. It was while on a visit to her friends Lucretia Mott and Jane Hunt that this denunciation took definite form, and she so fired her friends to action, as told in Mrs. Blatch's *Life*, that the call to convention was issued from that meeting.

That great landmark of the woman movement, Mill's *On the Subjection of Women* (1869), tells its story in the title, and the burden of the argument is summarized as follows:

> The disabilities of women are the only case, save one, in which laws and institutions take persons at their birth and ordain that they shall never in all their lives be allowed to compete for certain things. . . . Among all the lessons which men require for carrying on the struggle against the inevitable imperfections of their lot on earth, there is no lesson which they more need than not to add to the evils which nature inflicts, by their jealous and prejudiced restrictions on one another.

All negatives!

Freedom from Economic Disabilities

The next guidepost in the woman movement was *Women and Economics* (1896), Charlotte Perkins Gilman's epoch-making book. Women are oversexed (she says in substance), taught to rely on feline arts, restrained in their human impulse to do and to make, because their real disability is economic, not political. "The economic dependence of the human female on her mate," that "sexuo-economic relation," poisons love and marriage, family and social life, at their source. Hence, her program of economic independence is one of removing disabilities like the preceding. Much more, of course, is implied than is expressed, and Mrs. Gilman, in this and other writings, has anticipated most of the practical efforts for the management of women's lives which the new century has seen. Thus it would appear that the great interpreters of the woman's movement in the past have seen their goal as escape from a condition, rather than the establishment of a positive concept or ideal of women's nature and work.

That this idea has continued into the present and still largely dominates the woman movement is seen in the following words of Mrs. Carrie Chapman Catt in an article in *Current History*, for October, 1927:

> What is the woman movement and what is its aim? It is a demand for equality of opportunity between the sexes. It means that when and if a woman is as well qualified as a man to fill a position, she shall have an equal and unprejudiced chance to secure it. . . . What will bring the revolt to a close? . . . absolute equality of opportunity only will satisfy and therefore close the woman movement.

Progress in Removing Disabilities

Now it is certainly true that the successive practical steps by which women attained freedom from their disabilities in comparison with men, or, positively, the right to own property, to make contracts, to study and practice professions, to vote, have in every case been clearly set forth as objectives. From one point to another, then, there has been progress in this limited sense, that the immediate objective was clearly defined, and was attained. Mrs. Catt's own statement, however, is indubitable testimony to the fact that the positive "ideal condition" for women, which shall be a goal, a beacon, a guide to what she may, can, or shall do, or endeavor to do, has never as yet been a definite part of the woman's program. Progress in the full sense can, then, not be attributed to the woman movement, because no real objective has been set or attained. The "woman question" has never had an answer. And the proof of this is that never in the history of the woman movement were the conflicts in ethical motives more acute, the trends in education more contradictory, or the lack of clear thinking on fundamental meanings more notorious, than now.

This confusion was voiced by Dr. Harry Emerson Fosdick in sharper terms in a recent sermon, from a newspaper report of which I quote:

> There has been among us and there is now an insistence for freedom so widespread as to create the moral climate in which we all live. Many people, however, forget that there are two stages in the fight for freedom: first, the achievement of it; and, second, the using of it when you have achieved it.
>
> Think of the new freedom of woman. She has been emancipated in every realm of her life, legal, economic, and political. And yet has all this freedom solved a single ultimate problem for women? Only in the sense that it has presented American womanhood with an opportunity which may make womanhood or break it.

Wherein Past Objectives Have Been Inadequate

Dr. Fosdick is right. It is not too much to say that there is no more general grasp of these "ultimate problems" than in 1798, 1848, 1869, or 1920, when the vote was gained. Moreover, whereas a few years ago there was at least unanimity among thinking women as to the next step, that constituency is today facing two ways without realizing it.

There is, on the one hand, the original drive for ever wider opportunities for women: education to be carried to any point which a specific activity may require; with every *apparent* intention of serious pursuit of it—but with no least provision, either in professional machinery, in social framework, or even in current acknowledgment of need, for relating the individual occupation to the physical functions and emotional needs of women. The current rejoinder—"but we are now teaching women the basic arts of the family"—is precisely meaningless in this connection. The selective vocation is approached as if it were to be "the occupation of a celibate"—to paraphrase Herbert Spencer—until the moment comes, always by chance, when the use of training is abandoned, and the individual reverts to domestic pursuits. Education in home-making is of course good in itself; but it gives only the turn of the screw to what an English feminist calls "the intolerable choice" between married love and concrete achievement. The serious higher education or professional training of women today is literally founded on self-deception; a solemn farce in which all the actors consent to ignore the fact that the most natural, necessary, and valuable of human relations will in all probability soon ring down the final curtain. Of the inhibiting effect of this subconscious expectation of the break, both on education and achievement, I have written elsewhere. Suffice it to say that the most extraordinary and unexplained situation in the whole history of women is this ostrich-like attitude of women themselves, and women's educators above all, to the pressing need of conscious constructive control of the ever-imminent conflict between work and the love life.

This confusion in the objectives of women on the level of higher education is repeated in the field of women in industry. Not even the leaders of working women know what to advise for them, as is clearly set forth in a publication of the Women's Bureau.[2] They are said to be:

> . . . victims of an ever-changing public opinion. The least that the married woman who works should expect from industry is a consistent attitude toward her employment so that she may know what she is to expect. . . .

But, "the decrease in poverty incident to the employment of mothers," set over against the bad social consequences of the over-fatigue of the mother and the loss in childcare, has never been evaluated. The ultimate value for the industrial woman is still undetermined. Very recently a vivid picturing, by a social expert, of the dislocation in the personnel direction and organization of young women workers caused by their lack of real interest in anything but ultimate marriage, left the impression that this wholly natural interest was something which permanently vitiated the woman's labor situation. Rather would I say that the present

2. *Married Women in Industry*, Mary A. Winslow (1924).

impasse showed up the opportunity for constructive thinking on the part of the official leaders of women.

Alongside this age-old disregard of the fundamental impingement of nature on work, we have a recent tremendous efflorescence of the domestic and parental interests; a tendency to deprecate all systematic training except that for family living and to identify this with "training for life." This tendency derives, in the line of theory, from Rousseau's romantic view of woman's role, through Ellen Key and Havelock Ellis. Rousseau, who professed that education should be guided by the needs and rights of the personality of each individual, nevertheless applied this principle only to his *Émile*—his *Sophie* was never considered in any light save as Émile's life-companion.[3] Havelock Ellis is led by his studies in the differentia of sex to assume a complete fundamental difference in mentality and character and to expand this toward the conclusion that the whole end of woman is her biological and emotional activity. To quote from Havelock Ellis' account of Ellen Key, in which he voices his own agreement with her,

> Women, indeed, need free scope for their activities—and the earlier aspirations of feminism are thus justified—but they need it, not to wrest away any tasks that men may be better fitted to perform, but to play their own part in the field of creative life which is peculiarly their own. . . . The really fundamental difference between man and the woman is that he can usually give his best as a creator, and she as a lover, that his value is according to his work and hers according to her love. . . . Women are entitled to the same human rights as men [continues Ellis], and until such rights are attained "feminism" still has a proper task to achieve. But women must use their strength in the sphere for which their own nature fits them.[4]

Ellen Key's name is most widely associated with her special doctrines of "the cult of the child," "the right to motherhood." It may be questioned, however, if they will have as great importance for the concept of woman's function as the general trend of her teachings, which seek to lead women to abandon the field of varied creative opportunity and concentrate on family devotion. We get the reverberation of this plea in those new expressions of educators who are beginning to say, apparently to wide approval, "Let us now educate women *as women!*" This should not be thought to mean

3. Cp. Monroe, *History of Education.*
4. *The Task of Social Hygiene* (1912).

merely the desire to give women the necessary equipment for wifehood and motherhood—no, it is intended as a redirecting of women's education, and so of women's destiny. Here at least we have come to a foreshadowing of that ultimate concept for which we looked in vain before.

President Eliot [of Harvard] is forthright in his expression of this view:

> It is not the chief happiness or the chief end of woman, as a whole, to enter these new occupations, to pursue them through life. They enter many which they soon abandon; and that is good—particularly the abandonment. . . . The prime motive of the higher education of women should be recognized as the development in woman of the capacities and powers which will fit them to make family life more . . . productive in every sense, physically, mentally, and spiritually. To this modification of the higher education of women as we have seen it during the past generation may we not all look forward with abundant hope?

This was said by President Eliot in 1907[5] and it is now reprinted as a college publication by another president, with the comment that "it deserves a place in predictive prophecy."

Where We May Look for Progress in the Woman Movement

We have here at last the confrontation of two principles: the one, still confused, unfinished, entailing obvious conflict and contradiction; the other, definite enough, an "ultimate" in the sense required—if we can accept it. Where, then, shall we seek "progress" in the woman movement?

The people who want a quick return on their thinking are increasingly throwing in with the last view. It is so easy to rest in the dictum—since we all agree—that a woman's chief happiness is the vocation of wife and mother. But it needs only what Ellen Key calls "incorruptible realism" to see that the irresistible march of events is against it. First of all, the alleged sex division, in the effective sense, is gone. Science no longer sustains the dictum of Havelock Ellis; biology, genetics, and psychology are now on the side of the relative dissociation of abilities from sex characters. Secondly, we see the psychological impossibility of denying de-

5. *Women's Education*—A Forecast.

velopment to youth that is eager to learn, to act, and, for the most part, to work, or that needs to work. Thirdly, the psychological impossibility of restraining the *exercise* of a faculty which has once been developed, without danger of ill effects, even tragic ills. A hundred years ago, such a policy might have had some success, because women then did not as a class realize that their abilities were, broadly, equivalent to men's. But there is now no more chance of diverting those who thirst after knowledge and skill and the use of that skill, than of turning democracy permanently back to despotism. A real solution must be accepted in principle by at least the superior half of any class to be affected. Fourthly, the fact is inescapable that with early marriage and motherhood—an essential element in "the single vocation of motherhood" program—the termination of that active vocation will arrive just at the time when the woman herself is at the zenith of her powers. Result, either a frantic attempt to hold on to her vocation (with all the "fixation" and "mother-in-law" evils which modern mental hygiene has too fully shown us); or, resolute self-withdrawal, with the torture of twenty or more remaining years of futilities, social and cultural. Superfluous women! Every provocative magazine is full of stories about them.

No, the romantic program is a glorious picture of the possibilities of the wife and mother *relation*, but is not the solution of the ultimate destiny of the woman who has a mind, talents, energy and a long life to be lived in a world of creative doings. Therefore, it is to be hoped that the present distraction and uncertainty in the field of education, which this doctrine has mediated, will on sober second thought be overcome by its better understanding.

It is enough to read attentively Key's great book, *Love and Marriage*, to see the impossibility of releasing women's individual powers through education, and then diverting them completely from their end, without disaster.

Yet that disaster is what we are now inviting, not on principle, but through pure obstinate stupidity, in opening all doors to women, without providing for the woman's love life as the ordinary social setting does for man's. Various writers set up a straw woman, the "brain woman." It is as futile to deny that the present social framework does not allow the natural and necessary development of woman's affectional life, along with the natural continuous development and exercise of her individual powers. The man demands of life that he have love, home, fatherhood and the special work which his particular brain combination fits. Shall the woman demand less?

Here we are at the heart of the problem. I would say to Dr. Fosdick, that the reason why the emancipation of women has brought no "ultimate," is because women as a class have been too humble, too timid, to claim as an ultimate principle of life for themselves, what every man has without asking. The true concept of woman is of a being with a mind, with *specific* talents which need to be developed *and used;* and with a soul and body, a psychophysical organism which, too, needs to be developed *and used;* and until this principle is accepted as ultimate, as shaping not only education, but social forms, we shall look in vain for progress.

Whatever subvarieties of occupation of "the whole woman" develop, for individuals is immaterial. It may well be that nine-tenths of womankind will find fulfillment in the specific vocation of "collective motherliness," to use the phrase of Ellen Key. But this would be, on our view, merely one type of the general principle of integration. The ultimate principle of integration would demand full provision, in all educational plans, professional codes, and social arrangements for the ideally complete woman which would eliminate forever the necessity of an "intolerable choice."

Here is the place for John Dewey's definition of the problem of progress as one "of discovering the needs and capacities of collective human nature—and of inventing the social machinery which will set available powers operating for the satisfaction of those needs."

Inventing the Social Machinery

It is far from a small matter of special devices or personal adjustments by which women may participate in both professional and family life; it is a matter of transforming the whole social setting and the inner attitudes of men and women to accept the two-fold need of women as fundamental. The absolute first necessity is to see the problem for what it is; a fundamental one for education and ethics, not a mere question of management. The invention or achievement of successful methods by which, at various stages, adjustment may be assured, is important, indeed, but important primarily as a *vindication of possibility*, as *an illustration of meaning, as an aid to establishment of principle.*

A Practical Effort to Coordinate Women's Interests

"The individual can prescribe a life of reason more readily than he can follow it. But an environment can be formed in which desirable conduct becomes a reflex response."[6] It is toward the forming of the environment for successful integration (now in general effectively inhibited); to making integration both possible and natural, that the Institute for the Coordination of Women's Interests at Smith College is dedicated.

That is why the satisfactory organization, in a college project, of a new type of service for homes, of a cooperative nursery group, of a cooked food supply adjusted to moderate incomes, means not so many bits of ground won in home economics, but so many props in the social framework so necessary to any ultimate solution. All our analyses of the professions for their adjustment to women's needs, all our case histories of successful integrations of professional and home interests find herein their meaning and enter as elements into the synthesis.

The Institute's problem is thus intimately related to the fundamentals of education. The form which the principle of integration in women's lives takes, for collegiate education, is the principle of continuity in intellectual work. The practical corollaries of this principle are proving immense. It entails, for instance, replanning the curriculum for educational continuity, resulting in the new plan of the Graduate Project. It rescues women from the mental dryness of the post-college years from which so many women suffer.

We have only begun to realize that the true coordination of women's interests, the demand for integration, is a sword to cut such knotty problems of social ethics as partnership in marriage, the spacing of children, the objectives of women in research and administration, commerce and art. But the one unassailable ground won, from which all can ultimately be reached, is the acknowledgment of the principle of the integration of the full circle of the powers and needs of women.

6. Cattell, *A Statistical Study of American Men of Science.*

30. The Oppressive Climate for Literature in the United States: Sinclair Lewis

WELL FORTIFIED *with the finest liquor available in Stockholm, Sinclair Lewis stood before a distinguished audience at the Nobel Prize ceremonies in 1930 and delivered a polite but caustic rebuke to the undiscerning American public and to the remnants of what had been the American literary establishment. Going out of his way to speak generously of his chief competitors for the award—especially Theodore Dreiser—Lewis attributed most of the alleged deficiencies in American literature to the venerable members of the American Academy of Arts and Letters, to the nation's colleges and universities, to the deceased William Dean Howells, and to the elderly Hamlin Garland. As mediators between potential supporters of the arts in the United States and the country's writers, these representatives had failed miserably. As critics they had stifled intellectual boldness and rewarded timidity. In almost every conceivable fashion they had failed to provide constructive leadership for American writers. Yet, somehow, American literature not only survived, but thrived. Lewis proudly noted this phenomenon, but neglected to provide an explanation. His Nobel Prize, however, had been awarded for fictional satire, not for societal analysis.*

The American Fear of Literature

Members of the Swedish Academy; Ladies and Gentlemen: Were I to express my feeling of honor and pleasure in having been awarded the Nobel Prize in Literature, I should be fulsome and perhaps tedious, and I present my gratitude with a plain "Thank you."

I wish, in this address, to consider certain trends, certain dangers, and certain high and exciting promises in present-day American literature. To discuss this with complete and unguarded frankness—and I should not insult you by being otherwise than completely honest, however indiscreet—it will be necessary for me to

SOURCE: Sinclair Lewis, "The American Fear of Literature," *Why Sinclair Lewis Got the Nobel Prize* (New York, n.d.) pp. 9–23. Reprinted by permission of the estate of Sinclair Lewis.

be a little impolite regarding certain institutions and persons of my own greatly beloved land.

But I beg of you to believe that I am in no case gratifying a grudge. Fortune has dealt with me rather too well. I have known little struggle, not much poverty, many generosities. Now and then I have, for my books or myself, been somewhat warmly denounced —there was one good pastor in California who upon reading my "Elmer Gantry" desired to lead a mob and lynch me, while another holy man in the State of Maine wondered if there was no respectable and righteous way of putting me in jail. And, much harder to endure than any raging condemnation, a certain number of old acquaintances among journalists, what in the galloping American slang we call the "I Knew Him When Club," have scribbled that since they know me personally, therefore I must be a rather low sort of fellow and certainly no writer. But if I have now and then received such cheering brickbats, still I, who have heaved a good many bricks myself, would be fatuous not to expect a fair number in return.

No, I have for myself no conceivable complaint to make, and yet for American literature in general, and its standing in a country where industrialism and finance and science flourish and the only arts that are vital and respected are architecture and the film, I have a considerable complaint.

I can illustrate by an incident which chances to concern the Swedish Academy and myself and which happened a few days ago, just before I took ship at New York for Sweden. There is in America a learned and most amiable old gentleman who has been a pastor, a university professor, and a diplomat. He is a member of the American Academy of Arts and Letters and no few universities have honored him with degrees. As a writer he is chiefly known for his pleasant little essays on the joy of fishing. I do not suppose that professional fishermen, whose lives depend on the run of cod or herring, find it altogether an amusing occupation, but from these essays I learned, as a boy, that there is something very important and spiritual about catching fish, if you have no need of doing so.

This scholar stated, and publicly, that in awarding the Nobel Prize to a person who has scoffed at American institutions as much as I have, the Nobel Committee and the Swedish Academy had insulted America. I don't know whether, as an ex-diplomat, he intends to have an international incident made of it, and perhaps demand of the American Government that they land Marines in Stockholm to protect American literary rights, but I hope not.

I should have supposed that to a man so learned as to have been made a Doctor of Divinity, a Doctor of Letters, and I do not know how many other imposing magnificences, the matter would have seemed different; I should have supposed that he would have reasoned, "Although personally I dislike this man's books, nevertheless the Swedish Academy has in choosing him honored America by assuming that the Americans are no longer a puerile backwoods clan, so inferior that they are afraid of criticism, but instead a nation come of age and able to consider calmly and maturely any dissection of their land, however scoffing."

I should even have supposed that so international a scholar would have believed that Scandinavia, accustomed to the works of Strindberg, Ibsen, and Pontoppidan, would not have been peculiarly shocked by a writer whose most anarchistic assertion has been that America, with all her welahth and power, has not yet produced a civilization good enough to satisfy the deepest wants of human creatures.

I believe that Strindberg rarely sang the "Star-spangled Banner" or addressed Rotary Clubs, yet Sweden seems to have survived him.

I have at such length discussed this criticism of the learned fisherman not because it has any conceivable importance in itself, but because it does illustrate the fact that in America most of us—not readers alone but even writers—are still afraid of any literature which is not a glorification of everything American, a glorification of our faults as well as our virtues. To be not only a best-seller in America but to be really beloved, a novelist must assert that all American men are tall, handsome, rich, honest, and powerful at golf; that all country towns are filled with neighbors who do nothing from day to day save go about being kind to one another; that although American girls may be wild, they change always into perfect wives and mothers; and that, geographically, America is composed solely of New York, which is inhabited entirely by millionaires; of the West, which keeps unchanged all the boisterous heroism of 1870; and of the South, where every one lives on a plantation perpetually glossy with moonlight and scented with magnolias.

It is not today vastly more true than it was twenty years ago that such novelists of ours as you have read in Sweden, novelists like Dreiser and Willa Cather, are authentically popular and influential in America. As it was revealed by the venerable fishing Academician whom I have quoted, we still most revere the writers for the popular magazines who in a hearty and edifying chorus chant that the America of a hundred and twenty million population is still as simple, as pastoral, as it was when it had but forty million; that in an industrial plant with ten thousand employees, the relationship between the worker and the manager is still as neighborly and uncomplex as in a factory of 1840, with five employees; that the relationships between father and son, between husband and wife, are precisely the same in an apartment in a thirty-story palace today, with three motor cars awaiting the family below and five books on the library shelves and a divorce imminent in the family next week, as were those relationships in a rose-veiled five-room cottage in 1880; that, in fine, America has gone through the revolutionary change from rustic colony to world empire without having in the least altered the bucolic and puritanic simplicity of Uncle Sam.

I am, actually, extremely grateful to the fishing Academician for having somewhat condemned me. For since he is a leading member of the American Academy of Arts and Letters, he has released me, has given me the right to speak as frankly of that Academy as he has spoken of me. And in any honest study of American intellectualism today, that curious institution must be considered.

Before I consider the Academy, however, let me sketch a fantasy which has pleased me the last few days in the unavoidable idleness of a rough trip on the Atlantic. I am sure that you know, by now, that the award to me of the Nobel Prize has by no means been altogether popular in America. Doubtless the experience is not new to you. I fancy that when you gave the award even to Thomas Mann, whose "Zauberberg" seems to me to contain the whole of intellectual Europe, even when you gave it to Kipling, whose social significance is so profound that it has been rather authoritatively said that he created the British Empire, even when you gave it to Bernard Shaw, there were countrymen of those authors who complained because you did not choose another.

And I imagined what would have been said had you chosen some American other than myself. Suppose you had taken Theodore Dreiser.

Now to me, as to many other American writers, Dreiser more than any other man, marching alone, usually unappreciated, often hated, has cleared the trail from Victorian and Howellsian timidity and gentility in American fiction to honest and boldness and passion of life. Without his pioneering, I doubt if any of us could, unless we liked to be sent to jail, seek to express life and beauty and terror.

My great colleague Sherwood Anderson has proclaimed this leadership of Dreiser. I am delighted to join him. Dreiser's great first novel, "Sister Carrie," which he dared to publish thirty long years ago and which I read twenty-five years ago, came to housebound and airless America like a great free Western wind, and to our stuffy domesticity gave us the first fresh air since Mark Twain and Whitman.

Yet had you given the Prize to Mr. Dreiser, you would have heard groans from America; you would have heard that his style—I am not exactly sure what this mystic quality "style" may be, but I find the word so often in the writings of minor critics that I suppose it must exist—you would have heard that his style is cumbersome, that his choice of words is insensitive, that his books are interminable. And certainly respectable scholars would complain that in Mr. Dreiser's world, men and women are often sinful and tragic and despairing, instead of being forever sunny and full of song and virtue, as befits authentic Americans.

And had you chosen Mr. Eugene O'Neill, who has done nothing much in American drama save to transform it utterly, in ten or twelve years, from a false world of neat and competent trickery to a world of splendor and fear and greatness, you would have been reminded that he has done something far worse than scoffing—he has seen life as not to be neatly arranged in the study of a scholar but as a terrifying, magnificent and often quite horrible thing akin to the tornado, the earthquake, the devastating fire.

And had you given Mr. James Branch Cabell the Prize, you would have been told that he is too fantastically malicious. So would you have been told that Miss Willa Cather, for all the homely virtue of her novels concerning the peasants of Nebraska, has in her novel, "The Lost Lady," been so untrue to America's patent and perpetual and possibly tedious virtuousness as to picture an abandoned woman who remains, nevertheless, uncannily charming even to the virtuous, in a story without any moral; that

Mr. Henry Mencken is the worst of all scoffers; that Mr. Sherwood Anderson viciously errs in considering sex as important a force in life as fishing; that Mr. Upton Sinclair, being a Socialist, sins against the perfectness of American capitalistic mass production; that Mr. Joseph Hergesheimer is un-American in regarding graciousness of manner and beauty of surface as of some importance in the endurance of daily life; and that Mr. Ernest Hemingway is not only too young but, far worse, uses language which should be unknown to gentlemen; that he acknowledges drunkenness as one of man's eternal ways to happiness, and asserts that a soldier may find love more significant than the hearty slaughter of men in battle.

Yes, they are wicked, these colleagues of mine; you would have done almost as evilly to have chosen them as to have chosen me; and as a Chauvinistic American—only, mind you, as an American of 1930 and not of 1880—I rejoice that they are my countrymen and countrywomen, and that I may speak of them with pride even in the Europe of Thomas Mann, H. G. Wells, Galsworthy, Knut Hamsun, Arnold Bennett, Feuchtwanger, Selma Lagerlöf, Sigrid Undset, Verner von Heidenstam, D'Annunzio, Romain Rolland.

It is my fate in this paper to swing constantly from optimism to pessimism and back, but so is it the fate of any one who writes or speaks of anything in America—the most contradictory, the most depressing, the most stirring, of any land in the world today.

Thus, having with no muted pride called the roll of what seem to me to be great men and women in American literary life today, and having indeed omitted a dozen other names of which I should like to boast were there time, I must turn again and assert that in our contemporary American literature, indeed in all American arts save architecture and the film, we—yes, we who have such pregnant and vigorous standards in commerce and science—have no standards, no healing communication, no heroes to be followed nor villains to be condemned, no certain ways to be pursued and no dangerous paths to be avoided.

The American novelist or poet or dramatist or sculptor or painter must work alone, in confusion, unassisted save by his own integrity.

That, of course, has always been the lot of the artist. The vagabond and criminal François Villon had certainly no smug and comfortable refuge in which elegant ladies would hold his hand

and comfort his starveling soul and more starved body. He, veritably a great man, destined to outlive in history all the dukes and puissant cardinals whose robes he was esteemed unworthy to touch, had for his lot the gutter and the hardened crust.

Such poverty is not for the artist in America. They pay us, indeed, only too well; that writer is a failure who cannot have his butler and motor and his villa at Palm Beach, where he is permitted to mingle almost in equality with the barons of banking. But he is oppressed ever by something worse than poverty—by the feeling that what he creates does not matter, that he is expected by his readers to be only a decorator or a clown, or that he is good-naturedly accepted as a scoffer whose bark probably is worse than his bite and who probably is a good fellow at heart, who in any case certainly does not count in a land that produces eighty-story buildings, motors by the million, and wheat by the billions of bushels. And he has no institution, no group, to which he can turn for inspiration, whose criticism he can accept and whose praise will be precious to him.

What institutions have we?

The American Academy of Arts and Letters does contain, along with several excellent painters and architects and statesmen, such a really distinguished university president as Nicholas Murray Butler, so admirable and courageous a scholar as Wilbur Cross, and several first-rate writers: the poets Edwin Arlington Robinson and Robert Frost, the free-minded publicist James Truslow Adams, and the novelists Edith Wharton, Hamlin Garland, Owen Wister, Brand Whitlock and Booth Tarkington.

But it does not include Theodore Dreiser, Henry Mencken, our most vivid critic, George Jean Nathan who, though still young, is certainly the dean of our dramatic critics, Eugene O'Neill, incomparably our best dramatist, the really original and vital poets, Edna St. Vincent Millay and Carl Sandburg, Robinson Jeffers and Vachel Lindsay and Edgar Lee Masters, whose "Spoon River Anthology" was so utterly different from any other poetry ever published, so fresh, so authoritative, so free from any gropings and timidities that it came like a revelation, and created a new school of native American poetry. It does not include the novelists and short-story writers, Willa Cather, Joseph Hergesheimer, Sherwood Anderson, Ring Lardner, Ernest Hemingway, Louis Bromfield, Wilbur Daniel Steele, Fannie Hurst, Mary Austin, James Branch

Cabell, Edna Ferber, nor Upton Sinclair, of whom you must say, whether you admire or detest his aggressive socialism, that he is internationally better known than any other American artist whosoever, be he novelist, poet, painter, sculptor, musician, architect.

I should not expect any Academy to be so fortunate as to contain all these writers, but one which fails to contain any of them, which thus cuts itself off from so much of what is living and vigorous and original in American letters, can have no relationship whatever to our life and aspirations. It does not represent literary America of today—it represents only Henry Wadsworth Longfellow.

It might be answered that, after all, the Academy is limited to fifty members; that, naturally, it cannot include every one of merit. But the fact is that while most of our few giants are excluded, the Academy does have room to include three extraordinarily bad poets, two very melodramatic and insignificant playwrights, two gentlemen who are known only because they are university presidents, a man who was thrity years ago known as a rather clever humorous draughtsman, and several gentlemen of whom—I sadly confess my ignorance—I have never heard.

Let me again emphasize the fact—for it is a fact—that I am not attacking the American Academy. It is a hospitable and generous and decidedly dignified institution. And it is not altogether the Academy's fault that it does not contain many of the men who have significance in our letters. Sometimes it is the fault of those writers themselves. I cannot imagine that grizzly bear Theodore Dreiser being comfortable at the serenely Athenian dinners of the Academy, and were they to invite Mencken, he would infuriate them with his boisterous jeering. No, I am not attacking—I am reluctantly considering the Academy because it is so perfect an example of the divorce in America of intellectual life from all authentic standards of importance and reality.

Our universities and colleges, or gymnasia, most of them, exhibit the same unfortunate divorce. I can think of four of them, Rollins College in Florida, Middlebury College in Vermont, the University of Michigan, and the University of Chicago—which has had on its roll so excellent a novelist as Robert Herrick, so courageous a critic as Robert Morss Lovett—which have shown an authentic interest in contemporary creative literature. Four of them. But universities and colleges and musical emporiums and schools for the teaching of theology and plumbing and sign painting are as thick in America as the motor traffic. Whenever you see a public building with Gothic fenestration on a sturdy backing of Indiana concrete, you may be certain that it is another university, with anywhere from two hundred to twenty thousand students equally ardent about avoiding the disadvantage of becoming learned and about gaining the social prestige contained in the possession of a B.A. degree.

Oh, socially our universities are close to the mass of our citizens, and so are they in the matter of athletics. A great college football is passionately witnessed by eighty thousand people, who have paid five dollars apiece and motored anywhere from ten to a thousand miles for the ecstasy of watching twenty-two men chase one another up and down a curiously marked field. During the football season, a capable player ranks very nearly with our greatest and most admired heroes—even with Henry Ford, President Hoover, and Colonel Lindbergh.

And in one branch of learning, the sciences, the lords of business who rule us are willing to do homage to the devotees of learning. However bleakly one of our trader aristocrats may frown upon poetry or the visions of a painter, he is graciously pleased to endure a Millikan, a Michelson, a Banting, a Theobald Smith.

But the paradox is that in the arts our universities are as cloistered, as far from reality and living creation, as socially and athletically and scientifically they are close to us. To a true-blue professor of literature in an American university, literature is not something that a plain human being, living today, painfully sits down to produce. No; it is something dead; it is something magically produced by superhuman beings who must, if they are to be regarded as artists at all, have died at least one hundred years before the diabolical invention of the typewriter. To any authentic don, there is something slightly repulsive in the thought that literature could be created by any ordinary human being, still to be seen walking the streets, wearing quite commonplace trousers and coat and looking not so unlike a chauffeur or a farmer. Our American professors like their literature clear and cold and pure and very dead.

I do not suppose that American universities are alone in this. I am aware that to the dons of Oxford and Cambridge, it would seem rather indecent to suggest that Wells and Bennett and Galsworthy and George Moore may, while they commit the impropriety of continuing to live, be compared to any one so beautifully and safely dead as Samuel Johnson. I suppose that in the

Universities of Sweden and France and Germany there exist plenty of professors who prefer dissection to understanding. But in the new and vital and experimental land of America, one would expect the teachers of literature to be less monastic, more human, than in the traditional shadows of old Europe.

They are not.

There has recently appeared in America, out of the universities, an astonishing circus called "the New Humanism." Now of course "humanism" means so many things that it means nothing. It may infer anything from a belief that Greek and Latin are more inspiring than the dialect of contemporary peasants to a belief that any living peasant is more interesting than a dead Greek. But it is a delicate bit of justice that this nebulous word should have been chosen to label this nebulous cult.

Insofar as I have been able to comprehend them—for naturally in a world so exciting and promising as this today, a life brilliant with Zeppelins and Chinese revolutions and the Bolshevik industrialization of farming and ships and the Grand Canyon and young children and terrifying hunger and the lonely quest of scientists after God, no creative writer would have the time to follow all the chilly enthusiasms of the New Humanists—this newest of sects reasserts the dualism of man's nature. It would confine literature to the fight between man's soul and God, or man's soul and evil.

But, curiously, neither God nor the devil may wear modern dress, but must retain Grecian vestments. Oedipus is a tragic figure for the New Humanists; man, trying to maintain himself as the image of God under the menace of dynamos, in a world of high-pressure salesmanship, is not. And the poor comfort which they offer is that the object of life is to develop self-discipline—whether or not one ever accomplishes anything with this self-discipline. So this the whole movement results in the not particularly novel doctrine that both art and life must be resigned and negative. It is a doctrine of the blackest reaction introduced into a stirringly revolutionary world.

Strangely enough, this doctrine of death, this escape from the complexities and danger of living into the secure blankness of the monastery, has become widely popular among professors in a land where one would have expected only boldness and intellectual adventure, and it has more than ever shut creative writers off from any benign influence which might conceivably have come from the universities.

But it has always been so. America has never had a Brandes, a Taine, a Goethe, a Croce.

With a wealth of creative talent in America, our criticism has most of it been a chill and insignificant activity pursued by jealous spinsters, ex-baseball-reporters, and acid professors. Our Erasmuses have been village schoolmistresses. How should there be any standards when there has been no one capable of setting them up?

The great Cambridge-Concord circle of the middle of the Nineteenth Century—Emerson, Longfellow, Lowell, Holmes, the Alcotts—were sentimental reflections of Europe, and they left no school, no influence. Whitman and Thoreau and Poe and, in some degree, Hawthorne, were outcasts, men alone and despised, berated by the New Humanists of their generation. It was with the emergence of William Dean Howells that we first began to have something like a standard, and a very bad standard it was.

Mr. Howells was one of the gentlest, sweetest, and most honest of men, but he had the code of a pious old maid whose greatest delight was to have tea at the vicarage. He abhorred not only profanity and obscenity but all of what H. G. Wells has called "the jolly coarsenesses of life." In his fantastic vision of life, which he innocently conceived to be realistic, farmers and seamen and factory-hands might exist, but the farmer must never be covered with muck, the seaman must never roll out bawdy chanteys, the factory-hand must be thankful to his good kind employer, and all of them must long for the opportunity to visit Florence and smile gently at the quaintness of the beggars.

So strongly did Howells feel this genteel, this New Humanistic philosophy that he was able vastly to influence his contemporaries, down even to 1914 and the turmoil of the Great War.

He was actually able to tame Mark Twain, perhaps the greatest of our writers, and to put that fiery old savage into an intellectual frock coat and top hat. His influence is not altogether gone today. He is still worshipped by Hamlin Garland, an author who should in every way have been greater than Howells but who under Howells' influence was changed from a harsh and magnificent realist into a genial and insignificant lecturer. Mr. Garland is, so far as we have one, the dean of American letters today, and as our dean, he is alarmed by all of the younger writers who are so lacking in taste as to suggest that men and women do not always love in accordance with the prayer-book, and that common people sometimes use language which would be inappropriate at a women's literary club on Main Street. Yet this same Hamlin Garland, as a young man, before he had gone to Boston and become cultured and Howellsised, wrote two most valiant and revelatory works of realism, "Main-Travelled Roads" and "Rose of Dutcher's Coolie."

I read them as a boy in a prairie village in Minnesota—just such an environment as was described in Mr. Garland's tales. They were vastly exciting to me. I had realized in reading Balzac and Dickens that it was possible to describe French and English common people as one actually saw them. But it had never occurred to me that one might without indecency write of the people of Sauk Centre, Minnesota, as one felt about them. Our fictional tradition, you see, was that all of us in Midwestern villages were altogether noble and happy; that not one of us would exchange the neighborly bliss of living on Main Street for the heathen gaudiness of New York or Paris or Stockholm. But in Mr. Garland's "Main-Travelled Roads" I discovered that there was one man who believed that Midwestern peasants were sometimes bewildered and hungry and vile—and heroic. And, given this vision, I was released; I could write of life as living life.

I am afraid that Mr. Garland would be not pleased but acutely annoyed to know that he made it possible for me to write of America as I see it, and not as Mr. William Dean Howells so sunnily saw it. And it is his tragedy, it is a completely revelatory American tragedy, that in our land of freedom, men like Garland, who first blast the roads to freedom, become themselves the most bound.

But, all this time, while men like Howells were so effusively seeking to guide America into becoming a pale edition of an English cathedral town, there were surly and authentic fellows—Whitman and Melville, then Dreiser and james Huneker and Mencken—who insisted that our land had something more than tea-table gentility.

And so, without standards, we have survived. And for the strong young men, it has perhaps been well that we should have no standards. For, after seeming to be pessimistic about my own and much beloved land, I want to close this dirge with a very lively sound of optimism.

I have, for the future of American literature, every hope and every eager belief. We are coming out, I believe, of the stuffiness of safe, sane, and incredibly dull provincialism. There are young Americans today who are doing such passionate and authentic work that it makes me sick to see that I am a little too old to be one of them.

There is Ernest Hemingway, a bitter youth, educated by the most intense experience, disciplined by his own high standards, an authentic artist whose home is in the whole of life; there is Thomas Wolfe, a child of, I believe, thirty or younger, whose one and only novel, "Look Homeward, Angel," is worthy to be compared with the best in our literary production, a Gargantuan creature with great gusto of life; there is Thornton Wilder, who in an age of realism dreams the old and lovely dreams of the eternal romantics; there is John Dos Passos, with his hatred of the safe and sane standards of Babbitt and his splendor of revolution; there is Stephen Benét who, to American drabness, has restored the epic poem with his glorious memory of old John Brown; there are Michael Gold, who reveals the new frontier of the Jewish East Side, and William Faulkner, who has freed the South from hoopskirts; and there are a dozen other young poets and fictioneers, most of them living now in Paris, most of them a little insane in the tradition of James Joyce, who, however insane they may be, have refused to be genteel and traditional and dull.

I salute them, with a joy in being not yet too far removed from their determination to give to the America that has mountains and endless prairies, enormous cities and lost far cabins, billions of money and tons of faith, to an America that is as strange as Russia and as complex as China, a literature worthy of her vastness.

31. Prospects for American Intellectual Life: John Dewey

WHILE AMERICAN *intellectuals ridiculed William Jennings Bryan's performance on the courtroom stage at the Dayton, Tennessee, trial over the teaching of evolution, one of the most contemplative among them, philosopher-educator John Dewey, took a much more serious view of the situation. Bryan and his followers, Dewey conceded, could conduct only an unsuccessful holding action against biological inquiry. The antievolu-*

SOURCE: John Dewey, "The American Intellectual Frontier," *The New Republic*, 30 (May 10, 1922): 302–303.

tionists, however, represented something much more sinister to American intellectual life than the trial on a limited issue indicated. What the country actually was witnessing, Dewey declared, was a manifestation of "the fear of whatever threatens the security and order of a precariously attained civilization." Bryan's appeals, he warned, were "a symptom of the forces which are most powerful in holding down the intellectual level of American life." Since these Americans were protecting something much more precious than their antievolutionist biases: the foundations of their peculiar culture, their defense was apt to be tenacious. As a powerful minority—if not an outright majority—in the country they could be expected to maintain what Dewey termed "the fixed limit to thought" in the United States.

The American Intellectual Frontier

The campaign of William Jennings Bryan against science and in favor of obscurantism and intolerance is worthy of serious study. It demands more than the mingled amusement and irritation which it directly evokes. In its success (and it is meeting with success) it raises fundamental questions about the quality of our democracy. It helps us understand the absence of intellectual radicalism in the United States and the present eclipse of social and political liberalism. It aids, abets and gives comfort to the thoroughgoing critics of any democracy. It gives point to the assertion of our Menckens that democracy by nature puts a premium on mediocrity, the very thing in human nature that least stands in need of any extraneous assistance.

For Mr. Bryan is a typical democratic figure. There is no gainsaying that proposition. Economically and politically he has stood for and with the masses, not radically but "progressively." The most ordinary justice to him demands that his usefulness in revolt against privilege and his role as a leader in the late progressive movement—late in every sense of the word, including deceased—be recognized. His leadership in antagonism to free scientific research and to popular dissemination of its results cannot therefore be laughed away as a personal idiosyncrasy. There is a genuine and effective connection between the political and the doctrinal directions of his activity, and between the popular responses they call out.

What we call the middle classes are for the most part the churchgoing classes, those who have come under the influence of evangelical Christianity. These persons form the backbone of philanthropic social interest, of social reform through political action, of pacifism, of popular education. They embody and express the spirit of kindly goodwill toward classes which are at an economic disadvantage and toward other nations, especially when the latter show any disposition toward a republican form of government. The "Middle West," the prairie country, has been the center of active social philanthropies and political progressivism because it is the chief home of this folk. Fairly well to do, enough so at least to be ambitious and to be sensitive to restrictions imposed by railway and financial corporations, believing in education and better opportunities for its own children, mildly interested in "culture," it has formed the solid element in our diffuse national life and heterogeneous populations. It has been the element responsive to appeals for the square deal and more nearly equal opportunities for all, as it has understood equality of opportunity. It followed Lincoln in the abolition of slavery, and it followed Roosevelt in his denunciation of "bad" corporations and aggregations of wealth. It also followed Roosevelt or led him in its distinctions between "on the one hand and on the other hand." It has been the middle in every sense of the word and in every movement. Like every mean it has held things together and given unity and stability of movement.

It has never had an interest in ideas as ideas, nor in science and art for what they may do in liberating and elevating the human spirit. Science and art as far as they refine and polish life, afford "culture," mark stations on an upward social road, and have direct useful social applications, yes: but as emancipations, as radical guides to life, no. There is nothing recondite or mysterious or sinister or adverse to a reputable estimate of human nature in the causes of this state of mind. Historians of thought point out the difference between the fortunes of the new ideas of science and philosophy in the eighteenth century in England and France. In the former, they were accommodated, partially absorbed; they permeated far enough to lose their own inherent quality. Institutions were more or less liberalized, but the ideas were lost in the process. In France, the opposition was entrenched in powerful and inelastic institutions. The ideas were clarified and stripped to fighting weight. They had to fight to live, and they became weapons. What happened in England happened in America only on a larger scale and to greater depths. The net result is social and political liberalism combined with intellectual illiberality. Of the result Mr. Bryan is an outstanding symbol.

The fathers of our country belonged to an intellectual aristocracy; they shared in the intellectual enlightenment of the eighteenth century. Franklin, Jefferson, John Adams, in their beliefs and ideas were men of the world, especially of the contemporary French world. Their free-thinking ideas did not prevent their being leaders. A generation later and it is doubtful if one of them could have been elected town selectman, much less have become a powerful political figure. When Mr. Taft was a candidate for President, a professor of modern languages in a southern college was dismissed from his position because he remarked to a friend in private conversation that he did not think that the fact that Mr. Taft was a Unitarian necessarily disqualified him for service as President. The incident is typical of the change wrought in a century, a change which became effective, however, quite early in the century. There are histories of the United States written from almost every point of view; but the social and political consequences of the popular evangelical movement which began in the early years of the nineteenth century do not seem to have received the attention they deserve. A large part of what is attacked under the name of Puritanism has next to nothing to do with historic Puritanism and almost everything to do with that second "Great Awakening" which began in the border, southern and western frontier states in the first decade of the last century.

It is not without significance that Andrew Jackson, the first "church-going" President, was also the first political representative of the democratic frontier, the man who marks the change of the earlier aristocratic republic into a democratic republic. The dislike of privilege extended itself to fear of the highly educated and the expert. The tradition of higher education for the clergy was surrendered in the popular denominations. Religion was popularized, and thought, especially free thought which impinged adversely upon popular moral conceptions, became unpopular, too unpopular to consist with political success. It was almost an accident that even Lincoln could be elected President. Nominal tribute, at least, has had to be paid to the beliefs of the masses. When popular education was extended and colleges and "universities" were scattered towards the frontier, denominational agencies alone had sufficient social zeal to take part. When state universities were founded they were open to the suspicion of ungodliness; and generally protected themselves by some degree of conformity to the expectations imposed by the intellectual prejudices of the masses. They could go much further than denominational colleges, but they could not go so far as the cultivate the free spirit. There were reserves, reticences and accommodations.

The churches performed an inestimable social function in frontier expansion. They were the rallying points not only of respectability but of decency and order in the midst of a rough and turbulent population. They were the representatives of social neighborliness and all the higher interests of the communities. The tradition persisted after the incoming of better schools, libraries, clubs, musical organizations and the other agencies of "culture." There are still thousands of communities throughout the country where the church building is the natural meetinghouse for every gathering except a "show." The intensity of evangelical life toned down, and the asperities of dogmatic creeds softened. But the association of the church with the moral and the more elevated social interests of the community remained. The indirect power of the church over thought and expression increases as its direct power waned. The more people stopped going to church, the more important it became to maintain the standards for which the church stood. As the frontier ceased to be a menace to orderly life, it persisted as a limit beyond which it was dangerous and unrespectable for thought to travel.

What the frontier was to western expansion, slavery was for the South. After a period of genuine liberalism among the southern clergy, the church became largely a bulwark of support to the peculiar institution, especially as the battle took a sectional form. The gentry became at least nominally attached to the church in the degree in which clericalism attached itself to the support of slavery. The church was a natural outlet and consolation for the poor whites. It was upon the whole the most democratic institution within their horizon. It is notorious that the most reactionary theological tendencies have their home in the South. The churches there can thank God that they at least have not contaminated their theology with dangerous concessions to modern thought. In the South the movements to withhold public funds from public educational institutions which permit the teaching of evolution have their greatest success.

Mr. Bryan can have at best only a temporary triumph, a *succés d'estime*, in his efforts to hold back biological inquiry and teaching. It is not in this particular field that he is significant. But his appeals and his endeavors are a symptom and a symbol of the forces which are most powerful in holding down the intellectual level of American life. He does not represent the frontier democracy of Jackson's day. But he represents it toned down and cultivated as it exists in fairly prosperous villages and small towns that have inherited the fear of whatever threatens the security and order of a precariously attained civilization, along with pioneer impulses to neighborliness and decency. Attachment to stability and homogeneity of thought and belief seem essential in the midst of practical heterogeneity, rush and unsettlement. We are not Puritans in our intellectual heritage, but we are evangelical because of our fear of ourselves and of our latent frontier disorderliness. The depressing effect upon the free life of inquiry and criticism is the greater because of the element of soundness in frontier fear, and because of the impulses of good will and social aspiration which have become entangled with its creeds. The forces which are embodied in the present crusade would not be so dangerous were they not bound up with so much that is necessary and good. We have been so taught to respect the beliefs of our neighbors that few will respect the beliefs of a neighbor when they depart from forms which have become associated with aspiration for a decent neighborly life. This is the illiberalism which is deep-rooted in our liberalism. No account of the decay of the idealism of the progressive movement in politics or of the failure to develop an intelligent and enduring idealism out of the emotional fervor of the war, is adequate unless it reckons with this fixed limit to thought. No future liberal movement, when active liberalism revives, will be permanent unless it goes deep enough to affect it. Otherwise we shall have in the future what we have had in the past, revivalists like Bryan, Roosevelt and Wilson, movements which embody moral emotions rather than the insight and policy of intelligence.

32. The Decline of American Civilization —a Prophecy: Joseph Wood Krutch

SINCLAIR LEWIS and John Dewey were relatively optimistic about the future of civilization in the United States compared to Joseph Wood Krutch. It was symptomatic of the mood of American intellectuals during the 1920s that Krutch's gloomy The Modern Temper *exercised an appeal among them as powerful in its way as Bryan's theologic pronouncements were in the small towns. Krutch, born in 1893, had published* Our Changing Morals *in 1925 and, appropriately, a volume about Edgar Allen Poe in 1926, before writing* The Modern Temper, *the concluding chapter of which is reprinted below.*

It is not by thought that men live. Life begins in organisms so simple that one may reasonably doubt even their ability to feel, much less think, and animals cling to or fight for it with a determination which we might be inclined to call superhuman if we did not know that a will to live so thoughtless and so unconditional is the attribute of beings rather below than above the human level. All efforts to find a rational justification of life, to declare it worth the living for this reason or that, are, in themselves, a confession of weakness, since life at its strongest never feels the need of any such justification and since the most optimistic philosopher is less optimistic than the man or animal who, his belief that life is good being too immediate to require the interposition of thought, is no philosopher at all.

In view of this fact it is not surprising that the subtlest intellectual contortions of modern metaphysics should fail to establish the existence of satisfactory aims for life when, as a matter of fact, any effort to do so fails as soon as it begins and can only arise as the result of a weakening of that self-justifying vitality which is the source of all life and of all optimism. As soon as thought begins to seek the "ends" or "aims" to which life is subservient it has already confessed its inability to achieve that animal acceptance of life for life's sake which is responsible for the most determined efforts to

SOURCE: Joseph Wood Krutch, *The Modern Temper* (New York, 1929), pp. 233–249.

live and, in one sense, we may say that even the firmest medieval belief in a perfectly concrete salvation after death marks already the beginning of the completest despair, since that belief could not arise before thought had rendered primitive vitality no longer all-sufficient.

The decadent civilizations of the past were not saved by their philosophers but by the influx of simpler peoples who had centuries yet to live before their minds should be ripe for despair. Neither Socrates nor Plato could teach his compatriots any wisdom from which they could draw the strength to compete with the crude energy of their Roman neighbors, and even their thought inevitably declined soon after it had exhausted their vital energy. Nor could these Romans, who flourished longer for the very reason, perhaps, that they had slower and less subtle intellects, live forever; they too were compelled to give way in their time to barbarians innocent alike both of philosophy and of any possible need to call upon it.

The subhuman will to live which is all-sufficient for the animal may be replaced by faith, faith may be replaced by philosophy, and philosophy may attenuate itself until it becomes, like modern metaphysics, a mere game; but each of these developments marks a stage in a progressive enfeeblement of that will to live for the gradual weakening of which it is the function of each to compensate. Vitality calls upon faith for aid, faith turns gradually to philosophy for support, and then philosophy, losing all confidence in its own conclusions, begins to babble of "beneficent fictions" instead of talking about Truth; but each is less confident than what went before and each is, by consequence, less easy to live by. Taken together, they represent the successive and increasingly desperate expedients by means of which man, the ambitious animal, endeavors to postpone the inevitable realization that living is merely a physiological process with only a physiological meaning and that it is most satisfactorily conducted by creatures who never feel the need to attempt to give it any other. But they are at best no more than expedients, and when the last has been exhausted there remains nothing except the possibility that the human species will be revitalized by some race or some class which is capable of beginning all over again.

Under the circumstances it is not strange that decadent civilizations are likely to think that the collapse of their culture is in reality the end of the human story. Perhaps some of the last of the old Roman intelligentsia realized that the future belonged to the barbarians from the north and that it belonged to them for the very reason that they were incapable of assimilating ancient thought, but even among the early Christian theologians there was a widespread belief that the end of Rome could mean nothing except the end of the world, and, for similar reasons, it is difficult for us to believe in the possibility of anything except either the continuation of modern culture or the extinction of human life. But a glance at history should make us hesitate before asserting that either one of these alternative possibilities is likely to become a reality. On the one hand all cultures have ultimately collapsed and human life has, on the other hand, always persisted—not because philosophers have arisen to solve its problems but because naïver creatures, incapable of understanding the problems and hence not feeling the need to solve them, have appeared somewhere upon the face of the globe.

If modern civilization is decadent then perhaps it will be rejuvenated, but not by the philosophers whose subtlest thoughts are only symptoms of the disease which they are endeavoring to combat. If the future belongs to anybody it belongs to those to whom it has always belonged, to those, that is to say, too absorbed in living to feel the need for thought, and they will come, as the barbarians have always come, absorbed in the processes of life for their own sake, eating without asking if it is worth while to eat, begetting children without asking why they should beget them, and conquering without asking for what purpose they conquer.

Doubtless even those among the last of the Romans who had some dim conception of the fact that the centuries immediately to follow would belong to the barbarians were not, for the most part, greatly interested in or cheered by the fact. Thoughtful people come inevitably to feel that if life has any value at all, then that value lies in thought, and to the Roman it probably seemed that it was hardly worth while to save the human animal if he could be saved only by the destruction of all that which his own ancestors had achieved, and by the forgetting of everything which he cared to remember. The annihilation of ancient culture was to him equivalent to the annihilation of humanity, and a modern who has come to think in a similar fashion can have only a languid interest in a possible animal rejuvenation which would inevitably involve a blunting of that delicate sensibility and that exquisite subtlety of intellect upon which he has come to set the very highest value.

But doubtless this ancient Roman speculated idly, and it is impossible for us not to do the same. Whence will the barbarians (and we may use that word, not as a term of contempt, but merely as a way of identifying these people animated by vitally simple thoughts) come? We are not surrounded as the Romans were by childlike savages, and we can hardly imagine the black tribes of Africa pushing in upon us. Have we, within the confines of our own cities, populations quite as little affected by modern thought as the Goths were affected by Greek philosophy, and hence quite capable either of carrying peaceably on as the aristocracy dies quietly off at the top or of arising sometime to overwhelm us? Has China, having died once, lain fallow long enough to have become once more primitive, or are the Russians indeed the new barbarians, even if they are such in a somewhat different sense than that implied in the sensational literature of anticommunist propaganda?

II

These Russians are young in the only sense of the word which can have a meaning when applied to any part of the human family. If all men had a common ancestor, then all races are equally old in years, but those which have never passed through the successive and debilitating stages of culture retain that potentiality for doing so which constitutes them racially young, and the Russians, who have always lived upon the frontiers of Europe, are in this sense a primitive race, since European culture has never been for them more than the exotic diversion of a small class. For the first time in history the mass of the people is in a position to employ its constructive faculties, and it so happens that their domain is one which offers an enormous field for the employment of such faculties.

Young races like young individuals need toys to play with. Before the advent of the machine, the Romans amused themselves with military and social organization, pushing the boundaries of their empire farther and farther back into unknown territory until their energy was exhausted and they were compelled to begin a gradual retraction; today, the processes of industrial development are capable of absorbing much of the vitality which could formerly find an outlet only in conquest; but if modern people amuse themselves by building factories or digging mines they do so for exactly the same reason that the Romans annexed the British Isles—because, that is to say, there is little temptation to ask ultimate questions as long as there are many tangible things to do and plenty of energy to do them with. Russia has both, and for that very reason there is no other place in the world where one will find today an optimism so simple and so terrible.

We—particularly we in America—have done all that. We have dug our mines, piped our oil, built our factories, and, having done so, we have begun to settle down in our comfortable houses to ask what comes next. But the Russians are at least a century away from such a condition. They begin at a point at least as far back as we began a century ago and they are in the happy position of desiring certain things which they have good reason to believe ultimately achievable. Not only do they want to grow rich and to establish a form of society which will provide for an equitable distribution of their riches, but they find on every side some tangible task capable of being accomplished in such a way as to further their ambition. Perhaps when this ambition has been achieved, when all men are as materially comfortable as some few men are today, then the comfortable masses will discover what the comfortable few have discovered already, which is, of course, that comfort seems enough only when one happens not to have it. But that day is still long distant. Not only will the complete industrial development of the country occupy many years but the problems of the new society are themselves so complicated that they are not likely to be solved for generations and hence, in all probability, Russia will not grow ripe so rapidly as the United States did.

As a result of these conditions there has already developed in Russia a new philosophy of life which, in spite of the fact that it has taken a form influenced by modern industrial conditions, is easily recognizable as being essentially primitive in its simplicity. Sweeping aside the intellectual and emotional problems of Europe, refusing even in its art to concern itself with the psychology of the individual soul, Communism assumes that nothing is really important except those things upon which the welfare of the race depends, and in assuming that it is assuming exactly what a primitive society always assumes. Its drama and its poetry celebrate the machine exactly as the literature of a primitive people celebrates the process of hunting or of agriculture, and they do so for exactly the same reason, for the reason, that is to say, that agriculture on the one hand and industry on the other are the two fundamental processes by which the life of the people is sustained.

Communistic Utopianism is based upon the assumption that the only maladjustments from which mankind suffers are social in character and hence it is sustained by the belief that in a perfect state all men would be perfectly happy. Fundamentally materialistic, it refuses to remember that physical well-being is no guarantee of felicity and that, as a matter of fact, as soon as the individual finds himself in a perfectly satisfactory physical environment he begins to be aware of those more fundamental maladjustments which subsist, not between man and society, but between the human spirit and the natural universe. And though, for this reason, it must seem to the cultivated European essentially naïve, yet in that very naïveté lies its strength as a social philosophy. Thanks to the fact that the perfect Communist is not aware of the existence of any problems more subtle than those involved in the production and distribution of wealth, he can throw himself into the business of living with a firm faith in the value of what he is doing and he can display an energy in practical affairs not to be equaled by any one incapable of a similar belief in their ultimate importance.

All societies which have passed the first vigor of their youth reveal their loss of faith in life itself by the fact that they no longer consider such fundamental processes as other than means toward an end. Food, clothes, and warmth are considered merely as instruments, and the most eager attention is directed, not toward attaining them, but toward the activities which men are at liberty to pursue when such fundamental things are granted. Productive labor is regarded as an evil, and when anything is said concerning the possibility of improving the condition of the masses, such improvement is always thought of as consisting essentially in so shortening even their hours of labor as to make possible for them also certain hours of freedom. Primitive societies, on the other hand, have no desire to escape from such fundamental processes. They do not hunt in order to live but they live in order to hunt, because for them the value of life lies in the activities necessary to carry it on; and the communist philosophy of labor is based upon a similiarly primitive outlook. Factories are considered, not as a means toward an end, but as ends in themselves. A full life is to consist, not in one spent in the pursuit of those thoughts or the cultivation of those emotions which are possible only when productive labor has been reduced to a minimum, but in one completely absorbed by such labor.

Hence it is that to the good Communist, as to the good tribesman, any question concerning the meaning of life is in itself completely meaningless and he will live the complicated industrial life of today exactly as the tribesman lives the simple life of his tribe—not in thought but in action. He has a sort of God, but his God is in reality what anthropologists call a culture-god; merely, that is to say, the spirit which presides over and infuses itself with the germination of the seed, the ripening of the fruit, or the whirring of the machine.

Such a philosophy comes nearer than any other to that unformulated one by which an animal lives. It does not ask any of the questions which a weary people inevitably ask and it is, as a matter of fact, less a system of thought than a translation into simple words of the will to live and thrive. But it is, for all that, only the more impressive as an evidence of the vigorous youth of the Russian mind. The visitor to Moscow who sees how eagerly its inhabitants live under conditions which are still very difficult, how gladly they accept both labor and, when necessary, privation, cannot but realize that they are sustained by a fundamental optimism unknown anywhere else in the world. At the present moment the inhabitants of many European countries *have* much more but they *hope* much less, and they are incapable of any acceptance of life so vital and so complete.

If the Communistic experiment is economically a failure, then these hopes may be soon disappointed; if it becomes economically a success, then they will doubtless still be disappointed in that more distant day when, the perfect state having been achieved, its inhabitants come to realize that the natural universe is as imperfectly adapted as ever to human needs. But man-the-animal lives in Time. A hope is a hope up to the instant when it is dashed, and the Russia of today is filled with a confidence hardly less elementary than that of the animal which, under the influence of the vital urge, acts as though the litter which it has just brought into the world were so tremendously worth saving that nothing else which had occurred since the dawn of the first day were of equal importance.

Perhaps, then, Europe has good reason to speak of the "Bolshevik menace," but if so the events which she fears are not quite the ones most likely to occur. If Russia or the Russian spirit conquers Europe it will not be with the bomb of the anarchist but with the vitality of the young barbarian who may destroy many things but who destroys them only that he may begin over again. Such calamities are calamitous only from the point of view of a humanism which is values the complexity of its feelings and the subtlety of its intellect far more than Nature does. To her they are merely the reassertion of her right to recapture her own world, merely the process by which she repeoples the earth with creatures simple enough to live joyously there.

III

To us, however, such speculations as these are doubly vain. In the first place the future may belong, not to the Russians, but to some class of people not yet thought of in this connection, and in the second place none of these possible futures is one which can have anything to do with us or our traditions. Though the new barbarians may forget we will remember that the paradox of humanism and the tragic fallacy are not to be altered by the establishment of new societies and that the despair which was the fruit of both ancient and modern civilization must inevitably ripen again in the course of the development of any society which enters upon the pursuit of human values.

Some critics of communism have, to be sure, maintained that its tendencies were fundamentally antihuman and that, should it ever become established, it would so arrest the development of the humanistic spirit as to fix mankind forever in some changelessly efficient routine like that of an anthill. But even if this be true it does not alter the fact that its hopes are no hopes in which we can have any part, since we would be even more alien to such a society than to one which promised to recapitulate our own youth. The world may be rejuvenated in one way or another, but we will not. Skepticism has entered too deeply into our souls ever to be replaced by faith, and we can never forget the things which the new barbarians will never need to have known. This world in which an unresolvable discord is the fundamental fact is the world in which we must continue to live, and for us wisdom must consist, not in searching for a means of escape which does not exist, but in making such peace with it as we may.

Nor is there any reason why we should fail to realize the fact that the acceptance of such despair as must inevitably be ours does not, after all, involve a misery so acute as that which many have been compelled to endure. Terror can be blacker than that and so can the extremes of physical want and pain. The most human human being has still more of the animal than of anything else and no love of rhetoric should betray one into seeming to deny that he who has escaped animal pain has escaped much. Despair of the sort which has here been described is a luxury in the sense that it is possible only to those who have much that many people do without, and philosophical pessimism, dry as it may leave the soul, is more easily endured than hunger or cold.

Leaving the future to those who have faith in it, we may survey our world and, if we bear in mind the facts just stated, we may permit ourselves to exclaim, a little rhetorically perhaps,

> Hail, horrors, hail,
> Infernal world! and thou profoundest hell,
> Receive thy new possessor.

If Humanism and Nature are fundamentally antithetical, if the human virtues have a definite limit set to their development, and if they may be cultivated only by a process which renders us progressively unfit to fulfill our biological duties, then we may at least permit ourselves a certain defiant satisfaction when we realize that we have made our choice and that we are resolved to abide by the consequences. Some small part of the tragic fallacy may be said indeed to be still valid for us, for if we cannot feel ourselves great as Shakespeare did, if we no longer believe in either our infinite capacities or our importance to the universe, we know at least that we have discovered the trick which has been played upon us and that whatever else we may be we are no longer dupes.

Rejuvenation may be offered to us at a certain price. Nature, issuing her last warning, may bid us embrace some new illusion before it is too late and accord ourselves once more with her. But we prefer rather to fail in our own way than to succeed in hers. Our human world may have no existence outside of our own desires, but those are more imperious than anything else we know, and we will cling to our own lost cause, choosing always rather to know than to be. Doubtless fresh people have still a long way to go with

Nature before they are compelled to realize that they too have come to the parting of the ways, but though we may wish them well we do not envy them. If death for us and our kind is the inevitable result of our stubbornness then we can only say, "So be it." Ours is a lost cause and there is no place for us in the natural universe, but we are not, for all that, sorry to be human. We should rather die as men than live as animals.

33. Charles Lindbergh—the Lone Eagle: *New York Times*

No idol *of hero-worshipping Americans during the 1920s captured the national imagination so completely as Charles Lindbergh. Perhaps the most interesting aspect of the country's incredible infatuation with the modest aviator is that hardly anyone publicly questioned the sanity of the American public. Some of the details of Lindbergh's tumultuous welcome in New York City are described below from an article in the* New York Times. *On the day after Lindbergh arrived from Washington, the entire front page of the* Times *was given over to stories connected with Lindbergh, his mother, and the millions who trampled each other and filled the streets of the city with shredded paper while greeting the flyer.*

Millons Roar Welcome to Lindbergh

Colonel Charles A. Lindbergh descended modestly on New York yesterday on the waves of the greatest reception the city has ever accorded a private citizen. He came as he went, out of the clouds, on the wings of a swooping plane.

Millions beheld his blond, boyish head as he rode through six miles of streets and cheered from the depths of their hearts. There never was anything like it.

It began the moment his amphibian plane came to rest in the Narrows and it ran without break through the day. At the end, as he retired to a Long Island country estate for a few hours of social recreation, the flying Colonel was dazed but flushed with happiness.

He had had the vision of a city held by the thrall of a youth who

Source: *New York Times*, June 14, 1927, pp. 1–3.

had spanned the ocean in a single gallant gesture, a city that had only one interest and that to show him in every way possible that he had, as Mayor Walker phrased it, "won the city." He had only one regret and that was that he had been forced to abandon his flight here from Washington in his own beloved Spirit of St. Louis.

Arriving at 12:40 PM he found that the city had been awaiting him for hours. Lower Manhattan was packed at the Battery, along lower Broadway, at the City Hall. Up along the line of his procession millions were standing in line, hanging from windows, sitting in stands waiting to cheer "Lindy." The city had been drenched in bunting and in flags and ideal weather had come to add the final touch.

The pageant of his welcome was a series of pictures. There was the swoop down of his seaplane in the narrow water of the lower bay, where hundreds of vessels, dressed in a multitude of flags, closed in. Up through smoke and steam, while the harbor was rent by whistles he came to the Battery.

He stepped ashore there. Out in the broad expanse of the Battery Park was a tumultous mass of people. When he appeared a mighty roar of good will went up. Then he rode slowly up Broadway, in the wake of a glittering military display, and the thunder of his welcome grew more intense.

The slender young figure was at the City Hall and the Mayor was decorating him, telling how the city regarded him, and a hundred thousand were shouting plaudits. He passed again through a vast lane and the applause might have rocked his car. He turned from his perch at the back of his car to glance shyly but happily at his mother, Mrs. Evangeline Lindbergh, sharing in her son's greeting.

Then he was in Fifth Avenue, that thoroughfare of many parades, vivid in decorations and filled with a host. At the Public Library 10,000 children waved a welcome, while hundreds of thousands of their parents clustered near the steps shouted, waved hats, flourished sticks in happy gestures and gave cheer after cheer. At the end of his route in the greenery of the Mall in Central Park was the greatest single group of welcome: Upwards of 200,000 were assembled there to see Governor Alfred E. Smith place the State Medal of Valor about the flier's neck.

Bound for his surpassing reception, Colonel Lindbergh took off from Bolling Field at Washington at 9:54 AM. After attending a breakfast of aviators he had been whisked to the field and went immediately to the Spirit of St. Louis. He found that a valve would not function and an army pursuit plane was run out. He climbed in with a wave, in much the same serene manner he had stepped into his transoceanic airplane less than a month ago, and whirled upward.

The news was flashed to New York, where the crowds were already waiting. Quiet, orderly crowds, although super-enthusiastic, which gave the police a good-natured but comparatively easy task. Only one death was reported, that of a girl who died from heart disease, despite the magnitude of the crowds, estimated as numbering as many as 4,000,000 persons. Fewer than fifty persons were recorded by the police as requiring treatment, chiefly for faintness, although there were many minor sufferers.

The city waited, bands playing, flags flying. Then came word that Lindbergh was over Staten Island field he remarked: "Be sure to check up the gas feed on that ship before anybody flies it."

That was all the Colonel had to say about it. But an examination showed that he had traveled from the capital using an auxiliary gas tank. Before any one could question him on whether he had ever given a thought to the danger, the airman was in the amphibian *San Francisco*, which was one of the planes used in the Good-Will flight to South America. (Army officers at Washington explained later that Colonel Lindbergh must have misunderstood instructions and turned on the wrong gas switch.)

Lindbergh made for the Narrows. He came down smartly and taxied toward his marine guard of honor. There were 400 ships in the guard—excursion boats, yachts, tugs and motorboats—led by the municipal reception boat *Macom*, with Grover A. Whalen, Chairman of the Mayor's Committee on Reception, aboard. A police launch shot over to Lindbergh's plane and with a grip of the hand the Colonel was aboard. He was transshipped to the *Macom*, and the slow journey up the harbor was begun with "Lindy" on the bridge.

Sirens, shrill tooters, full-throated whistles on the flotilla burst into bedlam. Further up the bay and at the piers the deeper note of liners came in ear-splitting punctuations into the uproar. The birdman was getting his first installment of a typical New York welcome. The din was beyond description and the volume of it crept into the microphone placed at the end of Pier A, several miles from the main source of noise, and was carried to the ears of the radio audience, estimated at 15,000,000.

Then through a white mist of twisting paper, falling like silver flakes, the airman started up Broadway's canyon. Every window held spectators—waving, cheering spectators—and on either side he saw the thick masses of those on the sidewalks. Through this swaying, surging, eager throng he came to the City Hall, brilliant in the sunshine, resplendent with colors, and peopled by 100,000.

Preceding his arrival 15,000 soldiers and sailors had marched past the Mayor, his municipal administrative officers and 3,000 invited guest of the welcome committee, seated in two stands. Three white-robed women trumpeters sounded a piercingly clear signal as his car turned into the driveway to the Mayor's stand.

What an outburst of sound greeted him! He stepped from his car and was escorted to the Mayor to whom he was formally introduced by Mr. Whalen. The Chairman of the committee briefly recounted the circumstances of the famous take-off at Roosevelt Field and presented the flier as "the man who has won the love and admiration of the world." Before the Mayor gave his address of welcome, an illuminated scroll, testifying to the esteem in which the city held him, was read and presented to Colonel Lindbergh. He accepted it with his abrupt little bow and his quick-flashing smile.

Mayor Walker, veteran of many speeches of welcome, delivered an address which many considered a gem. He began with a reference to the naïve way in which the flier had sought letters of introduction to persons in Paris before he attempted his flight. Turning to the smiling, boyish figure at his side, the Mayor advised the flier that "if you have prepared yourself with any letters of introduction to New York City, they are not necessary."

Deftly the Mayor worked in Lindbergh's habit of referring to his plane and himself as "we," saying that he had "given to the world a flying pronoun." "The hearts of 6,000,000 citizens of New York were beating faster to the measure of the Colonel's courage and accomplishment," he said.

"Colonel Lindbergh," said the Mayor at another point, "New York City is yours—I don't give it to you: you won it."

He then proceeded up Fifth Avenue, with its sparkle of bunting, scathed building and shop. Never was such a crowd gathered in the avenue and it stretched solidly to Central Park and into the park and unbrokenly to the Mall where the hundreds of thousands, with the Governor in yet another stand, waited.

Colonel Lindbergh reached the Mall approximately four hours from the time he had made his landing in the Narrows.

Passing up Fifth Avenue the parade had parted to let the airman go to the head of the column. In this position he rode directly to the grand stand, and as he stepped to the side of Governor Smith the parade halted some distance down from the stand. A great outburst of enthusiasm came from the crowd—thousands of whom had been standing for seven or eight hours—as the tall form of the aviator came within vision.

The Mayor formally introduced the Colonel to the Governor and they exchanged a few remarks, both laughing. As they conversed, the Mayor disclosed that one of the things Lindbergh had said to him at the City Hall, when he and the flier had had a similar conversation, was relative to the spectators who had chosen the edges of skyscraper roofs for the vantage point. Lindbergh had expressed fear lest an overenthusiastic spectator might fall.

The Mayor also disclosed part of the conversation he had had with the flier on the trip from the City Hall to the Mall. At one point on the way up it was necessary to brush off some of the torn paper that had fallen into the car. Lindbergh picked up a piece of the paper and examined it. It was a tattered page from the telephone directory.

"I guess when I leave here," the Mayor quoted him as saying, "they'll have to print another edition of the telephone book."

"Well before you leave," replied the Mayor, "you'll have to provide us with another Street Cleaning Department."

During the procession, said the Mayor, Mrs. Lindbergh seemed visibly moved at times and there was more than one moment when her eyes filled, but otherwise she showed the same composure and gentle restraint that marked her demeanor in Washington.

Governor Smith put the blue ribbon, from which was suspended the State medal, over Lindbergh's head. The Governor read the inscription on the medal which was awarded for "courage and intrepidity of the highest degree in flying alone and unaided from New York to Paris to the glory of his country and his own undying fame."

"You are hailed," added Governor Smith, "in the Empire State as an ideal and an example for the youth of America."

V

Politics in the 1920s

34. The Apex of American Capitalism: Herbert Hoover

HERBERT HOOVER, *the only successful business executive ever to serve as President of the United States, made all too appropriate a symbol when the American business system collapsed almost completely during his administration. He contributed to the bitterness with which he was regarded by a generation of Americans by delivering glowing speeches like that reprinted below about the glorious triumphs and future of American business. Unfortunately for his reputation, Hoover continued to speak in similar terms after the economic decline started and while it continued.*

New York City

October 22, 1928

This campaign now draws near a close. The platforms of the two parties defining principles and offering solutions of various national problems have been presented and are being earnestly considered by our people.

After four months' debate it is not the Republican Party which finds reason for abandonment of any of the principles it has laid down or of the views it has expressed for solution of the problems before the country. The principles to which it adheres are rooted deeply in the foundations of our national life. The solutions which it proposes are based on experience with government and on a consciousness that it may have the responsibility for placing those solutions in action.

In my acceptance speech I endeavored to outline the spirit and ideals by which I would be guided in carrying that platform into administration. Tonight, I will not deal with the multitude of issues which have been already well canvassed. I intend rather to discuss some of those more fundamental principles and ideals upon which I believe the government of the United States should be conducted.

SOURCE: Herbert Hoover, "The New Day," *Campaign Speeches of Herbert Hoover* (Palo Alto, Calif., 1929), pp. 149–176. By permission of the Herbert Hoover Foundation, Inc.

Recent Progress as the Effect of Republican Policies

The Republican Party has ever been a party of progress. I do not need to review its seventy years of constructive history. It has always reflected the spirit of the American people. Never has it done more for the advancement of fundamental progress than during the past seven and one-half years since we took over the government amidst the ruin left by war.

It detracts nothing from the character and energy of the American people, it minimizes in no degree the quality of their accomplishments to say that the policies of the Republican Party have played a large part in recuperation from the war and the building of the magnificent progress which shows upon every hand today. I say with emphasis that without the wise policies which the Republican Party has brought into action during this period, no such progress would have been possible.

Confidence Restored

The first responsibility of the Republican administration was to renew the march of progress from its collapse by the war. That task involved the restoration of confidence in the future and the liberation and stimulation of the constructive energies of our people. It discharged that task. There is not a person within the sound of my voice who does not know the profound progress which our country has made in this period. Every man and woman knows that American comfort, hope, and confidence for the future are immeasurably higher this day than they were seven and one-half years ago.

Constructive Measures Adopted

It is not my purpose to enter upon a detailed recital of the great constructive measures of the past seven and one-half years by which this has been brought about. It is sufficient to remind you of the restoration of employment to the millions who walked your streets in idleness; to remind you of the creation of the budget system; the reduction of six billions of national debt which gave the powerful impulse of that vast sum returned to industry and commerce; the four sequent reductions of taxes and thereby the lift to the living of every family; the enactment of adequate protective tariff and immigration laws which have safeguarded our workers and farmers from floods of goods and labor from foreign countries; the creation of credit facilities and many other aids to agriculture; the building up of foreign trade; the care of veterans; the development of aviation, of radio, of our inland waterways, of our highways; the expansion of scientific research, of welfare activities; the making of safer highways, safer mines, better homes; the spread of outdoor recreation; the improvement in public health and the care of children; and a score of other progressive actions.

Delicacy of the Task

Nor do I need to remind you that government today deals with an economic and social system vastly more intricate and delicately adjusted than ever before. That system now must be kept in perfect tune if we would maintain uninterrupted employment and the high standards of living of our people. The government has come to touch this delicate web at a thousand points. Yearly the relations of government to national prosperity become more and more intimate. Only through keen vision and helpful cooperation by the government has stability in business and stability in employment been maintained during this past seven and one-half years. There always are some localities, some industries, and some individuals who do not share the prevailing prosperity. The task of government is to lessen these inequalities.

Never has there been a period when the Federal Government has given such aid and impulse to the progress of our people, not alone to economic progress but to the development of those agencies which make for moral and spiritual progress.

The American System

But in addition to this great record of contributions of the Republican Party to progress, there has been a further fundamental contribution—a contribution underlying and sustaining all the others—and that is the resistance of the Republican Party to every attempt to inject the government into business in competition with its citizens.

After the war, when the Republican Party assumed administration of the country, we were faced with the problem of determination of the very nature of our national life. During one hundred and fifty years we have builded up a form of self-government and a social system which is peculiarly our own. It differs essentially from all others in the world. It is the American system. It is just as definite and positive a political and social system as has ever been developed on earth. It is founded upon a particular conception of self-government in which decentralized local responsibility is the very base. Further than this, it is founded upon the conception that only through ordered liberty, freedom, and equal opportunity to the individual will his initiative and enterprise spur on the march of progress. And in our insistence upon equality of opportunity has our system advanced beyond all the world.

Suspended by the War

During the war we necessarily turned to the government to solve every difficult economic problem. The government having absorbed every energy of our people for war, there was no other solution. For the preservation of the state the Federal Government became a centralized despotism which undertook unprecedented responsibilities, assumed autocratic powers, and took over the business of citizens. To a large degree we regimented our whole people temporarily into a socialistic state. However justified in time of war, if continued in peacetime it would destroy not only our American system but with it our progress and freedom as well.

When the war closed, the most vital of all issues both in our own country and throughout the world was whether governments should continue their war-time ownership and operation of many instrumentalities of production and distribution. We were challenged with a peace-time choice between the American system of rugged individualism and a European philosophy of diametrically opposed doctrines—doctrines of paternalism and state socialism. The acceptance of these ideas would have meant the destruction of self-government through centralization of government. It would have meant the undermining of the individual initiative and enterprise through which our people have grown to unparalleled greatness.

Restored under Republican Direction

The Republican Party from the beginning resolutely turned its face away from these ideas and these war practices. A Republican

Congress cooperated with the Democratic administration to demobilize many of our war activities. At that time the two parties were in accord upon that point. When the Republican Party came into full power it went at once resolutely back to our fundamental conception of the state and the rights and responsibilities of the individual. Thereby it restored confidence and hope in the American people, it freed and stimulated enterprise, it restored the government to its position as an umpire instead of a player in the economic game. For these reasons the American people have gone forward in progress while the rest of the world has halted, and some countries have even gone backward. If anyone will study the causes of retarded recuperation in Europe, he will find much of it due to stifling of private initiative on one hand, and overloading of the government with business on the other.

Proposals Now Menacing This System

There has been revived in this campaign, however, a series of proposals which, if adopted, would be a long step toward the abandonment of our American system and a surrender to the destructive operation of governmental conduct of commercial business. Because the country is faced with difficulty and doubt over certain national problems—that is, prohibition, farm relief, and electrical power—our opponents propose that we must thrust government a long way into the businesses which give rise to these problems. In effect, they abandon the tenets of their own party and turn to state socialism as a solution for the difficulties presented by all three. It is proposed that we shall change from prohibition to the state purchase and sale of liquor. If their agricultural relief program means anything, it means that the government shall directly or indirectly buy and sell and fix prices of agricultural products. And we are to go into the hydroelectric power business. In other words, we are confronted with a huge program of government in business.

There is, therefore, submitted to the American people a question of fundamental principle. That is: shall we depart from the principles of our American political and economic system, upon which we have advanced beyond all the rest of the world, in order to adopt methods based on principles destructive of its very foundations? And I wish to emphasize the seriousness of these proposals. I wish to make my position clear; for this goes to the very roots of American life and progress.

Centralization Fatal to Self-Government

I should like to state to you the effect that this projection of government in business would have upon our system of self-government and our economic system. That effect would reach to the daily life of every man and woman. It would impair the very basis of liberty and freedom not only for those left outside the fold of expanded bureaucracy but for those embraced within it.

Let us first see the effect upon self-government. When the Federal Government undertakes to go into commercial business it must at once set up the organization and administration of that business, and it immediately finds itself in a labyrinth, every alley of which leads to the destruction of self-government.

Commercial business requires a concentration of responsibility. Self-government requires decentralization and many checks and balances to safeguard liberty. Our government to succeed in business would need become in effect a despotism. There at once begins the destruction of self-government.

Unwisdom of Government in Business

The first problem of the government about to adventure in commercial business is to determine a method of administration. It must secure leadership and direction. Shall this leadership be chosen by political agencies or shall we make it elective? The hard practical fact is that leadership in business must come through the sheer rise in ability and character. That rise can only take place in the free atmosphere of competition. Competition is closed by bureaucracy. Political agencies are feeble channels through which to select able leaders to conduct commercial business.

Government, in order to avoid the possible incompetence, corruption, and tyranny of too great authority in individuals entrusted with commercial business, inevitably turns to boards and commissions. To make sure that there are checks and balances, each member of such boards and commissions must have equal authority. Each has his separate responsibility to the public, and at once we have the conflict of ideas and the lack of decision which would ruin any commercial business. It has contributed greatly to the demoralization of our shipping business. Moreover, these commissions must be representative of different sections and different political parties, so that at once we have an entire blight upon coordinated action within their ranks which destroys any possibility of effective administration.

Moreover, our legislative bodies cannot in fact delegate their full authority to commissions or to individuals for the conduct of matters vital to the American people; for if we would preserve government by the people we must preserve the authority of our legislators in the activities of our government.

Thus every time the Federal Government goes into a commercial business, five hundred and thirty-one Senators and Congressmen became the actual board of directors of that business. Every time a state government goes into business one or two hundred state senators and legislators become the actual directors of that business. Even if they were supermen and if there were no politics in the United States, no body of such numbers could competently direct commercial activities; for that requires initiative, instant decision, and action. It took Congress six years of constant discussion to even decide what the method of administration of Muscle Shoals should be.

When the Federal Government undertakes to go into business, the state governments are at once deprived of control and taxation of that business; when a state government undertakes to go into business, it at once deprives the municipalities of taxation and control of that business. Municipalities, being local and close to the people, can, at times, succeed in business where federal and state governments must fail. We have trouble enough with logrolling in legislative bodies today. It originates naturally from desires of citizens to advance their particular section or to secure some necessary service. It would be multiplied a thousandfold were the federal and state governments in these businesses.

The effect upon our economic progress would be even worse. Business progressiveness is dependent on competition. New methods and new ideas are the outgrowth of the spirit of adventure, of individual initiative, and of individual enterprise. Without adventure there is no progress. No government administration can rightly take chances with taxpayers' money.

There is no better example of the practical incompetence of government to conduct business than the history of our railways.

During the war the government found it necessary to operate the railways. That operation continued until after the war. In the year before being freed from government operation they were not able to meet the demands for transportation. Eight years later we find them under private enterprise transporting fifteen percent more goods and meeting every demand for service. Rates have been reduced by fifteen percent and net earnings increased from less than one percent on their valuation to about five percent. Wages of employees have improved by thirteen percent. The wages of railway employees are today one hundred and twenty-one percent above prewar, while the wages of government employees are today only sixty-five percent above prewar. That should be a sufficient commentary upon the efficiency of government operation.

Dangers of Bureaucracy

Let us now examine this question from the point of view of the person who may get a government job and is admitted into the new bureaucracy. Upon that subject let me quote from a speech of that great leader of labor, Samuel Gompers, delivered in Montreal in 1920, a few years before his death. He said:

> I believe there is no man to whom I would take second position in my loyalty to the Republic of the United States, and yet I would not give it more power over the individual citizenship of our country. . . .
>
> It is a question of whether it shall be government ownership or private ownership under control. . . . If I were in the minority of one in this convention, I would want to cast my vote so that the men of labor shall not willingly enslave themselves to government authority in their industrial effort for freedom. . . .
>
> Let the future tell the story of who is right or who is wrong; who has stood for freedom and who has been willing to submit their fate industrially to the government.

I would amplify Mr. Gompers' statement. The great body of government employees which would be created by the proposals of our opponents would either comprise a political machine at the disposal of the party in power, or, alternatively, to prevent this, the government by stringent civil service rules must debar its employees from their full political rights as free men. It must limit them in the liberty to bargain for their own wages, for no government employee can strike against his government and thus against the whole people. It makes a legislative body with all its political currents their final employer and master. Their bargaining does not rest upon economic need or economic strength but on political potence.

But what of those who are outside the bureaucracy? What is the effect upon their lives?

The area of enterprise and opportunity for them to strive and rise is at once limited.

The government in commercial business does not tolerate amongst its customers the freedom of competitive reprisals to which private business is subject. Bureaucracy does not tolerate the spirit of independence; it spreads the spirit of submission into our daily life and penetrates the temper of our people not with the habit of powerful resistance to wrong but with the habit of timid acceptance of irresistible might.

Fatal to True Liberalism

Bureaucracy is ever desirous of spreading its influence and its power. You cannot extend the mastery of the government over the daily working life of a people without at the same time making it the master of the people's souls and thoughts. Every expansion of government in business means that government in order to protect itself from the political consequences of its errors and wrongs is driven irresistibly without peace to greater and greater control of the nation's press and platform. Free speech does not live many hours after free industry and free commerce die.

It is a false liberalism that interprets itself into the government operation of commercial business. Every step of bureaucratizing of the business of our country poisons the very roots of liberalism—that is, political equality, free speech, free assembly, free press, and equality of opportunity. It is the road not to more liberty, but to less liberty. Liberalism should be found not striving to spread bureaucracy but striving to set bounds to it. True liberalism seeks all legitimate freedom first in the confident belief that without such freedom the pursuit of all other blessings and benefits is vain. That belief is the foundation of all American progress, political as well as economic.

Liberalism is a force truly of the spirit, a force proceeding from the deep realization that economic freedom cannot be sacrificed if political freedom is to be preserved. Even if governmental conduct of business could give us more efficiency instead of less efficiency, the fundamental objection to it would remain unaltered and unabated. It would destroy political equality. It would increase rather than decrease abuse and corruption. It would stifle initiative and invention. It would undermine the development of leadership. It would cramp and cripple the mental and spiritual energies of our people. It would extinguish equality and opportunity. It would dry up the spirit of liberty and progress. For these reasons primarily it must be resisted. For a hundred and fifty years liberalism has found its true spirit in the American system, not in the European systems.

Flexibility of the American System

I do not wish to be misunderstood in this statement. I am defining a general policy. It does not mean that our government is to part with one iota of its national resources without complete protection to the public interest. I have already stated that where the government is engaged in public works for purposes of flood control, of navigation, of irrigation, of scientific research or national defense, or in pioneering a new art, it will at times necessarily produce power or commodities as a by-product. But they must be a by-product of the major purpose, not the major purpose itself.

Nor do I wish to be misinterpreted as believing that the United States is free-for-all and devil-take-the-hind-most. The very essence of equality of opportunity and of American individualism is that there shall be no domination by any group or combination in this republic, whether it be business or political. On the contrary, it demands economic justice as well as political and social justice. It is no system of laissez faire.

I feel deeply on this subject because during the war I had some practical experience with governmental operations and control. I have witnessed not only at home but abroad the many failures of government in business. I have seen its tyrannies, its injustices, its destructions of self-government, its undermining of the very instincts which carry our people forward to progress. I have witnessed the lack of advance, the lowered standards of living, the depressed spirits of people working under such a system. My objection is based not upon theory or upon a failure to recognize wrong or abuse, but I know the adoption of such methods would strike at the very roots of American life and would destroy the very basis of American progress.

Our people have the right to know whether we can continue to solve our great problems without abandonment of our American system. I know we can. We have demonstrated that our system is responsive enough to meet any new and intricate development in our economic and business life. We have demonstrated that we can meet any economic problem and still maintain our democracy as master in its own house, and that we can at the same time preserve equality of opportunity and individual freedom.

Practicability of Regulation

In the last fifty years we have discovered that mass production will produce articles for us at half the cost they required previously. We have seen the resultant growth of large units of production and distribution. This is big business. Many businesses must be bigger, for our tools are bigger, our country is bigger. We now build a single dynamo of a hundred thousand horsepower. Even fifteen years ago that would have been a big business all by itself. Yet today advance in production requires that we set ten of these units together in a row.

The American people from bitter experience have a rightful fear that great business units might be used to dominate our industrial life and by illegal and unethical practices destroy equality of opportunity.

Years ago the Republican administration established the principle that such evils could be corrected by regulation. It developed methods by which abuses could be prevented while the full value of industrial progress could be retained for the public. It insisted upon the principle that when great public utilities were clothed with the security of partial monopoly, whether it be railways, power plants, telephones, or what not, then there must be the fullest and most complete control of rates, services, and finances by government or local agencies. It declared that these businesses must be conducted with glass pockets.

As to our great manufacturing and distributing industries, the Republican Party insisted upon the enactment of laws that not only would maintain competition but would destroy conspiracies to destroy the smaller units or dominate and limit the equality of opportunity amongst our people.

One of the great problems of government is to determine to what extent the government shall regulate and control commerce and industry and how much it shall leave it alone. No system is perfect. We have had many abuses in the private conduct of business. That every good citizen resents. It is just as important that business keep out of government as that government keep out of business.

Nor am I setting up the contention that our institutions are perfect. No human ideal is ever perfectly attained, since humanity itself is not perfect.

The wisdom of our forefathers in their conception that progress can only be attained as the sum of the accomplishment of free individuals has been reinforced by all of the great leaders of the country since that day. Jackson, Lincoln, Cleveland, McKinley, Roosevelt, Wilson, and Coolidge have stood unalterably for these principles.

Effectiveness of the American System

And what have been the results of our American system? Our country has become the land of opportunity to those born without inheritance, not merely because of the wealth of its resources and industry but because of this freedom of inititaive and enterprise. Russia has natural resources equal to ours. Her people are equally industrious, but she has not had the blessings of one hundred and fifty years of our form of government and of our social system.

By adherence to the principles of decentralized self-government, ordered liberty, equal opportunity, and freedom to the individual, our American experiment in human welfare has yielded a degree of well-being unparalleled in all the world. It has come nearer to the abolition of poverty, to the abolition of fear of want, than humanity has ever reached before. Progress of the past seven years is the proof of it. This alone furnishes the answer to our opponents, who ask us to introduce destructive elements into the system by which this has been accomplished.

Let us see what this system has done for us in our recent years of difficult and trying reconstruction and then solemnly ask ourselves if we now wish to abandon it.

Postwar Recovery

As a nation we came out of the war with great losses. We made no profits from it. The apparent increases in wages were at the time fictitious. We were poorer as a nation when we emerged from the war. Yet during these last eight years we have recovered from these losses and increased our national income by over one-third, even if we discount the inflation of the dollar. That there has been a wide diffusion of our gain in wealth and income is marked by a hundred proofs. I know of no better test of the improved conditions of the average family than the combined increase in assets of life and industrial insurance, building and loan associations, and savings deposits. These are the savings banks of the average man. These agencies alone have in seven years increased by nearly one hundred percent to the gigantic sum of over fifty billions of dollars, or nearly one-sixth of our whole national wealth. We have increased in home ownership, we have expanded the investments of the average man.

Higher Standards of Living

In addition to these evidences of larger savings, our people are steadily increasing their spending for higher standards of living. Today there are almost nine automobiles for each ten families, where seven and one-half years ago only enough automobiles were running to average less than four for each ten families. The slogan of progress is changing from the full dinner pail to the full garage. Our people have more to eat, better things to wear, and better homes. We have even gained in elbow room, for the increase of residential floor space is over twenty-five percent, with less than ten percent increase in our number of people. Wages have increased, the cost of living has decreased. The job of every man and woman has been made more secure. We have in this short period decreased the fear of poverty, the fear of unemployment, the fear of old age; and these are fears that are the greatest calamities of humankind.

All this progress means far more than increased creature comforts. It finds a thousand interpretations into a greater and fuller life. A score of new helps save the drudgery of the home. In seven years we have added seventy percent to the electric power at the elbows of our workers and further promoted them from carriers of burdens to directors of machines. We have steadily reduced the sweat in human labor. Our hours of labor are lessened; our leisure has increased. We have expanded our parks and playgrounds. We have nearly doubled our attendance at games. We pour into outdoor recreation in every direction. The visitors at our national parks have trebled and we have so increased the number of sportsmen fishing in our streams and lakes that the longer time between bites is becoming a political issue. In these seven and one-half years the radio has brought music and laughter, education and political discussion to almost every fireside.

Springing from our prosperity with its greater freedom, its vast endowment of scientific research, and the greater resources with which to care for public health, we have according to our insurance actuaries during this short period since the war lengthened the average span of life by nearly eight years. We have reduced infant mortality, we have vastly decreased the days of illness and suffering in the life of every man and woman. We have improved the facilities for the care of the crippled and helpless and deranged.

Educational Progress

From our increasing resources we have expanded our educational system in eight years from an outlay of twelve hundred millions to twenty-seven hundred millions of dollars. The education of our youth has become almost our largest and certainly our most important activity. From our greater income and thus our ability to free youth from toil we have increased the attendance in our grade schools by fourteen percent, in our high schools by eighty percent, and in our institutions of higher learning by ninety-five percent. Today we have more youth in these institutions of higher learning twice over than all the rest of the world put together. We have made notable progress in literature, in art, and in public taste.

We have made progress in the leadership of every branch of American life. Never in our history was the leadership in our economic life more distinguished in its abilities than today, and it has grown greatly in its consciousness of public responsibility. Leadership in our professions and in moral and spiritual affairs of our country was never of a higher order. And our magnificent educational system is bringing forward a host of recruits for the succession to this leadership.

I do not need to recite more figures and more evidence. I cannot believe that the American people wish to abandon or in any way to weaken the principles of economic freedom and self-government which have been maintained by the Republican Party and which have produced results so amazing and so stimulating to the spiritual as well as to the material advance of the nation.

Significance to New York City

Your city has been an outstanding beneficiary of this great progress and of these safeguarded principles. With its suburbs it has, during the last seven and one-half years, grown by over a million and a half of people until it has become the largest metropolitan district of all the world. Here you have made abundant opportunity not only for the youth of the land but for the immigrant from foreign shores. This city is the commercial center of the United States. It is the commercial agent of the American people. It is a great organism of specialized skill and leadership in finance, industry, and commerce which reaches every spot in our country. Its progress and its beauty are the pride of the whole American people. It leads our nation in its benevolences to charity, to education, and to scientific research. It is the center of art, music, literature, and drama. It has come to have a more potent voice than any other city in the United States.

But when all is said and done, the very life, progress, and prosperity of this city is wholly dependent on the prosperity of the 115,000,000 people who dwell in our mountains and valleys across the three thousand miles to the Pacific Ocean. Every activity of this city is sensitive to every evil and every favorable tide that sweeps this great nation of ours. Be there a slackening of industry in any place, it affects New York far more than any other part of the country. In a time of depression one-quarter of all the unemployed in the United States can be numbered in this city. In a time of prosperity the citizens of the great interior of our country pour into your city for business and entertainment at the rate of one hundred and fifty thousand a day. In fact, so much is this city the reflex of the varied interests of our country that the concern of every one of your citizens for national stability, for national prosperity, for national progress, for preservation of our American system is far greater than that of any other single part of our country.

Unfinished Tasks

We still have great problems if we would achieve the full economic advancement of our country. In these past few years some groups in our country have lagged behind others in the march of progress. I refer more particularly to those engaged in the textile, coal, and agricultural industries. We can assist in solving these problems by cooperation of our government. To the agricultural industry we shall need to advance initial capital to assist them to stabilize their industry. But this proposal implies that they shall conduct it themselves, and not the government. It is in the interest of our cities that we shall bring agriculture and all industries into full stability and prosperity. I know you will gladly co-operate in the faith that in the common prosperity of our country lies its future.

In bringing this address to a conclusion I should like to restate to you some of the fundamental things I have endeavored to bring out.

The Coming Decision Fundamental

The foundations of progress and prosperity are dependent as never before upon the wise policies of government, for government now touches at a thousand points the intricate web of economic and social life.

Under administration by the Republican Party in the last seven and one-half years our country as a whole has made unparalleled progress and this has been in generous part reflected to this great city. Prosperity is no idle expression. It is a job for every worker; it is the safety and the safeguard of every business and every home. A continuation of the policies of the Republican Party is fundamentally necessary to the further advancement of this progress and to the further building up of this prosperity.

I have dwelt at some length on the principles of relationship between the government and business. I make no apologies for dealing with this subject. The first necessity of any nation is the smooth functioning of the vast business machinery for employment, feeding, clothing, housing, and providing luxuries and comforts to a people. Unless these basic elements are properly organized and function, there can be no progress in business, in education, literature, music, or art. There can be no advance in the fundamental ideals of a people. A people cannot make progress in poverty.

I have endeavored to present to you that the greatness of America has grown out of a political and social system and a method of control of economic forces distinctly its own—our American system—which has carried this great experiment in human welfare farther than ever before in all history. We are nearer today to the ideal of the abolition of poverty and fear from the lives of men and women than ever before in any land. And I again repeat that the departure from our American system by injecting principles destructive to it which our opponents propose will jeopardize the very liberty and freedom of our people, will destroy equality of opportunity not alone to ourselves but to our children.

The New Day

To me the foundation of American life rests upon the home and the family. I read into these great economic forces, these intricate and delicate relations of the government with business and with our political and social life, but one supreme end—that we reinforce the ties that bind together the millions of our families, that we strengthen the security, the happiness, and the independence of every home.

My conception of America is a land where men and women may walk in ordered freedom in the independent conduct of their occupations; where they may enjoy the advantages of wealth, not concentrated in the hands of the few but spread through the lives of all; where they build and safeguard their homes, and give to their children the fullest advantages and opportunities of American life; where every man shall be respected in the faith that his conscience and his heart direct him to follow; where a contented and happy people, secure in their liberties, free from poverty and fear, shall have the leisure and impulse to seek a fuller life.

Some may ask where all this may lead beyond mere material progress. It leads to a release of the energies of men and women from the dull drudgery of life to a wider vision and a higher hope. It leads to the opportunity for greater and greater service, not alone from man to man in our own land, but from our country to the whole world. It leads to an America, healthy in body, healthy in spirit, unfettered, youthful, eager—with a vision searching beyond the farthest horizons, with an open mind, sympathetic and generous. It is to these higher ideals and for these purposes that I pledge myself and the Republican Party.

35. A 100 percent American in the White House: Calvin Coolidge

One of the more widely circulated jokes about President Calvin Coolidge during his presidency concerned the woman who approached him at a party and allegedly gushed: "Mr. President, will you help me, I just bet that you'd say more than two words to me." Coolidge replied, "You lose," and turned away. While the story, even if fundamentally accurate, may have been more a reflection of Coolidge's Vermont humor than his fabled taciturnity, it does contain an element of symbolic reality. As this selection from Coolidge's autobiography illustrates, his values and emotional attachments remained those of a small town American. Actually Coolidge probably enjoyed ordinary gossip and banter; but the cosmopolitan society of Washington remained almost as foreign to him as that of Greenwich Village. Like Harding—and perhaps even Hoover, who was born in an Iowa town and raised on an Oregon farm—Coolidge was a President that the average Klan member could regard with comfort.

On Entering and Leaving the Presidency

It is a very old saying that you never can tell what you can do until you try. The more I see of life the more I am convinced of the wisdom of that observation.

Surprisingly few men are lacking in capacity, but they fail because they are lacking in application. Either they never learn how to work, or, having learned, they are too indolent to apply themselves with the seriousness and the attention that is necessary to solve important problems.

Any reward that is worth having only comes to the industrious. The success which is made in any walk of life is measured almost exactly by the amount of hard work that is put into it.

It has undoubtedly been the lot of every native boy of the United States to be told that he will some day be President. Nearly

Source: Calvin Coolidge, *The Autobiography of Calvin Coolidge* (New York, 1929), pp. 171–192. Reprinted by permission of John Coolidge.

every young man who happens to be elected a member of his state legislature is pointed to by his friends and his local newspaper as on the way to the White House.

My own experience in this respect did not differ from that of others. But I never took such suggestions seriously, as I was convinced in my own mind that I was not qualified to fill the exalted office of President.

I had not changed this opinion after the November elections of 1919, when I was chosen Governor of Massachusetts for a second term by a majority which had only been exceeded in 1896.

When I began to be seriously mentioned by some of my friends at that time as the Republican candidate for President, it became apparent that there were many others who shared the same opinion as to my fitness which I had so long entertained.

But the coming national convention, acting in accordance with an unchangeable determination, took my destiny into its own hands and nominated me for Vice-President.

Had I been chosen for the first place, I could have accepted it only with a great deal of trepidation, but when the events of August 1923, bestowed upon me the presidential office, I felt at once that power had been given me to administer it. This was not any feeling of exclusiveness. While I felt qualified to serve, I was also well aware that there were many others who were better qualified. It would be my province to get the benefit of their opinions and advice. It is a great advantage to a President, and a major source of safety to the country, for him to know that he is not a great man. When a man begins to feel that he is the only one who can lead in this republic, he is guilty of treason to the spirit of our institutions.

After President Harding was seriously stricken, although I noticed that some of the newspapers at once sent representatives to be near me at the home of my father in Plymouth, Vermont, the official reports which I received from his bedside soon became so reassuring that I believed all danger past.

On the night of August 2, 1923, I was awakened by my father coming up the stairs calling my name. I noticed that his voice trembled. As the only times I had ever observed that before were when death had visited our family, I knew that something of the gravest nature had occurred.

His emotion was partly due to the knowledge that a man whom

he had met and liked was gone, partly to the feeling that must possess all of our citizens when the life of their President is taken from them.

But he must have been moved also by the thought of the many sacrifices he had made to place me where I was, the twenty-five-mile drives in storms and in zero weather over our mountain roads to carry me to the academy and all the tenderness and care he had lavished upon me in the thirty-eight years since the death of my mother in the hope that I might sometime rise to a position of importance, which he now saw realized.

He had been the first to address me as President of the United States. It was the culmination of the lifelong desire of a father for the success of his son.

He placed in my hands an official report and told me that President Harding had just passed away. My wife and I at once dressed.

Before leaving the room I knelt down and, with the same prayer with which I have since approached the altar of the church, asked God to bless the American people and give me power to serve them.

My first thought was to express my sympathy for those who had been bereaved and after that was done to attempt to reassure the country with the knowledge that I proposed no sweeping displacement of the men then in office and that there were to be no violent changes in the administration of affairs. As soon as I had dispatched a telegram to Mrs. Harding, I therefore issued a short public statement declaratory of that purpose.

Meantime, I had been examining the Constitution to determine what might be necessary for qualifying by taking the oath of office. It is not clear that any additional oath is required beyond what is taken by the Vice-President when he is sworn into office. It is the same form as that taken by the President.

Having found this form in the Constitution I had it set up on the typewriter and the oath was administered by my father in his capacity as a notary public, an office he had held for a great many years.

The oath was taken in what we always called the sitting room by the light of the kerosene lamp, which was the most modern form of lighting that had then reached the neighborhood. The Bible which had belonged to my mother lay on the table at my hand. It was not officially used, as it is not the practice in Vermont or

Massachusetts to use a Bible in connection with the administration of an oath.

Besides my father and myself, there were present my wife, Senator Dale, who happened to be stopping a few miles away, my stenographer, and my chauffeur.

The picture of this scene has been painted with historical accuracy by an artist named Keller, who went to Plymouth for that purpose. Although the likenesses are not good, everything in relation to the painting is correct.

Where succession to the highest office in the land is by inheritance or appointment, no doubt there have been kings who have participated in the induction of their sons into their office, but in republics where the succession comes by an election I do not know of any other case in history where a father has administered to his son the qualifying oath of office which made him the chief magistrate of a nation. It seemed a simple and natural thing to do at the time, but I can now realize something of the dramatic force of the event.

This room was one which was already filled with sacred memories for me. In it my sister and my stepmother passed their last hours. It was associated with my boyhood recollections of my own mother, who sat and reclined there during her long invalid years, though she passed away in an adjoining room where my father was to follow her within three years from this eventful night.

When I started for Washington that morning I turned aside from the main road to make a short devotional visit to the grave of my mother. It had been a comfort to me during my boyhood when I was troubled to be near her last resting place, even in the dead of night. Some way, that morning, she seemed very near to me.

A telegram was sent to my pastor, Dr. Jason Noble Pierce, to meet me on my arrival at Washington that evening, which he did.

I found the Cabinet mostly scattered. Some members had been with the late President and some were in Europe. The Secretary of State, Mr. Hughes, and myself, at once began the preparation of plans for the funeral.

I issued the usual proclamation.

The Washington services were held in the rotunda of the Capitol, followed by a simple service and interment at Marion, Ohio, which I attended with the Cabinet and a large number of officers of the government.

The nation was grief-stricken. Especially noticeable was the deep sympathy every one felt for Mrs. Harding. Through all this distressing period her bearing won universal commendation. Her attitude of sympathy and affection towards Mrs. Coolidge and myself was an especial consolation to us.

The first Sunday after reaching Washington we attended services, as we were accustomed to do, at the First Congregational Church. Although I had been rather constant in my attendance, I had never joined the church.

While there had been religious services, there was no organized church society near my boyhood home. Among other things, I had some fear as to my ability to set that example which I always felt ought to denote the life of a church member. I am inclined to think now that this was a counsel of darkness.

This first service happened to come on communion day. Our pastor, Dr. Pierce, occupied the pulpit, and, as he can under the practice of the Congregational Church, and always does, because of his own very tolerant attitude, he invited all those who believed in the Christian faith, whether church members or not, to join in partaking of the communion.

For the first time I accepted this invitation, which I later learned he had observed, and in a few days without any intimation to me that it was to be done, considering this to be a sufficient public profession of my faith, the church voted me into its membership. This declaration of their belief in me was a great satisfaction.

Had I been approached in the usual way to join the church after I became President, I should have feared that such action might appear to be a pose, and should have hesitated to accept. From what might have been a misguided conception I was thus saved by some influence which I had not anticipated.

But if I had not voluntarily gone to church and partaken of communion, this blessing would not have come to me.

Fate bestows its rewards on those who put themselves in the proper attitude to receive them.

During my service in Washington I had seen a large amount of government business. Peace had been made with the Central Powers, the tariff revised, the budget system adopted, taxation reduced, large payments made on the national debt, the Veterans'

Bureau organized, important farm legislation passed, public expenditures greatly decreased, the differences with Colombia of twenty years' standing composed, and the Washington Conference had reached an epoch-making agreement for the practical limitation of naval armaments.

It would be difficult to find two years of peacetime history in all the record of our republic that were marked with more important and far-reaching accomplishments. From my position as President of the Senate, and in my attendance upon the sessions of the Cabinet, I thus came into possession of a very wide knowledge of the details of the government.

In spite of the remarkable record which had already been made, much remained to be done. While anything that relates to the functions of the government is of enormous interest to me, its economic relations have always had a peculiar fascination for me.

Though these are necessarily predicated on order and peace, yet our people are so thoroughly lawabiding and our foreign relations are so happy that the problem of government action which is to carry its benefits into the homes of all the people becomes almost entirely confined to the realm of economics.

My personal experience with business had been such as comes to a country lawyer.

My official experience with government business had been of a wide range. As Mayor, I had charge of the financial affairs of the City of Northampton. As Lieutenant-Governor, I was Chairman of the Committee on Finance of the Governor's Council, which had to authorize every cent of the expenditures of the Commonwealth before they could be made. As Governor, I was chargeable with responsibility both for appropriations and for expenditures.

My fundamental idea of both private and public business came first from my father. He had the strong New England trait of great repugnance at seeing anything wasted. He was a generous and charitable man, but he regarded waste as a moral wrong.

Wealth comes from industry and from the hard experience of human toil. To dissipate it in waste and extravagance is disloyalty to humanity. This is by no means a doctrine of parsimony. Both men and nations should live in accordance with their means and devote their substance not only to productive industry, but to the creation of the various forms of beauty and the pursuit of culture which give adornments to the arts of life.

When I became Presdient it was perfectly apparent that the key by which the way could be opened to national progress was constructive economy. Only by the use of that policy could the high rates of taxation, which were retarding our development and prosperity, be diminished, and the enormous burden of our public debt be reduced.

Without impairing the efficient operation of all the functions of the government, I have steadily and without ceasing pressed on in that direction. This policy has encouraged enterprise, made possible the highest rate of wages which has ever existed, returned large profits, brought to the homes of the people the greatest economic benefits they ever enjoyed, and given to the country as a whole an unexampled era of prosperity. This well-being of my country has given me the chief satisfaction of my administration.

One of my most pleasant memories will be the friendly relations which I have always had with the representatives of the press in Washington. I shall always remember that at the conclusion of the first regular conference I held with them at the White House office they broke into hearty applause.

I suppose that in answering their questions I had been fortunate enough to tell them what they wanted to know in such a way that they could make use of it.

While there have been newspapers which supported me, of course there have been others which opposed me, but they have usually been fair. I shall always consider it the highest tribute to my administration that the opposition have based so little of their criticism on what I have really said and done.

I have often said that there was no cause for feeling disturbed at being misrepresented in the press. It would be only when they began to say things detrimental to me which were true that I should feel alarm.

Perhaps one of the reasons I have been a target for so little abuse is because I have tried to refrain from abusing other people.

The words of the President have an enormous weight and ought not to be used indiscriminately.

It would be exceedingly easy to set the country all by the ears and foment hatreds and jealousies, which, by destroying faith and confidence, would help nobody and harm everybody. The end would be the destruction of all progress.

While every one knows that evils exist, there is yet sufficient good in the people to supply material for most of the comment that needs to be made.

The only way I know to drive out evil from the country is by the constructive method of filling it with good. The country is better off tranquilly considering its blessings and merits, and earnestly striving to secure more of them, than it would be in nursing hostile bitterness about its deficiencies and faults.

Notwithstanding the broad general knowledge which I had of the government, when I reached Washington I found it necessary to make an extensive survey of the various Departments to acquaint myself with details. This work had to be done intensively from the first of August to the middle of November, in order to have the background and knowledge which would enable me to discuss the state of the Union in my first Message to the Congress.

Although meantime I was pressed with invitations to make speeches, I did not accept any of them. The country was in mourning and I felt it more appropriate to make my first declaration in my Message to the Congress. Of course, I opened the Red Cross Convention in October, which was an official function for me as its President.

I was especially fortunate in securing C. Bascom Slemp as my Secretary, who had been a member of the House for many years and had a wide acquaintance with public men and the workings of legislative machinery. His advice was most helpful. I had already served with all the members of the Cabinet, which perhaps was one reason I found them so sympathetic.

Among its membership were men of great ability who have served their country with a capacity which I do not believe was ever exceeded by any former Cabinet officers.

A large amount was learned from George Harvey, Ambassador to England, concerning the European situation. He not only had a special aptitude for gathering and digesting information of that nature, but had been located at London for two years, where most of it centered.

I called in a great many people from all the different walks of life over the country. Among the first to come voluntarily were the veteran President and the Secretary of the American Federation of Labor, Mr. Gompers and Mr. Morrison. They brought a formal resolution expressive of personal regard for me and assurance of loyal support for the government.

Farm organizations and business men, publishers, educators, and many others—all had to be consulted.

It has been my policy to seek information and advice wherever I could find it. I have never relied on any particular person to be my unofficial adviser. I have let the merits of each case and the soundness of all advice speak for themselves. My counselors have been those provided by the Constitution and the law.

Due largely to this careful preparation, my Message was well received. No other public utterance of mine had been given greater approbation.

Most of the praise was sincere. But there were some quarters in the opposing party where it was thought it would be good strategy to encourage my party to nominate me, thinking that it would be easy to accomplish my defeat. I do not know whether their judgment was wrong or whether they overdid the operation, so that when they stopped speaking in my praise they found they could not change the opinion of the people which they had helped to create.

I have seen a great many attempts at political strategy in my day and elaborate plans made to encompass the destruction of this or that public man. I cannot now think of any that did not react with them and sometimes giving their proposed victim an opportunity to demonstrate his courage, strength and soundness, which increased his standing with the people and raised him to higher office.

There is only one form of political strategy in which I have any confidence, and that is to try to do the right thing and sometimes be able to succeed.

Many people at once began to speak about nominating me to lead my party in the next campaign. I did not take any position in relation to their efforts. Unless the nomination came to me in a natural way, rather than as the result of an artificial campaign, I did not feel it would be of any value.

The people ought to make their choice on a great question of that kind without the influence that could be exerted by a President in office.

After the favorable reception which was given to my Message, I stated at the Gridiron Dinner that I should be willing to be a candidate. The convention nominated me the next June by a vote which was practically unanimous.

With the exception of the occasion of my notification, I did not attend any partisan meeting or make any purely political speeches during the campaign. I spoke several times at the dedication of a monument, the observance of the anniversary of an historic event, at a meeting of some commercial body, or before some religious gathering. The campaign was magnificently managed by William M. Butler and as it progressed the final result became more and more apparent.

My own participation was delayed by the death of my son Calvin, which occurred on the seventh of July. He was a boy of much promise, proficient in his studies, with a scholarly mind, who had just turned sixteen.

He had a remarkable insight into things.

The day I became President he had just started to work in a tobacco field. When one of his fellow laborers said to him, "If my father was President I would not work in a tobacco field," Calvin replied, "If my father were your father, you would."

After he was gone some one sent us a letter he had written about the same time to a young man who had congratulated him on being the first boy in the land. To this he had replied that he had done nothing, and so did not merit the title, which should go to "some boy who had distinguished himself through his own actions."

We do not know what might have happened to him under other circumstances, but if I had not been President he would not have raised a blister on his toe, which resulted in blood poisoning, playing lawn tennis in the South Grounds.

In his suffering he was asking me to make him well. I could not.

When he went the power and the glory of the Presidency went with him.

The ways of Providence are often beyond our understanding. It seemed to me that the world had need of the work that it was probable he could do.

I do not know why such a price was exacted for occupying the White House.

Sustained by the great outpouring of sympathy from all over the nation, my wife and I bowed to the Supreme Will and with such courage as we had went on in the discharge of our duties.

In less than two years my father followed him.

At his advanced age he had overtaxed his strength receiving the thousands of visitors who went to my old home at Plymouth. It was all a great satisfaction to him and he would not have had it otherwise.

When I was there and visitors were kept from the house for a short period, he would be really distressed in the thought that they could not see all they wished and he would go out where they were himself and mingle among them.

I knew for some weeks that he was passing his last days. I sent to bring him to Washington, but he clung to his old home.

It was a sore trial not to be able to be with him, but I had to leave him where he most wished to be. When his doctors advised me that he could survive only a short time I started to visit him, but he sank to rest while I was on my way.

For my personal contact with him during his last months I had to resort to the poor substitute of the telephone. When I reached home he was gone.

It costs a great deal to be President.

36. Progressive Revolt, 1924: The Conference for Progressive Political Action

The coalition which came together in support of Robert La Follette's candidacy for the presidency in 1924 included the Socialist party, various state farmer-labor and Nonpartisan League parties, farmer organizations, the A. F. of L., the Railroad Worker Brotherhoods, and former Bull Moose Progressive party stalwarts. La Follette and the labor unions resolutely refused support from the Communists, almost as adamantly as the Communists, under orders from Moscow, declined to enter this bourgeois alliance. La Follette's coalition soon fell apart, but temporarily it did present a radical alternative to the major parties, as its platform illustrates.

For one hundred and forty-eight years the American people have been seeking to establish a government for the service of all and to

Source: The Conference for Progressive Political Action, *Report of the Committee on Resolutions of the Conference for Progressive Political Action, July 5, 1924.*

prevent the establishment of a government for the mastery of the few. Free men of every generation must combat renewed efforts of organized force and greed to destroy liberty. Every generation must wage a new war for freedom against new forces that seek through new devices to enslave mankind.

Under our representative democracy the people protect their liberties through their public agents.

The test of public officials and public alike must be: Will they serve, or will they exploit, the common need?

The reactionary continues to put his faith in mastery for the solution of all problems. He seeks to have what he calls the "strong men and best minds" rule and impose their decisions upon the masses of their weaker brethren.

The progressive, on the contrary, contends for less autocracy and more democracy in government and for less power of privilege and greater obligations of service.

Under the progressive principle of cooperation, that government is deemed best which offers to the many the highest level of average happiness and well-being.

It is our faith that we all go up or down together—that class gains are temporary delusions and that eternal laws of compensation make every man his brother's keeper.

In that faith we present our program of public service:

1. The use of the power of the federal government to crush private monopoly, not to foster it.

2. Unqualified enforcement of the constitutional guarantees of freedom of speech, press and assemblage.

3. Public ownership of the nation's water power and creation of a public superpower system. Strict public control and permanent conservation of all natural resources, including coal, iron and other ores, oil and timber lands, in the interest of the people. Promotion of public works in times of business depression.

4. Retention of surtaxes on swollen incomes, restoration of the tax on excess profits, taxation of stock dividends, profits undistributed to evade taxes, rapidly progressive taxes on large estates and inheritances, and repeal of excessive tariff duties, especially on trust-controlled necessities of life and of nuisance taxes on consumption, to relieve the people of the present unjust burden of taxation and compel those who profited by the war to pay their share of the war's costs, and to provide the funds for adjusted compensation solemnly pledged to the veterans of the World War.

5. Reconstruction of the Federal Reserve and Federal Farm Loan

System to provide for direct public control of the nation's money and credit to make it available on fair terms to all, and national and state legislation to permit and promote cooperative banking.

6. Adequate laws to guarantee to farmers and industrial workers the right to organize and bargain collectively through representatives of their own choosing for the maintenance or improvement of their standards of life.

7. Creation of a government marketing corporation to provide a direct route between farm producer and city consumer and to assure farmers fair prices for their products, and protect consumers from the profiteers in foodstuffs and other necessaries of life. Legislation to control the meat-packing industry.

8. Protection and aid of cooperative enterprises by national and state legislation.

9. Common international action to effect the economic recovery of the world from the effects of the World War.

10. Repeal of the Cummins-Esch law. Public ownership of railroads, with democratic operation, with definite safeguards against bureaucratic control.

11. Abolition of the tyranny and usurpation of the courts, including the practice of nullifying legislation in conflict with the political, social or economic theories of the judges. Abolition of injunctions in labor disputes and of the power to punish for contempt without trial by jury. Election of all federal judges without party designation for limited terms.

12. Prompt ratification of the child labor amendment and subsequent enactment of a federal law to protect children in industry. Removal of legal discriminations against women by measures not prejudicial to legislation necessary for the protection of women and for the advancement of social welfare.

13. A deep waterway from the Great Lakes to the sea.

14. We denounce the mercenary system of degraded foreign policy under recent administrations in the interests of financial imperialists, oil monopolists, and international bankers, which has at times degraded our State Department from its high service as a strong and kindly intermediary of defenceless governments to a trading outpost for those interest and concession seekers engaged in the exploitations of weaker nations, as contrary to the will of the American people, destructive of domestic development and provocative of war. We favor an active foreign policy to bring about a revision of the Versailles treaty in accordance with the terms of the armistice, and to promote firm treaty agreements with all nations to outlaw wars, abolish conscription, drastically reduce land, air and naval armaments, and guarantee public referendums on peace and war.

In supporting this program we are applying to the needs of today the fundamental principles of American democracy, opposing equally the dictatorship of plutocracy and the dictatorship of the proletariat.

We appeal to all Americans without regard to partisan affiliation and we raise the standards of our faith so that all of like purpose may rally and march in this compaign under the banners of progressive union.

The nation may grow rich in the vision of greed. The nation will grow great in the vision of service.

Separate Resolutions

1. Resolved, that we favor the enactment of the postal salary adjustment measure for the employes of the postal service passed by the first session of the 68th Congress and vetoed by President Coolidge.

2. Resolved, that we favor enforcement and extension of the merit system in the federal civil service to all its branches and transfer of the functions of the Personnel Classification Board to the United States Civil Service Commission.

3. Resolved, that we favor the immediate and complete independence of the Philippine Islands, in accordance with the pledges of the official representatives of the American people.

4. Resolved, that appropriate legislation be enacted which will provide for the people of the Virgin Islands a more permanent form of civil government such as will enable them to attain their economic, industrial and political betterment.

5. Resolved, that we deeply sympathize with the aspirations of the Irish people for freedom and independence.

6. Resolved, that in the prevailing starvation in Germany, which, according to authoritative evidence, is beyond the scope of private charity, and in the event of like destitution in any other country, we consider it humane and just, and in conformity with our traditions and former practices, that the aid of our government should be extended in the form of the delivery of surplus food supplies to a reasonable amount, and upon such conditions as the emergency may justify.

7. Resolved, that we denounce every such use of the armed forces of the United States to aid in the exploitation of weaker nations, as has occurred all too frequently in our relations with Haiti, San Domingo, Nicaragua and other nations of Central and South America.

37. Menace from the Tenements: James Cannon, Jr.

KLAN ORGANIZERS *found that white Protestant Americans' worst fears—at least those they could articulate—were connected to the threat that the fast-growing Catholic minority would take over the country politically and impose its cultural values upon those whose ancestors had created the nation. The known opposition of Catholic ethnic groups to public education and to prohibition encouraged these fears. The opposition of the Catholic hierarchy to birth control and the large proportion of Catholics among recent immigrants from Italy, Poland, Russia, and Germany, as well as Ireland, stimulated support from immigration restriction. When the Democratic party seemed to be on the verge of nominating Al Smith—a wet Catholic from the lower East Side of New York—for President, the probability mobilized some of the ugliest prejudice in the nation's history.*

Al Smith—Catholic, Tammany, Wet

If it were necessary to explain this in a single sentence, I should say: Governor Smith is personally, ecclesiastically, aggressively, irreconcilably Wet, and is ineradicably Tammany-branded, with all the inferences and implications and objectionable consequences which naturally follow from such views and associations. In the issue of *The Nation* of November 30, in an article discussing Governor Smith as a "Presidential possibility," Mr. Villard said:

> Do you believe in electing to the Presidency a man who drinks too much for his own good, and is politically a rampant Wet? . . . Does "Al" drink and does he drink too much? Well, I am reliably informed that he drinks every day, and the number of his cocktails and highballs is variously estimated at from four to eight. It is positively denied that he is ever intoxicated, much gossip to the contrary notwithstanding. He is a Wet, and he lives up to it, and for that consistency he is to be praised. . . . One may regret with all one's heart, as does the writer of these lines, that, being in an exalted position, he cannot set an example of abstinence to the millions whose State he governs, but at least one knows where he stands.

SOURCE: James Cannon, Jr., "Al Smith—Catholic, Tammany, Wet," *The Nation*, 127 (July 4, 1928): 9.

It is now over six months since that statement concerning Governor Smith's personal habits was printed and quoted, and there has been no official denial of its accuracy. It coincides with the private statements of other reliable persons. The facts certainly appear to warrant the asking of this question: Shall Dry America, a country with prohibition imbedded in its Constitution, elect a "cocktail President"?

It is true that a man's personal attitude toward the prohibition amendment and toward the use of intoxicants is not the only important question to be asked concerning his fitness for the office of President of the United States. But one's personal opinion on the principle of prohibition cannot be considered apart from the broader question of loyalty to the Constitution, as long as the prohibition amendment is a part of that Constitution. Furthermore, while it is true that the prohibition amendment does not prohibit the use of intoxicating liquor for beverage purposes, it is also true that it is the natural, logical consequence of the prohibition law that within a comparatively short time all legal use of beverage intoxicants will be eliminated. There are doubtless some law-abiding citizens who still use no intoxicants except those which they possessed at the time that prohibition went into effect, but that number is small and steadily decreasing. Can any lawabiding American citizen want a man to be elected President who not only disbelieves in the principle of prohibition, but, although sworn to uphold the Constitution of the United States, yet will continue to indulge his appetite for strong drink in the Executive Mansion? What an interesting public document for future generations to inspect would be the application of the President of the United States for a permit from the Prohibition Department to move from his residence to the White House an itemized list of the bottles, casks, barrels, and other containers of intoxicating liquor, traffic in which is prohibited by the Constitution which the said applicant is sworn to uphold!

But not only is Governor Smith personally Wet today, but his entire record is Wet. He was a frequenter of saloons while they existed; he put his foot on the brass rail and blew the foam off the glass; in his social and political activities he recognized the saloon as an important factor. As a legislator he not only opposed every measure to restrict the privileges of saloons, but endeavored to remove existing restrictions. He fought the ratification of the

Eighteenth Amendment and the passage of the Mullen-Gage State Law Enforcement Code, and after that code had been enacted by the New York State Legislature, he labored aggressively and persistently to obtain its repeal. He is now advocating modifications of the prohibition laws to permit each state to determine what shall be the legal alcoholic content of the beverages permitted.

When all his background is considered, it is not surprising that Governor Smith should have persistently and aggressively fought prohibition. Tammany-bred, a pupil, a follower, a protege of Croker, Foley, and Murphy, he is today the outstanding personality and most influential factor in Tammany Hall. It is true that Mr. George Olvaney, the titular head of Tammany Hall, declared on oath before the Senate Committee that Tammany was not a political organization at all, but simply a "patriotic society." But whatever it be called Tammany is, as was declared in *The Nation* for June 13, a "society held together by the cohesive power of public plunder." Governor Smith has for thirty-three years been a worker in or an official of that society. Nor has he condemned the Tammany graft and corruption which has recently come to light. Indeed, he has only recently been reinstated as a sachem.

Moreover, Governor Smith is ecclesiastically Wet. There was published in the secular press on January 2, 1928, a quotation which has not been denied from the *Osservatore Romano*, the official organ of the Vatican, stating that "the attempt to enforce prohibition in America has become so useless, not to say dangerous, that it would be better to abolish it, especially since upbridled passion is always more rampant as soon as there is an attempt to enforce complete abstinence." This attack upon the prohibition law of the United States by the Vatican organ is in full agreement with the open criticism of that law by the Cardinal Archbishop of New York and Boston and other Roman Catholic dignitaries.

I concede the right of the Pope, cardinals, archbishops, and other Roman Catholics to declare their attitude as freely as Methodist, Baptist, Presbyterian, or other Protestant bodies or ministers or laymen upon this question. Nor would I even intimate that these Roman Catholic leaders are not sincere in their opposition to the prohibition law. But it is not surprising, indeed it is to be expected, that this position of high dignitaries of the Roman church will be reflected in the attitude of many loyal Catholics who are members of legislatures, or of Congress, or who hold other official positions.

It is a fact that the attacks in Congress upon the prohibition law are made chiefly by men who are themselves Roman Catholics or who represent constituencies with large Roman Catholic populations. Certainly it is likely that Governor Alfred E. Smith is influenced by the views of the Pope and the cardinals on the subject of prohibition.

I repeat that because Governor Smith is personally, ecclesiastically, aggressively, irreconcilably Wet and is ineradicably Tammany-branded, the South's Dry Democrats will oppose him. It is unthinkable that the moral, religious leadership of the South could be a party to the nomination or election of such a man as Governor Smith, thus being guilty of an open betrayal of a great social, economic, and moral reform which was won after years of unselfish labor. If the Houston convention should nominate Governor Smith for President, multiplied thousands of life-long Democrats will decide that Democracy will be better served by the defeat of the Wet Tammany sachem than by his election, and will act accordingly.

VI

The Economy during the 1920s

38. Business and Jesus: Bruce Barton

A MARRIAGE *of the contemporary, impersonal, large-scale business firm with the small-town ethics still vital in the dominant American culture was consummated in a book by Bruce Barton (1886–1967),* The Man Nobody Knows. *Chairman of the Board of one of the most successful advertising agencies in the nation, Batten, Barton, Durstine, and Osborn, Barton attempted to show that Jesus Christ was "the founder of modern business." In the chapter reprinted below, Barton describes Jesus' executive abilities, based on principles just as effective in the twentieth century as in the first. The book, enormously successful, obviously served a need among Americans at least as strong as those filled by the new products that BBD and O publicized so ably.*

The Executive

It was very late in the afternoon.

If you would like to learn the measure of a man, that is the time of day to watch him. We are all half an inch taller in the morning than at night; it is fairly easy to take a large view of things when the mind is rested and the nerves are calm. But the day is a steady drain of small annoyances, and the difference in the size of men becomes hourly more apparent. The little man loses his temper; the big man takes a firmer hold.

It was very late in the afternoon in Galilee.

The dozen men who had walked all day over the dusty roads were hot and tired, and the sight of a village was very cheering, as they looked down on it from the top of a little hill. Their leader, deciding that they had gone far enough, sent two members of the party ahead to arrange for accommodations, while he and the others sat down by the roadside to wait.

After a bit the messengers were seen returning, and even at a distance it was apparent that something unpleasant had occurred. Their cheeks were flushed, their voices angry, and as they came nearer they quickened their pace, each wanting to be the first to explode the bad news. Breathlessly they told it—the people in the

SOURCE: Bruce Barton, *The Man Nobody Knows* (Indianapolis, Ind., 1925), pp. 1–31.

village had refused to receive them, had given them blunt notice to seek shelter somewhere else.

The indignation of the messengers communicated itself to the others, who at first could hardly believe their ears. This back-woods village refuse to entertain their master—it was unthinkable. He was a famous public character in that part of the world. He had healed sick people and given freely to the poor. In the capital city crowds had followed him enthusiastically, so that even his disciples had become men of importance, looked up to and talked about. And now to have this country village deny them admittance as its guests——

"Lord, these people are insufferable," one of them cried. "Let us call down fire from Heaven and consume them."

The others joined in with enthusiasm. Fire from Heaven—that was the idea! Make them smart for their boorishness! Show them that they can't affront *us* with impunity! Come, Lord, the fire——

There are times when nothing a man can say is nearly so powerful as saying nothing. Every executive knows that instinctively. To argue brings him down to the level of those with whom he argues; silence convicts them of their folly; they wish they had not spoken so quickly; they wonder what he thinks. The lips of Jesus tightened; his fine features showed the strain of the preceding weeks, and in his eyes there was a foreshadowing of the more bitter weeks to come. He needed that night's rest, but he said not a word. Quietly he gathered up his garments and started on, his outraged companions following. It is easy to imagine his keen disappointment. He had been working with them for three years . . . would they never catch a true vision of what he was about? He had so little time, and they were constantly wasting his time. . . . He had come to save mankind, and they wanted him to gratify his personal resentment by burning down a village!

Down the hot road they trailed after him, awed by his silence, vaguely conscious that they had failed again to measure up. "And they went to another village," says the narrative—nothing more. No debate; no bitterness; no futile conversation. In the mind of Jesus the thing was too small for comment. In a world where so much must be done, and done quickly, the memory could not afford to be burdened with a petty slight.

"And they went to another village."

Eighteen hundred years later an important man left the White House in Washington for the War Office, with a letter from the President to the Secretary of War. In a very few minutes he was back in the White House again bursting with indignation. The President looked up in mild surprise.

"Did you give the message to Stanton?" he asked.

The other man nodded, too angry for words.

"What did he do?"

"He tore it up," exclaimed the outraged citizen, "and what's more, sir, he said you are a fool."

The President rose slowly from the desk, stretching his long frame to its full height, and regarding the wrath of the other with a quizzical glance.

"Did Stanton call me that?" He asked.

"He did, sir, and repeated it."

"Well," said the President with a dry laugh, "I reckon it must be true then, because Stanton is generally right."

The angry gentleman waited for the storm to break, but nothing happened. Abraham Lincoln turned quietly to his desk and went on with his work. It was not the first time that he had been rebuffed. In the early months of the war when every messenger brought bad news, and no one in Washington knew at what hour the soldiers of Lee might appear at the outskirts, he had gone to call on General McClellan, taking a member of the Cabinet with him. Official etiquette prescribes that the President shall not visit a citizen, but the times were too tense for etiquette; he wanted first hand news from the only man who could give it.

The General was out, and for an hour they waited in the deserted parlor. They heard his voice at last in the hall and supposed of course that he would come in at once. But the "Young Napoleon" was too filled with his own importance; without so much as a word of greeting he brushed by, and proceeded on his haughty way upstairs. Ten minutes passed—fifteen—half an hour—they sent a servant to remind him that the President was still waiting. Obviously shocked and embarrassed the man returned. The General was too tired for a conference, he said; he had undressed and gone to bed!

Not to make a scene before the servants, the Cabinet member restrained himself until they were on the sidewalk. Then he burst forth, demanding that this conceited upstart be removed instantly from command. Lincoln laid a soothing hand on the other's shoulder. "There, there," he said with his deep, sad smile, "I will hold McClellan's horse if only he will bring us victories."

Other leaders in history have had that superiority to personal resentment and small annoyances which is one of the surest signs of greatness; but Jesus infinitely surpasses all. He knew that pettiness brings its own punishment. The law of compensation operates inexorably to reward and afflict us by and through ourselves. The man who is mean is mean only to himself. The village that had refused to admit him required no fire; it was already dealt with. No miracles were performed in that village. No sick were healed; no hungry were fed; no poor received the message of encouragement and inspiration—that was the penalty for its boorishness. As for him, he forgot the incident immediately. He had work to do.

Theology has spoiled the thrill of his life by assuming that he knew everything from the beginning—that his three years of public work were a kind of dress rehearsal, with no real problems or crises. What interest would there be in such a life? What inspiration? You who read these pages have your own creed concerning him; I have mine. Let us forget all creed for the time being, and take the story just as the simple narratives give it—a poor boy, growing up in a peasant family, working in a carpenter shop; gradually feeling his powers expanding, beginning to have an influence over his neighbors, recruiting a few followers, suffering disappointments and reverses, finally death. Yet building so solidly and well that death was only the beginning of his influence! Stripped of all dogma this is the grandest achievement story of all! In the pages of this little book let us treat it as such. If, in so doing, we are criticized for overemphasizing the human side of his character we shall have the satisfaction of knowing that our overemphasis tends a little to offset the very great overemphasis which has been exerted on the other side. Books and books and books have been written about him as the Son of God; surely we have a reverent right to remember that his favorite title for himself was the Son of Man.

Nazareth, where he grew up, was a little town in an outlying province. In the fashionable circles of Jerusalem it was quite the thing to make fun of Nazareth—its crudities of custom and speech, its simplicity of manner. "Can any good thing come out of Nazareth?" they asked derisively when the report spread that a new prophet had arisen in that country town. The question was regarded as a complete rebuttal of his pretensions.

The Galileans were quite conscious of the city folks' contempt, but they bore it lightly. Life was a cheerful and easy-going affair with them. The sun shone almost every day; the land was fruitful; to make a living was nothing much to worry about. There was plenty of time to visit. Families went on picnics in Nazareth, as elsewhere in the world; young people walked together in the moonlight and fell in love in the spring. Boys laughed boisterously at their games and got into trouble with their pranks. And Jesus, the boy who worked in the carpenter shop, was a leader among them.

Later on we shall refer again to those boyhood experiences, noting how they contributed to the vigorous physique which carried him triumphantly through his work. We are quite unmindful of chronology in writing this little book. We are not bound by the familiar outline which begins with the song of the angels at Bethlehem and ends with the weeping of the women at the cross. We shall thread our way back and forth through the rich variety of his life, picking up this incident and that bit of conversation, this dramatic contact and that audacious decision, and bringing them together as best to illustrate our purpose. For that purpose is not to write a biography but to paint a portrait. So in this first chapter we pass quickly over thirty years of his life, noting only that somehow, somewhere there occurred in those years the eternal miracle—the awakening of the inner consciousness of power.

The eternal miracle! In New York one day a luncheon was tendered by a gathering of distinguished gentlemen to David Lloyd George. There were perhaps two hundred at the tables. The food was good and the speeches were impressive. But what stirred one's imagination was a study of the men at the speakers' table. There they were—some of the most influential citizens of the present-day world; and *who* were they? At one end an international financier—the son of a poor country parson. Beside him a great newspaper proprietor—he came from a tiny town in Maine and landed in New York with less than a hundred dollars. A little farther along the president of a world-wide press association—a copy boy in a country newspaper office. And, in the center, the boy who grew up in the poverty of an obscure Welsh village, and became the commanding statesman of the British Empire in the greatest crisis of history.

When and how and where did the eternal miracle occur in the lives of those men? At what hour, in the morning, in the afternoon, in the long quiet evenings, did the audacious thought enter the mind of each of them that he was larger than the limits of a country town, that his life might be bigger than his father's? When did the thought come to Jesus? Was it one morning when he stood at the carpenter's bench, the sun streaming in across the hills? Was it late in the night, after the family had retired, and he had slipped out to walk and wonder under the stars? Nobody knows. All we can be sure of is this—that the consciousness of his divinity must have come to him in a time of solitude, of awe in the presence of Nature. The western hemisphere has been fertile in material progress, but the great religions have all come out of the East. The deserts are a symbol of the infinite; the vast spaces that divide men from the stars fill the human soul with wonder. Somewhere, at some unforgettable hour, the daring filled his heart. He knew that he was bigger than Nazareth.

Another young man had grown up near by and was beginning to be heard from the larger world. His name was John. How much the two boys may have seen of each other we do not know; but certainly the younger, Jesus, looked up to and admired his handsome, fearless cousin. We can imagine with what eager interest he must have received the reports of John's impressive success at the capital. He was the sensation of that season. The fashionable folk of the city were flocking out to the river to hear his denunciations; some of them even accepted his demand for repentance and were baptized. His fame grew; his uncompromising speeches were quoted far and wide. The businessmen of Nazareth who had been up to Jerusalem brought back stories and quotations. There was considerable head-wagging as there always is; these folk had known of John as a boy; they could hardly believe that he was as much of a man as the world seemed to think. But there was one who had no doubts. A day came when he was missing from the carpenter shop; the sensational news spread through the streets that he had gone to Jerusalem, to John, to be baptized.

John's reception of him was flattering. During the ceremony of baptism and for the rest of that day Jesus was in a state of splendid exultation. No shadow of a doubt darkened his enthusiasm. He was going to do the big things which John had done; he felt the power stirring in him; he was all eager to begin. Then the day closed and night descended, and with it came the doubts. The narrative describes them as a threefold temptation and introduces Satan to add to the dramatic quality of the event. In our simple story we need not spend much time with the description of Satan. We do not know whether he is to be regarded as a personality or as an impersonalization of an inner experience. The temptation is more real without him, more akin to our own trials and doubts. With him or without him, however, the meaning of the experience is clear.

This is its meaning; the day of supreme assurance had passed; the days of fearful misgiving had come. What man of outstanding genius has ever been allowed to escape them? For how many days and weeks do you think the soul of Lincoln must have been tortured? Inside himself he felt his power, but where and when would opportunity come? Must he forever ride the country circuit, and sit in a dingy office settling a community's petty disputes? Had he perhaps mistaken the inner message? Was he, after all, only a common fellow—a fair country lawyer and a good teller of jokes? Those who rode with him on the circuit testify to his terrifying moods of silence. What solemn thoughts besieged him in those silences? What fear of failure? What futile rebellion at the narrow limits of his life?

The days of Jesus' doubt are set down as forty in number. It is easy to imagine that lonely struggle. He had left a good trade among people who knew and trusted him—and for what? To become a wandering preacher, talking to folks who never heard of him? And what was he to talk about? How, with his lack of experience, should he find words for his message? Where should he begin? Who would listen? *Would* they listen? Hadn't he perhaps made a mistake? Satan, says the narrative, tempted him, saying: "You are hungry; here are stones. Make them into bread."—The temptation of material success. It was entirely unnecessary for him to be hungry ever. He had a good trade; he knew well enough that his organizing ability was better than Joseph's. He could build up a far more successful business and acquire comfort and wealth. Why not?

Satan comes in again, according to the narrative, taking him up into a high mountain and showing him the kingdoms of the world. "All these can be yours, if you will only compromise." He could go to Jerusalem and enter the priesthood; that was a sure road to distinction. He could do good in that way, and have the satisfaction of success as well. Or he might enter the public service, and seek political leadership. There was plenty of discontent to be capitalized, and he knew the farmer and the laborer; he was one of them; they would listen to him.

For forty days and nights the incessant fight went on, but once settled, it was settled forever. In the calm of that wilderness there came the majestic conviction which is the very soul of leadership—the faith that his spirit was linked with the Eternal, that God had sent him into the world to do a work which no one else could do, which—if he neglected it—would never be done. Magnify this temptation scene as greatly as you will; say that God spoke more clearly to him than to any who has ever lived. It is true. But to every man of vision the clear Voice speaks; there is no great leadership where there is not a mystic. Nothing splendid has evern been achieved except by those who dared believe that something inside themselves was superior to circumstance. To choose the sure thing is treason to the soul. . . . If this was not the meaning of the forty days in the wilderness, if Jesus did not have a *real* temptation which might have ended in his going back to the bench at Nazareth, then the forty days' struggle has no real significance to us. But the temptation *was* real, and he conquered. The youth who had been a carpenter stayed in the wilderness, a man came out. Not the full-fledged master who, within the shadow of the cross could cry, "I have overcome the world." He had still much growth to make, much progress in vision and self-confidence. But the beginnings were there. Men who looked upon him from that hour felt the authority of one who has put his spiritual house in order, and knows clearly what he is about.

Success is always exciting; we never grow tired of asking what and low. What, then, were the principal elements in his power over men? How was it that the boy from a country village became the greatest leader?

First of all he had the voice and manner of the leader—the personal magnetism which begets loyalty and commands respect. The beginnings of it were present in him even as a boy. John felt them. On the day when John looked up from the river where he was baptizing converts and saw Jesus standing on the bank, he drew back in protest. "I have need to be baptized of thee," he exclaimed, "and comest thou to me?" The lesser man recognized the greater instinctively. We speak of personal magnetism as though there were something mysterious about it—a magic quality bestowed on one in a thousand and denied to all the rest. This is not true. The essential element in personal magnetism is a consuming sincerity—an overwhelming faith in the importance of the work one has to do. Emerson said, "What you *are* thunders so loud I can't hear what you say." And Mirabeau, watching the face of the young Robespierre, exclaimed, "That man will go far; he believes every word he says."

Most of us go through the world mentally divided against ourselves. We wonder whether we are in the right jobs, whether we are making the right investments, whether, after all, anything is as important as it seems to be. Our enemies are those of our own being and creation. Instinctively we wait for a commanding voice, for one who shall say authoritatively, "I have the truth. This way lies happiness and salvation." There was in Jesus supremely that quality of conviction.

Even very successful people were moved by it. Jesus had been in Jerusalem only a day or two when there came a knock at his door at night. He opened it to find Nicodemus, one of the principal men of the city; a member of the Sanhedrin, a supreme court judge. One feels the dramatic quality of the meeting—the young, almost unknown, teacher and the great man, half curious, half convinced. It would have been easy to make a mistake. Jesus might very naturally have expressed his sense of honor at the visit; have said: "I appreciate your coming, sir. You are an older man and successful. I am just starting on my work. I should like to have you advise me as to how I may best proceed." But there was no such note in the interview—no effort to make it easy for this notable visitor to become a convert. One catches his breath involuntarily at the audacity of the speech:

"Verily, verily, I say to you, Nicodemus, except you are born again you can not see the kingdom of Heaven." And a few moments later, "If I have told you earthly things and you have not believed, how shall you believe if I tell you heavenly things?"

The famous visitor did not enroll as a disciple, was not invited to enroll; but he never forgot the impression made by the young man's amazing self-assurance. In a few weeks the crowds along the shores of the Sea of Galilee were to feel the same power and respond to it. They were quite accustomed to the discourses of the Scribes and Pharisees—long, involved arguments backed up by many citations from the law. But this teacher was different. He quoted nobody; his own word was offered as sufficient. He taught as "one having authority and not as the scribes." Still later we have yet more striking proof of the power that supreme conviction can carry. At this date he had become so large a public influence as to threaten the peace of the rulers, and they sent a detachment of soldiers to arrest him. They were stern men, presumably immune to sentiment. They returned, after a while, empty-handed.

"What's the matter?" their commander demanded angrily. "Why didn't you bring him in?"

And they, smarting under their failure and hardly knowing how to explain it, could make only a surly excuse.

"You'll have to send some one else," they said. "We don't want to go against him. *Never man so spake*."

They were armed; he had no defense but his manner and tone, but these were enough. In any crowd and under any circumstances the leader stands out. By the power of his faith in himself he commands, and men instinctively obey.

This blazing conviction was the first and greatest element in the success of Jesus. The second was his wonderful power to pick men, and to recognize hidden capacities in them. It must have amazed Nicodemus when he learned the names of the twelve whom the young teacher had chosen to be his associates. What a list! Not a single well-known person on it. Nobody who had ever made a success of anything. A haphazard collection of fishermen and smalltown business men, and one tax collector—a member of the most hated element in the community. What a crowd!

Nowhere is there such a startling example of executive success as the way in which that organization was brought together. Take the tax collector, Matthew, as the most striking instance. His occupation carried a heavy weight of social ostracism, but it was profitable. He was probably well-to-do according to the simple standards of the neighborhood; certainly he was a busy man and not subject to impulsive action. His addition to the group of disciples is told in a single sentence:

"And as *Jesus passed by*, he called Matthew."

Amazing. No argument; no pleading. A smaller leader would have been compelled to set up the advantages of the opportunity. "Of course you are doing well where you are and making money," he might have said. "I can't offer you as much as you are getting; in fact you may have some difficulty in making ends meet. But I think we are going to have an interesting time and shall probably accomplish a big work." Such a conversation would have been met with Matthew's reply that he would "have to think it over," and the world would never have heard his name.

There was no such trifling with Jesus. *As he passed by* he called Matthew. No executive in the world can read that sentence without acknowledging that here indeed is the Master.

He had the born leader's gift for seeing powers in men of which they themselves were often almost unconscious. One day as he was coming into a certain town a tremendous crowd pressed around him. There was a rich man named Zacchaeus in the town; small in stature, but with such keen business ability that he had got himself generally disliked. Being curious to see the distinguished visitor he had climbed up into a tree. Imagine his surprise when Jesus stopped under the tree and commanded him to come down saying, "Today I intend to eat at your house." The crowd was stunned. Some of the bolder spirits took it upon themselves to tell Jesus of his social blunder. He couldn't afford to make the mistake of visiting Zacchaeus, they said. Their protests were without avail. They saw in Zacchaeus merely a dishonest little Jew; he saw in him a man of unusual generosity and a fine sense of justice, who needed only to have those qualities revealed by some one who understood. So with Matthew—the crowd saw only a despised tax-gatherer. Jesus saw the potential writer of a book which will live forever.

So also with that "certain Centurion," who is one of the anonymous characters in history that every business man would have liked to meet. The disciples brought him to Jesus with some misgivings and apology. They said, "Of course this man is a Roman employee, and you may reprove us for introducing him. But really he is a very good fellow, a generous man and a respecter of our faith." Jesus and the Centurion looking at each other found an immediate bond of union—each responding to the other's strength. Said the Centurion:

"Master, my servant is ill; but it is unnecessary for you to visit my house. I understand how such things are done, for I, too, am an executive; I say to this man 'Go' and he goeth; and to another 'Come,' and he cometh; and to my servant, 'Do this,' and he doeth it. Therefore, speak the word only, and I know my servant will be healed."

Jesus' face kindled with admiration. "I have not found anywhere such faith as this," he exclaimed. This man understood him. Both were executives. They had the same problems and the same power; they talked the same language.

Having gathered together his organization, there remained for Jesus the tremendous task of training it. And herein lay the third great element in his success—his vast unending patience. The Church has attached to each of the disciples the title of Saint and thereby done most to destroy the conviction of their reality. They were very far from sainthood when he picked them up. For three years he had them with him day and night, his whole energy and resources poured out in an effort to create an understanding in them. Yet through it all they never fully understood. We have seen, at the beginning of this chapter, an example of their petulance. The narratives are full of similar discouragements.

In spite of all he could do or say, they were persuaded that he planned to overthrow the Roman power and set himself up as ruler in Jerusalem. Hence they never tired of wrangling as to how the offices should be divided. Two of them, James and John, got their mother to come to him and ask that her sons might sit, one on his right hand and one on his left. When the other ten heard of it they were angry with James and John; but Jesus never lost his patience. He believed that the way to get faith out of men is to show that you have faith in them; and from that great principle of executive management he never wavered.

Of all the disciples Simon was most noisy and aggressive. It was he who was always volunteering advice, forever proclaiming the staunchness of his own courage and faith. One day Jesus said to him, "Before the cock crows tomorrow you will deny me thrice." Simon was indignant. Though they killed him, he cried, he would never deny! Jesus merely smiled—and that night it happened. . . . A lesser leader would have dropped Simon. "You have had your chance," he would have said, "I am sorry but I must have men around me on whom I can depend." Jesus had the rare understanding that the same man will usually not make the same mistake twice. To this frail, very human, very likable ex-fisherman he spoke no word of rebuke. Instead he played a stroke of master strategy. "Your name is Simon," he said. "Hereafter you shall be called Peter." (A rock.) It was daring, but he knew his man. The shame of the denial had tempered the iron of that nature like fire; from that time on there was no faltering in Peter, even at the death.

The Bible presents an interesting collection of contrasts in this matter of executive ability. Samson had almost all the attributes of leadership. He was physically powerful and handsome; he had the great courage to which men always respond. No man was ever given a finer opportunity to free his countrymen from the oppressors and build up a great place of power for himself. Yet Samson failed miserably. He could do wonders singlehanded, but he could not organize. Moses started out under the same handicap. He tried to be everything and do everything; and was almost on the verge of failure. It was his father-in-law, Jethro, who saved him from calamity. Said that shrewd old man: "The thing that thou doest is not good. Thou wilt surely wear away, both thou and this people that is with thee, for this thing is too heavy for thee, for thou are not able to perform it thyself alone."

Moses took the advice and associated with himself a partner, Aaron, who was strong where he was weak. They supplemented each other and together achieved what neither of them could have done alone.

John, the Baptist, had the same lack. He could denounce, but he could not construct. He drew crowds who were willing to repent at his command, but he had no program for them after their repentance. They waited for him to organize them for some sort of effective service, and he was no organizer. So his followers drifted away and his movement gradually collapsed. The same thing might have happened to the work of Jesus. He started with much less reputation than John and a much smaller group of followers. He had only twelve, and they were untrained simple men, with elementary weakness and passions. Yet because of the fire of his personal conviction, because of his marvelous instinct for discovering their latent powers, and because of his unwavering faith and patience, he molded them into an organization which carried on victoriously. Within a very few years after his death, it was reported in a far-off corner of the Roman Empire that "these who have turned the world upside down have come hither also." A few decades later the proud Emperor himself bowed his head to the teachings of this Nazareth carpenter, transmitted through common men.

39. The Gladiators: Raymond L. Summers

THE SIZE *of potential audiences for entertainment—athletic contests, movies, even concerts—increased enormously between 1900 and 1920 as a result of economic changes. Automobiles, radio, higher incomes, a shorter work week, and new publicity techniques all combined to draw Americans toward stadiums and theaters where they could see the spectacles and heroes they had heard and read about. The largest crowds consistently gathered to watch football contests. Men and boys who never had left New York felt as though they were alumni of Notre Dame and never missed an opportunity to cheer for the "Fighting Irish" when they played in Yankee Stadium. Young men whose ability to run fast and hard with a football in one arm far exceeded all their other talents became national heroes, almost on the order of Charles Lindbergh or Calvin Coolidge. Some of the effects on America's citadels of learning, which subsidized these teams, are summarized in the article below.*

The Football Business

A few days ago, the Carnegie Foundation for the Advancement of Teaching startled the country by publishing a report showing that most of the country's universities are buying athletes to participate in their intercollegiate contests, and especially football. The following article is written by a member of the faculty in a leading American college, and describes from first-hand experience, and in detail, the activities which are the basis of the Foundation's report. For obvious reasons, the author finds it necessary to write under a pseudonym.

I am an associate professor of English at an eastern university whose football teams have been beaten with monotonous regularity during the past four years. I have been alumni secretary for five years and, for an equal length of time, the so-called preparatory school contact-man. For the past decade I have served on the faculty committee which awards scholarships to deserving students. As a result of these experiences I have been brought into intimate contact with the question of professionalism in intercollegiate athletics.

SOURCE: Raymond L. Summers, "The Football Business," *The New Republic* (November 6, 1929), pp. 319–322.

The big majority of the articles in newspapers and magazines on the subject of proselyting have been written by men who are simply observers. In common parlance they are on the outside looking in, and although they speak with apparent authority, the truth of the matter is that they do not know what they are talking about. They will tell you that athletics in our American colleges and universities are cleaner than they have been in the past, that the practice of proselyting is dying out and that, except in a few exceptional cases, varsity football teams are composed of bona fide students who are attending college for the sole purpose of securing an education.

As a matter of fact, competition among our colleges for the acquisition of preparatory and high school gridiron stars is keener than ever before, and it is practically impossible for a college to have consistently successful football teams unless it bids in the open market for the services of outstanding players in secondary schools.

Intercollegiate football has become a business proposition. The expenses of a season, even for a minor college, are surprisingly large. The salaries of the head coach and his staff, the cost of trainers and training table, guarantees, equipment and the care of the playing field total many thousands of dollars. The money must come from somewhere. A winning team draws large gate receipts; a losing team is a financial failure. Therefore, it behooves a college to have a winning team. Otherwise there is a large deficit at the end of the season and no money with which to finance basketball, baseball, track and other nonpaying sports.

So the graduate manager of athletics takes upon himself the task of producing a winner. He engages the best coach procurable, encourages prep school football players to enter his college, makes frantic pleas for alumni support, and hopes for the best.

The problem of schedule making confronts him. For the early season he arranges games with minor colleges, paying them large guarantees for appearance on the home field. He requests places on the schedules of the larger universities, but is courteously informed that their lists have long since been filled. He writes to So-and-so College, which has had a winning team for years and one which draws large crowds in New York or Philadelphia. The graduate manager of So-and-so replies that before expecting consideration of any kind, Blank College should go out and get a reputation. So the harassed graduate manager of Blank fills in with whatever teams he can get, announces his schedule, and braces himself for the wave of protest which is certain to overwhelm him.

By letter, telegram and personal visit, he is requested, courteously and otherwise, to explain why Blank has to play Squedunk and Schoolville. Why didn't he sign up with Princeton or Yale? How about some of these colleges no bigger than Blank which play before thirty thousand people in New York? What's the big idea, anyhow?

The graduate manager explains patiently that Blank has had a poor record in football for the past several years, and that it isn't a drawing card for the money-making colleges. "If we want to play big-league football," he says, "we've got to have a winning team."

"Well, then," reply the alumni, "let's *get* a winning team."

Sometimes, if a college happens to be blessed with wealthy graduates, a sum of money is contributed for the express purpose of paying the expenses of star athletes. A coach of national reputation is secured. In his first year, the varsity does poorly, but the freshmen finish the season undefeated. In the second year, the varsity team shows surprising improvement; in the third year, it is a near champion.

Sport writers wax enthusiastic over the success of the system which Coach Hocus-pokus has installed. The alumni puff out their chests, hurry down to the office and make nuisances of themselves among their associates. The following season—those miraculously strong freshmen are seniors now—the team plays in New York before forty thousand people who have paid $3 each to see the near champions in action. From the net returns of the season, totaling over $100,000, the wealthy graduates are given back their initial investment, with interest. The graduate manager doesn't need to worry now about his schedule. The team is a headliner, a winner. And the problem is solved.

It all seems simple enough. But it so happens that at Blank College, which is my own university, the leaders among our alumni body are men of rather old-fashioned ideas of honor and fair play. Any one of a dozen I might mention is financially able to buy a winning football team. A few years ago we seriously considered the advisability of going into the *business* of football on a large scale—and voted it down. We decided that the primary purpose of a university is to educate young men. Many of our recent graduates, who are "razzed" in the office whenever we are beaten, emit indignant howls of protest, and demand the coach's scalp.

What they don't understand is that Blank is playing the game according to the rules, that our football players are paying the same tuition as other students and are meeting exactly the same scholastic requirements. And they have no knowledge whatever of the practices employed by other colleges of our own size who are defeating us year after year with monotonous regularity.

We have three major opponents on our football schedule. Of the twelve games played with them since 1924, we have won two and lost ten. One of these major opponents has an amateur football team, and in our series of four games we have broken even. The other two teams have beaten us by from one to twelve touchdowns. They have their victories, but we have our self-respect.

We would drop them from our schedule were it not for the fact that it would mean financial suicide. Our athletic association has a note for forty thousand dollars in a local bank, the accumulated deficits of the past five years. The games with these two major opponents—whose teams are unquestionably semi-professional—are our only hope of ultimate solvency. If by a miracle we could reach either game undefeated, we would draw a gate large enough to pay off the note. And then, too, there is the traditional aspect of the case. We have played against both of these opponents for twenty years.

And so we continue to be an amateur team in a league which is composed mainly of professionals. There are some colleges with which we will not schedule games, colleges which are placed on the blacklist of every respectable institution. They accept for entrance candidates who are not qualified to carry college work. These men enroll in special courses, attend classes when the spirit moves them, and receive a salary every Saturday night for jobs which include jumping over a chair, managing a nonexistent laundry, or acting as salesman for a real estate firm many miles away. These "salesmen" receive advance commissions for parcels of land which are to be sold some time in the future.

Class two on our list includes those colleges which require their football players to qualify for entrance, although occasionally mechanical training and music are accepted for admission. These football players attend classes more or less regularly, but their professors make allowances for their services on the gridiron and "go easy" on them. They are given a scholarship covering tuition and all fees, the fraternities provide board and room free of charge, and the athletic association helps out if necessary in the matter of spending money. These men are, to all appearances, bona fide students and simon-pure amateur athletes; but they are receiving a college education, or what goes for a college education, without cost; and the peculiar thing about them is that no matter how poor they may be as students, they are never reported deficient during football season.

Then, of course, there are the large universities whose entrance requirements are stringent and whose scholastic standards are above reproach. These universities have adopted a code of ethics which is a model of its kind. So far as the administrative officers and faculty are concerned, their hands are clean.

But they have no control over their alumni body. Magnus University, for instance, remains in complete ignorance if an interested graduate chooses to dip into his pocket and provide the funds for the education of a deserving boy. The fact that the boy in question happens to be an outstanding athlete is of no concern to the university. He pays his tuition, maintains satisfactory class standing and is an admirable young man in every way.

Probably I can best describe this system of alumni support of athletes by recounting an incident which came to my attention a few years ago. A high school graduate applied for admission to Blank University and was accepted. Because of his exceptional record in school, both as a leader and an athlete, he was awarded a scholarship valued at $250 a year. We have five such scholarships given on the basis of the Rhodes Scholarships to Oxford.

This boy—let us call him McCormick—had friends at Blank. They found a job for him waiting on table downtown and arranged to have him pay his room rent by tending furnace in a private house near the campus. He had saved $200, which was enough to see him through the first year. Naturally we expected great things of him at Blank, for he was a football and basketball player of unusual ability.

Our consternation can be imagined, therefore, when, two weeks before the opening of college, we learned that McCornick had decided not to attend Blank after all. We next heard of him as the star halfback in one of the leading preparatory schools of the East. The tuition at that school is approximately $2,000 a year.

McCormick remained there for two years, then entered Magnus University as a freshman. He was captain of the yearling football team, and last season earned all-American mention as halfback on the varsity. And McCormick, we must remember, had exactly $200 to his name when he applied for admission to Blank.

What really happened is this. Because of his football ability, the boy was "staked" to two years in preparatory school and four years in college by a wealthy alumnus of Magnus University. I happen to know that each year, ten outstanding athletes have their way paid at this preparatory school by alumni of Magnus. But the university authorities know nothing about it, and Magnus stands in the forefront of our American universities, with a reputation for clean athletics and unquestioned good sportsmanship.

The case of McCormick is only one of many with which I have had intimate personal contact. About five years ago we had at Blank a student whom we shall call Larry Jones. He came from a small high school unheralded and unsung, but in sophomore year, he won his varsity letter in football, basketball and baseball. He was one of those rare athletes who enjoy perfect coordination of mind and muscle, and he was probably the best halfback on the Atlantic Coast.

But he remained at Blank for only two years. The next season saw him as a backfield star at West Point, where he achieved the ambition of all football players—a position on Walter Camp's all-American team.

He has a brother Jimmy, who was ready for college in 1926. Jimmy, who wanted to enter Blank, visited the scholarship committee at my office in the university. His father had suffered financial reverses and could give him no help. We offered him a memorial scholarship covering tuition and fees.

"That's fine," he said, "but where am I going to live and how am I going to eat?"

We suggested a job downtown, but he explained to us that he wouldn't be required to work at other colleges. So we let him go, and now, if I should tell you his real name, you would recognize him as quarterback on the football team and shortstop on the baseball nine of a large eastern university. He must have found there an answer to his question concerning food and lodging.

Then there is the case of Swede Swanson. Swede was six feet tall and weighed 190 pounds. As a high school fullback he was the sensation of scholastic circles, and because he lived within thirty miles of Blank, we tried, in our amateurish way, to interest him in entrance. Only two things prevented the success of the plan: he had no money and he was able to offer only six of the fifteen credits required for admission. And so we lost contact with Swede until two years later, when he blossomed forth as the star fullback on the varsity team of a large metropolitan college.

I could recount at least a score of incidents of this type, but those mentioned above should provide sufficient proof of our contention that all is not as it should be in the world of intercollegiate athletics. There is no question whatever that the practice of proselyting is rampant in our colleges and universities, but even more surprising is the fact that there are a few institutions which actually offer financial assistance to young men already in college.

Some years ago there was a football player at Blank whom we shall call Charley Hinds. He was a big, strapping chap with the shoulders of a Hercules. He played end on our varsity team, but because of financial difficulties was forced to leave college after completing his sophomore year. His scholastic record was bad, but his record as an athlete was far above the average.

He went to work as a swimming instructor in an amusement park; he married and had a child. But the next year he entered a university which is known throughout the country for the excellence of its football teams. His play during the season gained him national recognition. In the winter, as manager of the university's indoor track team, he spent several weeks in New York. His wife and baby lived in an apartment on the West Side. Hinds had very little money, but he supported his wife and child and paid his own college expenses. Here at Blank University we should like to know how he did it. Our graduate manager knows, but he won't tell.

Charley Hinds, however, isn't our only athlete to transfer to another college. There is, for instance, Ben Gibbons. Ben was our most promising freshman tackle two years ago. He was a poor boy, commuting to college from his home fifteen miles away. He held a scholarship awarded in open competition and was an exceptional student. He would reach the campus at eight o'clock in the morning, go without lunch because he couldn't afford to buy it and was too proud to bring his own, attend football practice and take the 7:40 train home. It was a hard struggle, but he plugged along grimly.

He wanted very much to live on the campus in his sophomore

year, but he did not see how he could possibly do it without long hours of manual labor. And then, a classmate of his in high school who was an undergraduate at a small college in Pennsylvania announced to Ben that he could attend Smalltown without any expense whatever.

Ben entered into correspondence with the Smalltown coach and showed us the letters, which promised him tuition, board, room rent and spending money. There didn't seem to be any special secrecy about it. The Smalltown coach wrote to our graduate manager, whom he knew personally:

"I hate to dish you out of a good man, Bill, but we sure do need a tackle down here."

Ben Gibbons, balancing release from financial worry against hours of hard work, decided to go to Smalltown. Last season he made a splendid record as varsity tackle.

All of which leads us to speculate about the effect of such practices upon the boys themselves. Hinds and Gibbons, of course, were older men and decided only after careful deliberation to trade their athletic ability for a bachelor's degree. Gibbons is still at Smalltown taking an engineering course and doing well. It isn't a very good course, but he hopes later to attend Massachusetts Institute of Technology. Hinds is a teacher of physical training at a minor college, and word reaches us that he is earning less money now than he did as an undergraduate, although he is able to add to his income by playing professional football.

But what about the high school and prep school stars who sell themselves to the highest bidder? Their football coaches have given them an exaggerated idea of their own importance, and the fact that there are many colleges which will take them at their face value leads naturally to the assumption that so long as they make good on the football field, they have nothing to worry about. Many of them, I should say about 50 percent, receive classroom training which will stand them in good stead in future years. The others remain in college for a year or two, and then pass out of the picture. They play professional football and baseball for a time, but eventually they are forced to accept a minor position with some business concern. I have never known of any so-called athletic-scholarship man who has risen to a position of prominence.

But the practice of proselyting, of bidding in the open market for outstanding football players, goes merrily on; and the college which plays fair, which maintains its self-respect in spite of a long succession of defeats, finds itself in an unhappy position. It must either accept defeat as inevitable or risk the loss of alumni support. The college whose football team loses consistently erects no stadium or gymnasium with funds raised by its graduates. Contributions to the alumni associations lag; the "loyalty fund," which should enjoy normal growth, actually becomes smaller. Influential graduates lose interest, and the administration finds it increasingly difficult to meet the yearly deficit.

There is, fortunately, at my own university, a small group in our alumni body which is willing to pay the price of self-respect. But the big majority of our graduates, especially those of the past ten years, hate to be beaten. They are bringing an increasingly strong pressure to bear upon our athletic authorities. They are tired of getting licked, they explain, and they want us to climb on the band wagon and make some noise in the big parade.

So what are we going to do about it? What is going to be done by the other colleges which play the game according to the rules? That is the question which faces us at the present time. And the answer? Well, we haven't any idea of what the answer will be. That depends, to a great extent, on the American public, and on the alumni of our colleges and universities. Possibly the situation will be clarified in a few years.

But meanwhile, what is a college to do?

40. The State of the Economy, 1929: Wesley C. Mitchell

NOT ALL *Americans were completely swept away by the wave of supreme optimism that rolled over the country as wages, profits, even farm prices, but especially values of well-known common stocks, soared in 1929. A committee headed by economist Wesley Mitchell, head of the National Bureau of Economic Research, presented President Hoover and the nation with a remarkably balanced economic report in mid-1929, part of the conclusion of which is reprinted below.*

SOURCE: Wesley C. Mitchell, "A Review," *Recent Economic Changes in the United States* (New York, 1929), pp. 874–889. Reprinted by permission of McGraw-Hill Book Company.

The Competition of New Products and New Tastes

Scarcely less characteristic of our period than unit-cost reductions is the rapid expansion in the production and sale of products little used or wholly unknown a generation or even a decade ago. Among consumers' goods, the conspicuous instances are automobiles, radios and rayon. But the list includes also oil-burning furnaces, gas stoves, household electrical appliances in great variety, automobile accessories, antifreezing mixtures, cigarette lighters, propeller pencils, wristwatches, airplanes, and what not. Among producers' goods we have the truck and the tractor competing with the horse and the mule, reinforced concrete competing with brick and lumber, the high-tension line competing with the steam engine, fuel oil competing with coal, not to mention excavating machines, belt conveyors, paint sprayers, and "automatics" of many sorts competing with manual labor.

Changes in taste are in large part merely the consumers' response to the solicitation of novel products, effectively presented by advertising. But that is not all of the story; the consumer is free to choose what he likes among the vociferous offerings, and sometimes reveals traces of initiative. In what other terms can one explain the changes in diet pointed out in the first chapter? Americans are consuming fewer calories per capita; they are eating less wheat and corn but more dairy products, vegetable oils, sugar, fresh vegetables and fruit. More families than ever before are sending their sons and daughters to college—surely that is not a triumph of "high-powered" salesmanship. Young children, girls and women, are wearing lighter and fewer clothes. The short skirt, the low shoe, the silk or rayon stocking, "athletic" underwear, the soft collar, sporting suits and sporting goods, have an appeal which makers of rival articles have not been able to overcome. And, in a sense, every consumers' good, from college to candy, is a rival of every other consumers' good, besides being a rival of the savings bank.

"When the makers of one product get a larger slice of the consumer's dollar, the slices left for the makers of other products get smaller." This way of accounting for the hardships met by certain long-established industries in 1922–1927, such, for example, as the leather and woolen trades, is popular and sound, so far as it goes.

But it does not take account of the fact that desire for new goods, or the pressure of installment purchases once made, may lead people to work harder or more steadily, and so get more dollars to spend. Presumably the enticements of automobiles and radios, of wrist watches and electric refrigerators, of correspondence courses and college, have steadied many youths, set many girls hunting for jobs and kept many fathers of families to the mark. Also a considerable part of the country's former bill for intoxicants has been available to spend in other ways. How much allowance we should make for these factors nobody knows. All one can say with assurance is that consumption per capita has increased in volume to match the increased per capita output of consumers' goods taken altogether. Yet the increase in consumption has not been rapid enough to prevent shifts in the kind of goods bought from pressing hard upon the makers of articles waning in popular favor.

So too in the realm of producers' goods. Despite the active building campaign, the lumber industry has had hard sledding. Coal mining has not prospered, and can attribute part of its difficulties to other fuels, water power, and more economical ways of burning coal itself. Breeders of draft animals have found their markets cut into by motor vehicles. Railways have lost traffic to trucks and omnibusses—though the loss in freight tonnage is held by Professor Cunningham to be less than the public supposes. Steam-engine builders have had to change their products or reduce their output. It is not necessary to multiply examples; most technical improvements reduce the demand for some other good, and so create difficulties for those who supply the latter.

Geographical Shifts in Industry and Trade

Just as definite a gain may be made in productivity by shifting factories to better locations, or by reorganizing channels of supply, as by installing automatic machines. Besides the drift of cotton manufacturing to the South, of which everyone thinks, and the more recent drift of shoe manufacturing to the West, the chapter on industry shows a prevailing tendency toward geographical decentralizing of production. The proportion of the output of many goods coming from the old headquarters is on the decline. The chapter on agriculture indicates a parallel development in farming. The cotton belt is stretching west, the wheat belt west and north-west; the dairying and the market-garden areas are moving in various directions. Finally, the chapter on marketing shows a concentration of trade in cities and towns at the expense of villages.

Doubtless these changes are to the advantage of those who make them. If they proved unprofitable, they would be abandoned. But it is equally clear that we have here another feature of increasing efficiency which brings losses as well as gains. New England may not lose as much as North Carolina and St. Louis gain from the shifts in the cotton and shoe trades—that is a question of the totals. And New England may devise new ways of using her labor, her capital, her manufacturing sites, and her ingenuity, more profitable than the old—necessity is often the mother of invention. If these efforts succeed, they may create fresh difficulties felt elsewhere. Similar truisms might be recited concerning the other cases in point. But whatever happens in the future, we must not let the dazzle of the high lights blind us to the sectional shadows.

"Technological Unemployment"

Among all the hardships imposed by increasing efficiency, most publicity has been given to the decline in the number of wage earners employed by factories. That is a matter of the gravest concern in view of the millions of families affected or threatened by the change, and in view of their slender resources. To it special attention has been paid in this investigation.

The new phrase coined to describe what is happening, "technological unemployment," designates nothing new in the facts, though the numbers affected may be large beyond precedent. Ever since Ricardo shocked his rigid disciples by admitting that the introduction of "labor-saving" machinery may cause a temporary diminution of employment, economists have discussed this problem. Granting Ricardo's admission, they have nevertheless held that, in the long run, changes in method which heighten efficiency tend to benefit wage earners. English experience since Ricardo's day seems to bear out this contention. The power looms, which put an end to hand-loom weaving after tragic struggles, have not reduced the number of British workers employed in weaving, or cut their average earnings. The railways, which displaced the old mail coaches and carters, have not reduced the number of transport workers or made them poorer. And the new trades of building and caring for the elaborate modern equipment must not be forgotten. There doubtless are cases in which improvments in methods have caused what promises to be a permanent reduction in the number of persons employed in an industry. By defining industry narrowly, these cases can be made numerous. But the broad result plainly has been that the industrial triumphs of the nineteenth century increased the demand for labor and increased its rewards. "Labor-saving" machinery has turned out to be job-making machinery.

To recall these familiar facts should not diminish by one jot our rating of the hardships suffered by men who are thrown out of jobs. They and their families often undergo severe privation before new employment can be found; the new jobs may pay less than the old or be less suitable; too often the displaced man never finds a new opening. Technical progress is continually made at cost to individuals who have committed no fault and committed no avoidable error of judgment. No organized plan has been evolved for preventing such hardships, aside from the schemes devised by some trade unions for tiding their members over mechanical revolutions in their crafts. The nations have left the remedy to "natural forces"; they have trusted that the expansion of production, which improvements bring about, will presently open new places for the displaced workers.

The problem of what happened in the short period 1922–1927, then, is to find how many wage earners were displaced in that time, how many of the displaced found new jobs promptly, and what these new jobs were. To answer these questions accurately would require far better data than are to be had. There are few branches of statistics in which the United States lags further behind the leaders than in statistics of employment. What we have been able to learn comes to this:

Starting with the 1920 census of occupations and reckoning forward, it is estimated that by 1927 there had been an increase of about 5,100,000 employees 16 years of age and over, who looked to nonagricultural occupations for a living. The figure allows for the fact that some 860,000 persons had left the farms to seek livelihoods elsewhere, and the more than offsetting fact that the number of pupils over 15, enrolled in schools and colleges, had risen by 1,430,000 between 1920 and 1927.

Of the 5,100,000 net additions to nonagricultural job seekers, a few turned to mining and allied occupations; 100,000 entered public services, over 600,000 engaged in construction work of some sort, nearly a million attached themselves to "transportation and communication," 1,400,000 became mercantile employees, and more than two and a half millions took to miscellaneous occupations in hotels, restaurants, garages, repair shops, moving-picture places, barber shops, hospitals, insurance work, professional offices, and the like. Manufacturing is the only large occupational group, aside from farming, to show a decline. There the number of employees fell from about 11,200,000 in 1920 to about 10,600,000 in 1927—a drop of 600,000. . . .

All these data are estimates of the net changes in numbers of persons "attached to" the occupations in question. They show that American wage earners met "technological unemployment" in manufacturing mainly by turning to other ways of making a living. The decline from 1920 to 1927 in the number of persons actually at work in manufacturing enterprises is put at 825,000, but the number of *unemployed* among the people who depended on factory work for a living increased only 240,000 between 1920 and 1927, according to the best figures available. If these estimates are approximately correct, then some 585,000 of the workers laid off by factories had taken up other occupations. That is, 71 percent of the workers displaced had attached themselves to new trades by 1927.

Adopting a new occupation, however, does not guarantee getting a new job. The surplus workers from our farms and factories who hunted for fresh openings increased unemployment in other fields. The expansion of business, particularly the expansion of miscellaneous and mercantile occupations, made places for perhaps four and a half million new wage earners. But the supply of new jobs has not been equal to the number of new workers plus the old workers displaced. Hence there has been a net increase of unemployment, between 1920 and 1927, which exceeds 650,000 people.

The number of the unemployed has varied from year to year with cyclical changes in business activity. It surpassed all previous records in the depression of 1921; it declined rather slowly in the revival of 1922; even in the busy year 1923 it remained higher than in 1920; it rose in the mild recession of 1924, declined on the return of activity in 1925–1926, and then mounted again in 1927. The final estimates presented in the chapter on labor may be summarized as follows:

TABLE 1 ESTIMATED AVERAGE MINIMUM VOLUME OF UNEMPLOYMENT IN THE UNITED STATES, 1920–1927

Year	Nonagricultural wage and salary earners	Average minimum number unemployed	Percentage unemployed
1920	27,558,000	1,401,000	5.1
1921	27,989,000	4,270,000	15.3
1922	28,505,000	3,441,000	12.1
1923	29,293,000	1,532,000	5.2
1924	30,234,000	2,315,000	7.7
1925	30,941,000	1,775,000	5.7
1926	31,808,000	1,669,000	5.2
1927	32,695,000	2,055,000	6.3

It must be emphasized that these figures are merely the best estimates which it is possible to make from the scattered and imperfect materials available. They are subject to considerable margins of error. They minimize the seriousness of unemployment. Finally, even as minimum figures, these estimates do not profess to show the high points reached by unemployment in bad seasons—they give only yearly averages.

One may wonder at the versatility, initiative and mobility of Americans, as evidenced afresh by their prompt shifting of occupations on so great a scale in recent years. One may wonder also at the rapid expansion of the trades which have absorbed some five million employees in seven years without reducing wage rates. But one must not forget that these shiftings have been compulsory in large measure; men have been forced out of farming and forced out of factories as well as pulled into automobile services, shops and restaurants. And the employment balance is on the unfavorable side. While our economic progress has meant larger per capita earnings for all workers taken together, it has imposed severe suffering upon hundreds of thousands of individuals.

THE DOMESTIC DIFFICULTIES OF AGRICULTURE

It was noted above that American farming owes part of its difficulties in 1922–1927 to reductions in foreign demand and increases in foreign supply. It must now be added that fresh difficulties have been created for farmers by changes in domestic demand, and by the successful efforts of farmers to increase their own efficiency as producers.

All in all, the standard of living has been rising in the United States of late. But Americans have been eating less food per capita than once they did. The greater diversification of diet has been advantageous to dairymen, market gardeners and fruit growers; but the bulk of farmers have lost more than they have gained from the changes. Americans have also been wearing less clothing than formerly, and that hurts the market for cotton planters and wool growers. Moreover, there has been a shift from cotton and woolen fabrics toward silk and rayon. Finally, the goods on which American families have spent freely—automobiles and their accessories, gasoline, household furnishings, and equipment, radios, travel, amusements and sports—are goods in which little agricultural produce is used.

To make matters harder, the firmness of wage rates in the flourishing industries has forced farmers to pay relatively high wages for such hired labor as they have needed. Taxes on farm property have risen in every year covered by the record. While the prices farmers had to pay for operating supplies and equipment, as well as for consumers' goods, dropped sharply in 1921, they did not drop nearly so much as the prices which farmers received for their products. Fluctuations in the two sets of prices since 1921 have redressed the inequality only in part.

It is a grave error to think of American farmers as the passive but complaining victims of calamity. They have exhibited as vigorous a capacity for self-help as any other large section of the community. The qualities which enabled their forerunners to subdue the wilderness reappear in the efforts of the present generation to work a way out of the postwar tangle.

But agriculture is a business of very slow turnover. Agriculture is also an extrahazardous business, which depends for results on averages over a series of harvests. The dislocations it faces at present are partly the result of continuing secular trends, rather than cyclical fluctuations which reverse themselves every few years. And agriculture is a business in which millions of producers are working each on his own account. A concerted policy is exceedingly difficult to organize. What one farmer does to help himself often makes matters harder for other farmers. That is the aspect of the farm problem which requires attention here.

The individual farmer, hard pressed by low prices and high fixed costs, has tried several ways to better his fortunes. One way alleviates the lot of other farmers, whether it turns out well for himself or not. It is to give up farming. Dr. C. J. Galpin estimates that there was a net decrease of farm population amounting to 460,000 persons in 1922, perhaps a larger number in 1923, 182,000 in 1924 when city jobs were harder to get, and 479,000 in 1926. We have already noticed Dr. M. B. Givens' estimate that in 1920–1927 upwards of a million migrants from the farm sought other occupations. So far as reduction in number of workers goes, there is a close parallel between the record of farming and of manufacturing.[1]

This considerable shift in population has been accompanied by a much slighter decline in the area of land cultivated. The abandonment of poor farms has unquestionably been accelerated by hard times, though we lack comprehensive data to show on what scale. On the other hand, wide tracts of former waste lands have been reclaimed and wider tracts of former cattle ranges have been brought under the plow. The net outcome of these contrary movements is perhaps best shown by the Department of Agriculture's report of the acreage in 19 principal crops. From 351 million acres in 1919, the area declined unsteadily to 342 millions in 1924, rose above 350 millions in 1926, and then shrank by three-quarters of a million acres in 1927.

But the smaller numbers of workers left on farms, cultivating slightly less land, have increased their output—again paralleling developments in manufacturing. The Department of Agriculture's index showing "mass of crop production" mounted from 100 in 1919—a year of fair harvests—to 102 in 1922, 104 in 1925, and 106 in 1927. If these figures were reduced to a per capita basis, the rate of increase would be decidedly greater. Of course, every farmer who has enlarged his output has contributed his mite toward keeping down prices. Agricultural depression had forced the individual farmer to meet his narrow margins above cost by raising more units to sell, and selling more units has tended to make these margins narrower still.

Increased productivity per worker in agriculture has been achieved in the same way as increased productivity per worker in

1. Commenting upon this passage, Dr. E. G. Nourse suggests that this shrinkage in the number of farm workers seems likely to continue. Agriculture bids fair definitely and permanently to lose numbers as a result of changes in technique. The new branches of farming which are growing up take many less hands than are displaced in the old staple lines. Thus the industry as a whole is giving up workers to other callings.

manufacturing—by putting more intelligence into the work. For decades, agricultural experiment stations, colleges, state bureaus, farm papers, and the Department of Agriculture in Washington have been actively seeking to learn and to teach better methods of farming. From drainage to the choice of crops, the breeding of stock and the building of fireplaces, scarcely any feature of farming as a technical process, as a business enterprise, or as a way of making a home but has been studied intensively and written up extensively. Slowly the lessons have been learned by an increasing number of farmers and farmers' wives. The pressure of hard times speeded up the application of knowledge to practice, despite the fact that hard times cut down the farmers' ability to accumulate the capital which many of the changes require.

One of the conspicuous changes in methods of farming has reacted most unfavorably upon the demand for farm products. The number of tractors in use on farms is estimated to have increased from 80,000 in January, 1918, to 380,000 in 1922, and 770,000 in January, 1928. This change has been accompanied by a decrease in the number of horses and mules on farms from about 26,400,000 in 1918 and 1919 to 20,100,000 in 1928. An even greater decline was occurring at the same time in the number of horses and mules in cities. A not inconsiderable branch of animal husbandry thus lost much of its market. What was worse, at least 15 to 18 million acres of hay and grain land lost its market also.

That with all their courage and ability farmers have not yet succeeded in regaining their former measure of prosperity, must be ascribed partly to the slowness of agricultural processes themselves, partly to the halting recuperation of Europe and its reactions on other countries, and partly to the fact that increasing efficiency has added to the supply of farm products or cut down the demand.

Agricultural depression has not been confined to the United States. In many other countries, the tillers of the soil have been engaged in a similar struggle with unfavorable conditions of supply and demand. Their efforts to make up for the relatively low prices received for their products by marketing larger quantities, and their compulsory retrenchments of expenditure, have reacted unfavorably upon the fortunes of American farmers, just as the similar actions of American farmers have made conditions harder for them. Round a good part of the globe, the productivity of agriculture has been rising, while in most of the leading industrial nations other branches of production have grown slowly if at all. The effect upon prices in the great world markets has been striking. The demand for agricultural products as a whole is inelastic compared with the demand for many industrial products. That is, a relatively small increase in the current supply of foodstuffs, the great agricultural staple, brings a relatively large decline in market prices. Hence the change in the international balance of agricultural and nonagricultural output has created a difficult situation for farmers, even in the few countries, like the United States, where production in other lines has increased rapidly.

What has been the net effect of all the factors, domestic and foreign, influencing the economic fortunes of American farmers, is hard to ascertain. The preceding chapters on agriculture and on national income present the facts from various angles. That is desirable; for no simple summary of so complicated a situation can be adequate. But perhaps the following figures, which purport to show the changing relations between the average per capita incomes of farmers and of the whole population, are as significant as any which might be chosen.

Though the estimates from which these percentages are drawn . . . are the best results our investigators have been able to get from the available data, they are subject to an uncertain margin of error. That the figures differ in certain respects from what most people, including our investigators themselves, would expect to find is not seriously disturbing; for expectations in such matters are notoriously biased by cases which have impressed our minds because of their striking character.

TABLE 2 ESTIMATED PER CAPITA INCOMES OF AMERICAN FARMERS AS PERCENTAGES OF ESTIMATED PER CAPITA INCOMES OF THE TOTAL POPULATION, IN VARIOUS YEARS

Prewar years		Postwar years	
1913	39 percent	1919	57 percent
1914	39 percent	1920	46 percent
		1921	34 percent
		1922	35 percent
		1923	36 percent
		1924	37 percent
		1925	39 percent

On the face of these returns, American farmers gained greatly in relative economic status between the beginning and the end of the war, though, even at their peak, agricultural incomes per capita remained far below the national average. The catastrophic drop from 1919 to 1921 wiped out all of this gain and considerably more. If our estimates are reliable, by 1925 farmers had won back to their prewar position in comparison with average per capita incomes in other occupations, but they were by no means so well off as in 1919–1920. Unfortunately, the data for similar computations in years since 1925 are not yet available.

Even if these results be accepted as probably more reliable than general impressions, they do not represent adequately the farmer's relative position in the national economy. In particular, they show nothing of the financial entanglements into which many of the most enterprising American farmers were drawn in the flush years. A man may make as good a current income now as before the war and still be far worse off, if he is carrying a greatly increased load of debts. And quite apart from that, the not unfavorable income comparison which 1925 makes with prewar years is due to the use of shrinking per capita figures for farmers and swelling per capita figures for the total population. An industry which keeps up its per capita quota of the national income because thousands of workers withdrew from it cannot be regarded as flourishing.

The Interrelations among Economic Changes

The Factors Already Discussed

So far, the contrasts noted at the outset of this chapter between the economic fortunes of different income groups, different industries, and different sections of the United States in 1922–1927, have been traced to three factors—or rather to three great complexes of factors. (1) Foreign conditions on the whole have been none too favorable to American business, and they have been eminently unfavorable to American agriculture. Important branches of industry have enjoyed a large increase in foreign sales; but had Europe been prosperous, American prosperity would have been less "spotty" and more intense.[2] (2) Such prosperity as we have enjoyed has been earned by many-sided and strenuous efforts, in which millions of people have shared, to improve our technical methods, our business management, our trade-union policy, and our government administration. (3) While increasing efficiency

2. Once more the reader is reminded that this summary deals only with broad features. Important details, passed by in silence here, are brought out in the preceding chapters.

has added to real income, it has put pressure, often rising to severe hardship, upon competitors, direct and indirect. The factory hand competing with the "automatic" machine, the horse farmer competing with the tractor farmer, the lumber industry competing with the cement industry, the New England cotton mill competing with the North Carolina cotton mill, the independent retailer competing with the chain store, the clothing trade competing with the makers of automobiles and radios for slices of the consumers' dollars, have had a hard time.

The analysis is not simple, but it is still too schematic. There is no hope of learning and telling the whole story in realistic detail. Yet one further factor of great moment and two sets of "economic ractions" must be introduced before a summing up is attempted.

Retardation in the Growth of Population and Its Effects

The additional factor to be taken into account concerns population growth. In sketching the main lines of nineteenth-century experience, it was noted that the fruits of the tree of applied knowledge can be consumed in several ways. One way is to increase population as fast as the tree increases its yield. If that course is pushed to the limit, there can be no reduction of working hours and no advance in the standard of living. The latter gains are contingent upon keeping the growth of population slower than the gain in productive efficiency. And before the close of the century the European stock had sensibly reduced its birth rate.

This reduction of birth rates has been going on during our period in most of the states of the union. The decline seems to be more rapid than the decline in death rates. Moreover, first the war and then legislation restricted immigration. The chapter on labor sums up the results in the following way:

	Net immigration into the United States	Average per year
Prewar period July 1, 1907–June 30, 1914	4,645,590	663,656
War and early postwar period July 1, 1914–June 30, 1921	1,253,652	179,093
Quota-restriction period July 1, 1921–June 30, 1927	1,873,311	312,219

Combined, the birth-rate and death-rate changes and the changes in migration reduced the average annual increase of population from 1,800,000 in 1920–1925 to 1,545,000 in 1925–1928.

The retardation in population growth has affected the whole social situation profoundly in ways which concern the student of sociology and politics quite as deeply as they concern the economist. It will be long before the full effects upon national life become clear. But certain prompt economic consequences must be noted.

At the close of the war, when a fall in the price level like that of 1865 was expected by many, business executives frequently said that the first task of reorganization was to "liquidate labor." The great buying campaign of 1919 and the accompanying uprush of prices caused a postponement of this program. For a time it was hard to get men enough, even at rising rates. When prices fell precipitously in 1920–1921 and unemployment was rife, the moment to insist on wage reductions seemed to have come. But the trade unions offered strenuous resistance, despite the number of the temporarily idle. Their resistance was more effective than it could have been had not the growth of population been retarded for some years. The prices of labor were cut, to be sure, but not cut as much as the prices of consumers' goods. Hence, when employment became tolerably full again toward the close of 1922, wage earners found themselves in possession of relatively large purchasing power. Then the economic advantages of a broad consumers' market began to appear. Employers discovered that their inability to "liquidate labor" had been fortunate for themselves, as well as for their employees. The doctrine of high wages found conspicuous champions among the business leaders, and their formulations favored its spread. Discoveries in science, as well as in practical life, have often been made thus by observing the consequences of a thwarted effort.

In most periods of prosperity, wage rates lag somewhat behind living costs on the rise. The indications are that these paradoxical "prosperity losses" to wage earners have not cut much figure during 1922–1927. Wholesale prices have sagged slightly, and living costs have advanced but little. Though the percentage of unemployment has risen since 1923, wage rates have been firmly maintained on the whole, if not increased somewhat.

This result also must be ascribed in part to the relatively slow increase in the number of job hunters. Had there been no legal check on immigration in 1922–1927, unemployment would have attained large proportions, and the difficulty of maintaining wage rates would have been greater.

Moreover, it seems sound to ascribe a part of the gains in technical efficiency, which have been so characteristic of recent years, to the high price of labor. An employee to whom one pays high wages may represent low labor cost. But if he is to be so efficient as to be cheap, he must be provided with good equipment and aided by good management. More horse power per man and better management per man, to twist Mr. Dennison's flexible phrase, are needed to secure more production per man; and more production must be had per man when more wages are paid per man.

All this discussion on a per capita basis is proper; to make clear how proper, consider the effect of retardation in population growth upon aggregate production and wealth. Had there been no reduction in birth rates and no restriction of immigration, the United States would contain several millions more people than it does. As large or a larger fraction of the greater population would be "engaged in gainful occupations," and, despite more unemployment and a less advanced stage of industrial technique, the workers would probably be producing a greater volume of goods. Thus, the national income would be rising faster than it is; but per capita income would be growing slower than it is. Since birthrate restriction seems to be voluntary, and since immigration restriction certainly is, we must conclude that Americans are preferring to raise the economic level of average life rather than to maximize national wealth.

Mutually Moderating and Mutually Intensifying Reactions

The two sets of economic reactions still to be noted may be thought of as the mutually moderating effects of factors opposing each other, and as the mutually intensifying effects of factors working in the same direction.

Like the set of economic reactions already discussed—the pressure exerted on competitors by those who increase their own efficiency—these moderating and intensifying effects arise from the basic feature of economic organization. Though modern society accepts the principle of individual responsibility, each individual gets his money income wholly by serving others, and gets his real income mainly by consuming goods other people have made. Thus everyone depends both on the buying power of other consumers and on the efficiency of other producers. And what is true of every individual is true, *mutatis mutandis,* of every business enterprise. These intricate relations of interdependence tangle the skein of economic causes and effects beyond the present power of man to unravel. Every development is the net resultant of numerous causes and also the cause of numerous effects. But though we cannot disentangle all the crisscrossing influences of the factors which have shaped American fortunes in 1922–1927, we can follow certain of their salient reactions upon each other.

To take first the moderating effects of opposing factors: American prosperity in 1922–1927, in nonagricultural lines, would have been decidedly greater had the six million American farmers been flourishing. Every man thrown out of work has subtracted an iota from the national dividend and an iota from the demand for goods. Every business that has failed has made a tiny difference in our ability to provide for our wants and to market our products. The United States as a whole would have been better off if all foreign countries had enjoyed fortunes equal to its own.

On the other hand, the farmers would have been in far worse plight if the majority of Americans had not been receiving relatively large incomes, and if American factories and railways had not been highly efficient as servants of agriculture. So too, the unemployed would have been more numerous, and their difficulties in getting new jobs greater, had the country suffered from industrial depression. Finally, other countries would have been worse off, had we not been in position to import freely, and to make large loans.

There can be no doubt about the reality or the importance of these reactions of hardship in diminishing prosperity, and of prosperity in diminishing hardship. But there seems to be no way of measuring such complicated influences with the data available.

Clearer still are the effects of one favorable development in reinforcing other favorable developments, and the corresponding intensification of misfortune by misfortune. In this period and in our country, the former set of cumulations has been more in evidence than the latter. And it is necessary to bring these reactions of favorable developments upon each other into the foreground of our final picture. For we cannot understand any single factor in the situation, such as increasing technological efficiency, the rising standard of living, the relatively stable price level, the large volume of construction, the abundance of capital and credit, or large income disbursements, without noting how other factors favored its development.

Take, for example, keener intelligence applied to the day's work, which increased the physical output of goods. That has meant the possibility of larger average real incomes per capita. To distribute these goods, market experts cultivated the desires of the people for a freer and more varied consumption, they developed plans by which the eager could satisfy wants before they could pay. A sound monetary and banking system provided the requisite currency and credit to run this whole process of producing and distributing a swelling river of goods. Price fluctuations were held within narrow limits by a combination of prudence among business men, unit-cost reductions by technical experts, skill on the part of bankers, and the course of foreign markets. This relative stability of prices reinforced the pressure upon all parties to exercise caution, calculate closely, and watch costs; it also helped to keep world prices relatively stable. Since prices were not buoyant, business enterprises had to maintain a high level of efficiency in order to make profits, and that fact intensified the application of intelligence with which this paragraph started. By the aid of the reinforced efficiency, it has been possible to pay high wages and salaries, meet interest and rental charges, distribute liberal dividends, and still retain large surpluses for protecting or expanding business ventures. The large income disbursements provided the purchasing power to which the market experts appealed for the purchase of the increased physical output of goods. Meanwhile, the considerable profits reaped by the large number of efficient enterprises made them eager to grow. At the same time, prosperous families wanted better housing; prosperous communities wanted larger schools; prosperous states wanted hard-surfaced roads. So the routine business of providing current income was supplemented by an exceptional volume of new construction to provide industrial equipment of all kinds, office buildings, single dwellings, apartments, hotels, theaters, schools and highways. That required capital running into billions of dollars. The demand was met without strain from the surpluses of business enterprises and the savings of individuals whose higher standards of living had not absorbed all of their money incomes. And of course the construction work, as it proceeded, enlarged the market for a vast variety of goods, and enlarged the disbursements of income.

So one might go on indefinitely, tracing the fashion in which each of the prosperity-producing factors in the situation has increased the activity out of which it grew, and thus promoted conditions which heightened its own efficiency. The broad facts, however, are patent. And no elaboration would lead to a convincing evaluation of what credit belongs to any single factor taken by itself. Drop out any of the developments recalled in the preceding paragraph, and the process as a whole would be altered. It is just as impossible to say what high wages, large construction, skillful marketing, railroad efficiency, or abundant credit contributed to prosperity, as it is to say how much agricultural depression, technological unemployment, or the lingering troubles of Europe have diminished the prosperity which might have been attained but for these drawbacks.

Net Effects upon Average Per Capita Income

Reasons were given above for accepting the estimate of per capita income, expressed in dollars of constant purchasing power, as the most inclusive, and probably the most reliable, summary of the net results flowing from all the myriad changes which affect the economic welfare of the country's people. Accordingly, we return to these figures as the best general conclusion of the whole investigation. Two series of figures are given. The first shows income received in money; the second "disbursed income"—that is, money receipts plus the value of income yielded by homes occupied by their owners and by household goods, the value of farm produce consumed by the producers and minor items of similar nature. The first series corresponds closely to the common conception of income, but the other is a better index of economic welfare. The following comments refer to the second series.[3]

From the trough in which the war and the war-dominated cycle of 1919–1921 left the country, Americans raised their average for-

3. The difference between income received in money and disbursed income appears to be decreasing rapidly in relation to total income, with some indications of an absolute decrease as well. Presumably this change is explained, in part, by the increasing percentage of the population that lives in rented quarters.—Note by M. C. Rorty, Director.

TABLE 10 PER CAPITA INCOME IN THE UNITED STATES EXPRESSED IN 1925 DOLLARS

	Income received in money	Disbursed income
1913	$554	$621
1917	579	656
1919	510	611
1920	520	600
1921	500	576
1922	557	625
1923	616	679
1924	628	697
1925	647	714
1926	659[a]	733[a]

[a] Preliminary.

tunes to the prewar level in a single year of reviving activity. A second year of great gains left the old records far behind. Since 1923, progress has been steady, but less rapid.

Unless these figures are very far in error, not only absolutely but also relatively, the final verdict upon the years 1922–1926, and presumably upon 1927 and 1928, for which the income record is yet incomplete, must be that they brought good times to the majority of our people—though by no means to all.

41. Disaster on Wall Street: *New York Times*

LINDBERGH'S FLIGHT, *it turned out, was not the most publicized event of the 1920s. That honor went to the terrible stock market crash that took place from mid-September to mid-November, 1929, with the phase of most rapid decline in late October. An article from the* New York Times, *Friday, October 30, describes the damage of the previous day.*

Stocks Collapse

Stock prices virtually collapsed yesterday, swept downward with gigantic losses in the most disastrous trading day in the stock market's history. Billions of dollars in open market values were

SOURCE: *New York Times*, October 30, 1929.

wiped out as prices crumbled under the pressure of liquidation of securities which had to be sold at any price.

There was an impressive rally just at the close, which brought many leading stocks back from 4 to 14 points from their lowest points of the day.

Trading on the New York Stock Exchange aggregated 16,410,030 shares; on the Curb, 7,096,300 shares were dealt in. Both totals far exceeded any previous day's dealings.

From every point of view, in the extent of losses sustained, in total turnover in the number of speculators wiped out, the day was the most disastrous in Wall Street's history. Hysteria swept the country and stocks went overboard for just what they would bring at forced sale.

Efforts to estimate yesterday's market losses in dollars are futile because of the vast number of securities quoted over-the-counter and on out-of-town exchanges on which no calculations are possible. However, it was estimated that 880 issues, on the New York Stock Exchange, lost between $8,000,000,000 and $9,000,000,000 yesterday. Added to that loss is to be reckoned the depreciation on issues on the Curb Market, in the over-the-counter market and on other exchanges.

There were two cheerful notes, however, which sounded through the pall of gloom which overhung the financial centres of the country. One was the brisk rally of stocks at the close, on tremendous buying by those who believe that prices have sunk too low. The other was that the liquidation has been so violent, as well as widespread, that many bankers, brokers and industrial leaders expressed the belief last night that it now has run its course.

A further note of optimism in the soundness of fundamentals was sounded by the directors of United States Steel Corporation and the American Can Company, each of which declared an extra dividend of $1 a share at their late afternoon meetings.

Banking support, which would have been impressive and successful under ordinary circumstances, was swept violently aside, as block after block of stock, tremendous in proportions, deluged the market. Bid prices placed by bankers, industrial leaders and brokers trying to halt the decline were crashed through violently, their orders were filled, and quotations plunged downward in a day of disorganization, confusion and financial impotence.

While even the tremendous buying power of the banking group

was unable to turn the tide of selling in yesterday's market, the group did not relax its concern over the situation on the Exchange. Two meetings were held during the day, one at noon and one at 4:30 P.M., the latter lasting until 6:30 P.M.

After the evening meeting Thomas W. Lamont of J. P. Morgan & Co. spoke to reporters.

"I want to take occasion," Mr. Lamont said, "to explain again, as heretofore, that the banking group was organized to offer certain support in the market and to act as far as possible as somewhat of a stabilizing factor.

"It was not the intention of the group to attempt to maintain prices, but to maintain a free market; in other words, to correct the condition that prevailed last Thursday.

"The group has continued and will continue in a cooperative way to support the market and has not been a seller of stocks."

The statement was issued at the request of reporters to quiet rumors which had been abroad that the banking group had been selling stocks instead of supporting them.

These rumors were, of course, without foundation, for the group is known to have purchased heavily in directions where the force of its buying power would be most effective in stemming demoralization. It was reliably reported that in many instances when no bids could be obtained on the floor for large blocks of stocks forced on the market the group had supplied the necessary bids and in other instances had acted as a stabilizing influence upon the list as a whole.

Yesterday's market crash was one which largely affected rich men, institutions, investment trusts and others who participate in the stock market on a broad and intelligent scale. It was not the margin traders who were caught in the rush to sell, but the rich men of the country who are able to swing blocks of 5,000, 10,000 up to 100,000 shares of high-priced stocks. They went overboard with no more consideration than the little trader who was swept out on the first day of the markets upheaval, whose prices, even at their lowest of last Thursday, now look high in comparison.

The market on the rampage is no respecter of persons. It wasted fortune after fortune away yesterday and financially crippled thousands of individuals in all parts of the world. It was not until after the market had closed that the financial district began to realize that a good-sized rally had taken place and that there was a stopping place on the down-grade for good stocks.

The market has now passed through three days of collapse, and so violent has it been that most authorities believe that the end is not far away. It started last Thursday, when 12,800,000 shares were dealt in on the Exchange, and holders of stocks commenced to learn just what a decline in the market means. This was followed by a moderate rally on Friday and entirely normal conditions on Saturday, with fluctuations on a comparatively narrow-scale and with the efforts of the leading bankers to stabilize the market evidently successful. But the storm broke anew on Monday, with prices slaughtered in every direction, to be followed by yesterday's tremendous trading of 16,410,030 shares.

Sentiment had been generally unsettled since the first of September. Market prices had then reached peak levels, and, try as they would, pool operators and other friends of the market could not get them higher. It was a gradual downward sag, gaining momentum as it went on, then to break out into an open market smash in which the good, the bad and indifferent stocks went down alike. Thousands of traders were able to weather the first storm and answered their margin calls; thousands fell by the wayside Monday and again yesterday, unable to meet the demands of their brokers that their accounts be protected.

There was no quibbling at all between customer and broker yesterday. In any case where margin became thin a peremptory call went out. If there was no immediate answer the stock was sold out "at the market" for just what it would bring. Thousands sold out on the decline and amid the confusion, found themselves in debt to their brokers last night.

42. Unemployment in 1931: Jacob Billikopf

In most respects the economic depression reached a reasonably stable bottom—like a ship on the ocean floor—during the summer of 1932. Conditions among the unemployed and those reduced to part-time or sporadic work already were awful in mid-1931, but hope existed even among realistic observers that further suffering could be alleviated and that the situation soon would improve. A realistic appraisal of the contemporary economic travail, mixed with a remnant of optimism is presented below. It was difficult to imagine then that the conditions described could and would become much worse.

In the day of prosperity be joyful, and in the day of adversity consider. Ecclesiastes 7:14.

With the possible exception of the World War, no phenomenon has arisen in our contemporary life fraught with such consequences as the unemployment problem. There are now between six and seven million men and women out of work in this country. Perhaps as many are working part time. And there are millions whose wages, by a process of nibbling, have been reduced during the past eighteen months from 10 to 30 percent, these reductions being more severe and widespread in the nonprofit, unstable industries, such as textiles. All this has come about despite the sincere and well-meant gestures of President Hoover and his Cabinet, demanding that employers should live up to the wage truce, alleged to have been entered into in January 1930—a promise which, in the nature of subsequent developments, could not have been worth the paper on which it was written.

In this connection I should like to remind those now urging that wage earners should share in the deflation, that real wages—by which is meant wages in relation to cost—never were inflated. Dr. Julius Klein is my authority for the statement that from 1921 to 1929 real wages increased only 13 percent; that during the same

Source: Jacob Billikopf, "What Have We Learned about Unemployment?," *Proceedings of the National Conference of Social Work* (Chicago, 1931), pp. 25–49. Reprinted by permission of The University of Chicago Press.

period returns to industrialists grew 72 percent. Meantime, dividends on industrial and rail stocks increased 256 percent.

The subject of wages might be approached from the purely personal angle. During the past eight years it has been my privilege to act as impartial chairman of the men's clothing industry in the City of New York. Week after week I am called upon to adjudicate disputes between capital and labor in a complicated and unstable industry. Naturally, the question of wages frequently comes up. I should like to invite the president of the American Bankers Association—and there are many like him who honestly and sincerely believe the quickest way to the restoration of prosperity lies in a reduction of wages—to sit in at one of our industrial sessions and advise me whether, in his judgment, any further cuts should be made in the wages of the coat maker, the pants maker and vest maker, bearing in mind that at no time in the history of the clothing industry during the past decade, even in the most prosperous years, have these workers averaged, in the City of New York, more than thirty or thirty-one weeks' employment a year. What is true of those in the garment industries, both men's and women's—and they constitute the largest single industry in the City of New York—is likewise true of a number of other industries throughout the country. I would have my distinguished guest remember that, during the past year, the garment workers, with the exception of the cutters, were fortunate to be engaged as many as eighteen full weeks. So much, then, for the question of wages, and I am not concerning myself at this moment with a presentation of the firmly established premise that our national prosperity is predicated, in large measure, on a high-wage basis.

Now, whatever may have been the original cause or causes of the severe depression which began two years ago, today the situation is so complicated that it would be the height of folly to select one, two, or even three major causes and say: "Let us solve these and end the depression." But, because there is such a growing public belief that our difficulties are largely, if not entirely, mental or psychic, that all we have to do is to practice the formula of Coué, I should like to present for consideration only two out of a large number of purely external economic factors which are constantly affecting our national situation and which complicate the many problems growing out of unemployment.

A year ago Owen D. Young delivered a notable address in San

Francisco, under the auspices of the National Electric and Light Association. In it, among other things, Mr. Young said:

> What is to be our National policy with regard to our surplus? Take the surplus of our mines and factories. We cannot overlook the fact that in 1927 we produced 51 percent of the world's copper, 72 percent of its oil and 42 percent of its pig iron. The output per man in our factories has been rapidly increasing since 1917. Using that year as 100, in the electrical manufacturing industry it is in excess of 164, and in the automotive industry it is approximately 200. It is therefore clear that as our production per man increases in our factories, and goes beyond the power of our consumption, we must export that surplus or have corresponding unemployment in those industries.

On May 25, 1930, 1,066 leading American economists and students of international relations submitted to President Hoover a memorandum, two essential features of which were these: Already our factories supply our people with over 96 percent of the manufactured goods they consume. Our producers look to foreign markets to absorb the increasing output of their machines. Many of our citizens have invested their money in foreign enterprises. The Department of Commerce has estimated that such investments, quite aside from the war debts, amounted to nearly $14,000,000,000 on January 1, 1929. These investors, too, would suffer if restrictive duties were to be increased, since such action would make it still more difficult for foreign debtors to pay the interest due them.

In a word, there was a large body of intelligent public opinion to the effect that increased restrictive duties, such as were contemplated by the Smoot-Hawley Bill, would not only seriously impair our export trade, but would also encourage concerns with higher costs to increase production and thus compel the consumer to subsidize waste and inefficiency in industry.

What was the response to Mr. Young's plea and to the memorandum of the 1,066 economists? We proceeded to establish a high, fantastic tariff structure, which tended further to complicate our already disturbed situation. Let me illustrate. In 1910 our exports to South American countries amounted to $300,000,000. By 1930 they had risen to more than $2,000,000,000. Shortly after his election, Mr. Hoover went to South America on what was euphoniously termed a "good will mission"—in reality, an effort to consolidate and strengthen our favorable trade relations with Latin

American countries. Those of us who are fairly familiar with sentiment in the twenty-one South American republics are only too poignantly aware of their resentment and bitterness as to our tariff legislation, already expressing itself in the Argentine and neighboring countries in the following slogan: "We will buy from those who buy from us."

Take the automobile industry. One out of every ten persons in this country is, directly or indirectly, dependent for a livelihood on the automotive industry. The drop in our automobile exports alone, in a year, amounted to a sum sufficient to keep the entire motor industry of the United States running on full time for a month. The operation of that one industry affects dozens of others, and the consequent loss in wages represents a huge sum.

And there is our neighbor to the north—Canada. During the Canadian election campaign of 1930, many Canadians were led to believe that the Hawley-Smoot Tariff is a menace to the Dominion's economic independence, and that absorption by the United States was inevitable unless there were reprisals. The Liberal administration was defeated and the Conservative government now in power is pledged to a policy of economic nationalism. The new Canadian government is erecting tariff barriers which they hope will ultimately cut off two-thirds of the $900,000,000 of imports from the United States. If this comes about Canada will have ceased to be our best customer. Moreover, our higher tariffs already have led to the establishment of American branch plants in Canada—nearly a hundred—with further loss of employment by American workers.

> Today the whole nation has more profound reason for solicitude in the promotion of our foreign trade than ever before . . . to insure continuous employment and maintain our wages we must find a profitable market. Every nation loses by the poverty of another. Every nation gains by the prosperity of another.

These words were uttered by Herbert Hoover, then a candidate for the presidency, at Boston, October 15, 1928.

Let me present still another external economic factor which has been endangering and will continue increasingly to imperil our national situation. If I speak to you about Russia it is because I agree with Senator Borah that Russia is the most stupendous reality in international affairs. It is unnecessary to belabor the point that Russian Communism or State Capitalism, as I view it, is a challenge or a menace to our American civilization. Although I would not sympathize with the procedure to which I shall refer, I can readily understand why the forty capitalist countries in the world might wish to band themselves together and try in every way possible to eliminate that menace. Before me, then, I have a mental picture of the delegates of these forty countries, gathered in Washington, London, or Paris, and being appealed to by Winston Churchill, with his caustic logic and impeccable English, or by Hamilton Fish—the less said about his logic, the better. I visualize one of these gentlemen addressing the delegates in the following manner:

Russian communism is a monster which threatens to destroy us. It threatens our morals, our religion, our system of ethics. It is particularly dangerous to our system of private property, which has taken three hundred years to build up. In a word, it is a serious menace to our glorious civilization.

In 1918 and 1919, those of us who represented the Allies spent hundreds of millions of dollars to equip the armies of Kolchak, Denikin, Wrangle, Yudenich, and other Russian ex-generals, to help them destroy the Bolsheviki. True, as they were marching from the Crimea to Petrograd, some of these White Armies, led by Denikin and Yudenich, butchered tens of thousands of innocent Jewish men, women and children. This is deplorable. But, had they gained their objective, the price would not, perhaps, have been too high. However, when they reached Petrograd, that vagrant and irresponsible journalist, Leon Trotsky—he who, though in exile, is carrying on some vicious propaganda through the radical columns of the *Saturday Evening Post*—consolidated the various scattered armies and stiffened their resistance, with the result that on the military front we were a complete failure.

At this moment Russia is engaged in her five-year diabolical plan. When it was first conceived we belittled it. We looked upon it with contempt. We said the Russian peasant was so constituted physically and psychologically that it would be at least a quarter or half century before he could become oriented to our civilization, our industrial technique and our technological devices. But, so great has been its progress and so alarming its developments, that this monster threatens to destroy us and we must kill it.

There are two ways of effectively proceeding: first, let us cease selling goods to Russia; second, let us place an embargo on her products.

Speaking for myself, continues Hamilton Fish, I shall use whatever influence I possess to withdraw the 2,500 American engineers now in Russia and the $225,000,000 worth of investments on the part of such American enterprises as General Motors, General Electric, Ford, etc. And to show you what actually could be achieved, I am proud to say that already the Washington Chapter of the Daughters of the American Revolution has served notice on some of the shopkeepers in the capital that unless they cease selling Russian candy they will be boycotted!

All of which sounds reasonable and quite practical. But let us look into the currents and crosscurrents to see what actually has happened in the Russian situation. After 1925 our exports to Russia increased year by year, so that during the fiscal year 1929–1930, they amounted to nearly $150,000,000, giving employment to tens of thousands of people. During the past two fiscal years Soviet imports from the United States have been about 45 percent of Soviet imports from all of Europe. More significant is the fact that during 1930 our exports to the Soviet increased 35 percent, while our total exports were declining 27 percent. Russia is the only important nation that increased its purchases here during the depression. But, a year or so ago, Congressman Hamilton Fish discovered that there were Communists on every corner and he was determined to rid our country of a "pernicious political phantasmagoria." A congressional committee was appointed. At a cost of $60,000 a report of twenty volumes was submitted. It created considerable hysteria throughout the country and naturally produced repercussions in Russia. Our trade with that country has fallen off sharply since January, 1931, and is likely to dwindle to small proportions.

Should we be greatly concerned about the loss of $150,000,000 worth of trade with Russia? Not at all, if we can only exterminate Bolshevism. Perhaps the loss of even a billion dollars' worth of trade would not be an excessive price for such a consummation! is the plea of men like Ambassador Edge, who insists that "for the sake of passing profits we must not be parties to economic suicide."

Let us now see how the other capitalist countries in Europe are responding to the pleas of Winston Churchill or Hamilton Fish. Within the past six months virtually every important one has entered into trade relations with Russia, and on terms highly favorable to that country. Some of them are guaranteeing exporters against loss to the extent of 75 percent of the value of the goods produced for export to Russia. Only a few days ago, credits of more than $25,000,000 were extended to the Soviet government under partial guaranty of the British Treasury. These moneys will be used for "heavy engineering." The government guarantees 60 percent of the Soviet purchase and the manufacturers concerned the remaining 40 percent, and the credit is for thirteen months. With Italy the Soviets recently concluded a trade agreement under which Italy will take cheap oil, grain, coal, and timber against delivery of machinery, automobiles, cables, and electrical goods. Under the present agreement the German Reich guarantees 75 percent of the credits extended by industry to Russia over a period of eighteen months. Mind you, these credits by Italy, Germany, England, France, and other countries are extended to Russia out of the billions you and I have loaned to the continental countries during the past decade.

Did I say that it was Winston Churchill, most brilliant, most bitter, and most Chauvinist British archenemy of the Bolsheviks; did I say it was he who urged the delegates of the forty capitalist countries not to trade with Russia? I was mistaken, because only several weeks ago Winston Churchill concluded a debate in the House of Commons with an argument which, boiled down, meant this: "Let us break our diplomatic relations with the Soviet Union, for if we do we shall receive more Soviet orders. America proves it."

And Commander Locker-Lampson, who believed Lenin was paid by the Germans and Gandhi by the Bolsheviks, said in the House of Commons: "There is no one on this side of the House who is against trade with Russia. We signed the trade agreement of 1921 and voted for it. We would vote again for agreements that would facilitate and encourage trade with that great country. We are ready to trade with morons or with anybody else who is ready to pay." And, during the year 1930, Russia exported to European countries nearly $350,000,000 worth of goods.

Hugh Cooper, the noted American engineer, responsible for that great engineering project over the Dnieper, is obviously on sound ground when he says that world economic prosperity and, to an even greater extent, world peace, depends on what we decide to do about Russia.

> It will not suffice to formulate discriminative embargoes and boycotts simply out of dislike for the Soviet Government; hate never produced any collective or individual good in the world and never will. It is time to realize that the Soviet Union is a fact that has got

to be reckoned with, that it cannot be made to disappear by incantations.

In any event it must be obvious that while we are talking about embargoes, the Soviet Union—and I am quoting Max Litvinoff—"has concluded the most important industrial contracts in Germany and Italy, is extending trade with England and other European industrial countries and is entering into negotiations with countries which have hitherto hesitated in this respect." All of which has a direct bearing on our unemployment situation.

Whatever one may think of Russia and its dictatorship, so ruthless at times that no lover of democracy can sympathize, Russia is today the only world group working on a plan for industry as a whole.

> And public, not individual interest, is the base on which that plan rests. It makes no difference to us industrially whether that plan is being forced upon Russia by a minority or a majority: it exists and that is our one concern. The man who believes that unenlightened small units, the fulcrum for whose mental levers is self-interest alone, can meet and beat that menace, unaided by close and hearty cooperation, lacks intelligence. The real problem is this—under our system can such cooperation be obtained through education of the units as to permit us successfully to compete with an industry where the operation of units is commanded by a single voice—the government—and in the public interest, without much regard to the profit of the individual.

The views just expressed are the sentiments—and I quote him literally—of Thomas L. Chadbourne, noted corporation lawyer and author of the "Chadbourne Plan" for the control of sugar production. Mr. Chadbourne has arrived at the conclusion, which so many of us share, that the advocates of unrestrained and unenlightened competition, as it exists today, are the best friends of the Russian Bolshevik theory, while the advocates of collective leadership in each industry are the best foes of the Bolshevists.

As I see the situation in this country, I am firmly convinced that sooner or later we, too, will have to heed the advice of such splendid economists as George Soule, Stuart Chase, Charles Beard, and Louis Lorwin, and introduce the element of control in our processes of production and distribution, if we are ever to stabilize employment.

Now, what has been the attitude of our national government

toward those external economic factors of which I have mentioned only two, and which are constantly affecting our national situation? What about the great variety of purely internal economic factors, such as technological unemployment, our agrarian problem, etc.? Just what has been the reaction of our national government? It has been a policy of laissez faire—leave things alone and they will right themselves. This theory was born in the minds of Adam Smith and other economists, who saw industry as a spinning wheel, a hand loom, a blacksmith at his anvil, and the farmer with his scythe.

Let me state here, lest what is to follow is misunderstood, that there is no man in American life for whom I have greater sympathy than for Mr. Hoover. He came to the presidency heralded as one of the greatest humanitarians of all time. Hailed as an engineer and administrator of the highest constructive genius, he was not only going to consolidate all the then existing elements in our prosperity but to usher in a new era of unprecedented prosperity. Few presidents before him can have suffered so many slings and arrows of outrageous fortune. Yet, as one who believes that the doctrine of laissez faire died long ago, I deplore the fact that in these days of strain and stress, of social, political and economic flux, our official thinking should still be dominated by the philosophy contained in *American Individualism*, a book Mr. Hoover wrote in 1923. In fact, those of you who read the president's recent speeches at the Clara Barton Memorial Exercises and his "Odyssey" at Valley Forge, must have discovered that whatever Liberalism was contained in *American Individualism* has virtually evaporated.

For a period of twelve or fifteen months we were told that if we only repeated the formula of Coué—every day in every way industrial conditions are getting better and better—the depression would come to an end. Some mental experts there were, and still are, in Washington, who even insist that a repetition of the formula was unnecessary; all we had to do was to go around the corner and there we would find abundant prosperity. It is my opinion, although I have no statistical data on which to base it, that as a result of this imperturbable and stupid optimism, tens of thousands of men and women rushed back into the stock market, not in a spirit of gambling, but to recoup their lost fortunes or equalize their holdings, with the result that hundreds of millions of dollars must have been lost in the two or three major breaks which followed the Wall Street debacle of October 1929.

On the occasion of the first anniversary of that disastrous event, Mr. Hoover lifted the moratorium, and we were told that there was such a thing as "honest distress," although I have never been able to determine just what that phrase implied. The services of Colonel Arthur Woods were requisitioned to mobilize various forces in the country, so that "honest distress" might be relieved. No sooner had he reached Washington than social workers began to furnish him with statistics to the effect that the situation was well in hand; that suffering would be relieved during the approaching winter months. Did not many community chests in the country reach their quotas? Did not some of them exceed the quotas of previous years? Look at Florence, South Carolina. Look at Pottstown, Pennsylvania. Look at Scranton, Pennsylvania, where the employee group contributed a larger share to the chest than the previous year, almost one-half of the total. And even Detroit, so severely hit by the economic depression, managed to fill its quota. All such favorable indexes that the Woods Committee had the situation under effective control!

Well, I am not altogther unhappy to say—and I speak for myself only—that we, in Philadelphia, did not reach our objective. Had we secured the $3,800,000 asked for the 120 member agencies, the first citizens of the community would have gathered around the festive tables and congratulated themselves upon this great achievement. We might even have succeeded in inducing one of the greatest industrialists in the world to come to the City of Brotherly Love and give us the same assurance which he gave the Prosser Committee in New York, that by our achievements we have "succeeded in equalizing the impact of a great 'national disaster.' " But, unfortunately, Philadelphia fell short by $600,000. Whereupon our Committee of One Hundred on Unemployment, of which it was my privilege to be chairman, became quite active, and we petitioned the city council to set aside the modest sum of $300,000 for the unemployed. In a grandiloquent message to the City Fathers, the Mayor said: "My heart goes out to the poor, but the City is my client. I would rather be just than generous."

This did not dampen our efforts. On November 7, 1930, our Committee arranged a luncheon at the Bellevue-Stratford. It was attended by 192 of Philadelphia's celebrities and salubrities. After listening to the pleas, in behalf of the unemployed, of Mr. Karl de Schweinitz and myself, one prominent corporation lawyer arose and, with tears in his eyes, described the tragic story of Marie Antoinette, who mercilessly turned away folk who came to her for bread, saying: "If they have no bread, why don't they eat cake?" Two weeks later she was beheaded. A striking moral to that story! Another gentleman, a prominent merchant prince, described vividly the Russian Revolution—how it could have been averted if only the Romanov family had been more sympathetic to the plight of the common people! So before us we had the picture of two revolutions likely to arise at anytime. Why, they were virtually around the corner!—the very corner, in fact, where only a few days before, the ex-Secretary of Labor, Senator James J. Davis, told us, awaited abundant prosperity! The upshot of the meeting was this. As chairman I was authorized to appoint a number of committees. Instead, I went to see Mr. Horatio Gates Lloyd, of Drexel & Company and one of the partners of J. P. Morgan & Company, and appealed to him to head the Committee on Unemployment Relief. He accepted and the Committee proceeded to organize relief activities under the effective guidance of Mr. Karl de Schweinitz, who, in turn, mobilized various social workers, in an attempt to relieve distress in a community in which there were nearly 250,000 persons out of work. Within a period of several months, nearly $2,000,000 was raised, more than half of which was contributed by employees, who, it might be stated in passing, only two or three months before had given generously to the Welfare Federation Campaign. An impasse was reached. It seemed as though all resources had been exhausted. No more funds were in sight and all the activities—the feeding of 10,000 school children; subsidies to the leading, but virtually bankrupt, relief organizations; loan bureau, made-work, shelter for the homeless—would have to be closed. Whereupon Mr. Lessing J. Rosenwald, president of the Federation of Jewish Charities, in addition to a contribution already made, offered $100,000, provided five other individuals would respond similarly by March 11. This offer produced an electric effect and six other Philadelphians met the challenge, with the result that considerable momentum was given to the campaign. Altogether nearly $4,000,000 was raised. A keen and penetrating psychologist could write an interesting analysis of the various motivations which entered into this, as they enter into so many campaigns—motivations which have little, if anything, to do with the intrinsic merit of the cause in behalf of which funds are obtained.

Anticipating that the $4,000,000 would be spent by June 1, the Committee of One Hundred on Unemployment, in conjunction with the Lloyd Committee, began to agitate, as early as February, for a municipal appropriation for the care of the unemployed. The mayor of the city, who only a few months before "would rather be just than generous," and the City Fathers, who were desperately opposed to the "iniquitous dole system" we were trying to perpetrate on the community, finally yielded to public pressure. No longer did we refer to that modest item of $300,000, which we asked the mayor to incorporate in his budget. We talked in terms of millions because millions were actually needed to see us through until January 1, 1932. Without going into detail, absorbingly interesting as they are, the legislature granted our city council permission to borrow $3,000,000 for the unemployed, to be spent during the remainder of the calendar year, the fund to be administered under the direction of Mr. Horatio Gates Lloyd, a dollar-a-year man. In fact, Governor Pinchot told the City Fathers that, in view of the tragedies facing us the coming winter, he would not sign the bill unless it was for $3,000,000.

By the first of the year, then, Philadelphia will have spent $7,000,000 for the unemployed, in addition to what the various private relief organizations will have received from the Welfare Federation and the Federation of Jewish Charities. Seven million dollars—eighteen times the amount our Welfare Federation has been allocating to the Family (Relief) Society and nine times the amount spent jointly by this organization and the Jewish Welfare Society, the two largest relief-giving agencies in the community. Are those of us who were largely instrumental in obtaining the $4,000,000 from private sources, the $3,000,000 from the city council, and an interim subvention of $500,000 by the city council to its department of public welfare, happy over the outcome? Again, speaking for myself, I cannot say that I am thrilled. Obviously, to arouse the giving public, the City Fathers, and our legislators to a realization of the tragedies in our midst, we were compelled to resort to considerable propaganda. The publicity given to the "human interest" stories led, in some quarters, to hysteria. That hysteria resulted in the creation of 75 bread lines and neighborhood relief societies. A study of these bread lines by our Community Council revealed what we social workers might have anticipated, namely, that 86 percent of the recipients of relief were obtaining help from one, two, three, or more sources. Picture "the American System," with all the demoralizing features which we associate with the term "dole," as it supposedly exists in England—and bear in mind that in Philadelphia, at least, we had the situation under such control that we became the envy of other communities! And, has it occurred to those who preach the doctrine that our depression is due largely to psychic causes, that the type of publicity to which we are compelled to resort in behalf of the unemployed further accentuates the gloom and militates strongly against such efforts as "Buy-Now" campaigns?

But, what about the future? What will happen after January 1, when our funds shall have been exhausted? The legislature will not be in session to grant further permission for the city to borrow funds. What about New York? What about Chicago? What about Detroit, which has spent about $20,000,000 for public relief in the last twelve months? Last winter, food, clothing, medical attention and, in many cases, rent money were provided for more than 40,000 families in that city. The average monthly outlay per family was $40. On account of the desperate financial position in which the city finds itself, the council has already voted to limit the total of family relief expenditures to $300,000 monthly, which means that the normal American family in Detroit, during the coming winter months, will be asked to keep alive on $7.50 a month!

What, I ask, will happen after January 1? The President's Emergency Committee for Employment has come to our Conference with a project involving the national mobilization of social welfare and fund-raising resources, so that the nearly four hundred community chests throughout the country may, next October or November, raise amounts sufficient to care for the vast army of the unemployed. We will certainly cooperate with the President's Committee. Certainly, we are happy to have the President's blessing. Having attained extraordinary skill in developing enthusiasm, even in moribund communities, we propose to make abundant use of the words of encouragement from the President and the members of his Cabinet. But—and what I am about to say cannot be underscored too strongly—I want to warn you, my fellow social workers, that we will be guilty of duplicity; we will be betraying the interests of the millions of unemployed who expect us to articulate their needs, if, in our vast enthusiasm to fill our community chests, we should give the impression, directly or even inferentially, that all a community has to do is to raise its chest quota and the unemployed will be provided for. This is the way I see the situation. As a result of the policy of drift, and of utter lack of mastery in directing it, our government will be compelled, by the logic of inescapably cruel events ahead of us, to step into the situation and bring relief on a large scale—a scale commensurate with the vast importance and the tragedies of our problem. Private philanthropy is no longer capable of coping with the situation. It is virtually bankrupt in the face of great disaster. With the bravest of intentions, the community chests, comprising as they do a multiplicity of institutions, are altogther unequal to the task ahead of us. Let us be honest, therefore, and say so—not wait until the disaster assumes larger proportions. Let us be frank and admit that if any American method of meeting unemployment is ever devised, it will be something more fundamental than relief. If the spirit of irony, says Paul Douglas, were hovering over this land, he would find a source of sardonic amusement in the spectacle of a country which for a decade has protested that it did not want unemployment insurance because it was a dole, and which still so protests, slowly realizing that under its boasted American methods all that it can offer to those who are in great need from unemployment is the real dole of public or private charity.

In order to avoid the flood, the dikes which hold back the waters must be complete and coextensive with its needs. Although there are many dikes to withstand the waters of disaster, the one I wish to dwell on at this time is unemployment insurance in the clothing industry, primarily because, as chairman of the New York Clothing Unemployment Fund, I have had a body of sufficient experience to justify my speaking on this subject a bit more authoritatively than on others.

During the war, the men's clothing industry in Chicago experienced a marked expansion. New factories were built and staffs increased. Since 1920, the Chicago market, in common with the entire industry, has passed through a period of drastic deflation. It was in the spring of 1923 that the Amalgamated Clothing Workers of America, now with a membership of 120,000, and the clothing manufacturers in Chicago, entered into an agreement providing for the establishment of unemployment funds in that city. When unemployment insurance came into force, May 1, 1923, 413 firms, with 27,000 employees, began to contribute. By 1926 the number of firms had dwindled to 206 and the number of employees to fewer than 20,000. By May, 1929, the number of workers had been still further reduced—possibly to 13,000.

Unemployment insurance, like all other forms of insurance, must be based on payment of premiums or contributions. By the terms of this agreement which became effective May 1, 1923, the contributions were fixed at 3 percent of the weekly payroll, divided equally between employer and employee. Thus, an employer contributed each week 1½ percent of his total wage bill, and each union employee 1½ percent of his total weekly wages. To establish an adequate reserve it was agreed that the funds be allowed to accumulate for a year before any benefits should be paid. On the first of May, 1924, one year later, the unemployment funds in Chicago amounted to one and one-half million dollars.

Under the Chicago plan, eligibility to benefit was limited to members of the union who had worked in the industry for a specified time. The rate of benefit was fixed first at 40 percent of the full-time weekly earnings of the worker, with a maximum benefit of $20 a week, and later was reduced to 30 percent and a maximum of $15. The maximum period for benefits was placed at seven and a half weeks a year.

With minor changes in administration, the scheme has remained unaltered since its inception in 1923, except that the funds were increased from 3 to 4½ percent of the payroll on May 1, 1928, when the employers agreed to raise their contributions from 1½ to 3 percent. In the seven years of its existence, the funds have distributed to the members of the union in Chicago more than $6,000,000 in unemployment benefits. During the past two years, 1929 and 1930, benefits have been distributed at the rate of $1,000,000 a year, among about 15,000 employees. This sum invites comparison with the $8,000,000 collected by the Prosser Committee in New York for the benefit of some 750,000 people out of employment, and the $4,000,000 collected by the Lloyd Committee in Philadelphia for the care of about 250,000 people out of work.

Although the plan was first conceived as a plan only for mitigating the effects of seasonal unemployment, it was soon learned that unemployment funds of this nature could be put to other uses as well. The clothing industry has in the past decade experienced the same technological revolution that has characterized the postwar history of all American industry. During this process of mechanization, many workers lose their jobs and face long periods of idleness before they find new jobs for which they have the requisite skill and training. When changes of this kind took place in the Chicago clothing industry, funds were drawn from the unemployment insurance funds and were used in the form of discharge wages for these displaced workers. In the case of some 500 highly skilled operatives, employed by a large firm, the discharge wage was fixed at $500 a person and the money needed for the purpose was taken partly from the insurance fund and made up by additional contribution from the employer.

This first attempt to create unemployment insurance in the clothing industry was regarded in 1923 as an experiment. Little then was known in this country about either the theory or practice of unemployment insurance. The experience of the first five years was so satisfactory that the Amalgamated succeeded in 1928 in reaching agreements with the manufacturers of New York City and of Rochester, which provided for creation of similar unemployment funds in those cities. Started later than in Chicago, the Rochester and the New York unemployment funds amount only to 1½ percent of the payroll, contributed entirely by the employers. During the year 1930, one of general depression in nearly all American industries, the unionized clothing workers in those three cities received in unemployment benefits the sum of $1,500,000.

Aside from the fairly substantial benefits which this plan has yielded to clothing workers, the experiment is of significance to all industry because it has proved the administrative practicability of unemployment insurance in this country. Tried in the most unstable of all American industries, the unemployment funds of the Amalgamated have remained solvent through several severe depressions and through a period of drastic and continuous internal reorganization of the industry. At the close of 1930, the unemployment funds of Chicago, New York, and Rochester were left with combined reserves of more than $1,000,000.

Plans similar to this one have been in operation in individual firms for some years. Only a few months ago the General Electric Company announced the establishment of a scheme of unemployment insurance for its 100,000 employees. Again, quite recently, fourteen companies in Rochester, each employing from 4,500 to 13,000 workers—one a public utility, the others manufacturing products as varied as cameras and heavy machinery—have joined in an unemployment benefit plan to give workers some degree of income security in future hard times.

Under the Rochester scheme, the fourteen companies will build up individual unemployment reserve funds, to which management but not employees will contribute. Based on its own experience and the degree of stabilization it has achieved, each company will put into its fund an annual amount not to exceed 2 percent of the payroll until the unemployment reserve amounts to five yearly appropriations. No benefits will be paid until January 1, 1933.

Of the forty-odd million gainful employed workers in the United States only about 150,000 are provided with protection against unemployment.

If the present situation, says Dr. Leo Wolman, could be regarded as an isolated phenomenon, unknown in the past and unlikely to appear again in the future, we might look upon it with equanimity—as an unpleasant but passing phase in the healthy readjustment of business and industry. Unfortunately, there are no sound reasons to support this attitude. The same factors in competitive industry which have made for succeeding cycles of boom, depression, and recovery in the history of business are operating at this time, perhaps in an aggravated degree, in both the national and international business situation.

Some industrialists still insist that there are methods of regularizing industry and stabilizing employment which may obviate the need for unemployment insurance. This may be true in the case of industries which produce standardized products, such as the General Electric Company, Procter & Gamble, the Standard Oil Company of New Jersey, the Columbia Conserve, the Fels-Naphtha Soap, the Dennison Manufacturing Company, the International Harvester, and others. There are about two hundred American concerns now using permanent employment regularization plans with a fair degree of success. A notable instance of stabilization is presented by the American Soap and Glycerine Producers, which manufacture fairly standardized articles. In the case of the General Electric Company, there is the incandescent lamp, made in five styles, and the styles do not change, unless the management so decrees. Such an article lends itself to standardization. For many years seasonal variations have been avoided by making new lamps in summer and then selling them in the winter. When it comes to large engineering projects, in which General Electric is engaged, the company, according to Mr. Gerard Swope, is not so fortunate. It is unreasonable to expect the individual business or industry to stabilize itself in the face of deep economic forces before which we stand helpless and unprepared. The instances of regularization to which, until recently, we have pinned high hopes, have at no time affected as much as 1 percent of the total working forces of the country. In fact, a committee of six outstanding business executives submitted a report to the American section of the International Chamber of Commerce, in which they pointed out that, while further intensive efforts on the part of the responsible heads of industry would result in greater regularization, yet the remedies for insecurity in employment which can be applied by the individual employer to his own situation are equally as complex as the forces which produce intermittent unemployment.

In a vast economic crisis, then, such as confronts us today, our alternatives are reliance on hastily devised machinery for the distribution of relief, or sympathetic provision for unemployment compensation out of reserves set aside for this purpose in advance.

There would seem to be no sound reason—and I am speaking now on the strength of my observations in the clothing industry—why unemployment insurance cannot be universally adopted in American industry. Sidney Hillman, President of the Amalgamated Clothing Workers of America, whose ingenuity was largely responsible for the introduction of insurance in his industry, properly observes that if all industries were on the same basis as the Chicago Unemployment Insurance Fund, paying 4½ to 5 percent of the total wage bill, one year's reserve for all industries in the country would amount to nearly two and one-half billion dollars. If this provision had been made, there would have been two and one-half billion dollars available at the onset of this depression. A restoration of such purchasing power might have acted like a balance of a flywheel.

Again and again we are cautioned against measures which, while ostensibly providing insurance, would bring about the "iniquitous dole." Such a contention implies, first, that those engaged in industry can prevent unemployment, or, at least, reduce its severity, and secondly, that this is a matter in which the industry, acting as a unit, can best achieve the object. May I repeat that the principal causes of unemployment are quite beyond the control of a single industry; that the sphere in which the improved organization of an individual industry can prevent unemployment is very limited.

Try as hard as we may, we cannot escape the conclusion that we must have compulsory unemployment insurance, which would impose the entire cost of the fund on industry, with each industry being permitted, under state supervision, to set up and administer its own reserves. As a further proof of the need for a compulsory feature, we might borrow a chapter from our experiences in the field of industrial pensions in the United States. In 1925, a friend of mine, a highly competent student of economics, was asked by an important national organization to make a study of industrial pensions in the United States. The author of that study told me only a few days ago that he was not permitted to incorporate in his book the statement made to him by so high an authority as Mr. Ingalls Kimball, of the Metropolitan Life Insurance Company, to the effect that at the time, in 1925, there was not a single pension plan in the United States which was actually solvent. This opinion was supported by other actuaries. Which goes to show that while such unemployment insurance plans as those supported by the Amalgamated, the General Electric, and the Rochester group of employers, may succeed on account of the social vision and fine leadership back of them, purely voluntary schemes, especially in industries composed of unskilled labor, and in which collective bargaining does not play a part, are likely to fail. When the United States Chamber of Commerce, the American Engineering Council, and kindred bodies tell us that our "attempt to do by law that which industry can much better do for itself" should be frowned upon, it should not be forgotten that the English government did not organize a scheme of unemployment insurance until employers as a body showed that they were unwilling to deal with it. And, when Colonel Arthur Woods issues the vehement warning that "under no circumstances should this country adopt the dole system, but that we must pursue the 'American way,' because they, in Europe, do not have, as we have, large resources of private contributions," I should like to remind Colonel Woods that such lofty sentiments are meaningless and self-deluding when applied to actual conditions; that men, women, and children should not be allowed to go hungry because a certain social theory is to be exalted; and that there seems to be no good reason for applying a word of reproach to what the English are doing. They set out on a scheme of insurance against unemployment which, to be sure, has had its actuarial calculations vitiated by the war and by the long depression, but which has, in general, commended itself to all thoughtful students of the subject. As the *New York Times* states editorially:

> To intimate that the plan of cooperative workingmen's insurance is nothing but handing out money personally from the public treasury, is merely to seize upon the term "dole" in order to discredit what most of us believe in or are getting ready to adopt in one form or another.

Not for a single moment would I have you believe that, in our efforts to deal with so great a catastrophe, unemployment insurance is the only or even chief desideratum. While we cannot prevent unemployment in the present state of knowledge and in the present characteristics of our economic order, yet our knowledge is sufficiently adequate to indicate many points at which the severity may be greatly lessened.

If time permitted, I should like to discuss the necessity for exercising greater control over credits; for the common planning of industry; for further types of research; and for expansion of public works. A word about the latter. While the significance of public works is perhaps a bit overplayed, yet I am in accord with that group of sound economists who believe that a federal bond issue of at least three billion dollars should be floated and spent on construction work as quickly as possible. This would give employment to nearly 750,000 workmen, thus stimulating private business. Any such quickening of the process of economic recovery through government intervention along economically sound lines is bound to be productive of a great deal of good.

It must be borne in mind, too, that the federal government is in a better position to borrow and increase its expenditures than are the state governments, because its system of taxation is less antiquated. It is hardly fair to urge the average workman who faces an uncertain future, to dissipate his resources by "buying now," when the government itself sets exactly the opposite example, despite the fact that money can be borrowed at bargain rates, especially by government bodies. As a member of the Committee on Unemployment and Industrial Stabilization of the Progressive Conference headed by Senator Robert M. LaFollette, I readily subscribe, therefore, to the statement issued by the LaFollette Committee, that "unless the federal government spends now, the cost of healing the injuries which are bound to occur during the coming twelve months, will be many times more than what may be saved by our present policy of federal economy."

Again, we are beginning to see in this country that connecting men with jobs is a great primary need in modern industrial life. The Wagner Bill, which finally passed in the closing days of Congress, but which the president vetoed just after March 4, was essentially a constructive measure, intended to create a nationwide system operated by the states and stimulated by federal grants which would speed up and set going an adequate structure of services everywhere. There is grave doubt that the present makeshift moves on the part of the federal Department of Labor will result in any such system. Clearly, there is need for new enabling legislation by the next Congress to devise such a system—either reenactment of the Wagner Bill or of an equally broad-gauge and effective measure.

Now, what is the duty and the responsibility that rests upon us social workers? Heretofore there has been too great a tendency among us to emphasize the adjustment of the individual to his environment rather than the improvement of the environment for the sake of the individual. The unemployment crisis furnishes overwhelming evidence that this emphasis has been mistaken. As early as thirty years ago, that great economist, Simon Patten, expressed the hope that there was one word which would die—"rehabilitation." Instead of striving to restore the fallen, we should let no one sink to a level where rehabilitation is necessary. If, contended Patten, we cut this word out of the social conditions that its use implies, new programs would grow up in harmony with modern needs.

Many social agencies that are dealing with psychiatric behavior, health, and character building in other activities outside the rim of relief work, have gradually had it driven home to them that they have been living in a fool's paradise, having nothing to do with the main economic footholds of life. They have begun to realize that we cannot deal effectively with even an inferiority complex on an empty stomach.

During the past twelve months we have heard some devastating comments about our economic order which has occasioned so much distress. There is William McAdoo, ex-Secretary of the

Treasury, who presents a severe indictment of what Tawney calls our "acquisitive society." We have Daniel Willard, president of the Baltimore & Ohio Railroad and chairman of the Board of Trustees of Johns Hopkins University, telling a distinguished group of faculty men and students, that there is nothing more deplorable than the condition of a man, able and anxious to work, but unable to secure work; with no resources but his labor and perhaps with others even more helpless dependent upon him. And, added Willard quite significantly, "While I do not like to say so, I would be less than candid if I did not say that in such circumstances I would steal before I would starve." There is Nicholas Murray Butler, who fortunately has given up the idea of becoming President of the United States and has joined the ranks of the great liberal thinkers of the country, calling attention to the fact that great masses of men will not indefinitely sit quietly by and see themselves and those dependent upon them reduced to penury and want, while what we call civilization has so much to offer; commands such stupendous resources; and seems capable of accomplishing almost anything. There is Owen D. Young, with his pronouncement that unemployment is the greatest economic blot on our capitalistic system, and that business, if it is to fulfil its ideal, owes men an opportunity to earn a living.

There is hardly a commencement or baccalaureate orator who is not at this moment crying for enlightened leadership; for an industrial statesmanship which will solve some of the vexing problems confronting us. But let me remind you what William James once said: "abstract conceptions are notoriously weak in impulsive action." I repeat: "abstract conceptions are notoriously weak in impulsive action." If, therefore, you and I believe in unemployment insurance, let us not merely talk about it abstractly, but in our respective communities let us advocate it, and let us get back of the Commission for the Study of Unemployment Insurance, created as a result of the Conference of Seven Governors called by Governor Roosevelt in Albany last January. If we believe in a three and a half billion dollar loan to finance important national public works, at a time when great multitudes of unemployed workers are in need of jobs, let us say so.

If we believe that mothers' assistance funds—(and, by the way, it was my privilege to sponsor the first legislation for mothers' assistance as early as 1912, in Missouri, when even many social workers opposed the proposed laws because they said: "they constituted an insidious attack upon the family, inimical to the welfare of the children and injurious to the character of the parents")—if we believe that mothers' assistance funds should be so modified in their scope as to include not only widows and orphans, not only families whose chief breadwinners are committed to penal or mental institutions, but also those families in which there is acute suffering resulting from involuntary idleness, let us say so, and in no unmistakable language. If we believe in shortening the hours of labor as a means of combatting the evils resulting from technological unemployment, let us speak our minds. If we believe in old age pensions as offering to old folks the certainty of greater economic security, let us support such measures, not as an act of charity, but of elemental justice.

My friends, the time has come when you and I, who are so closely in touch with the tragedies of unemployment—the tragedies of despair arising from still other causes—must articulate the needs of those under our care. Unless we do so, millions of men and women and children, who look to us for such articulation, will, in the classic words of Job, say to us:

> Sorry (and hypocritical) comforters are ye all.
> When will your windy words have an end?

72 73 74 75 12 11 10 9 8 7 6 5 4 3 2 1